Annual Editions:
Human Development, 44/e

Edited by
Claire N. Rubman

http://create.mheducation.com

ISBN-10: 125934939X ISBN-13: 9781259349393

Contents

Preface

The authors of this collection of articles collectively challenge the notion of the status quo: They question overindulgent parenting, bullying in homes and across college campuses, standardized tests, and the pervasiveness of cheating in our educational system. They raise provocative questions such as:

- Is it possible to create artificial sperm or have a womb transplant?
- When an infant is left alone, forgotten, and strapped in to the infant seat in the rear of a car, is it because the parent was too busy multitasking, too emotionally and physically exhausted, or too absent minded?
- Should an adolescent be tried as an adult when the prefrontal cortex has clearly not yet matured?
- Did Harvard college students cheat en masse on a recent exam?

This Annual Editions in anthology generates new perspectives on a wide range of topics from life of the infertile Iranian woman to the benefits and limitations of the iPad. Read about current research on the pain and feelings of loneliness and isolation that the adolescent brain experiences. Learn about the myths and dangers of multitasking and why many professors say that their students are ill prepared for the workplace. Find out what happens to the human brain as we age and discover techniques to keep our aging brains more dynamic.

These articles were compiled to promote thought and discussion using the Socratic Method (Socrates, 470–399 B.C.E.) to generate critical thinking as a powerful tool for learning. They are the ideal catalyst for student-led discussions and student-centered learning. They can be the stimulus for a debate, student presentations, or larger class discussions.

The topics were selected to motivate and inspire you to think, read, discuss, and learn in an interactive environment. Take ownership of these issues and themes in human lifespan development. Using Bronfenbrenner's Ecological Model (1994), think about how they impact you as an individual as well as society at large.

Editor

Dr. Rubman is a Cognitive Developmental Psychologist. She has numerous publications and radio interviews to her credit. She is frequently requested to present guest lectures, keynote addresses, and workshop presentations both within the United States and internationally.

Uniquely qualified to talk and write about cognitive development, Dr. Rubman has a refreshingly novel approach that appeals to students, teachers, parents, and experts in the field. Her conference presentations include titles such as

- "What's Next: Calculus in Kindergarten?"
- "Youface and MyTube: Teens and Technology"
- "Time Out Doesn't Work"
- "Pixels in the Classroom"
- "The 21st Century Brain and Other Stories"
- "A Line in the Sandbox"

Magazine articles include such titles as

- "Read-iculous: The Challenges of Reading through the Eyes of a Child"
- "The Big Fat Question of Obesity"
- "It's Never Too Soon to Plan for Kindergarten, Is It?"

Dr. Rubman is a Professor at Suffolk County Community College in Selden, New York, where she has taught for the past 14 years. She has also spent time in the classroom as a kindergarten teacher in London, England, and California, USA.

Born and raised in Glasgow, Scotland, she earned her PhD and MA degrees in Cognitive Developmental Psychology from the State University of New York in Stony Brook. She holds a BA degree from Glasgow University, and she also earned her FLCM, LLCM (Teacher's Diploma) degrees from the London College of Music in London, England, where she currently serves as an external examiner.

Dr. Rubman can be contacted through her website www.clairerubman.com or through her website "Education and Parenting Matters."

Academic Advisory Board

Members of the Academic Advisory Board are instrumental in the final selection of articles for *Annual Editions* books and ExpressBooks. Their review of the articles for content, level, and appropriateness provides critical direction to the editor(s) and staff. We think that you will find their careful consideration reflected here.

Unit 1

UNIT

Prepared by: Claire N. Rubman, *Suffolk County Community College*

Genetics and Prenatal Influences on Development

Have you ever spent time at a family gathering and wondered about your genetic inheritance? Who in your family do you look like and who do you act least like? Through this collection of articles, we can learn about new discoveries in our DNA. We can also trace the X chromosome and look at the maternal influence among male offspring.

It is important to consider our parents, grandparents, and other relatives, but what do you think about when you pause to consider your future? Perhaps, you fantasize about your potential family or maybe you dread the thought of ever having children. This collection of articles looks from both perspectives. It also takes into account the new technologies that are available to assist infertile couples.

Perhaps, you already have children and are wondering about how your pregnancy behavior impacted your children's development. Did you gain too much "baby weight"? Did that, somehow, affect your unborn child? It is possible pregnancy behavior influence later development in your child's adolescent years?

Each of these issues is addressed within this collection of articles that takes a closer look at genetics and prenatal influences on development.

We are learning about genetics at a staggering rate, and along with our new knowledge comes a deeper understanding of our mistakes from the past. One misunderstanding that has generated misinformation is the concept of "junk DNA." Hall's article "Journey to the Genetic Interior" will allow the reader to better understand the ENCODE project's discoveries that have reshaped our understanding of DNA.

The focus our discussion shifts to prenatal development for the remainder of this unit, however, we pause to consider women who cannot have children or who choose not to procreate. "The No-Baby Boom" by Kingston allows us to think about the one in five woman who remains childless into her 40s. Why has this number doubled in just one generation? Why is this indicative of women in many developed countries around the world? The concept of "social infertility" is discussed.

As excitement continues to build around the first, and soon to be second "Royal Baby" in the United Kingdom, the genetic legacy of Princess Diana may live on in Prince William and Kate's children. The role of the X chromosome is explored in this context in Badcock's "The Incredible Expanding Adventures of the X Chromosome."

For women who would like to become pregnant but experience difficulties along the way, "Making Babies" by Alexis Madrigal explores the many and varied options that today's technology has made possible including a uterus transplant, artificial gametes, and the use of mitochondrial DNA.

With the advent of new technologies comes the potential for misuse including the sex-selection abortion in countries such as India, Taiwan, Azerbaijan, Albania, China, and the United States. Mara Hvistendahl explores the many and varied reasons for gender selection in her article "Unnatural Selection." Dowries, population control, and genetic diseases have contributed to sex selection in many countries around the world. Hvistendahl discusses the impact of these choices in many countries.

These technological advances have created new possibilities for some women whose religion used to preclude this type of intervention. In Iran, for example, the issuing of a fatwa on donor eggs or sperm by the Ayatollah Ali Khamenei cleared the way for the 20 percent of that nation's infertile couples to try new reproductive techniques. Moaveni's "The Islamic Republic of Baby-Making" explores the growth of 70 fertility clinics and takes a closer look at the root causes including male infertility, which he describes as "the hidden story of the Middle East."

The final article in this unit, "Beyond the Baby Weight" by Eric Reither, looks at the impact of maternity weight gain or "baby weight" on the child. The link between the weight gained during pregnancy and a child's potential for obesity are explored. Factors such as prenatal care and socio-economic status are the basis of this study of Hawaiian and non-Hawaiian women. The relationship between maternal obesity, high birth weight, and obesity in adolescence is teased apart.

Article

Prepared by: Claire N. Rubman, *Suffolk County Community College*

Journey to the Genetic Interior

What was once known as "junk DNA" turns out to hold hidden treasures, says computational biologist Ewan Birney.

STEPHEN S. HALL

Learning Outcomes

After reading this article, you will be able to:

- Explain why the term "junk DNA" should be expunged from our lexicon.
- Discuss why finding out how much we do not understand about human DNA is good.

In the 1970s, when biologists first glimpsed the landscape of human genes, they saw that the small pieces of DNA that coded for proteins (known as exons) seemed to float like bits of wood in a sea of genetic gibberish. What on earth were those billions of other letters of DNA there for? No less a molecular luminary than Francis Crick, co-discoverer of DNA's double-helical structure, suspected it was "little better than junk."

The phrase "junk DNA" has haunted human genetics ever since. In 2000, when scientists of the Human Genome Project presented the first rough draft of the sequence of bases, or code letters, in human DNA, the initial results appeared to confirm that the vast majority of the sequence—perhaps 97 percent of its 3.2 billion bases—had no apparent function. The "Book of Life," in other words, looked like a heavily padded text.

But beginning roughly at that same time, a consortium of dozens of international laboratories embarked on a massive, unglamorous and largely unnoticed project to annotate what one biologist has called the "humble, unpretentious non-gene" parts of the human genome. Known as the Encyclopedia of DNA Elements (ENCODE for short), the project required scientists, in essence, to crawl along the length of the double helix as they attempted to identify anything with a biological purpose. In 2007 the group published a preliminary report hinting that, like the stuff all of us park in the attic, there were indeed treasures aplenty amid the so-called junk.

Now, in a series of papers published in September in *Nature* (*Scientific American* is part of Nature Publishing Group) and elsewhere, the ENCODE group has produced a stunning inventory of previously hidden switches, signals and signposts embedded like runes throughout the entire length of human DNA. In the process, the ENCODE project is reinventing the vocabulary with which biologists study, discuss and understand human inheritance and disease.

Ewan Birney, 39, of the European Bio-informatics Institute in Cambridge, England, led the analysis by the more than 400 ENCODE scientists who annotated the genome. He recently spoke with *Scientific American* about the major findings. Excerpts follow.

SCIENTIFIC AMERICAN: The ENCODE project has revealed a landscape that is absolutely teeming with important genetic elements—a landscape that used to be dismissed as "junk DNA." Were our old views of how the genome is organized too simplistic?

BIRNEY: People always knew there was more there than protein-coding genes. It was always clear that there was regulation. What we didn't know was just quite how extensive this was.

Just to give you a sense here, about 1.2 percent of the bases are in protein-coding exons. And people speculated that "maybe there's the same amount again involved in regulation or maybe a little bit more." But even if we take quite a conservative view from our ENCODE data, we end up with something like 8 to 9 percent of the bases of the genome involved in doing something like regulation.

Thus, much more of the genome is devoted to regulating genes than to the protein-coding genes themselves?
And that 9 percent can't be the whole story. The most aggressive view of the amount we've sampled is 50 percent. So certainly it's going to go above 9 percent, and one could easily argue for something like 20 percent. That's not an unfeasible number.

Should we be retiring the phrase "junk DNA" now?
Yes, I really think this phrase does need to be totally expunged from the lexicon. It was a slightly throwaway phrase to describe very interesting phenomena that were discovered in the 1970s. I am now convinced that it's just not a very useful way of describing what's going on.

What is one surprise you have had from the "junk"?
There has been a lot of debate, inside of ENCODE and outside of the project, about whether or not the results from our experiments describe something that is really going on in nature. And then there was a rather more philosophical question, which is whether it matters. In other words, these things may biochemically occur, but evolution, as it were, or our body doesn't actually care.

That debate has been running since 2003. And then work by ourselves, but also work outside of the consortium, has made it much clearer that the evolutionary rules for regulatory elements are different from those for protein-coding elements. Basically the regulatory elements turn over a lot faster. So whereas if you find a particular protein-coding gene in a human, you're going to find nearly the same gene in a mouse most of the time, and that rule just doesn't work for regulatory elements.

In other words, there is more complex regulation of genes, and more rapid evolution of these regulatory elements, in humans?
Absolutely.

That's a rather different way of thinking about genes—and evolution.
I get this strong feeling that previously I was ignorant of my own ignorance, and now I understand my ignorance. It's slightly depressing as you realize how ignorant you are. But this is progress. The first step in understanding these things is having a list of things that one has to understand, and that's what we've got here.

Earlier studies suggested that only, say, 3 to 13 percent of the genome had functional significance—that is, actually did something, whether coding for proteins, regulating how the genes worked or doing something else. Am I right that the ENCODE data imply, instead, that as much as 80 percent of the genome may be functional?
One can use the ENCODE data and come up with a number between 9 and 80 percent, which is obviously a very big range. What's going on there? Just to step back, the DNA inside of our cells is wrapped around various proteins, most of them histones, which generally work to keep everything kind of safe and happy. But there are other types of proteins called transcription factors, and they have specific interactions with DNA. A transcription factor will bind only at 1,000 places, or maybe the biggest bind is at 50,000 specific places across the genome. And so, when we talk about this 9 percent, we're really talking about these very specific transcription-factor-to-DNA contacts.

On the other hand, the copying of DNA into RNA seems to happen all the time—about 80 percent of the genome is actually transcribed. And there is still a raging debate about whether this large amount of transcription is a background process that's not terribly important or whether the RNA that is being made actually does something that we don't yet know about.

Personally, I think everything that is being transcribed is worth further exploration, and that's one of the tasks that we will have to tackle in the future.

There is a widespread perception that the attempts to identify common genetic variants related to human disease through so-called genome-wide association studies, or GWAS, have not revealed that much. Indeed, the ENCODE results now show that about 75 percent of the DNA regions that the GWAS have previously linked to disease lie nowhere near protein-coding genes. In terms of disease, have we been wrong to focus on mutations in protein-coding DNA?
Genome-wide association studies are very interesting, but they are not some magic bullet for medicine. The GWAS situation had everyone sort of scratching their heads. But when we put these genetic associations alongside the ENCODE data, we saw that although the loci are not close to a protein-coding gene, they really are close to one of these new elements that we're discovering. That's been a lovely thing. In fact, when I first saw it, it was a slightly too-good-to-be-true moment. And we spent a long time double-checking everything.

How does that discovery help us understand disease?
It's like opening a door. Think about all the different ways you can study a particular disease, such as Crohn's: Should we look at immune system cells in the gut? Or should we look at the neurons that fire to the gut? Or should we be looking at the stomach and how it does something else?

All those are options. Now suddenly ENCODE is letting you examine those options and say, "Well, I really think you should start by looking at this part of the immune system—the helper

T cells—first." And we can do that for a very, very big set of diseases. That's really exciting.

Now that we are retiring the phrase "junk DNA," is there another, better metaphor that might explain the emerging view of the genetic landscape?
What it feels like is genuinely a jungle—a completely dense jungle of stuff that you have to work your way through. You're trying to hack your way to a certain position. And you're really not sure where you are, you know? It's quite easy to feel lost in there.

Over the past 20 years the public has been repeatedly told that these big genomic projects—starting with the Human Genome Project and going on through various other projects—were going to explain everything we needed to know about the "book of life." Is ENCODE simply the latest in this sequence?
I think that each time we always said, "These are foundations. You build on them." Nobody said, "Look, the human genome bases, that's it. It's all done and dusted—we've just got a bit of code breaking to do here." Everybody said, "We're going to be studying this for 50 years, 100 years. But this is the foundation that we start on." I do get the feeling that the ENCODE project is the next layer in that foundational resource for other people to stand on top of and look further. The biggest change here is in our list of known unknowns. And I think people should understand that although finding out how much you don't know can feel regressive and frustrating, identifying the gaps is really good.

Ten years ago we didn't know what we didn't know. There is no doubt that ENCODE poses many, many, many more questions than it directly answers. At the same time, for Crohn's disease, say, and lots of other things, there are some effectively quick wins and low-hanging fruit—at least for researchers—where you start to say to people, "Oh my gosh, have you looked there?"

It's just one more step. It's an important step, but nowhere near the end, I'm afraid.

You sometimes refer to yourself as ENCODE's "cat herder in chief." How many people were involved in the consortium, and what was it like coordinating such a massive effort?
This is very much a different way of doing science. I am only one of 400 investigators, and I am the person who is charged to make sure that the analysis was delivered and that it all worked out. But I had to draw on the talents of many, many people.

So I'm more like the cat herder, the conductor, necessarily, than someone whose brain can absorb all of this. It comes back to that sense that it's a bit of a jungle out there.

Well, you deserve a lot of credit. It's more than just cats. They're pretty opinionated cats.
Yeah, they are. What scientists are not are dogs. Dogs naturally run in packs. Cats? No. And I think that sums up the normal scientific phenotype. And so you have to cajole these people sometimes into sort of taking the same direction.

Do you see a point where all this complex information will resolve into a simpler message about human inheritance and human disease? Or do we have to accept the fact that complexity is, as it were, in our DNA?
We are complex creatures. We should expect that it's complex out there. But I think we should be happy about that and maybe even proud about it.

Critical Thinking

1. What is the goal of the ENCODE project?
2. How do protein-coding elements differ from regulatory elements in humans?

Create Central

www.mhhe.com/createcentral

Internet References

Basic Neural Processes
www.psych.hanover.edu/Krantz/neurotut.html

Scientific American Online
www.ScientificAmerican.com/oct2012/genes

The ENCODE Project: Encyclopedia of DNA Elements
www.genome.gov/10005107

Stephen S. Hall has written about science for *The Atlantic*, *The New York Times Magazine*, *New Yorker* and many other magazines.

Article Prepared by: Claire N. Rubman, *Suffolk County Community College*

The No-Baby Boom

Social infertility, baby regret and what it means that shocking numbers of women aren't having children

ANNE KINGSTON

Learning Outcomes

After reading this article, you will be able to:

- Understand the nuances of social infertility.
- Explain the acronym "PANK."
- Describe how childless women are depicted in the media.

Catherine-Emmanuelle Delisle does not seem, at first glance, like a social firebrand. The 37-year-old schoolteacher in Saint-Bruno, a Montreal suburb, is a thoughtful, sensitive woman who exudes gamine charm. She enjoys jewellery making, design, and cinema—and she really loves children, enough to devote her life to teaching drama and French in primary school. But Delisle knew as a teenager she couldn't have kids, a fact she was in denial about for years, she says. Grappling with never giving birth was painful, and required time to grieve. As she began to reframe her life as a **childless** woman, she observed a lack of role models or even discussion of the subject. "We are non-existent in the media, in cinema, in art, in magazines," she says. When **childless** women are depicted, it's characters like Breaking Bad's Marie, who deals with the unhappiness of her domestic situation by going to open houses and making up elaborate stories about herself, many involving fictional children. And of course there's 45-year-old actress Jennifer Aniston, the mother of all non-mothers, whose uterus is a chronic subject of tabloid fretting. (Last week, OK continued the "sad, barren Jen" narrative: "Jen agrees to fertility treatment to have kids," it claimed.)

Delisle is hell-bent on reframing the way women like her are depicted. "We're seen as selfish, or treated as if our lives lack meaning or value," she says with a bemused laugh, knowing well it's imagery that can be insidiously absorbed by women themselves.

Delisle's blog, FemmeSansEnfant.com, launched in 2012, provides a counterpoint, a place for women to connect and support one another. Interviewees share stories on video: the journalist Pénélope McQuade explains she never felt the "visceral" need for children; singer Marie Denise Pelletier speaks of dreaming of being a singer, not a mother. "My goal is to get women without children, whether by choice or circumstance, known and valued," Delisle says.

The schoolteacher is part of a growing global movement that's giving voice to a misunderstood phenomenon whose repercussions are personal and societal. "We think there is a room called childlessness with two doors: 'didn't want' or 'can't have,'" says Jody Day, the writer and social entrepreneur behind Gatway-Women.com, a network based in London, England, for the "**childless**-by-circumstance" (dubbed "NoMos"). "But there are many ways to end up not being a mother."

That millions of women are discovering this is reflected in statistics: one out of five women in the U.K., Ireland, the U.S., Canada, and Australia are reaching their mid-40s without having had children—twice as many as a generation ago. The 2010 U.S. census revealed 47.1 percent of women of child-bearing age don't have children—up from 35 percent in 1976.

To put those developments in historical context, Daly notes that the last time the **childless** rate was one in five, it was in a generation of so-called "surplus women" born at the turn of the 20th century. "The fact it took a war with unprecedented loss of life and global depression to cause such an increase in childlessness gives you some idea of the social change we're going through now," she says.

Yet discussion of childlessness remains mired in handwringing, pity and judgment—either concern over the consequences of a reduced tax base and diminishing social supports, as explored in Jonathan Last's "What to Expect When No One's Expecting: America's Coming Demographic Disaster," or coverage of the militant "child-free" movement seen in books like Jen Kirkman's *I Can Barely Take Care of Myself: Tales from a Happy Life without Kids*. Virtually ignored in the conversation is the impact of "social infertility"—Day's coinage for the growing number of women who don't have a partner or the right partner while they can have children. It's a big problem for women born in the '70s, says Day, who experienced social infertility herself: she married at 23 and tried to get pregnant in her late 20s; her 16-year marriage ended when she was 39 and considering IVF. "I couldn't find a suitable person to do IVF with," she says. "Now I know it was probably way too late by then anyway."

Social infertility is such a new concept that data are scarce. A 2013 study out of Australia's Deakin University published in the *Journal of Social Inclusion* reports there has been a "general failure to examine women's reasons for childlessness beyond [medical] infertility." It found that more than half of the surveyed women without children listed having never been in the "right" relationship, being in a relationship where the partner did not want to have children—what some bloggers call "infertility by marriage"—or never having wanted children as the reason.

The emerging topography of childlessness is also delineated in Melanie Notkin's new memoir, *Otherhood: Modern Women Finding a New Kind of Happiness*, an insightful, anecdotal account of the challenges facing professional Manhattan women who dream of finding the right partner and having children. (Think *Sex and the City* with IVF.) Notkin discusses the "dating Bermuda Triangle" faced by over-30 women and the fertility snatchers who end long-term relationships as a woman's reproductive life is ending.

The 44-year-old, Montreal-born, McGill-educated, New York City-based former marketing executive has made a career of focusing on **childless** women. In 2008, she launched the "multiplatform lifestyle brand" SavvyAuntie.com targeted at "PANKs" (her acronym for "professional aunt, no kids")—the 23 million **childless** American women who are invested both emotionally and financially in the children in their lives. Savvy Auntie suggests gifts, details activities from making dough animals to "Skype dance-offs," and even confers the "Savvy Auntie Best Toy Award" on worthy merchandise. **Childless** women, invisible to marketers in the past, are now appearing on the radar, Notkin says. A 2012 Weber Shandwick/KRC survey of 2000 women in U.S. and Canada, titled "The Power of the PANK," estimated total spending of $9 billion annually by PANKs on children in their lives, with an average of $387 per child. Thirty-four percent were also contributing to a child's education—hence the emergence of the "aunt" demographic. A commercial for Huggies released this month depicts a loving aunt being flown to meet her sister's newborn on the diaper-maker's dime.

Notkin's focus may be on tapping a new market, but she also exposes something more profound underlying it. Most women start out expecting to have children, she says, citing a recent Centers for Disease Control and Prevention study that found 80 percent of single women are **childless,** but that 81 percent of that group said they hope or plan to have children. She rejects the "career woman" label used to describe **childless** women: "It implies we have chosen work over love, marriage, children. I know no woman who has done that." Social infertility—or "circumstantial infertility" to use Notkin's term—forces women to recalibrate expectations in ways not discussed publicly, she says: "At 25, a woman expects to have children, at 35 she hopes to, and at 45 she says she's happy she doesn't."

Women don't broadcast wanting a child for fear of being lectured that they shouldn't wait, Notkin says. But they're well aware of the tick-tock, she says: "Every 28 days offers a reminder." The upshot is that women are being forced to make a tactical decision in their 30s: resort to solo motherhood, partner with someone simply to procreate, freeze their eggs, or rely on IVF. All are "choices" that are not fully choices. How many women have the resources to keep working while paying child care on a single salary—or to not work at all? How many can afford to freeze their eggs, and then pay for IVF too? Advances in fertility technology have created false perceptions, says Notkin, who writes that people talk about freezing eggs as if it's picking up a carton of milk. "The assumption is that if you wanted a kid, you would have a kid and go it alone. But that's not viable for a lot of women." People see Halle Berry giving birth at 47 and think it's the new norm, she notes. IVF is misrepresented in the media, says Day. "All we hear is miracle stories, not that it usually doesn't work over age 40."

The fact that discussion about childlessness is framed in terms of personal choice, failure and medical infertility shuts down conversation, says Day. So do the cultural narratives of motherhood and womanhood, a spectacle Notkin calls "mom-opia"—"seeing motherhood as the only normal, natural way to be a woman." It's a fixation reflected in manic coverage of celebrity "baby bumps" and loss of pregnancy weight—as well as photos of stars with their kids. We see it too in Michelle Obama's transformation from accomplished professional and activist to supermom, not only to her own kids, but to the nation—overseeing how it eats and encouraging it to exercise.

Women outside the maternal matrix are suspect—former Australian PM Julia Gillard was termed "deliberately barren" and unfit for leadership by a political opponent. In 2012, Wildrose Party Leader Danielle Smith's childlessness was questioned on Twitter by a PC staffer, who later resigned. Actress Helen Mirren's declaration that she has "no maternal instinct" was viewed as a salvo in an unnamed war. "**Childless** women represent a threat to the status quo," says Day. "We're seen as a destabilizing influence. If one does well in her career—and doesn't have children—she can do as well as a man." Against this grain, women don't speak up for fear of sounding shrill or pathetic or desperate or being defined by one aspect of their lives—disappointment in not having children.

But that is changing, particularly over the past year, as **childless** women are increasingly vocal, says Lisa Manterfield, the Los Angeles-based author of *I'm Taking My Eggs and Going Home: How One Woman Dared to Say No to Motherhood,* her 2011 memoir that chronicles how she was 34 by the time she met the man she wanted to raise a family with, then wrestled with infertility before coming to the difficult decision that motherhood wasn't in her future. When Manterfield launched LifeWithoutBaby.com 4 years ago, she says, there were only a few voices—Pamela Tsigdinos at SilentSorority.com and Tracey Cleantis at LaBeletteRouge.com—telling their personal stories to a small audience. Now more women are willing to talk about a loss others can't see, she says, one that forced her to confront how much of female identity is tied to motherhood. "The loss isn't tangible, so most women feel alone, their grief compounded by the attitude that they 'should be over it,' " she says. Adding to the isolation is the feeling of being "locked out of the Mommy Clubhouse," as one blogger put it on LifeWithoutBaby .com. "Women without children not only lose a future family," says Day, "but can lose their peer group who have moved to a country called motherhood where we don't speak the language."

The fact that the archetype of the most pitied and shamed woman has, in one generation, gone from single mother to single woman over 40 without children reflects fundamental societal shifts, says Day, who thinks it's not a coincidence that the "fetishization of motherhood"—from pregnancy studio shots to the ideal birth (at home! in water! without meds!)—comes at a time of rising childlessness. "There's so much cultural anxiety around what it means; there's reflexive nostalgia for a simpler time: women at home and gender roles more clearly defined." This isn't only societal pressure; some of it comes from women recognizing the increasing precariousness of motherhood. Day likens it to propaganda used to lure women home from the workforce after the Second World War. It can be seductive, she says. "It seems such a solid identity, being a mother; being **childless** is fluid, nebulous: 'What are you?'"

Rising childlessness is often blamed on feminism selling women a "bill of goods" about "having it all." But Betty Friedan's 1963 manifesto *The Feminine Mystique* presumed that women would continue to marry and have children. "The assumption of your own identity, equality and even political power does not mean you stop needing to love, and be loved by, a man, or that you stop caring for your kids," she wrote.

What no one could have predicted is that women born in the '60s and '70s would become what Day terms the "shock absorber" cohort, living through the most extraordinary changes in dating and mating in one generation. That's the result of a confluence of forces—the pill, women's access to higher education and professions—running headlong into a rigid corporate model that remains based on the husband-provider, male-fertility model—working hard in your 20s and 30s to establish a reputation, leaving kids to the stay-at-home wife. "But that doesn't work for women," says Day. "If you make it work, it's as much luck as good judgment."

Today's "surplus women" are not war widows but young professional women for whom there aren't enough suitable male partners—a phenomenon referred to in China derisively as "A1 women and D4 men." Yet the blame invariably falls on them for being "too choosy," a motif of the booming advice-to-female-professionals book genre, the latest being Susan Patton's new *Marry Smart: Advice for Finding THE ONE,* in which the "Princeton Mom" advises women to snag their "MRS" in university as they'll never have access to such an elite dating pool again.

But the issue is more structural: we're transitioning from an old social model in which women are expected to "marry up" socially or economically that runs parallel to an emerging one examined in Lisa Mundy's *The Richer Sex: How the New Majority of Female Breadwinners Is Transforming Sex, Love and Family.* Mundy concludes that if successful millennial women want to marry and have children, they'll have to marry down. That's happening globally, but slowly, Mundy told *Maclean's.* Many women she spoke to admitted lying about what they did when they met a man, either fearing the truth would be intimidating or wanting to seem more feminine, she says. Notkin, too, chronicles how modern dating rituals can have one foot in traditional rom-com expectations: women want chivalry as well as a socially enlightened man. They have no problem "leaning in" at work, per Sheryl Sandberg's instruction, she says. "We lean in every day; we're almost falling over." Yet when dating, they want to lean back and let men do some of the heavy lifting. Notkin always envisioned "motherhood as part of the romantic wholeness of marriage and family," she writes, and was unwilling to settle for less.

Reconciling a new reality with the Vaseline-lens myth is the central theme of the **childless**-by-circumstance movement. Navigating unchartered waters requires a "plan B," Day writes in her 2013 book *Rocking the Life Unexpected.* **Childless** women feel pressure to have a big compensatory life, she says. "It's as though if you're not a mother, you have to become Mother Teresa. But you don't need a big life on the outside, just on the inside." Notkin describes her situation this way: "While it's not the life I expected, it's the life I directed."

But childlessness is not only a personal issue to be grappled with, it's a social one requiring new models, says Day—the most pressing being caregiving in old age. "It isn't just about childlessness," says Day. "The ratio of people around to take care of aging persons is changing, and daughters are not necessarily available to give that care because they're working." She'd like to see an intergenerational dialog among older women without children, mothers in her generation and their daughters. "We need to discuss not just what we did wrong but what we've learned, so it doesn't take them by surprise."

Looking around, there's no shortage of role models, including Aniston, who is finally voicing her frustration with the

childless stigma. When the actress interviewed the feminist activist Gloria Steinem at the Maker's Conference in California in February, Aniston noted that for women in the public eye, "our value and worth is dependent on our marital status and/or if we've procreated." Steinem, who is also **childless,** shot back, "Well, I guess we're in deep s—t!" The audience laughed uproariously—with them, not at them.

Critical Thinking

1. Why has the rate of childlessness increased in recent years?
2. How has corporate America capitalized on the "childless" market?
3. How does feminism relate to the 21st-century woman and her childbearing choices?

Create Central

www.mhhe.com/createcentral

Internet References

CNN Health U.S. women having fewer children

http://thechart.blogs.cnn.com/2013/12/06/u-s-women-having-fewer-children

Ranker.com Childless Celebrities | List of Famous People without Children

http://www.ranker.com/list/childless-celebrities/celebrity-lists?var=2&utm_expid=16418821-48.w4XvOttHQz-Kl88l1iLzhA.1&utm_referrer=http%3A%2F%2Fwww.google.com%2Furl%3Fsa%3Dt%26rct%3Dj%26q%3D%26esrc%3Ds%26source%3Dweb%26cd%3D1%26sqi%3D2%26ved%3D0CB4QFjAA%26url%3Dhttp%253A%252F%252Fwww.ranker.com%252Flist%252Fchildless-celebrities%252Fcelebrity-lists%26ei%3DWrsYVJifJI_gsAS6y4KADg%26usg%3DAFQjCNFKy6rJjGCDAmm8CyU5dnhaYFriWA%26sig2%3Dzq8aq1kdh_mtMRsWRy2cHQ%26bvm%3Dbv.75097201%2Cd.cWc

savvyauntie.com PANK: Professional Aunt No Kids

http://savvyauntie.com/About.aspx?GroupId=389&Name=PANK:%20Professional%20Aunt%20No%20Kids

Kingston, Anne. "The No-Baby Boom." *Maclean's* 127. 12 (March, 31, 2013): 48–50.

Article Prepared by: Claire N. Rubman, *Suffolk County Community College*

The Incredible Expanding Adventures of the X Chromosome

Genes housed on the powerhouse X chromosome shed new light on the human mind, including why identical female twins differ more than their male counterparts, why there are more male geniuses and male autists, and why you may have mom to thank for your brains.

CHRISTOPHER BADCOCK

Learning Outcomes

After reading this article, you will be able to:

- Distinguish between the genetic potential of the X compared to the Y chromosome.
- Explain why you may have your mother to thank for your intelligence.

In the early 1980s I met and began an unofficial training with Anna Freud—Sigmund Freud's youngest daughter, and his only child to follow him into psychoanalysis. I was a young social scientist who had been carrying out a self-analysis for some years.

Anna Freud's couch was a daybed on which I lay, with her seated in a chair at its head. On one or two occasions I couldn't help but think that the voice I heard coming from her chair was in fact that of her father, speaking to me from beyond the grave.

I can even recall her exact words in one case. I had been free-associating about my attempt to analyze myself when Anna Freud remarked, "In your self-analysis you sank a deep but narrow shaft into your unconscious. Here we clear the whole area, layer by layer." This produced a spine-tingling reaction in me, and I surprised Miss Freud (as I called her) by stating that her remark reminded me of her father, because he was particularly fond of archaeological metaphors in his published writings. Most people would simply attribute her statement to the influence of her father's writing on her own choice of words. Thirty years ago, I would probably have said the same. But today, having spent decades researching the links between genetics and psychology, I can offer a different hypothesis, one that goes to the core of all we now know about the inheritance and expression of genes in the brain.

The Royal X

Everyone inherits 23 chromosomes from each parent, 46 in all, making 23 matched pairs—with one exception. One pair comprises the chromosomes that determine sex. Female mammals get an X chromosome from each parent, but males receive an X from their mother and a Y sex chromosome from their father.

The X chromosome a woman inherits from her mother is, like any other chromosome, a random mix of genes from both of her mother's Xs, and so does not correspond as a whole with either of her mother's X chromosomes. By contrast, the X a woman inherits from her father is his one and only X chromosome, complete and undiluted. This means that a father is twice as closely related to his daughter via his X chromosome genes as is her mother. To put it another way: Any X gene in a mother has a 50/50 chance of being inherited by her daughter, but every X gene in a father is certain to be passed on to a daughter.

These laws of genetic transmission have major implications for family lineages. When it comes to grandparents, women are always most closely X-related to their paternal grandmother and less related to their paternal grandfather. Consider how this plays out in the current British royal family. The late Diana, Princess of Wales, will be more closely related to any daughter born to William and Kate than will Kate's parents, thanks to

William's passing on his single X from her. Kate's mother's X genes passed on to a granddaughter, by contrast, will be diluted by those of Kate's father in the X this girl would receive from Kate, meaning that the X-relatedness of the Middletons to any granddaughter would be half that of Princess Diana. Prince Charles, however, would be the least related of all four grandparents to Prince William's daughters because he confers no sex chromosome genes on them.

Prince Charles would be the least related grandparent to any daughters of prince William and Kate because he confers no sex chromosome to girls.

Of course, if William and Kate produce a son, the situation is reversed, and now Prince Charles is most closely related to his grandson, via his Y chromosome. Princess Diana will have no sex-chromosome relatedness to William and Kate's sons because the X she bequeathed William will not be passed on to the grandsons.

Calculations of X-relatedness may seem abstract, but they have probably played a huge role in European history, thanks to the fact that Queen Victoria passed on hemophilia, an X-chromosome disorder that was in the past fatal to males. Victoria and her female descendants were protected by a second, unaffected X, but princes in several European royal houses—not least the Romanovs—were affected, with disastrous consequences for successions based on male primogeniture.

The X in Sex

Not only are X chromosomes bequeathed and inherited differently, depending on whether you are male or female, they also have different patterns of expression in the body. For example, in 1875, Darwin described a disorder that appeared in each generation of one family's male members, affecting some but sparing others: "... small and weak incisor teeth ... very little hair on the body ... excessive dryness of the skin. ... Though the daughters in the ... family were never affected, they transmit the tendency to their sons; and no case has occurred of a son transmitting it to his sons."

Today we know this to be anhidrotic ectodermal dysplasia (AED), a disorder involving sweat glands, among other things, that affects males and females differently. Because AED is carried on an X chromosome, affected males have no sweat glands whatsoever. They express their one and only X in all their cells. Affected females with the AED gene on only one X have different patterns of expression because areas of their body randomly express one or the other of their two X chromosomes. It is perfectly possible for an affected woman to have one armpit that sweats and one that doesn't.

X chromosome expression can explain not only differences between males and females but also differences between identical female twins. Such twins may routinely differ more than their male counterparts, because in each woman, one of their two X chromosomes is normally silenced. Identical twins result when the cells of the fertilized egg have divided only a few times and the egg then splits into two individuals. The pattern of differential X expression in cells is set at this stage. In females, an X chromosome gene called Xist effectively tosses a coin and decides which of the two X chromosomes will be expressed and which silenced in any particular cell.

Differential X chromosome gene expression explains why one of a pair of living Americans is a successful athlete yet her identical twin sister suffers from Duchenne muscular dystrophy (DMD), an X-linked genetic disease that predominantly affects males and leaves sufferers unable to walk. In this case only one twin was unfortunate enough to inherit the cell lineages that expressed the DMD gene from one parental X chromosome, while the other twin inherited those expressed from the other parent's unaffected X.

A predisposition to sex-linked disorders is just one of the ways female identical twins differ more than males. A recent study found that compared with male twins, female identical twins vary more on measures of social behavior and verbal ability. This is also due to differential expression of genes on their two X chromosomes in contrast to male twins' single, truly identical X. In the past, such differences between identical twins would have been attributed to nongenetic or environmental factors, but now we know that these dissimilarities are in fact the result of gene expression. Where X chromosome genes are concerned, what once seemed to be nurture now turns out to be nature.

The X Factor in IQ

Another important factor in sex chromosome expression is the huge dissimilarity between the information carried on the X and Y chromosomes. The Y has a mere 100 or so genes, and there is no evidence that any of them are linked to cognition. This contrasts sharply with the 1,200-odd genes on the X chromosome. There is mounting evidence that at least 150 of these genes are linked to intelligence, and there is definite evidence that verbal IQ is X-linked. It suggests that a mother's contribution to intelligence may be more significant than a father's—especially if the child is male, because a male's one and only X chromosome always comes from his mother. And in females, the X chromosome derived from the father is in fact bequeathed directly from the father's mother, simply setting the maternal X-effect back one generation, so to speak.

The Case against "Genius" Sperm Banks

IF INTELLIGENCE IS X-linked to the degree that some researchers speculate, there are important implications for our views of the heritability of talent—and even genius. The Repository for Germinal Choice was a California sperm bank that operated in the 1980s and 1990s and claimed that its donors reflected a range of Nobel laureates. (In fact the only confirmed Nobel Prize-winning donor was William Shockley, and most donors are now known not to have been laureates at all.) But beyond the actual composition of the sperm bank, there is a fundamental problem with an enterprise founded on the belief that Nobel Prize-winning talent might be heritable from the father, given the likely role of the X chromosome in intelligencê.

In the case of a "genius" sperm bank, only half the sperm donated would on average be carrying the Nobel laureate's X chromosome, and any child resulting from such a fertilization would be female, and so would have a second X from the mother to dilute its effect. In the beginning, mothers receiving Nobel laureates' sperm from the Repository for Germinal Choice had to be members of Mensa, and so would have had high IQs to pass on to their offspring of either sex via their X chromosomes. Indeed, this in itself might explain any apparent heritability of Nobel laureate "genius" via the Repository.

The other half of the preserved sperm would have a Y chromosome instead of an X. These sperm assuredly would produce sons, but there is no evidence that the Y is implicated in intelligence. On the contrary, the sole X of sons conceived this way would increase their vulnerability to intellectual impairment in the way that it does for all males, and would also mean that any "genius" seen in them most likely came from their single, undiluted maternal X.

Finally, there is the environmental factor in IQ. Clearly this too would be wholly attributable to the mothers in the case of a sperm bank, because the father provides only his genes.

Ironically then, mothers with children of "genius" sperm-bank fathers were probably laboring under something of a delusion. Any intellectual talent in their children was most likely predominantly attributable to them, both via their X chromosome genes and the home environment they provided. However, the single mothers who nowadays constitute the major clientele for sperm banks may not be too displeased to realize that, where heritability of intelligence is concerned, Mother Nature is something of a feminist.

The fact that males have only a single X, uniquely derived from the mother, has further implications for variations in intelligence. Look at it this way: If you are the son of a highly intelligent mother and if there is indeed a major X chromosome contribution to IQ, you will express your one and only maternal X chromosome without dilution by the second X chromosome that a female would inherit. The effects cut both ways: If you are a male with a damaged IQ-linked gene on your X, you are going to suffer its effects much more obviously than a female, who can express the equivalent, undamaged gene from her second X chromosome. This in itself likely explains why there are more males than females with very high and very low IQs: males' single X chromosome increases variance in IQ, simply because there is not a second, compensatory X chromosome.

If you are the son of a highly intelligent mother and there is indeed a major X chromosome contribution to IQ, you're in luck.

The inheritance of intelligence is not limited to the influence of sex-linked genes. Non-sex-chromosome genes can also vary in their pattern of expression depending on which parent they come from (so-called genomic imprinting). One such gene on chromosome 6 (IGF2R) has been found to correlate with high IQ in some studies. The mouse version of this gene is expressed only from the maternal chromosome, and to that extent such genes resemble X chromosome ones in their maternal bias. Although it remains highly controversial to what extent the same is true of the human version of this gene, several syndromes that feature mental retardation are associated with imprinted genes on others of the 22 non-sex chromosomes.

X Expression in Autism

Autism spectrum disorder is yet another phenomenon that can be clarified through the prism of X chromosome inheritance and expression. Researchers have recently begun to suspect that autism is X-linked, in part because more males than females are affected by ASD, particularly at the high-functioning end of the spectrum—Asperger's syndrome—where males outnumber females by at least 10 to 1. Asperger's syndrome impairs pro-social behavior, peer relations, and verbal ability (among other deficits)—the very same traits that vary between identical female as opposed to identical male twins, and all of which are thought to have some linkage to the X chromosome. Because males have only a single X, they could be much more vulnerable to such X-linked deficits than are females, who normally have a second X chromosome to compensate and dilute the effect.

Indeed, women afflicted with autism spectrum disorders may be among the minority of females who disproportionately express one parent's X. Women on the autism spectrum are probably among the 35 percent of women who have a greater than 70:30 skew in their pattern of X expression in favor of one rather than the other parent's X. Indeed, 7 percent of women have more than a 90:10 skew. Such a hugely one-sided expression of one X would closely resemble the single X chromosome found in males. And if X expression peculiarities affect critical genes implicated in autism in the case of these women, Asperger's would result, just as it does in males. Furthermore, the fact that only a small minority of females have such highly skewed X expression could explain why so many more males than females are affected. Most females have more equitable patterns of X expression and are therefore protected by their second X.

The peculiarities of X chromosome gene expression might even explain the often-remarked variability of the symptoms in Asperger's. Classically heritable single-gene disorder like anhidrotic ectodermal dysplasia or Duchenne muscular dystrophy usually have strikingly consistent symptoms because only one gene is affected, often in the same way. But if variable expression of several X-linked genes is the norm in Asperger's syndrome, the outcome in each case might be surprisingly different, and the combined effects highly variable—just as researchers find.

Female identical twins differ more than their male counterparts, because in each woman one of their two X chromosomes is normally silenced.

X Marks the Spot in the Brain

What light might this shed on Anna Freud's eerie use of metaphors favored by her father? In her case, the woman who became a psychoanalyst just like her father might have been among the minority of women who disproportionately express one parent's set of X-linked genes in the brain. We saw earlier that anhidrotic ectodermal dysplasia affects only some areas of a woman's skin, depending on where the affected X is expressed. Both the skin and the brain develop from the same layer in the ball of cells (or blastocyst) from which the embryo first forms. We also saw that in females this can result in some cells expressing one parent's X and some expressing the other's, and if this can happen to the skin, then it could also occur in the brain: Some parts might express the father's X and some parts the mother's. Indeed, there is persuasive evidence that this occurs in mice, and circumstantial evidence that it also does in humans.

Given the possibility of an extreme skew in the pattern of X expression, such as likely occurs in women with Asperger's syndrome, we can envisage a situation in which critical parts of a woman's brain are built entirely by one parent's genes. And if that parent is the father, then the same genes that constructed his brain would be expressed in his daughter's brain. Theoretically, a woman could be an X chromosome clone of her father in that each and every X gene he has would be inherited and expressed by her, perhaps in exactly the same regions of the brain. This could result in a daughter's mind being very like her father's—and surprisingly dissimilar to her mother's.

Freud emphasized the importance of the relationship between mothers and sons, but in my experience it pales in comparison to that between many fathers and daughters, who often seem to have a close emotional bond that intensifies with time.

Sigmund Freud's own relationship with his daughter Anna certainly seems a case in point, as I was able to observe firsthand—at least in the daughter at the end of her life. At the time, I felt I was hearing the voice of Freud speaking from beyond the grave. But of course only a person's DNA can survive his or her death, and even then it has to be packaged in a living descendant. So today I am more inclined to think that the words I heard may indeed have been those of Sigmund Freud, but expressed from his daughter's paternal X chromosome.

Critical Thinking

1. Identify the approximate number of genes found on each X chromosome and the approximate number on each Y chromosome.
2. Explain why genius and autism are related to the X chromosome, and why they both are more common in males.
3. How can identical female twins differ on traits related to genes on their X chromosomes?

Create Central

www.mhhe.com/createcentral

Internet References

Biological Basis of Heredity: Sex Linked Genes
http://anthro.palomar.edu/biobasis/bio_4.htm

Genetic Science Learning Center
www.learn.genetics.utah.edu

Identical Twins Facts
www.ask.com/Identical+Twins+Facts

Christopher Badcock, PhD, is the author of *The Imprinted Brain*. He retired this year as a Reader in Sociology at the London School of Economic and Political Science.

Article

Prepared by: Claire N. Rubman, *Suffolk County Community College*

Making Babies

Five predictions about the future of reproduction

ALEXIS MADRIGAL

Learning Outcomes

After reading this article, you will be able to:

- Explain how technology such as "GLOW" and "FETUS CARE" can enhance the reproductive process.
- Describe how stem cells may enhance reproduction in the future through the use of artificial gametes.
- Articulate the issue with the "slippage" that occurs as a result of screening and the potential paradox that may arise.

Forty years ago, there was exactly one way for humans to reproduce. A man's sperm would combine with a woman's egg, inside of her body. Together they would form a zygote, which would become an embryo, and then a fetus. With any luck, the woman would carry the fetus to term, and a baby would be born. The process had not changed since long before anyone could call us human. Until one day, after years of trial and error, Dr. Patrick Steptoe and Dr. Robert Edwards combined an egg from Lesley Brown with sperm from her husband, John, in a petri dish and implanted the resulting embryo in her uterus. On July 25, 1978, Louise Brown came squalling into the world, heralding a revolution not just in the mechanics of reproduction but in the surrounding culture.

At the time, James Watson, a co discoverer of DNA's double-helix structure, warned that if in vitro fertilization were allowed to proceed on a broader scale, "all hell will break loose, politically and morally, all over the world." Since then, not only has reproductive technology gone ahead, it has headed in previously unthinkable directions, and with little public scrutiny. For example, over the past 20 years, a new procedure called intracytoplasmic sperm injection has allowed fertility clinicians to select an individual sperm and insert it into an egg. It is the only reliable option for men with very low sperm counts or low-quality sperm, and for the hundreds of thousands of men it's enabled to have children, it's been life-changing. Happily, the procedure appears to cause only a relatively minor increase in the risk of birth defects.

Future reproductive innovations are likely to develop in similar ways—led by practitioners, with little U.S. government oversight. Few people, it seems, want to stand in the way of someone who desires a biological family. And so far, almost no one has. But some of the reproductive technologies on the horizon could test our flexibility. Here, drawn from interviews with scholars, doctors, and entrepreneurs are a handful of guesses about how the future may change what's involved in making a person—from the ease of getting pregnant, to the mechanics of procreation, to our very definition of family.

1 It Will Take a Village to Make a Child

Sperm and egg donation and surrogacy have already enabled unusual parental configurations. In some cases—say, a father contracting with an egg donor and a separate surrogate mother—a new baby could be said to have three biological parents. But this is only the beginning of what science may make possible in the near future. One new IVF procedure would combine the nucleus of a patient's egg with mitochondrial DNA from a donor's egg. The FDA is mulling approving the technique, which could prevent diseases that originate in mitochondrial DNA; it's already been successfully tested in monkeys.

Or take uterus transplants, in which one woman's healthy uterus is implanted in someone else's abdomen. Since 2012, nine Swedish women have received a uterus donation from a relative—in most cases their own mother. They're now under going IVF treatment, to see whether they can conceive and carry a baby. If successful, they'll be the first women to bear a child with another person's womb. Not only that: their children will in effect be sleeping in the same "room" that they once did. The implications are fascinating. As Charis Thompson, a sociologist at the London School of Economics who has written a book about IVF, observes, "Parenthood is multiplying."

2 Your Biological Clock Will Be Personalized . . .

One of the key problems in fertility research is how to help women who wish to start families later in life. Many women in their late 30s and beyond turn to IVF, usually with little sense of whether the physically demanding and expensive treatments are likely to work. Services like Univfy are trying to help women under stand their own fertility better. One of Univfy's co founders, the ob-gyn and fertility researcher Mylene Yao, says that women are entitled to a better read on their chances of conceiving through IVF than the rough age-based estimates that most fertility clinics provide. "There is no such thing as an average 38-year-old woman," Yao told me. Her company draws on detailed data from a 5-year study of IVF patients and other predictive models to provide personalized information about an individual's likelihood of conception. She compares the effort to those of Netflix and Amazon: "We're all, as consumers, getting better predictive information with online shopping than with health care."

3 . . . And Procreation Will Be Precisely Timed

Max Levchin is a co founder of Glow, a fertility-tracking app that helps users time sex for the greatest chance of conception. This isn't so revolutionary—solid knowledge of the menstrual cycle, a thermometer, a pen, and paper will let you do much the same thing—but by allowing users to pool data anonymously, it could lead to a better understanding of population-wide fertility patterns. There have been surprisingly few large-scale studies of couples' efforts to conceive; Levchin hopes that data from Glow can help change that.

The problem is, the data that people record are not very reliable. For example, slight temperature variations are key to predicting ovulation, and deviations in exactly when a woman takes her temperature can add noise to a data set. Down the road, Levchin sees simple sensors having a big effect on a couple's odds of conception and, ultimately, on our understanding of fertility patterns. He envisions a sticker-like thermometer that could "sit in some place, like the small of the back," he says. "You'll have a continuous feed of someone's temperature."

Such monitoring could be even more important for expectant mothers. Already, Taiwanese designers are working on an app called Fetus Care, which they say will use data from a sensor to detect worrisome uterine contractions or an abnormal fetal heart rate. Perhaps one day implantable sensors will track the interior state of the womb. After all, the FDA has approved ingestible data-logging sensors for use in other parts of the body.

4 Synthetic Sperm Will Save the Nuclear Family

As long as we're entertaining far-out but technically feasible scenarios, the most radical revision in reproduction could be the creation of artificial gametes, aka sperm, and egg cells. Researchers may ultimately be able to take a cell from an adult man or woman, turn it into a stem cell, then change that stem cell into a sperm or an egg. Doctors have already succeeded in breeding same-sex laboratory animals in this way.

Timothy Murphy is a philosophy professor at the University of Illinois College of Medicine at Chicago whose work focuses on the bioethical implications of reproductive technologies for gay, lesbian, and transgender people. He points out that creating artificial sperm and eggs could, rather than leading to radical social change, actually preserve a normative family structure. "For gay and lesbian couples, the synthetic gametes would eliminate the need for a third party," Murphy notes. This kind of assisted reproductive technology—"unnatural" as it might be—would allow same-sex couples to keep reproduction solely within the family.

5 Genotyping Will Breed Conformity

Here's a final paradox: even as reproductive freedom increases, enabling more types of parents to have children, these parents may choose children who ft a narrower and narrower notion of normal. Charis Thompson, the sociologist, told me about a conversation she recently had with a British in fertility doctor, who gave a disturbing preview of where we might be headed.

"You start out offering these prenatal screenings for certain conditions that everybody agrees are very severe. It is not particularly eugenic, but about alleviating the suffering of the child and the parents. But there is slippage," she said. "The more you can test for and screen out, the more people do. And the example this person gave was the high number of people who will abort a fetus that is found to have an extra digit."

A mere 11 years after the completion of the Human Genome Project, it is technically possible to scan an embryo's entire genome during the IVF process. If parents are already aborting pregnancies to avoid extra fingers, how many will resist the temptation to implant only the embryo with the "best" genome?

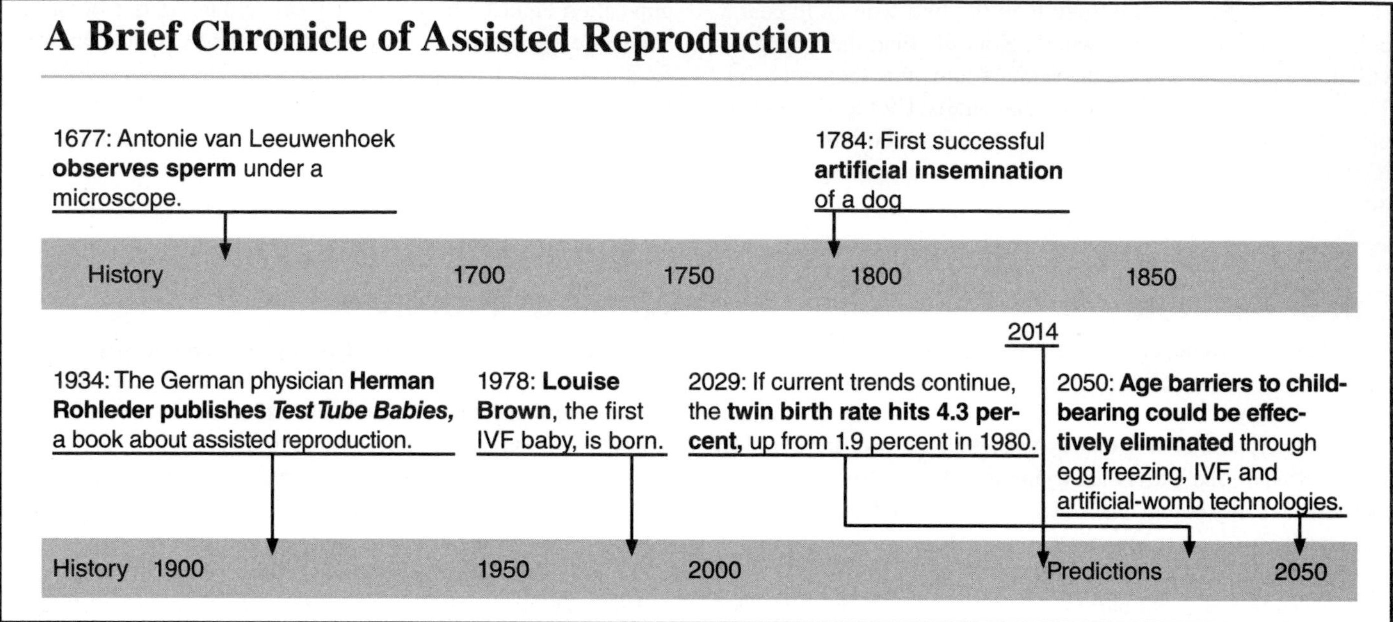

A Brief Chronicle of Assisted Reproduction
1677: Antonie van Leeuwenhoek observes sperm under a microscope.
1784: First successful artificial insemination of a dog
History
1700
1750
1800
1850
2014
1934: The German physician Herman Rohleder publishes Test Tube Babies, a book about assisted reproduction.
1978: Louise Brown, the first IVF baby, is born.
2029: If current trends continue, the twin birth rate hits 4.3 percent, up from 1.9 percent in 1980.
2050: Age barriers to child-bearing could be effectively eliminated through egg freezing, IVF, and artificial-womb technologies.
History
1900
1950
2000
Predictions
2050

Which is to say, the future of reproduction might be increasingly diverse families making increasingly similar babies.

Critical Thinking

1. Why does Madrigal suggest that babies created using these new technological advances may be "increasingly similar"?
2. What are some of the potential legal issues with these new reproductive technologies?
3. What safeguards can be put in place to keep each of these innovations ethical and in the best interests of each potential child?

Create Central

www.mhhe.com/createcentral

Internet References

NCBI "Emotions and Ethical Considerations of Women Undergoing IVF"

http://www.ncbi.nlm.nih.gov/pmc/articles/PMC3258403/

RH Reality Check "Nine Women Receive Uterus Transplants in Sweden Raising Ethical Questions"

http://rhrealitycheck.org/article/2014/01/23/nine-women-receive-uterus-transplants-sweden-raising-ethical-questions/

The New York Times "Ethics Questions Arise as Genetic Testing of Embryos Increases"

http://www.nytimes.com/2014/02/04/health/ethics-questions-arise-as-genetic-testing-of-embryos-increases.html

The Telegraphy "Stem Cells Used to Make Artificial Sperm"

http://www.telegraph.co.uk/science/science-news/8682142/Stem-cells-used-to-make-artificial-sperm.html

Madrigal, Alexis. "Making Babies." *The Atlantic* 313. 5 (June 2014): 32–34.

Article

Prepared by: Claire N. Rubman, *Suffolk County Community College*

Unnatural Selection

The gaping gender gap in Asia—the result of sex-selective abortion—has a burgeoning (and to some, equally alarming) counterpart here in the U.S.

MARA HVISTENDAHL

Learning Outcomes

After reading this article, you will be able to:

- Identify developmental disabilities more common in children born prematurely.
- Evaluate a future with one-third more males than females.

New Delhi, India

For Dr. Puneet Bedi, the intensive care unit in Apollo Hospital's maternity ward is a source of both pride and shame. The unit's technology is among the best in Delhi—among the best, for that matter, in all of India. But as a specialist in high-risk births, he works hard so that babies can be born. The fact that the unit's technology also contributes to India's skewed sex ratio at birth gnaws at him. Seven out of 10 babies born in the maternity ward, Bedi says, are male. He delivers those boys knowing that many of them are replacements for aborted girls.

A tall, broad-shouldered man with a disarmingly gentle voice, Bedi stands in the unit's control room, gazing into a sealed, temperature-controlled room lined with rows of cribs. He performs abortions himself. For sex-selective abortions, however, he reserves a contempt bordering on fury. To have his work negated by something as trifling as sex preference feels like a targeted insult. "You can choose whether to be a parent," he says. "But once you choose to be a parent, you cannot choose whether it's a boy or girl, black or white, tall or short."

A broad interpretation of parental choice, indeed, is spreading throughout India—along with China, Taiwan, Vietnam, Georgia, Azerbaijan, and Albania. Preliminary results from India's 2011 census show a sex ratio of only 914 girls for every 1,000 boys ages 6 and under, a decline from 2001. In some Chinese counties the sex ratio at birth has reached more than 150 boys for every 100 girls. "We are dealing with genocide," Bedi says. Sex-selective abortion, he adds, is "probably the single most important issue in the next 50 years that India and China are going to face. If you're going to wipe out 20 percent of your population, nature is not going to sit by and watch."

If you're going to wipe out 20 percent of your population, nature will not sit by and watch.

Bedi speaks with an immaculate British accent that hints at years spent studying at King's College London. The accent helps in this part of Delhi, where breeding can trump all else. His patients are the sort who live in spacious homes tended by gardeners, belong to bucolic country clubs, and send their children to study in the United States. India's wealthy are among the most frequent practitioners of sex selection, and in their quest to have a son Bedi is often an obstacle. His refusal to identify sex during ultrasound examinations disappoints many women, he says: "They think it's just a waste of time and money if you don't even know whether it's a boy or a girl."

India outlawed fetal sex identification and sex-selective abortion in 1994, but so many physicians and technicians break the law that women have little trouble finding one willing to scan fetal sex. Bedi says sex-selective abortion has caught on in Delhi because it bears the imprint of a scientific advance. "It's sanitized," he says. The fact that sex selection is a medical act, he adds, neatly divides the moral burden between two parties: Parents tell themselves their doctor knows best, while doctors point to overwhelming patient demand for the procedure.

Hospital administrators, for their part, have little incentive to do anything about the problem because maternity wards bring in substantial business. (At Apollo, a deluxe delivery suite outfitted with a bathtub, track lighting, a flat screen television, and a large window looking out onto landscaped grounds runs to $200 a night.) "When you confront the medical profession, there is a cowardly refusal to accept blame," Bedi says. "They say, 'We are doctors; it's a noble profession.' This is bullshit. When it comes to issues like ethics and morality, you can have an opinion, but there is a line which you do not cross. Everybody who [aborts for reasons of sex selection] knows it's unethical. It's a mass medical crime."

For as long as they have counted births, demographers have found an average of 105 boys born for every 100 girls. This is our natural sex ratio at birth. (The small gap neatly makes up for the fact that males are more likely to die early in life.) If Asia had maintained that ratio over the past few decades, the continent would today have an additional 163 million women and girls.

For Westerners, such a gender gap may be difficult to fathom: 163 million is more than the entire female population of the United States. Walk around Delhi's posh neighborhoods, or visit an elementary school in eastern China, and you can see the disparity: Boys far outnumber girls.

At first glance, the imbalance might seem to be the result of entrenched gender discrimination and local practices. Scholars and journalists typically look to the Indian convention of dowry, which makes daughters expensive, and to China's one-child policy, which makes sons precious, to explain sex selection in Asia. (Sons have long been favored in China, as in many other parts of the world.) But this logic doesn't account for why South Koreans also aborted female fetuses in large numbers until recently, or why a sex ratio imbalance has lately spread to the Caucasus countries—Azerbaijan, Georgia, and Armenia—and the Balkans, or why sex-selective abortion occurs among some immigrant communities in the United States.

What impact will hundreds of million of "surplus" men have on everything from health care to crime?

The world's missing females are an apparent paradox: Sex selection is occurring at a time when women are better off than ever before. "More and more girls are going to school and getting educated," says T.V. Sekher, a demographer at the International Institute for Population Studies in Mumbai. And in India, educated women are more likely to have a son than those with no degree. The women who select for sex include lawyers and doctors and businesspeople. Economic development has accompanied a drop in fertility rates, which decreases the chances of a couple getting the son they want without resorting to technology.

We might have seen this coming. Decades ago, Western hysteria over what many saw as an impending "population explosion" led American scholars and policymakers to scour the world for solutions to reducing the global birth rate. Studies from India and East Asia showed the major barrier to acceptance of contraception was that couples wanted at least one son. The advocates of population control saw that the barrier might be turned into an opportunity, however: If parents could be guaranteed a son the first time around, they might happily limit themselves to one or two children.

Beginning in the late 1960s, influential U.S. experts sounded their approval for sex selection everywhere from the pages of major scientific journals to the podiums at government sponsored seminars. "[I]f a simple method could be found to guarantee that first-born children were males," Paul Ehrlich wrote in *The Population Bomb* in 1968, "then population control problems in many areas would be somewhat eased."

Meanwhile, another group of scientists was figuring out how to determine fetal sex. These scientists' efforts focused on amniocentesis, which entails inserting a needle through a pregnant women's abdomen into the amniotic sac surrounding the fetus and removing a small amount of protective amniotic fluid, a substance rich with fetal cells that reveal its sex. They saw sex determination as a way to help women carrying sex-linked diseases like hemophilia have healthy children. But when amniocentesis, and later ultrasound, found their way to Asia decades later, it was their use as a population-control tool that stuck.

Sex selection's proponents argued that discrimination against women and girls wouldn't endure. As women became scarce, several prominent Western theorists proposed, they would also become more valuable, prompting couples to have daughters again. But in fact the opposite has happened. In their scarcity, women are being turned into commodities to be sold to and exploited by what demographers call "surplus men": the ones left over in an imagined world in which everyone who can marry does so. Scholars have begun to calculate the impact hundreds of millions of such men will have on everything from health care to crime.

Suining County, China

In a village in eastern China's agricultural belt, I meet Zhang Mei, a 37-year-old woman clad in men's pants and a black-and-white polka-dot shirt that billows around her thin frame. Zhang is from distant Yunnan province, a poor mountain region near the border with Tibet. Her neighbors say she arrived 20 years ago, after a long journey in which a trafficker took her east to deliver her into marriage. She had no idea where she was headed beyond the vague promise that she would find work there, and yet she had some faith in the trafficker, for she hadn't been kidnapped. Her parents had sold her.

The man who became her husband was gentle, but 15 years her senior, undeniably ugly, and one of the poorest residents of the village. Zhang learned that she had to work hard to make ends meet, and that she could not leave, even for a short trip home. Soon after she married, she found herself under pressure to have a son. One came on the third try, after two girls. But as the children grew, her husband complained it cost too much to educate their daughters, and since it is sons that matter in Suining, he sent one of the girls back to Yunnan to be raised by Zhang's parents: a return, one generation later, of a lost girl.

Today Zhang copes with lifelong detention by gambling at raucous *majiang* games, burying herself in soap operas, and praying. (She is Christian.) "I carry some burdens," she tells me, as we sit on the couch in her one-room home. "If I didn't pray, I would keep them all in my heart."

Zhang's story is perhaps the most obvious way in which the gender imbalance is altering societies in Asia. The U.S. Department of State lists the dearth of women in Asia as one of the principal causes of sex trafficking in the region. Some of those women, like Zhang, are sold into marriage. Others become prostitutes. But what happens to the men who can't find partners is significant as well.

Nothing can fully predict the effect of gathering tens of millions of young bachelors in one place for years on end. But preliminary conclusions can be drawn from places where the first generation touched by sex selection has reached adulthood. One line of speculation centers on testosterone, which occurs in high levels among young unmarried men. While testosterone does not directly cause violence in a young man, it can elevate existing aggressive tendencies, serving as a "facilitative effect" that predicts whether he will resort to violence. Gauging whether millions of high-testosterone men together spark more violence is complicated, particularly in China and India, which have experienced great social change in the past few decades. But some answers can be found through breaking down crime rates by region and time period.

In a 2007 study, Columbia University economist Lena Edlund and colleagues at Chinese University of Hong Kong used the fact that China's sex ratio at birth spiked in some provinces earlier than others to explore a link between crime rates and a surplus of men. The researchers found a clear link, concluding a mere 1 percent increase in sex ratio at birth resulted in a 5- to 6-point increase in an area's crime rate.

Other scholars speculate the gender imbalance is yielding depression and hopelessness among young men—which may explain why China has lately been hit with the sort of senseless violence that was once America's domain. In 2004 and 2010 the country saw separate waves of attacks on elementary schools and child care centers in which murderers went on rampages and bludgeoned and stabbed children to death.

Eight out of the 10 killers (all male) lived in eastern Chinese provinces with high sex ratios at birth; several were unemployed. One man told neighbors, before he was arrested and summarily executed, that he was frustrated with his life and wanted revenge on the rich and powerful. Another apparently told police he was upset because his girlfriend had left him.

Los Angeles, U.S.

"Be certain your next child will be the gender you're hoping for," promises the Web site of L.A.'s Fertility Institutes. Dr. Jeffrey Steinberg founded the clinic in 1986, just as in-vitro fertilization was taking off.

Today 70 percent of his patients come to select the sex of their baby. Steinberg's favored method is preimplantation genetic diagnosis, PGD, an add-on to in-vitro fertilization that allows parents to screen embryos before implanting them in the mother. Like amniocentesis and ultrasound before it, PGD was developed to test for defects or a propensity toward certain diseases.

But lab technicians working with eight-celled embryos can also separate XY embryos from XX ones, thus screening for sex—the first nonmedical condition to be turned into a choice. PGD thus attracts Americans who are perfectly capable of having babies the old-fashioned way but are hell-bent on having a child of a certain sex. So determined are they that they're willing to submit to the diet of hormones necessary to stimulate ovulation, pay a price ranging from $12,000 to $18,000, and live with IVF's low success rate. Decades after America's elite introduced sex selection to the developing world, they have taken it up themselves.

High-tech sex selection has its critics. They point to a litany of ethical issues: that the technology is available only to the rich, that it gives parents a degree of control over their offspring they shouldn't have, that it marks the advent of designer babies. But in surveys of prospective American parents over the past 10 years, 25 to 35 percent say they would use sex selection techniques if they were readily available; presumably that means more affordable and less invasive.

A squat, balding man who exudes a jovial confidence, Dr. Steinberg talks as if he has all the time in the world, peppering his stories with Hollywood gossip. (To wit: The producers of the show *CSI* once stopped by the clinic to evaluate a sperm cryopreservation tank's potential as a weapon.) The patient response to his clinic offering sex selection, Steinberg tells me after ushering me into a spacious corner office, has been "crazy."

The fertility doctors who perform preimplantation sex selection take care to distinguish it from sex-selective abortion. In America, they point out, patriarchy is dead, at least when it comes to choosing the sex of our children. As late as the 1970s, psychologists and sociologists found that Americans were far more likely to prefer sons to daughters. Not anymore.

National figures are not available, but two of America's leading clinics—HRC Fertility in Los Angeles and Genetics and IVF Institute in Fairfax, Virginia—independently report that between 75 and 80 percent of their patients want girls. The demand for daughters may explain why at Steinberg's clinic everything from the entrance wall to the scrubs worn by the laboratory workers are pink.

For the most part, however, Americans don't talk about gender preference. We say "family balancing," a term that implies couples have an inherent right to an equal number of boys and girls. (Many patients seeking sex selection via PGD already have a child of the opposite sex.) We talk about "gender disappointment," a deep grief arising from not getting what we want. The author of the reproductive technology guide *Guarantee the Sex of Your Baby* explains: "The pain that these mothers feel when they fail to bear a child of the 'right' sex is more than just emotional angst. The longing that they hold in their hearts can translate into real physical pain."

Rhetorical differences aside, "family balancing" is not in fact all that different from what is happening in China and India. In Asia, too, most parents who select for sex do so for the second or third birth. And examining why American parents are set on girls suggests another similarity: Americans who want girls, like Asians who opt for boys, have preconceived notions of how a child of a certain gender will turn out.

Bioethicist Dena S. Davis writes that people who take pains to get a child of a certain sex "don't want just the right chromosomes and the attendant anatomical characteristics, they want a set of characteristics that go with 'girlness' or 'boyness.' If parents want a girl badly enough to go to all the trouble of sperm sorting and artificial insemination, they are likely to make it more difficult for the actual child to resist their expectations and follow her own bent."

When Dr. Sunita Puri surveyed Bay Area couples undergoing PGD for sex selection, most of them white, older, and affluent, 10 out of 12 wanted girls for reasons like "barrettes and pink dresses."

Some mention that girls do better in school, and on this point the research backs them up: Girls are more likely to perform and less likely to misbehave, while boys have lately become the source of a good deal of cultural anxiety. Others mention more noble goals. They talk about raising strong daughters; women mention having the close relationship they had—or didn't have—with their own mother.

But regardless of the reason, bioethicists point out, sex selection prioritizes the needs of one generation over another, making having children more about bringing parents satisfaction than about responsibly creating an independent human being.

At stake with preimplantation sex selection is much more than the global balance of males and females, as if that weren't enough. If you believe in the slippery slope, then sex-selective embryo implantation definitely pushes us a little further down it.

In 2009 Jeffrey Steinberg announced that the clinic would soon offer selection for eye color, hair color, and skin color. The science behind trait selection is still developing, and some later doubted whether he in fact was capable of executing it. Still, Steinberg might have eventually gone through with the service had his advertisement not set off an uproar. The press descended, the Vatican issued a statement criticizing the "obsessive search for the perfect child," and couples who had used PGD for medical reasons balked, fearing frivolous use of reproductive technology would turn public sentiment against cases like theirs. For the moment, at least, Americans had problems with selecting for physical traits, and Steinberg retreated.

Having children has become more about bringing parents satisfaction than creating independent human beings.

"The timing was off is all," he tells me. "It was just premature. We were ahead of our time. So we said, 'OK, fine. We'll put it on the back burner.'" In the meantime, he says, couples obsessed with blue or green eyes continue to call the office. He keeps their names on a mailing list.

Critical Thinking

1. Differentiate between sex-selective abortion and preimplantation sex selection.
2. What are some negative consequences in a society where males far outnumber females?
3. Why would selection for offspring traits (e.g., skin color, eye color, hair color) create ethical issues in a society?
4. If you could afford it, would you choose to preselect traits for your own offspring using preimplantation genetic diagnosis (PGD)?

Create Central

www.mhhe.com/createcentral

Internet References

American Academy of Pediatrics
www.aap.org

Medicine Plus Health Information/Prenatal Care
www.nim.nih.gov/medicineplus/prenatalcare.html

National Children's Study
www.nationalchildrensstudy.gov

Mara Hvistendahl is a China-based correspondent with *Science* magazine. She's also written for *Harper's, Scientific American,* and *Popular Science*. This piece is adapted from her new book, *Unnatural Selection: Choosing Boys Over Girls, and the Consequences of a World Full of Men* (PublicAffairs, 2011).

Article

Prepared by: Claire N. Rubman, *Suffolk County Community College*

The Islamic Republic of Baby-Making

How the supreme leader's revolutionary acceptance of cutting-edge fertility treatments is changing lives in Iran—and unsettling the deeply conservative Sunni Middle East

AZADEH MOAVENI

Learning Outcomes

After reading this article, you will be able to:

- Detail the consequences of infertility before the Ayatollah's fatwa in 1999.
- Explain the outcome of "consanguineous" marriages in Iran.
- Describe how the "hidden story" of the Middle East has impacted the Shiite and Sunni communities.

On a sultry evening last fall, a private fertility clinic in the southern Iranian city of Shiraz was so busy that the harried receptionist struggled to accommodate all the women seeking its services. On a mantelpiece rested a framed fatwa from Ayatollah Ali Khamenei providing religious sanction for **sperm** and **egg** donations—placed there, perhaps, to reassure these women that they had the supreme leader's approval for what they were about to do. Many had traveled long distances from smaller towns to reach the clinic, and the packed waiting area was abuzz with conversation, as women swapped stories about treatment, drugs, and their shared struggles to conceive a child.

"I couldn't afford this five years ago, but I've saved up now and am ready to try," said one 30-year-old woman seated in the waiting room.

While the world's attention has been focused on Iran's nuclear program, the country has been quietly working on a different sort of breakout capacity. The Islamic Republic—governed by its strict mullahs, who've managed to botch progress in fields ranging from domestic manufacturing to airport construction—has unexpectedly transformed itself into the fertility treatment capital of the Muslim Middle East. Iran now boasts more than 70 clinics nationwide, which attract childless couples, Sunni and Shiite alike, from throughout the region. This initiative has raised challenges to traditional views on parenthood and marriage and has helped chip away at taboos about sexual health—even as it has left some of Iran's conservative Sunni neighbors aghast.

"Doctors in the Gulf are horrified by the way the Iranians have allowed this," says Soraya Tremayne, an Oxford University professor and an expert on fertility in Iran. "They say, 'We would never allow this among us.'" For generations of Iranians, infertility was once a marriage-unraveling, soul-decaying trauma. It was memorialized in films like Dariush Mehrjui's *Leila,* in which a conniving mother bullies her son into taking a second wife when his first fails to conceive. The first wife, ashamed of her infertility and still in love with her husband, goes along with the plan, but the emotional strain destroys their marriage and the husband is ultimately left with a child, but bitterly alone. The film screened just a few years before Khamenei's 1999 fatwa and was a major hit, resonating with the multitude of Iranian women and men facing the prospect of a childless marriage and the intolerable alternative of polygamy.

Iran, like other Middle Eastern countries, has an extremely high infertility rate. More than 20 percent of Iranian couples cannot conceive, according to a study conducted by one of the country's leading fertility clinics, compared with the global rate of between 8 and 12 percent. Experts believe this is due to the prevalence of consanguineous marriages, or those between cousins. Male infertility is "the hidden story of the Middle East," says Marcia Inhorn, a Yale University medical anthropologist and a specialist on assisted reproduction in the region. Couple that with a shocking, multidecade decline in the average number of children born per woman, and it means that fertility treatment is needed in Iran more than ever.

Still, the pressure on a married couple—and particularly the woman—to produce children remains intense.

"We live in an Eastern society, and having children remains a very significant thing in our culture," says Sara Fallahi, a physician who practices in one of Shiraz's three fertility clinics. "Even for this generation that's getting married later and wanting smaller families, most still definitely want one child."

Iran's first in vitro fertilization (IVF) clinic opened up in Yazd, a desert city in central Iran, more than 20 years ago. It immediately found itself inundated with clients. By the mid-2000s, it was so popular that lines stretched out the door. Couples who had traveled from rural areas would camp outside in hopes of getting an appointment. More clinics soon opened in Tehran and across the country.

IVF quickly gained acceptance in other parts of the Middle East, but physicians ran into religious restrictions prohibiting more advanced forms of fertility treatment. Standard IVF involves fertilizing an **egg** with **sperm** in a laboratory and then returning the embryo into the womb, a process requiring that both the **egg** and **sperm** of the respective partners be viable, which is not always the case. The next step in treating infertility requires a third party—that is, an **egg** or **sperm** donor from outside the couple. In Islam, the ethics of such treatment are murky: Patients initially worried they might be committing adultery or that children born of such unions would be illegitimate.

But childless couples continued to demand a way to conceive. In Iran, medical specialists set about finding a religious solution, seeking the support of sympathetic mujtahids (clerics qualified to read and interpret the Quran).

The Shiite tradition of reinterpreting Islamic law was central to the clerics' willingness to go along—in stark contrast to Sunni jurisprudence's focus on scholarly consensus and literal readings of the Quran, which has meant few fresh legal rulings on modern matters.

Although, to Westerners, Iran's Shiite clerics might appear reactionary, they are downright revolutionary when it comes to bioethics. In recent years, they have handed down fatwas allowing everything from stem-cell research to cloning.

Their edicts did necessitate some Quranic contortions, however. The religiously acceptable solutions offered at first, like temporary marriage between an **egg** donor and the fertile male partner, proved too complicated, requiring a married donor to endure a flurry of divorces and remarriages. And some clerics who disagree with Khamenei's fatwa still advocate temporary marriage as a way of avoiding the adulterous implications of third-party donations. But this approach is easier for husbands, who can contract a temporary marriage with a female **egg** donor without needing to divorce the infertile wife; for a fertile wife to be able to receive **sperm** from a donor, she must divorce her husband, wait a religiously mandated 3 months before marrying the **sperm** donor, then divorce him, and finally remarry her original husband.

Iranian clerics' willingness to issue innovative religious rulings coincided with a changing political and demographic climate that also spurred fertility treatments. In the wake of the 1979 revolution, the country embarked on a quest to boost population, but by the late 1980s and early 1990s, as Iran struggled to rebuild in the aftermath of its devastating war with Iraq and with the baby boom in full effect, many questioned whether the country's economy, schools, and cities could handle the population growth. So the authorities reversed course, implementing a set of policies that gently persuaded traditional Iranians to have fewer children.

According to Oxford's Tremayne, authorities carefully avoided words like "reduction" and "control" and instead proposed "regulation of the family," emphasizing that the policy was intended not only to reduce family size but also to enable infertile couples to have families. The bargain worked, as traditionalists embraced the government's antinatal policies and Iran's fertility treatment centers multiplied. By promoting contraception and vasectomies, among other strategies, and withdrawing state subsidies after the second child, Iran managed to reduce its population growth rate from 3.8 percent in 1986 to 1.5 percent in 1996. But it may have worked too well: today, Iran finds itself below the replacement rate of 2.1 children per woman.

In 1999, Khamenei issued his landmark fatwa making third-party **sperm** and **egg** donation permissible. "Both the **egg** donor and the infertile mother must abide by the religious codes regarding parenting," the ayatollah decreed, setting out the various conditions that made the act permissible before God. Through Khamenei's edict, the Islamic Republic had made clear at the highest level that the state was ready to sanction Iranians' efforts to make babies—whatever it took.

Today, the era when infertility was discussed in hushed tones is giving way to a lively culture of intervention and openness. Women chat openly about IVF on state television, couples recommend specialists and trade stories on Internet message boards, and practitioners have begun pushing insurance companies to cover treatment. And the state runs subsidized clinics, so the cost for treatment is lower than almost anywhere else in the world: a full course of IVF, including drugs, runs the equivalent of just $1,500, according to Fallahi.

Khamenei's fatwa was revolutionary for Shiite Muslims everywhere, and it cleared the way for many clinics in Lebanon, which has a significant Shiite population, to follow suit. But according to Yale's Inhorn, Sunnis are also responding to the ruling, with some infertile couples from the Arab world heading to Tehran clinics that employ Arabic interpreters. Sunni countries like Egypt, Turkey, and the United Arab Emirates practice classic IVF widely, but offer no treatment options for men and women who require third-party reproductive assistance to conceive.

"Some Sunni couples have been able to wrap their minds around **egg** donation," says Inhorn. "They can tell themselves, 'Well, at least there's one fatwa that says it's OK. Some branch of Islam says so.' This makes them more at ease."

Still, Fallahi, the physician, says that anxious clients at her clinic in Shiraz often raise the question of religious approval. "They want to be sure what they're doing is not haram," or forbidden by Islamic law, she says. Parliament legalized embryo donation in 2003, providing some legal backing to the supreme leader's religious ruling. Fallahi stresses, however, that Khamenei's edict is the opinion of one marja, or source of emulation, and that not all ayatollahs agree. "We tell people that parliament has approved this, but that they need to check with the marja they follow to see if he gives permission." In some ways, fertility treatment may be the rare area where the Iranian regime has moved forward before society is ready. Although legislators approved embryo donation, they overruled Khamenei on **sperm** donation, banning the procedure in 2003. As a result, the practice was pushed underground, and those clinics that quietly offer the treatment are vulnerable to prosecution. Sara Bamdad, a researcher in Shiraz who conducted a survey on public attitudes about assisted reproduction, found that only 34 percent of respondents approved of **egg** donation. "Lawmakers should be thinking about the future and what is going to happen to these children when they're older," says Bamdad. "If a society can't accept a child that's born of assisted reproduction, then there'll be so many problems in the future."

Iran's legal system has yet to catch up with the implications of third-party fertility treatments. Under Iran's Islamic family law, babies born of **sperm** or **egg** donation fall into the legal category of adopted children and stepchildren, who are not permitted to inherit property from non biological parents. Couples thus must find alternative ways to put aside assets to provide for these kids, and the rights and responsibilities of biological parents (the **egg** or **sperm** donors, who are meant to remain confidential but whose identities are sometimes disclosed in practice) remain unclear. But if religious rulings are still murky, the baby-making revolution may be gently removing cultural taboos around other areas of sexual health. The Avicenna Infertility Clinic in Tehran, the country's most prominent fertility treatment center, has recently opened a health clinic that treats sexual dysfunction and sexually transmitted diseases.

Tremayne recounts visiting a fertility clinic where a large room full of men and women sat watching a video transmission of a surgery to fertilize a woman's **egg** on a giant television screen. "Our intention is to create a new culture so that people understand how babies are conceived and how infertility can be treated," a doctor told Tremayne. Scenes like this are part of a broader effort to educate the public, and while it may take years for infertility to lose its stigma in Iranian culture, the discussion of bodies and their biological functions and failings may be gradually helping Iranian men and women share responsibility for what has for centuries been the profound nang, or dishonor, laid at the feet of women.

The pursuit of cutting-edge baby-making has launched a process that could ultimately change what it means to be married and infertile, what it means to be a parent, even what it means to be kin in the Islamic Republic. As Iran struggles with the collision between its people's evolving values and the tenets of Islamic law, its success with fertility treatment suggests that it just may be possible to reconcile these competing pressures. But whether it will catch on in the Sunni Middle East is an open question.

"Iran is surging ahead using [these technologies] in all their forms," Tremayne says, "going places where the Sunni countries in the region cannot follow."

Critical Thinking

1. How do infertility rates in Iran compare with other countries such as the United States?
2. How do marriage laws in Iran conflict with fertility treatments that are currently available and future treatments such as artificial sperm or uterus transplants?

Create Central

www.mhhe.com/createcentral

Internet References

Central Intelligence Agency The World Fact Book Total Fertility Rates
https://www.cia.gov/library/publications/the-world-factbook/field

faculty.washington.edu Modernization and Consanguineous Marriage in Iran
http://faculty.washington.edu/charles/pubs/1994-ModernizationConsanguineousMarriageIran.pdf

Islamweb.net Infertility: the Struggle to Conceive
http://www.islamweb.net/womane/nindex.php?page=readart&id=149490s/2127.html

IVF.net IVF Clinics Middle East
http://www.ivf.net/ivf/royan-institute-o3899.html

The National Center for Biotechnology Information Making Muslim babies: IVF and gamete donation in Sunni versus Shi'a Islam
http://www.ncbi.nlm.nih.gov/pmc/articles/PMC1705533

UN.org Recent Changes and the Future of Fertility in Iran
http://www.un.org/esa/population/publications/completingfertility/2RevisedABBASIpaper.PDF

Moaveni, Azadeh. "The Islamic Republic of Baby-Making." *Foreign Policy*. 204 (January, 2014): 1–8.

Article Prepared by: Claire N. Rubman, *Suffolk County Community College*

Beyond the Baby Weight

Most expectant mothers know that how they take care of their body during pregnancy will affect the health of their newborn child. Now, new research suggests that some aspects of prenatal care, specifically maternal weight gain, may impact a child's health well into adolescence.

ERIC REITHER

Learning Outcomes

After reading this article, you will be able to:

- Articulate why children born to obese women are more likely to be obese as adolescents.
- Discuss the "troubling intergenerational cycle" among native Hawaiian and Pacific women.
- Explain the term *epigenetics* and its effect on a developing fetus' body weight in later life.

Using the Utah Population Database, Utah State University Associate Professor Eric Reither and his colleagues have been able to tease out links between timing of prenatal care and obesity rates among different ethnic groups in the state of Utah. The Utah Population Database is one of the most comprehensive population records in the nation, tracking information including timing of initial prenatal care, mother's and child's weights at time of birth, weight of a child upon receiving their driver's license, and ethnicity.

Reither's research divided information from the population database along ethnic lines for three groups: Native Hawaiian and other Pacific Islanders (NHOPI), Asians, and non-Hispanic Whites. The researchers decided to focus on these groups because their lifestyles, access to health care, and rates of disease vary greatly.

"Their socioeconomic characteristics tend to be different," said Reither. "So, for example, levels of education, levels of income tend to be different across those groups. Also, groups from mainland Asia in the U.S. have some of the lowest levels of obesity observed among any ethnic group. Conversely, Native Hawaiians and Pacific Islanders tend to have quite high levels of obesity and diabetes. A lot of research examines these groups as a single entity, obscuring their considerable differences."

Having such a large and diverse population sample allowed researchers to compare many variables. "We were interested in the effects that prenatal care could have in narrowing some pretty stark ethnic differences in obesity," said Reither. Among other important influences like mother's education and family structure, two major factors appear to influence a child's rate of obesity during their adolescent years: a mother's weight during pregnancy and her access to prenatal care.

"We suspect that timely prenatal care encourages mothers to adopt healthy behaviors early," said Reither. "Overweight women are more likely to have larger babies and are more likely to gain weight in excess of doctors' recommendations during pregnancy." In their article, "Prenatal Care, Childhood Obesity, and Ethnic Health Disparities: Analyses from a Unique Population Database" published in the *Journal of Heath Care for the Poor and Underserved,* the researchers suggested that the best way for overweight women to achieve optimal health outcomes for their babies was to gain a limited but healthy amount of weight during pregnancy.

As upward trends in obesity continue, teaching women about the risks of being obese during pregnancy may be more important than ever. According to the Utah Population Database, rates of obesity in expectant mothers were 4 percent among Asians, 9 percent among non-Hispanic Whites, and 14 percent among NHOPIs. Of course, an overweight mother does not guarantee that a child will become obese, leading the researchers to believe that something else about prenatal care plays a role in children's lives.

Results from analyses of the population database suggest that children of obese women are far more likely to be obese during adolescence—especially if their mother did not receive prenatal care until after the first trimester. "Women who initiated prenatal care at an early stage of pregnancy were much less likely to have offspring who struggled with obesity in adolescence," Reither pointed out.

Timing appears to be key for pregnant women seeking prenatal care. Reduced adolescent obesity was only seen in mothers who visited doctors during their first trimester. Even women who received the same quality of care and visited the doctor the same number of times, but who waited to begin visits until later in their pregnancies were more likely to have children who were overweight during adolescence than women who initiated prenatal care early on.

"If expectant mothers can prevent obesity and other health complications during pregnancy, their offspring will have better chances for healthy lives down the road."

—Eric Reither

What occurs in a mother's body during the first trimester is known to have a significant effect on the developing fetus. "If expectant mothers can prevent obesity and other health complications during pregnancy, their offspring will have better chances for healthy lives down the road," Reither said.

Although the genes that a child receives from their parents are fixed, the structure of the genes is not. Changes in structure can be caused by environmental factors which can turn individual genes on or off. These small changes in the genome—known as epigenetics—can have large effects throughout a person's lifetime. A woman's weight during her first trimester of pregnancy may change which genes are activated in her child, possibly increasing the child's risk for obesity later in life.

Reither suggests that changes in gene expression happen early in pregnancy, which is why healthy changes to a mother's diet have a bigger effect if they are implemented in the first trimester. "Doctors now will recommend early in pregnancy—and in fact, even before considering pregnancy—that women do certain things to improve their health," Reither said. "Actually, that both partners do certain things for a period of time to maximize potential health outcomes."

Although it doesn't appear that these epigenetic changes can be reversed with healthy lifestyle changes in later months of pregnancy, Reither does not want to dissuade mothers from making changes if they miss the first trimester window. "I think that if halfway through a pregnancy a woman realized that she could do a little better in terms of diet and exercise that, of course, is preferable to no changes in behavior," he said.

Rates of obesity can vary widely between ethnic groups. In Utah, NHOPI women were more likely than women of other ethnicities to be obese and were about 20 percent less likely to initiate prenatal care in their first trimester of pregnancy. This relationship between maternal obesity, high birth weight, and adolescent obesity is what Reither referred to as a "troubling intergenerational cycle" in his article.

"The idea is that after a few generations, both from an epigenetic standpoint and from a sociological standpoint, these things can become fairly entrenched," Reither said. For researchers trying to determine how to best break this intergenerational cycle, determining where changes need to be made can be difficult, as both social and genetic factors influence a person's weight. "You start looking for interventions—ways that you can break through cycles and you know there's no simple answer to that, no magic bullet, but it seems that early adoption of prenatal care could be one useful tool to help break these cycles of obesity among certain ethnic groups."

Reither and his colleagues hope that this study will encourage insurance companies and public health agencies to adopt programs that encourage all pregnant women to visit with their doctors as early as possible. "The evidence suggests that early initiation of prenatal care really does help. Doctors are well positioned to encourage good nutrition, reasonable levels of physical activity, and appropriate weight gain to help women and their offspring avoid obesity and related health complications."—ET

Critical Thinking

1. How does the use of the longitudinal research paradigm in this study enhance our understanding of pregnancy and weight gain?
2. How can this important information about weight gain during pregnancy be disseminated to all ethic groups?

Create Central

www.mhhe.com/createcentral

Internet References

How a Pregnant Woman's Choices Could Shape a Child's Health

http://www.npr.org/blogs/health/2013/09/23/224387744/how-a-pregnant-womans-choices-could-shape-a-childs-health

Pregnancy weight gain: What's healthy?—Mayo Clinic

http://www.mayoclinic.org/healthy-living/pregnancy-week-by-week/in-depth/pregnancy-weight-gain/art-20044360

Reither, Eric. "Beyond the Baby Weight." *Utah Science* 67. 1 (Spring/Summer 2013): 16–19.

Unit 2

UNIT

Prepared by: Claire N. Rubman, *Suffolk County Community College*

Development During Infancy and Early Childhood

When you look at a newborn baby, what is he or she capable of? How long will it be until this little bundle of joy steals, plays video games, or feels sorry for a friend? Whether this is our child or a child we are taking care of, what can we do to enhance development? What are the best decisions in terms of vaccinations at the doctor's office or toys in the toy box?

Looking at neonates, or newborns, in a hospital nursery, they may all appear to be relatively similar. Alice Sterling Honig looks at the differences between newborns and the relative care that each personality type requires. The emotional connections that a caregiver forms with an infant can "unlock the treasures of loving kindness, thoughtful, and eloquent use of language, intensive active curiosity to learn and willingness to cooperate, and the deep desire to work hard to master new tasks." With the importance of this care in mind, Honig gives specific guidelines to optimize learning and development in several key areas. A caregiver should nurture the emotional nature of an infant. Stress should be addressed to encourage better attachment bonds. Learning should be from an infant-centered perspective, and games should be used as learning tools. This type of respectful childcare is more likely to develop an infant with empathy and a solid social, emotional, and cognitive foundation for development.

Turning to a child's medical wellbeing, to provide our infants with the best possible start in life, the potential exists to vaccinate them against such childhood diseases as polio, measles, mumps, and rubella. Is it possible, however, that the very vaccines that were developed to protect our infants from disease could, instead, be harming our children? Mooney's article titled "Vaccination Nation" explores the relationship between a component in some vaccinations, thimerosal, and the increased rates of autism in young children. He reviews the debate that reaches back to 1998 that was fueled in part by a researcher in England, Dr. Andrew Wakefield. Wakefield claimed that the vaccine itself caused intestinal damage and a release of toxins that affected the brain. Since thimerosal has been removed from children's vaccinations, the rates of autism have not decreased accordingly, lending credence to the notion that it was not the root cause of autism. Mooney addresses the potential risk to young children who are not vaccinated as a result of this "vaccination scare."

Empathy is the focus of Pariakian and Lerner's article titled "How to Help Your Toddler Begin Developing Empathy." They give suggestions to parents and caregivers that can nurture this skill in young children. Because infants and toddlers are extremely self-centered at this age, this is a skill that will, according to Pariakian and Lerner, take time to develop. It serves to separate popular from rejected children. It is a complex skill that takes years of time and much experience and social interaction to develop. Empathy in early childhood relies on a child's understanding of the separation of the self from others, and it develops in conjunction with a child's theory of the mind between ages 18 and 24 months. This is a time when toddlers begin to recognize their own unique thoughts and feelings that can be different from other people's feelings or thoughts.

Whether we are sitting in the doctor's waiting room or in our living rooms at home, children love to be entertained. In our technologically savvy world, children's toys have become increasingly more advanced. Stephen Gass compares blocks and dolls with iPads and computers. Children born in the technological era, known as "digital natives," are anticipated to take initiative, respond to their own natural curiosity, and persist longer in difficult tasks. Despite this initial allure of technology, it may not be an ideal educational tool, according to recent research. Gass recommends playing, exploration, and experimentation as ideal learning tools for optimal cognitive development. He concludes that simplicity is the best tool for children's learning, reminding the reader that the focus should not be on what the adult brings to the child—digital versus traditional toys per se—but rather what the child takes away from the experience.

Hanna Rosin's article, "The Touch-Screen Generation," continues this discussion in more detail. She discusses technology from a cognitive and social perspective citing such issues as the "video deficit," that is, children can remember significantly more information if it is presented by a real person rather than a video screen. To explain this phenomenon, she cites Troseth's research, which concludes that children seek out "socially relevant information," but they learn from an early age that the television screen does not provide any actual interaction because it lacks this "two way exchange of information." Rosin alludes to the American Academy of Pediatrics guidelines of 2011 that children under the age of two should not watch any television, but she doesn't seem convinced! She challenges this notion by presenting possible educational gains from educational television or iPad apps. She questions what Maria Montessori, the founder of the Montessori approach, would have thought of this technology. Rosin, a mother herself, decides to allow her (almost) 2-year-old son to follow the "Prensky Rules"—basically, technology without time limits. She claimed that for 10 days her son played with an iPad for two-hour stretches several times per day, then he lost interest in it altogether. What can we conclude about technology and the role of research in child psychology?

Rosin experimented, albeit informally, on her youngest child. Would she have been as cavalier with her first or second child? What role does birth order play in the development of a child? Does it matter if you are the firstborn or the youngest child in the family? Ogden addresses birth order in her article, "Luck of the Draw." Are firstborn children more cautious but more intelligent? Is it possible that they are taller and have larger waists and higher blood pressure, making them more susceptible to heart disease, strokes, or hypertension? Similarly, Rosin discusses that younger brothers may be more likely to be homosexuals and younger children in general were more likely to end up in the emergency room with asthma. Are these statistical anomalies or does birth order really matter?

The final article in this unit looks to the safety and well-being of our infants and toddlers. "No Child Locked Inside" by Jorge Rossi addresses the tragic loss of life when a child is locked inside a car because he or she was forgotten by a parent or child minder. Perhaps, the advent of airbags has increased this tragic epidemic because infant and toddler seats must be placed in the rear of a car where they can be forgotten more easily. It is also possible that parents are multitasking, working more hours, and are so exhausted that this type of tragic mistake is more common. Rossi describes one state's action and awareness plan to combat this social phenomenon.

Article

Prepared by: Claire N. Rubman, *Suffolk County Community College*

Keys to Quality Infant Care

Nurturing Every Baby's Life Journey

ALICE STERLING HONIG

Learning Outcomes

After reading this article, you will be able to:

- Distinguish between three infant temperament types and explain why each baby's unique personality should be explored.
- Defend the author's assertion that love and intimate connections are paramount requirements for quality infant care.

Teachers of infants need a large bunch of key ideas and activities of all kinds to unlock in each child the treasures of loving kindness, thoughtful and eloquent use of language, intense active curiosity to learn, willingness to cooperate, and the deep desire to work hard to master new tasks. Here are some ideas that teachers can use during interactions with infants to optimize each child's development.

Get to Know Each Baby's Unique Personality

At 4 months, Luci holds her hands in front of her face and turns them back and forth so she can see the curious visual difference between the palms and backs. Jackson, an 8-month-old, bounces happily in accurate rhythm as his teacher bangs on a drum and chants, "Mary had a little lamb whose fleece was white as snow!" Outdoors, 1-year-old Jamie sits in an infant swing peering down at his feet sticking out of the leg holes. How interesting! Those are the same feet he has watched waving in the air while being diapered and has triumphantly brought to his mouth to chew on.

Teachers can tune in to each child's special personality—especially the child's temperament. There are three primary, mostly inborn, styles of temperament (Honig 1997). Some babies are more low-key; they tend to be slow to warm up to new caregivers, new foods, and new surroundings. They need reassuring hand-holding and more physical supports to try a new activity. Others are more feisty and sometimes irritable. They tend to be impetuous, intense in their emotional reactions, whether of anger or of joy. Easygoing babies are typically friendly, happy, accept new foods and caregivers without much fuss, and adapt fairly quickly and more flexibly after experiencing distress or sudden change. Try to find out whether each baby in your care tends to be shy and slow to warm up *or* mostly feisty and intense *or* easygoing. A caring adult's perceptive responses in tune with individual temperament will ease a child's ability to adapt and flourish in the group setting.

Physical Loving

Your body is a safe haven for an infant. Indeed, some babies will stay happy as a clam when draped over a shoulder, across your belly as you rock in a rocking chair, or, especially for a very young baby, snuggled in a sling or carrier for hours. As Montagu (1971) taught decades ago, babies need *body loving:* "To be tender, loving, and caring, human beings must be tenderly loved and cared for in their earliest years. . . . caressed, cuddled, and comforted" (p. 138).

As you carry them, some babies might pinch your neck, lick your salty arm, pull at your hair, tug at eyeglasses, or show you in other ways how powerfully important your body is as a sacred and special playground. Teach gentleness by calmly telling a baby you need your glasses on to read a story. Use the word *gently* over and over and over. Dance cheek-to-cheek with a young child in arms to slow waltz music—good for dreary days! Also carry the baby while you do a routine task such as walking to another room to get something.

Provide lap and touch times generously to nourish a child's sense of well-being. Slowly caress a baby's hair. Rub a tense shoulder soothingly. Kiss one finger and watch as a baby offers every other finger to kiss. Rock a child with your arms wrapped around him for secure comfort. Babies learn to become independent as we confirm and meet their dependency needs in infancy. A sense of well-being and somatic certainty flows from cherishing adults who generously hold, caress, and drape babies on shoulders and tummies.

Create Intimate Emotional Connections

Scan the environment so you can be close to every baby. Notice the quiet baby sitting alone, mouthing a toy piece and rocking back and forth with vacant eyes. Notice shy bids for attention, such as a brief smile with lowered lids. The child with an easy or cautious temperament needs your loving attention as much as the one who impulsively climbs all over you for attention.

A caring adult's perceptive responses in tune with individual temperament will ease a child's ability to adapt and flourish in the group setting.

Shine admiring eyes at the children, whether a baby is cooing as she lies in her crib, creeping purposefully toward a toy she desires, or feeding herself happily with messy fingers. Speak each child's name lovingly and frequently. Even if they are fussing, most babies will quiet when you chant and croon their names.

Although babies do not understand the meanings of the words, they do understand *tonal* nuances and love when your voice sounds admiring, enchanted with them, and happy to be talking with them. While diapering, tell the baby he is so delicious and you love his plump tummy and the few wispy hairs on that little head. Watch him thrust out his legs in delight on the diapering table. Your tone of voice entrances him into a deep sense of pleasure with his own body (Honig 2002).

Harmonizing Tempos

Tempo is important in human activities and is reflected in how abruptly or smoothly adults carry out daily routines. Because adults have so many tasks to do, sometimes we use impatient, too-quick motions, for example, while dressing a baby to play outdoors. When dressing or feeding, more leisurely actions are calming. They signal to children that we have time for them. Rub backs slowly and croon babies into soothing sleep.

A baby busily crawling across the rug sees a toy, grasps it, then plops himself into a sitting position to examine and try to pull it apart. He slowly looks back and forth at the toy as he leisurely passes it from hand to hand. He has no awareness that a teacher is about to interrupt because she is in a hurry to get him dressed because his daddy is coming to pick him up. Young children need time and cheerful supports to finish up an activity in which they are absorbed. If they are hurried, they may get frustrated and even have a tantrum.

Enhance Courage and Cooperation

Your presence can reassure a worried baby. Stay near and talk gently to help a child overcome his fear of the small infant slide. Pascal sits at the top, looking uncertain. Then he checks your face for a go-ahead signal, for reassurance that he can bravely try to slide down this slide that looks so long to him. Kneeling at the bottom of the slide, smile and tell him that you will be there to catch him when he is ready to slide down.

Be available as a "refueling station"—Margaret Mahler's felicitous term (Kaplan 1978). Sometimes a baby's independent learning adventure comes crashing down—literally. Your body and your lap provide the emotional support from which a baby regains courage to tackle the learning adventure again.

Create loving rituals during daily routines of dressing, bath times, nap times, feeding times. Babies like to know what will happen and when and where and how. Babies have been known to refuse lunch when their familiar, comfortable routines were changed. At cleanup times, older babies can be more flexible and helpful if you change some chores into games. Through the use of sing-song chants, putting toys away becomes an adventure in finding the big fat blocks that need to be placed together on a shelf and then the skinny blocks that go together in a different place.

Young children need time and cheerful supports to finish up an activity in which they are absorbed. If they are hurried, they may get frustrated and even have a tantrum.

Address Stress

Attachment research shows that babies who develop secure emotional relationships with a teacher have had their distress signals noticed, interpreted correctly, and responded to promptly and appropriately (Honig 2002). At morning arrival times, watch for separation anxiety. Sometimes holding and wordlessly commiserating with a baby's sad feelings can help more than a frenzied attempt to distract her (Klein, Kraft, & Shohet 2010). As you become more expert at interpreting a baby's body signals of distress and discomfort, you will become more sensitively attuned in your responses (Honig 2010).

Learn Developmental Milestones

Learning developmental norms helps teachers figure out when to wonder, when to worry, and when to relish and feel overjoyed about a child's milestone accomplishments. Day and night toilet learning can be completed anywhere from 18 months to 5 years. This is a *wide* time window for development. In contrast, learning to pick up a piece of cereal from a high chair tray with just thumb and forefinger in a fine pincer grasp is usually completed during a *narrow* time window well before 13 months. By 11 months, most babies become expert at using just the first two fingers.

Hone Your Detective Skills

If a baby is screaming and jerking knees up to his belly, you might suspect a painful gas bubble. Pick up the baby and jiggle and thump his back until you get that burp up. What a relief, for you as well as baby. Maybe an irritable, yowling baby just needs to be tucked in quietly and smoothly for a nap after an expert diaper change. Suppose baby is crying and thrashing about, and yet he has been burped and diapered. Use all your detective skills to determine the cause. Is it a hot day? He might be thirsty. A drink of water can help him calm down.

Notice Stress Signs

Scan a child's body for stress signs. Dull eyes can signal the need for more intimate loving interactions. Tense shoulders and a grave look often mean that a child is afraid or worried (Honig 2010). Compulsive rocking can mean a baby feels forlorn. Watch for lonesomeness and wilting.

Some babies melt down toward day's end. They need to be held and snuggled. Murmur sweet reassurances and provide a small snack of strained applesauce to soothe baby's taste buds and worries. Check his body from top to bottom for signs of stresses or tensions, such as eyes avoiding contact, teeth grinding, fingernail chewing, frequently clenched fists, so that you can develop an effective plan for soothing. Be alert, and tend to children's worrisome bodily signs; these will tell you what you need to know long before children have enough language to share what was stressful (Honig 2009).

Play Learning Games

Parents and teachers are a baby's preferred playmates. While playing learning games with infants, pay attention to their actions. Ask yourself if the game has become so familiar and easy that it is time to "dance up the developmental ladder" (Honig 1982) and increase the game's challenge. Or perhaps the game is still too baffling and you need to "dance down" and simplify the activity so that the child can succeed.

Provide safe mirrors at floor level and behind the diapering table so children can watch and learn about their own bodies. Hold babies in arms up to a mirror to reach out and pat the face in the mirror. Lying on the floor in front of a securely attached safety mirror, a young child twists and squirms to get an idea of where his body begins and ends.

Your body can serve as a comforting support for some early learning activities. Sit an infant on your lap and watch as he coordinates vision and grasp to reach and hold a toy you are dangling. Babies love "Peek-a-boo! I see you!" These games nurture the development of object permanence—the understanding that objects still exist even when they are out of sight. Peek-a-boo games also symbolically teach that even when a special adult is not seen, that dear person will reappear.

Provide Physical Play Experiences

Play pat-a-cake with babies starting even before 6 months. As you gently hold a baby's hands and bring them out and then back together, chant slowly and joyously, "Pat-a-cake, pat-a-cake, baker's man; bake me a cake just as fast as you can. Pat it, and roll it, and mark it with a *B*, and put it in the oven for [baby's name] and me." Smile with joy as you guide the baby's hands rhythmically and slowly through the game, and use a high-pitched voice as you emphasize her name in the sing-song chant. Over the next months, as soon as you begin chanting the words, the baby will begin to bring hands to the midline and do the hand motions that belong with this game. Babies who are 9 to 11 months old will even start copying the hand-rolling motions that belong with this game.

To encourage learning, try to arrange games with more physical actions. Sit on the floor with your toes touching the baby's toes, then model how to roll a ball back and forth.

Introduce Sensory Experiences

Safe sensory and tactile experiences are ideal for this age group. As he shifts a toy from hand to hand, turns it over, pokes, tastes, bangs, and even chews on it, a baby uses his senses to learn about the toy's physical properties. Teachers can blow bubbles so babies can reach for and crawl after them. Provide play-dough made with plenty of salt to discourage children from putting it in their mouths. Older babies enjoy exploring finger paints or nontoxic tempera paint and fat brushes.

Play Sociable Games

Give something appealing to a seated baby. Put out your hand, smile, and say "Give it to me, please." The baby may chew on the "gift," such as a safe wooden block or chunky plastic cylinder peg. After the baby passes it to you, say thank you, then give the object back with a smile. Give-and-take games with you are a sociable pleasure for babies and teach them turn-taking skills that are crucial for friendly social interchanges years later.

Seated on a chair, play a bouncing game, with the baby's back resting snuggly against your tummy. After you stop bouncing and chanting "Giddyup, horsie," a baby often bounces on his or her tush as if to remind you to start this game over and over. An older baby vigorously demands "More horsie!" to get you to restart this game. Babies enjoy kinesthetic stimulation too, such as when you swing them gently in a baby swing. A baby will grin with glee as you pull or push him in a wagon around the room or playground.

Observe Babies' Ways of Exploring and Learning

Observe a baby to learn what and how she is learning, then adapt the activity to offer greater challenge. Observation provides information that lets teachers determine when and how to arrange for the next step in a child's learning experience. Watch quietly as a baby tries with determination to put the round wood top piece for a ring stack set on the pole. His eyes widen in startled amazement as he gradually realizes that when the hole does not go through the middle, then that piece will not go down over the pole—a frustrating but important lesson. Calmly, a teacher can demonstrate how to place the piece on top of the pole while using simple words to describe how this piece is different. She can also gently guide the baby's hands so he feels successful at placing the piece on top.

Enhance Language and Literacy in Everyday Routines

Talk back and forth with babies; respond to their coos and babbles with positive talk. When the baby vocalizes, tell her, "What a terrific talker you are. Tell me some more."

The diapering table is a fine site for language games. With young babies, practice "parentese"—a high-pitched voice, drawn-out vowels, and slow and simple talk. This kind of talk fires up the brain neurons that carry messages to help a baby learn (Doidge 2007). Cascades of chemicals and electrical signals course down the baby's neural pathways. A baby responds when you are an attentive and delighted talking partner. Pause so the baby gets a turn to talk too, and bring the game to a graceful close when baby fatigue sets in.

Talk about body parts on dolls, stuffed animals, yourself, and the babies in the room. Talk about what the baby sees as you lift her onto your lap and then onto your shoulders. Talk at mealtimes. Use every daily routine as an opportunity to enhance oral language (Honig 2007).

Daily reading is an intimate one-on-one activity that young babies deeply enjoy in varied spaces and at varied times of the day (Honig 2004). Hook your babies on books as early as possible. Frequent shared picture-book experiences are priceless gifts. Early pleasurable reading experiences empower success in learning to read years later in grade school (Jalongo 2007).

Cuddle with one or several children as you read and share books together every day. Use dramatic tones along with loving and polite words. You are the master of the story as you read aloud. Feel free to add to or to shorten picture-book text according to a particular child's needs. Group reading times can be pleasurable when infants lean against you as you sit on the rug and share a picture book. Teachers often prefer the intimacy of individual reading times with babies (Honig & Shin 2001). Individual reading can help a tense or fussy baby relax in your lap as he becomes deeply absorbed in sharing the picture-book experience.

Encourage Mastery Experiences

Children master many linguistic, physical, and social skills in the first years of life. Watch the joy of mastery and self-appreciation as a baby succeeds at a task, such as successfully placing Montessori cylinders into their respective sockets. Babies enjoy clapping for their own efforts. Mastery experiences arranged in thoughtful doses bring much pleasure, such an eagerness to keep on exploring, trying, and learning. Watch the baby's joy as he proudly takes a long link chain out of a coffee can and then stuffs it slowly back in the can. He straightens his shoulders with such pride as he succeeds at this game of finding a way to put a long skinny chain into a round container with a small diameter opening.

Mastery experiences arranged in thoughtful doses bring much pleasure, such an eagerness to keep on exploring, trying, and learning.

Vygotsky taught that the *zone of proximal development* is crucial for adult-child coordination in learning activities. You the teacher are so important in helping a child to succeed when a task may be slightly too difficult for the child to solve alone. Hold the baby's elbow steady when she feels frustrated while trying to stack one block on top of another. For a difficult puppy puzzle, a teacher taped down a few of the pieces so a baby could succeed in getting the puppy's tail and head pieces in the right spaces. If a baby has been struggling with a slippery nesting cup for a while, just steady the stack of cups so he can successfully insert a smaller cup into the next largest one.

Promote Socioemotional Skills

Babies learn empathy and friendliness from those who nurture them. Empathy involves recognizing and feeling the distress of another and trying to help in some way. A young baby who sees another baby crying may look worried and suck his thumb to comfort himself. Fifteen-month-old Michael tussles over a toy with Paul, who starts to cry. Michael looks worried and lets go of the toy so Paul has it. As Paul keeps crying, Michael gives him his own teddy bear. But Paul continues crying. Michael pauses, then runs to the next room and gets Paul's security blanket for him. And Paul stops crying (Blum 1987).

When teachers showed deeply respectful caregiving, then they observed that babies did develop early empathy and internalize the friendly interactions they had experienced.

Friendliness includes making accommodations so children can play together. For example, move a child over to make room for a peer, or make overtures to invite other babies to engage in peer play. Perhaps they could take turns toddling in and out of a cardboard house. Babies act friendly when they sit near each other and companionably play with toys, happy to be close together. McMullen and colleagues (2009) observed that positive social-emotional interactions were rare in some infant rooms. But when teachers showed deeply respectful caregiving, then they observed that babies did develop early empathy and internalize the friendly interactions they had experienced. One teacher is described below:

> Her wonderful gentle manner, the way she speaks to the babies, how they are all her friends . . . only someone who utterly respects and values babies could put that kind of effort into this the way she does, almost like she is setting a beautiful table for honored guests each and every morning. (McMullen et al. 2009, p. 27)

Conclusion

Later in life, a baby will not remember your specific innumerable kindly caring actions in the earliest years. However, a child's *feelings* of being lovable and cherished will remain a body-memory for life. These feelings of having been loved will permeate positive emotional and social relationships decades later.

Keep your own joy pipes open. How brief are the years of babyhood. All too soon young children grow into the mysterious world of teenagers who prefer hanging out with peers to snuggling on an adult lap. Reflect with deep personal satisfaction on your confidence and delight in caring for tiny ones—hearing the first words, seeing the joy at a new accomplishment, watching the entranced look of an upturned face as you tell a story, feeling the trust as a baby sleepily settles onto your lap for refreshment of spirit, for a breath of the loving comfort that emanates from your body.

Life has grown more complicated in our technological, economically difficult, and more and more urbanized world. But you, the teacher, remain each baby's priceless tour guide into the world of "growing up!" You gently take each little person by the hand—literally and figuratively—and lure each and every baby into feeling the wonder and the somatic certainty of being loved, lovable, and cherished so that each baby can fully participate in the adventure of growing, loving, and learning.

Your nurturing strengthens a baby's determination to keep on learning, keep on cooperating, keep on being friendly, and keep on growing into a loving person—first in the world of the nursery and later in the wider world. You can give no greater gift to a child than to be the best guide possible as each child begins his or her unique life journey.

References

Blum, L. 1987. Particularity and responsiveness. In *The emergence of morality in young children,* eds. J. Kagan & S. Lamb, 306–37. Chicago: University of Chicago Press.

Doidge, N. 2007. *The brain that changes itself.* New York: Penguin.

Honig, A.S. 1982. *Playtime learning games for young children.* Syracuse, NY: Syracuse University Press.

Honig, A.S. 1997. Infant temperament and personality: What do we need to know? *Montessori Life* 9 (3): 18–21.

Honig, A.S. 2002. *Secure environments: Nurturing infant/toddler attachment in child care settings.* Washington, DC: NAEYC.

Honig, A.S. 2004. Twenty ways to boost your baby's brain power. *Scholastic Parent and Child* 11 (4): 55–56.

Honig, A.S. 2007. Oral language development. *Early Child Development and Care* 177 (6): 581–613.

Honig, A.S. 2009. Stress and young children. In *Informing our practice: Useful research on young children's development,* eds. E. Essa & M.M. Burnham, 71–88. Washington, DC: NAEYC.

Honig, A.S. 2010. *Little kids, big worries: Stress-busting tips for early childhood classrooms.* Baltimore: Brookes.

Honig, A.S., & M. Shin. 2001. Reading aloud to infants and toddlers in childcare settings: An observational study. *Early Childhood Education Journal* 28 (3): 193–97.

Jalongo, M.R. 2007. *Early childhood language arts.* 4th ed. New York: Pearson.

Kaplan, L. 1978. *Oneness and separateness: From infant to individual.* New York: Simon & Schuster.

Klein, P.S., R.R. Kraft, & C. Shohet. 2010. Behavior patterns in daily mother-child separations: Possible opportunites for stress reduction. *Early Child Development and Care* 180: 387–96.

McMullen, M.B., J.M. Addleman, A.M. Fulford, S. Moore, S.J. Mooney, S.S. Sisk, & J. Zachariah. 2009. Learning to be *me* while coming to understand *we.* Encouraging prosocial babies in group settings. *Young Children* 64 (4): 20–28. www.naeyc.org/files/yc/file/200907/McMullenWeb709.pdf

Montagu, A. 1971. *Touching: The human significance of the skin.* New York: Harper & Row.

Critical Thinking

1. Identify the three primary, inborn styles of temperament.
2. Why is physical contact an important aspect of quality infant care?
3. What are ways to enhance language development in infants?

Create Central

www.mhhe.com/createcentral

Internet References

Baby Center
www.babycenter.com

Early Childhood Care and Development
www.ecdgroup.com

Project Viva
www.dacp.org/viva

The National Association for the Education of Young Children (NAEYC)
www.naeyc.org

Zero to Three: National Center for Infants, Toddlers, and Families
www.zerotothree.org

Alice Sterling Honig, PhD, is professor emerita of child development in the College of Human Ecology at Syracuse University, where she has taught the QIC (Quality Infant/Toddler Caregiving) Workshop for 34 years. She is the author or editor of more than two dozen books and more than 500 articles and chapters on early childhood. As a licensed New York State clinician, she works with children and families coping with a variety of troubles, such as divorce or learning difficulties. ahonig@syr.edu.

Article

Prepared by: Claire N. Rubman, *Suffolk County Community College*

Vaccination Nation

The decadelong controversy surrounding the safety of vaccines is over—or is it? A fierce debate continues wover what really puts our children at risk.

CHRIS MOONEY

Learning Outcomes

After reading this article, you will be able to:

- Defend the pro-vaccine group's position of "Every Child by Two."
- Explain the apparent increase in autistic spectrum disorders today.

Vaccines do not cause autism. That was the ruling in each of three critical test cases handed down on February 12 by the U.S. Court of Federal Claims in Washington, D.C. After a decade of speculation, argument, and analysis—often filled with vitriol on both sides—the court specifically denied any link between the combination of the MMR vaccine and vaccines with thimerosal (a mercury-based preservative) and the spectrum of disorders associated with autism. But these rulings, though seemingly definitive, have done little to quell the angry debate, which has severe implications for American public health.

The idea that there is something wrong with our vaccines—that they have poisoned a generation of kids, driving an "epidemic" of autism—continues to be everywhere: on cable news, in celebrity magazines, on blogs, and in health news stories. It has had a particularly strong life on the Internet, including the heavily trafficked *The Huffington Post,* and in pop culture, where it is supported by actors including Charlie Sheen and Jim Carrey, former *Playboy* playmate Jenny McCarthy, and numerous others. Despite repeated rejection by the scientific community, it has spawned a movement, led to thousands of legal claims, and even triggered occasional harassment and threats against scientists whose research appears to discredit it.

You can see where the emotion and sentiment come from. Autism can be a terrible condition, devastating to families. It can leave parents not only aggrieved but desperate to find any cure, any salvation. Medical services and behavioral therapy for severely autistic children can cost more than $100,000 a year, and these children often exhibit extremely difficult behavior. Moreover, the incidence of autism is apparently rising rapidly. Today one in every 150 children has been diagnosed on the autism spectrum; 20 years ago that statistic was one in 10,000. "Put yourself in the shoes of these parents," says journalist David Kirby, whose best-selling 2005 book, *Evidence of Harm,* dramatized the vaccine-autism movement. "They have perfectly normal kids who are walking and happy and everything—and then they regress." The irony is that vaccine skepticism—not the vaccines themselves—is now looking like the true public-health threat.

The decadelong vaccine-autism saga began in 1998, when British gastroenterologist Andrew Wakefield and his colleagues published evidence in *The Lancet* suggesting they had tracked down a shocking cause of autism. Examining the digestive tracts of 12 children with behavioral disorders, nine of them autistic, the researchers found intestinal inflammation, which they pinned on the MMR (measles, mumps, and rubella) vaccine. Wakefield had a specific theory of how the MMR shot could trigger autism: The upset intestines, he conjectured, let toxins loose in the bloodstream, which then traveled to the brain. The vaccine was, in this view, effectively a poison. In a dramatic press conference, Wakefield announced the findings and sparked an instant media frenzy. For the British public, a retreat from the use of the MMR vaccine—and a rise in the incidence of measles—began.

In the United States, meanwhile, fears would soon arise concerning another means by which vaccines might induce autism. Many vaccines at the time contained thimerosal, a preservative introduced in the 1930s to make vaccines safer by preventing bacterial contamination. But thimerosal is 50 percent mercury by weight, and mercury is known to be a potent neurotoxin, at least in large doses. In 1999 new federal safety guidelines for mercury in fish stirred concerns about vaccines as well.

The U.S. government responded by ordering that thimerosal be removed from all vaccines administered to children under age 6, or reduced to trace amounts. (Some inactivated influenza vaccines were exempted.) The step was described as a "precautionary" measure. There was no proof of harm, government researchers said, just reason to worry that there might be. Meanwhile, scientists launched numerous studies to determine whether thimerosal had actually caused an autism epidemic, while some parents and their lawyers started pointing fingers and developing legal cases.

Within weeks of this year's federal court decisions—which examined and vindicated both the MMR vaccine and thimerosal environmental lawyer Robert F. Kennedy Jr. wrote a column in *The Huffington Post* in which he continued to press his case that the government has peddled unsafe vaccines to an unsuspecting public. It is a cause he has championed since 2005, when he published "Deadly Immunity" in *Rolling Stone* and *Salon* magazines. The article was a no-holds-barred denunciation of the U.S. public-health establishment, purporting to tell the story of how "government health agencies colluded with Big Pharma to hide the risks of thimerosal from the public . . . a chilling case study of institutional arrogance, power, and greed." Half a decade after the original thimerosal concerns were first raised, Kennedy claimed to have found the smoking gun: the transcript of a "secret" 2000 meeting of government, pharmaceutical, and independent researchers with expertise in vaccines. Kennedy's conclusion: The generational catastrophe was real; our kids had been poisoned. If true, it would be perhaps the greatest biomedical catastrophe in modern history.

But for Kennedy to be right, a growing consensus in the medical establishment had to be wrong. Indeed, Kennedy blasted a leading organ of science that had just vindicated both the MMR vaccine and thimerosal, the Institute of Medicine (IOM). "The CDC [Centers for Disease Control and Prevention] paid the Institute of Medicine to conduct a new study to whitewash the risks of thimerosal," Kennedy wrote, "ordering researchers to 'rule out' the chemical's link to autism." In reality, the IOM—a branch of the National Academy of Sciences (NAS), the government's top independent scientific adviser—carefully creates firewalls between the funding it receives to conduct scientific assessments and the results it ultimately produces. "Funders don't control the composition of the committee, and they don't meet with the committee," says Harvard public-health researcher Marie McCormick, who chaired the IOM vaccine-safety committee in question. "And on no NAS or IOM committee are the members paid; they all work pro bono. There's no reason for them not to look at the data."

The same year Kennedy's article came out, journalist David Kirby published *Evidence of Harm—Mercury in Vaccines and the Autism Epidemic: A Medical Controversy.* He followed a group of parents from the Coalition for SafeMinds, an autism activist organization. They had grown convinced that vaccines and other environmental factors had caused their children's conditions. Kirby's chronicle of the parents' efforts to publicize the dangers of vaccines became a best seller and greatly advanced SafeMinds' cause.

"It's not hard to scare people," says pediatrician and leading vaccine advocate Paul Offit. "But it's extremely difficult to unscare them."

Yet even as vaccine hysteria reached a fever pitch in the wake of Kennedy's and Kirby's writings, the scientific evidence was leaning strongly in the other direction. In discounting the dangers of both the MMR vaccine and thimerosal, the IOM had multiple large epidemiological studies to rely on. For MMR, the IOM examined 16 studies. All but two, which were dismissed because of "serious methodological flaws," showed no evidence of a link. For thimerosal, the IOM looked at five studies, examining populations in Sweden, Denmark, the United Kingdom, and the United States (studies that vaccine critics contend were flawed). Since then, further research has strengthened and vindicated the committee's original conclusion. It is a conclusion that has been "independently reached by scientific and professional committees around the world," as a recent science journal commentary noted. Either the scientific community has found a clear, reassuring answer to the questions raised about thimerosal in vaccines, or there is a global scientific conspiracy to bury the truth.

Whether the public is hearing the scientific community's answer is another matter. "It's not hard to scare people," says pediatrician and leading vaccine advocate Paul Offit, who himself coinvented a vaccine. "But it's extremely difficult to unscare them."

A backlash against vaccine skeptics is beginning to mount. Standing up to fellow celebrities, actress Amanda Peet, who recently vaccinated her baby daughter, has become a spokeswoman for the provaccine group Every Child by Two. Offit's book *Autism's False Prophets* has further galvanized vaccine defenders—not only by debunking the science of those who claim vaccines are dangerous but also by contending that the parents of autistic children and the children themselves are indeed victims, not of vaccines but of medical misinformation.

The provaccine case starts with some undeniable facts: Vaccines are, as the IOM puts it, "one of the greatest achievements of public health." The CDC estimates that thanks to vaccines, we have reduced morbidity by 99 percent or more for smallpox, diphtheria, measles, polio, and rubella. Averaged over the course of the 20th century, these five diseases killed nearly 650,000 people annually. They now kill fewer than 100. That is not to say vaccines are perfectly safe; in rare cases they can cause serious, well-known adverse side effects. But what researchers consider unequivocally unsafe is to avoid them. As scientists at the Johns Hopkins Bloomberg School of Public Health recently found while investigating whooping cough outbreaks in and around Michigan, "geographic pockets of vaccine exemptors pose a risk to the whole community."

When it comes to autism, vaccine defenders make two central claims. First, the condition is likely to be mostly genetic rather than environmentally caused; and second, there are reasons to doubt whether there is really a rising autism epidemic at all.

It is misleading to think of autism as a single disorder. Rather, it is a spectrum of disorders showing great variability in symptoms and expression but fundamentally characterized by failed social development, inability to communicate, and obsessive repetitive behavior. Autism generally appears in children at early ages, sometimes suddenly, and its genetic component has long been recognized. Studies have shown that if one identical twin has autism, there is at least a 60 percent chance that the other also does. "From my point of view, it's a condition associated with genetic defects and developmental biology problems," says Peter Hotez, a George Washington University microbiologist and father of an autistic child. Hotez, who is also president of the Sabin Vaccine Institute, says, "I don't think it's possible to explain on the basis of any vaccine toxin that is acquired after the baby is born." Still, scientists cannot fully rule out environmental triggers—including various types of toxicity—that might interact with a given individual's preexisting genetic inclination. Autism is a complex disorder with multiple forms of expression and potentially multiple types of causation that are incompletely understood.

As for whether autism is rising, a number of experts say it is hard to know. Is the increase real, or is it largely the result of more attention to the condition, an expansion of the autism spectrum to embrace many different heterogeneous disorders, a new focus on children classified as autistic in federal special education programs during the 1990s, and other factors? It could be some combination of all these things.

But if environmental triggers of autism cannot be ruled out, the idea that those triggers can be found in the MMR vaccine or in thimerosal has crumbled under the weight of scientific refutation. Epidemiological studies have cast grave doubt on Andrew Wakefield's MMR hypothesis—and so have subsequent scandals. Nearly all of Wakefield's coauthors have since retracted the autism implications of their work; *The Lancet* has also backed away from the study. A series of investigative stories published in *The Times* of London unearthed Wakefield's undisclosed ties to vaccine litigation in the U.K. and, more recently, suggested he fabricated his data (which Wakefield denies).

As for thimerosal, government precautions notwithstanding, it was never clear how threatening it might be. The federal mercury standards that first heightened concern were developed for methylmercury, not ethylmercury, the form contained in thimerosal. Ethylmercury has less risk of accumulating to a toxic dose because it does not last as long in the body. And, according to the IOM's 2004 report, there had never been any evidence of a major incident of mercury poisoning leading to autism.

The strongest argument against the idea that thimerosal poisoned a generation of children does not emerge from the body of published studies alone. There is the added detail that although thimerosal is no longer present in any recommended childhood vaccines save the inactivated influenza vaccine—and hasn't been, beyond trace amounts, since 2001—no one is hailing the end of autism. "If you thought thimerosal was related to autism, then the incidence of autism should have gone down," Harvard's McCormick explains. "And it hasn't."

Children who would have been classified as mentally retarded or learning disabled were now being classified on the autism spectrum.

In 2005 David Kirby stated that if autism rates didn't begin to decline by 2007, "that would deal a severe blow to the autism-thimerosal hypothesis." But as McCormick notes, despite the absence of thimerosal in vaccines, reports of autism cases have not fallen. In a 2008 study published in *Archives of General Psychiatry,* two researchers studying a California Department of Developmental Services database found that the prevalence of autism had actually continued increasing among the young. Kirby concedes that these findings about the California database represent a "pretty serious blow to the thimerosal-causes-autism hypothesis," though he does not think they thoroughly bury it. In an interview, he outlined many problems with relying on the California database, suggesting potential confounding factors such as the state's high level of immigration. "Look, I understand the desire to try to end this and not scare parents away from vaccination," Kirby says. "But I also feel that sometimes that desire to prove or disprove blinds people on both sides."

Kirby says—and even some vaccine defenders agree—that some small subgroup of children might have a particular vulnerability to vaccines and yet be missed by epidemiological studies. But the two sides disagree as to the possible size of that group. "If one or two or three children every year are getting autism from vaccines, you would never pick that up," Offit says. Kirby, in contrast, feels that while the idea of thimerosal as the "one and only cause of autism has gone out the window," he still believes there is an "epidemic" with many environmental triggers and with thimerosal as a possible contributing factor.

Meanwhile, in the face of powerful evidence against two of its strongest initial hypotheses—concerning MMR and thimerosal—the vaccine skeptic movement is morphing before our eyes. Advocates have begun moving the goalposts, now claiming, for instance, that the childhood vaccination schedule hits kids with too many vaccines at once, overwhelming their immune systems. Jenny McCarthy wants to "green our vaccines," pointing to many other alleged toxins that they contain. "I think it's definitely a response to the science, which has consistently shown no correlation," says David Gorski, a cancer surgeon funded by the National Institutes of Health who in his spare time blogs at Respectful Insolence, a top medical blog known for its provaccine stance. A hardening of antivaccine attitudes, mixed with the despair experienced by families living under the strain of autism, has heightened the debate—sometimes leading to blowback against scientific researchers.

Paul Shattuck did not set out to enrage vaccine skeptics and the parents of autistic children. Currently an assistant professor at the George Warren Brown School of Social Work at Washington University in St. Louis, he has dedicated the last decade of his professional life to helping people with autism in their families. "Some of my dearest friends have kids with autism," he says.

But in 2006 Shattuck came under fire after he published an article in the journal *Pediatrics* questioning the existence of an autism epidemic. No one doubts that since the early 1990s the number of children diagnosed with autism has dramatically increased, a trend reflected in U.S. special education programs, where children enrolled as autistic grew from 22,445 in 1994–1995 to 140,254 in 2003–2004. Yet Shattuck's study found reasons to doubt that these numbers were proof of an epidemic. Instead, he suggested that "diagnostic substitution"—in which children who previously would have been classified as mentally retarded or learning disabled were now being classified on the autism spectrum—played a significant role in the apparent increase.

Shattuck did not reject the idea that rising autism levels might be in part due to environmental causes; he merely showed the increase was largely an artifact of changing diagnostic practices, which themselves had been enabled by rising levels of attention to autism and its listing as a diagnostic category in special education. Yet simply by questioning autism epidemic claims in a prominent journal, he became a target. "People were obviously Googling me and tracking me down," he recalls. Shattuck emphasizes that most e-mails and calls merely delivered "heartfelt pleas from people with very sick kids who've been led to believe a particular theory of etiology." The bulk weren't menacing, but a few certainly were.

Others attacked Shattuck's research on the Web and insinuated that he had fabricated his data or committed scientific misconduct. "It was dismaying to feel like people were calling me a traitor to autistic kids and families," he says.

"If there has been a more harmful urban legend circulating in our society than the vaccine-autism link," University of Pennsylvania bioethicist Arthur Caplan wrote in *The Philadelphia Inquirer,* "it's hard to know what it might be." One type of harm, as Shattuck's story shows, is to individual scientists and the scientific process. There is a real risk that necessary research is being held back as scientists fear working in such a contested field. Shattuck's experience is not unique. Offit cannot go on a book tour to promote *Autism's False Prophets* because of the risk involved in making public appearances. He has received too many threats.

Yet another cost comes in the rush toward unproven, and potentially dangerous, alternative therapies to treat autism. It is easy to sympathize with parents of autistic children who desperately want to find a cure, but this has led to various pseudoremedies whose efficacy and safety have been challenged by science. These include facilitated communication, secretin infusion, chelation therapy (which involves pumping chemicals into the blood to bind with heavy metals such as mercury), and hormonal suppression. It is estimated that more than half of all children with autism are now using "complementary and alternative" treatments.

Disease, however, is the greatest danger associated with holding back vaccines amid the ongoing investigation of dubious claims. Both the vaccinated and the unvaccinated populations are placed at greater risk. Given enough vaccine exemptions and localized outbreaks, it is possible that largely vanquished diseases could become endemic again. (That is precisely what happened with measles in 2008 in the U.K., following the retreat from the MMR vaccine in the wake of the 1998 scare.) The public-health costs of such a development would be enormous—and they would not impact everyone equally. "If vaccine rates start to drop, who's going to get affected?" Peter Hotez asks. "It's going to be people who live in poor, crowded conditions. So it's going to affect the poorest people in our country."

Paradoxically, the great success of vaccines is a crucial reason why antivaccination sentiment has thrived, some scientists say. Most of the diseases that vaccines protect against have largely been licked. As a consequence, few people personally remember the devastation they can cause. So with less apparently on the line, it is easier to indulge in the seeming luxury of vaccine skepticism and avoidance. Even before the recent spike in attention to thimerosal, members of the public were alarmingly skeptical of vaccines. In a 1999 survey, 25 percent felt their children's immune systems could be harmed by too many vaccinations, and 23 percent shared the sentiment that children receive more vaccinations than are healthy. There is every reason to think that those numbers—gathered before the vaccine-autism controversy reached anything like its current intensity—have risen since.

In the United States, population pockets with low vaccination rates (such as in Boulder, Colorado, and Ashland, Oregon) have existed for some time, and the great fear among many governmental medical authorities is that high-profile claims about vaccine dangers will widen the phenomenon, with potentially disastrous consequences. Already, medical and religious vaccination exemptions are climbing: In New York State they totaled 4,037 in 2006, nearly twice as many as in 1999. In New Jersey they came to 1,923 in 2006 versus only 727 in 1990. It is not just exemptors: The far larger concern, according to McCormick and others, is those parents referred to as "vaccine hesitaters." They have heard all the noise about vaccines and will probably get their children shots because they feel they have to, but their skepticism is growing.

Offit points to still another threat: litigation. The wave of autism-related claims filed with the U.S. government's Vaccine Injury Compensation Program is unprecedented. Since 2001 autism claims have outnumbered nonautism cases almost four to one. Following the science, the court has now dismissed many of them, but there is the possibility that civil litigation will follow. "I still think it's going to be another 10 years before this really washes out in litigation," Offit says. If the legal atmosphere becomes too difficult for vaccine manufacturers, they could stop producing them or be forced out of business.

Ultimately, that is why the vaccine-autism saga is so troubling—and why it is so important to explore how science and so many citizens fell out of touch.

"It wouldn't have been possible without the Internet," says journalist Arthur Allen, who has covered the vaccine-autism story since 2002, when he wrote a high-profile *The New York Times Magazine* article that took the thimerosal risk seriously. Over time Allen changed his mind, coming to reject the idea that vaccines are to blame. Still, he recognizes why it persists. "If people believe something happened to them, there are so many people on the Web you can find who believe the same thing." The Internet has become a haven for a number of autism support groups that continually reinforce the vaccine-autism argument. This has led to the radicalization of some elements who have denounced scientists as "vaccine barbarians," "pharmaceutical and medical killers," and so on. And after all we have heard about environmental and chemical risks—some accurate, some not—people are now easily persuaded about all manner of toxin dangers.

But if the Internet has made it easier for pockets of antiscience feeling to grow and flourish, scientific authorities also deserve some of the blame. "I don't think they woke up that this was a serious problem until maybe 2008," David Gorski says about the growing antivaccine sentiment. George Washington University's Hotez notes that "the office of the surgeon general, the secretary of Health and Human Services, and the head of the CDC have not been very vocal on this issue." True, the CDC, the Food and Drug Administration, and other governmental organizations feature accurate and up-to-date information about vaccine risks on their websites. But that is very different from launching a concerted communications campaign to ensure that the public retains faith in vaccination.

Some outspoken scientists may have actually increased the polarization on this issue. For example, calling those against vaccines "scientifically illiterate"—or, as CDC vaccine expert Stephen Cochi reportedly put it to one journalist, "junk scientists and charlatans"—may just lead to a further circling of the wagons.

The most promising approach to the vaccine-autism issue comes from the government itself. Consider the work of Roger Bernier, a CDC scientist who turned to emphasizing the public-engagement aspects of the vaccine problem after hearing one parent declare any new government research on the topic "dead on arrival." The central problem Bernier has confronted: how to deal with a situation in which so many parents are unswervingly convinced that their children have been harmed, in which they could be harming their children even more by using untested therapies, and in which dangerous misinformation abounds.

"There's no end to the kind of noise people can make about vaccines," he observes. "And so if you're in the vaccine community, what's the best approach to this? I don't think it is ignoring people." Instead, Bernier has headed up a series of award-winning projects that bring together average citizens with scientists and policymakers to reach joint recommendations on vaccines, holding public dialogues across the country to break down boundaries between the experts and everybody else, literally putting multiple perspectives around a table. His example suggests that while science's first and greatest triumph in this area was to develop vaccinations to control or eradicate many diseases, the challenge now—not yet achieved, and in some ways even more difficult—is to preserve public support for vaccine programs long after these scourges have largely vanished from our everyday lives.

"The problem is not only research," Bernier says. "The problem is trust."

Critical Thinking

1. Explain why some people still believe that vaccinations cause autism.
2. Identify known factors which are correlated with autistic spectrum disorders.
3. Provide reasons why every child should have vaccinations.

Create Central

www.mhhe.com/createcentral

Internet References

Autism
www.autism-society.org

Autism Information
www.hhs.gov/autism

Autism Signs May Show Up as Early as First Month
www.keyt.com/news/health/study-autism

Chris Mooney will continue to report on the vaccine—autism controversy on his blog. The Intersection, at blogs.discovermagazine.com/intersection.

Article

Prepared by: Claire N. Rubman, *Suffolk County Community College*

How to Choose the Right Apps for Early Learning

STEPHEN GASS

Learning Outcomes

After reading this article, you will be able to:

- Explain the term *digital native.*
- Articulate the educational outcome of technological "bells and whistles" on student learning.
- Define the acronym P.L.A.Y.

Expert Perspective

Young Children Learn Best from Carefully Vetted Content

"Make no mistake about why these babies are here—they are here to replace us."
—Jerry Seinfeld

Good news: Babies are born wired to learn. Instinctively, our youngest "digital natives" (those who have only ever lived in a technocentric, screen-centric world) will:

- Take initiative
- Act on their natural curiosity
- Make clear choices
- Try different approaches
- Stick to a task to persist at a goal
- Share their discoveries and seek social interaction

At minimum, it sounds as if babies are ready to take on the four C's of the 21st century curriculum (creativity, critical thinking, communication, collaboration). Good news, again.

While these nascent skills will form the foundations for all future learning, they require scaffolding and exercise to insure the viability of the foundation. With the inextricable link between technology and 21st century success, an ever-growing library of baby/toddler/preschool apps and e-books, and the ubiquity of tots holding tablets and phones, the inevitable question becomes this: How might we use these digital tools to best build those foundations?

What the Research Tells Us

Currently, much of the data about young **children** and digital devices is device-oriented. As this literature review shows, several studies report on kids' average hours of screen time per day (2.2 to 4.6 hours for 2- to 5-year-olds); others reflect a strong and positive attitude about the educational value of digital devices among a majority of parents; still others confirm toddlers' and preschoolers' ability to demonstrate the requisite motor and cognitive skills for clicking, tapping, swiping (at the older ages), and navigating through experiences of interest.

Unfortunately, we know less about the efficacy of the content or experience to deliver on the software's educational promises. While a few studies in the literature review above show students improving in certain skill areas after using particular pieces of software, a set of generalizable rules, hallmarks, and features that might guide early educators' choices is scant.

One study that does examine user experience looks at the design of the clickable hot spots found in most **children's** interactive experiences. The findings suggest that when hot spots support, reinforce, or extend the e-story **children** are reading, the **children** are better able to retell the story. Extraneous or incidental "bells and whistles" had the opposite effect. While the former approach is quite common, more than likely as an educator, you are not surprised to learn that extraneous information, regardless of its entertainment value, can sabotage a well-constructed lesson.

In the context of the paucity of interactive content research, the point of this example is to illustrate that as educators, armed only with your instincts and knowledge of best practices, you are able to identify the resource best suited to any given learning goal and learner.

With that in mind, and with reinforcement from the vast archive of early childhood research literature that suggests that playing, exploring, and experimenting with open-ended materials (as well as building concepts through direct experience with people and objects) are essential for healthy growth and development, here are some guidelines for navigating the landscape of 21st century digital early learning.

Playground vs. Playpen

In order to be in the best possible position to effectively "replace" us, today's **children** must be active learners who can readily go beyond producing the right short answer to knowing where, when, why, and how to apply information. Yet, the majority of today's digital experiences stop short, simply offering countless opportunities to identify, catch, and capture letters, shapes, numbers, and colors. Many, perhaps in an effort to prepare early learners for life in an agrarian society, also focus on naming favorite barnyard animals and noises.

Since the foundations of and attitudes toward learning are forged during the early years, it's essential that a **child's** digital learning play is built on more than naming things and receiving "good job" rewards, no matter how charmingly animated. When considering skill-building products in math or language, for example, look for digital equivalents of math manipulatives, such as Tangrams HD by Visual Learning Aids, that allow the **child** to play with math concepts; or seek out storytelling props that invite language play, such as Sock Puppets.

Toy vs. Tool

Classic toys such as dolls, blocks, balls, and role-playing sets (play kitchen, work bench, garage/roadway—all gender stereotypes aside) are familiar learning tools in many preschool and pre-preschool environments. In addition to providing opportunities for **children** to exercise certain motor skills, these types of materials are dependable standards for nurturing social, language, and a range of problem solving skills.

Many of the digital counterparts for these activities, however, are right-answer oriented, rather than allowing for truly open-ended play and exploration. Look for play experiences that avoid rigid rules, allow for exploration, and offer more than sound effects and easy cleanup, such as the Balls app by Iotic.

Real vs. Virtual

While hands-on interactions with objects and people in the real world are generally considered the preferred way for young **children** to learn, it's hard to resist the allure of a **child** at peace with a tablet.

A myriad of electronic "paint" and music-making products promise countless hours of creative play. Look for those that, like a master arts teacher, can provoke a little exploration that may lead to a deeper understanding of how to build a piece of music or create an image to express an idea. A good example is Singing Fingers, an iPad app developed at MIT that lets the users finger-paint sounds (including their voice) on the screen, then play and explore the graphic musically.

Try to determine how readily these virtual explorations come off the screen and onto the floor, into the room, or on the walls through conversation, display, or live performance. And keep in mind that even the most profound curriculum or magical material is best served when there's a teacher, parent, or mentor to guide, interpret, narrate, scaffold, or extend the experience.

Today and Tomorrow

Despite the complexities of an increasingly digital world, it's often best to keep it simple. Regardless of the **child's** real world experience—from ducks to fire trucks—or the specific curricular goal, teachers can always just gather their group around the glow of the screen, do an image search, and compare, contrast, describe, and imagine away.

As early educators evaluate and wend their way through the mountain of apps, games, and digital "solutions," just remember that it's not about what technology can deliver, but what the **child** takes away.

P.L.A.Y. WORKS

When choosing apps or any other educational tool for young kids, early childhood expert Stephen Gass suggests keeping in mind the acronym P.L.A.Y.:

P is for position: Make sure the **child** is in a position where he or she can see what's happening.

L is for language: Whatever you do with a **child,** describe what's happening.

A is for action: Whether it's swiping or tapping, bring the **child** into the action as much as possible.

Y is for yuks: Have a good time, be silly, use silly voices. And if things go wrong, laugh about it!

Critical Thinking

1. What is the essence of play in early childhood and can technology capture it successfully?
2. Why is technology so appealing to parents as a learning tool?
3. What are the shortcomings of technology in early childhood education?

Create Central

www.mhhe.com/createcentral

Internet References

Hands-on Learning for Young Children
http://msue.anr.msu.edu/news/hands-on_learning_for_young_children

Pinterest
http://www.pinterest.com/margaretapowers/ece-tech/

Technology and Interactive Media as Tools in Early Childhood Programs Serving Children from Birth through Age 8
http://www.naeyc.org/files/naeyc/file/positions/PS_technology_WEB2.pdf

To iPad or not to iPad
http://www.academia.edu/4117396/To_iPad_or_not_to_iPad_iPads_in_Early_Childhood_Education

Using Technology in the Early Childhood Classroom
http://teacher.scholastic.com/professional/bruceperry/using_technology.htm

---

STEPHEN GASS has more than 20 years of experience in the design, development, and distribution of learning products, including **computer** software, online applications, toys, games, books, and video. He is president of Every Baby Company, an organization he founded for the development of early learning products, the first of which is Eebee's Adventures.

Gass, Stephen. "How to Choose The Right Apps for Early Learning." *T.H.E. Journal* 40. 9 (September, 2013): 20–22.

Article

Prepared by: Claire N. Rubman, *Suffolk County Community College*

The Touch-Screen Generation

HANNA ROSIN

Learning Outcomes

After reading this article, you will be able to:

- Evaluate what tablets, iPads, and smartphones are doing to young children's brains.
- Distinguish between digital natives and digital immigrants and give characteristics of each.

On a chilly day last spring, a few dozen developers of children's apps for phones and tablets gathered at an old beach resort in Monterey, California, to show off their games. One developer, a self-described "visionary for puzzles" who looked like a skateboarder-recently-turned-dad, displayed a jacked-up, interactive game called Puzzingo, intended for toddlers and inspired by his own son's desire to build and smash. Two 30-something women were eagerly seeking feedback for an app called Knock Knock Family, aimed at 1-to-4-year-olds. "We want to make sure it's easy enough for babies to understand," one explained.

The gathering was organized by Warren Buckleitner, a longtime reviewer of interactive children's media who likes to bring together developers, researchers, and interest groups—and often plenty of kids, some still in diapers. It went by the Harry Potter-ish name Dust or Magic, and was held in a drafty old stone-and-wood hall barely a mile from the sea, the kind of place where Bathilda Bagshot might retire after packing up her wand. Buckleitner spent the breaks testing whether his own remote-control helicopter could reach the hall's second story, while various children who had come with their parents looked up in awe and delight. But mostly they looked down, at the iPads and other tablets displayed around the hall like so many open boxes of candy. I walked around and talked with developers, and several paraphrased a famous saying of Maria Montessori's, a quote imported to ennoble a touch-screen age when very young kids, who once could be counted on only to chew on a square of aluminum, are now engaging with it in increasingly sophisticated ways: "The hands are the instruments of man's intelligence."

What, really, would Maria Montessori have made of this scene? The 30 or so children here were not down at the shore poking their fingers in the sand or running them along mossy stones or digging for hermit crabs. Instead they were all inside, alone or in groups of two or three, their faces a few inches from a screen, their hands doing things Montessori surely did not imagine. A couple of 3-year-old girls were leaning against a pair of French doors, reading an interactive story called *Ten Giggly Gorillas* and fighting over which ape to tickle next. A boy in a nearby corner had turned his fingertip into a red marker to draw an ugly picture of his older brother. On an old oak table at the front of the room, a giant stuffed Angry Bird beckoned the children to come and test out tablets loaded with dozens of new apps. Some of the chairs had pillows strapped to them, since an 18-month-old might not otherwise be able to reach the table, though she'd know how to swipe once she did.

Not that long ago, there was only the television, which theoretically could be kept in the parents' bedroom or locked behind a cabinet. Now there are smartphones and iPads, which wash up in the domestic clutter alongside keys and gum and stray hair ties. "Mom, everyone has technology but me!" my 4-year-old son sometimes wails. And why shouldn't he feel entitled? In the same span of time it took him to learn how to say that sentence, thousands of kids' apps have been developed—the majority aimed at preschoolers like him. To us (his parents, I mean), American childhood has undergone a somewhat alarming transformation in a very short time. But to him, it has always been possible to do so many things with the swipe of a finger, to have hundreds of games packed into a gadget the same size as *Goodnight Moon.*

In 2011, the American Academy of Pediatrics updated its policy on very young children and media. In 1999, the group had discouraged television viewing for children younger than 2, citing research on brain development that showed this age group's critical need for "direct interactions with parents and other significant care givers." The updated report began by acknowledging that things had changed significantly since then. In 2006, 90 percent of parents said that their children younger than 2 consumed some form of electronic media. Nonetheless, the group took largely the same approach it did in 1999, uniformly discouraging passive media use, on any type of screen, for these kids. (For older children, the academy noted, "high-quality programs" could have "educational benefits.") The 2011 report mentioned "smart cell phone" and "new screen" technologies, but did not address interactive apps. Nor did it broach the possibility that has likely occurred to those 90 percent of American parents, queasy though they might be: that some good might come from those little swiping fingers.

I had come to the developers' conference partly because I hoped that this particular set of parents, enthusiastic as they were about interactive media, might help me out of this conundrum, that they might offer some guiding principle for American parents who are clearly never going to meet the academy's ideals, and at some level do not want to. Perhaps this group would be able to articulate some benefits of the new technology that the more cautious pediatricians weren't ready to address. I nurtured this hope until about lunchtime, when the developers gathering in the dining hall ceased being visionaries and reverted to being ordinary parents, trying to settle their toddlers in high chairs and get them to eat something besides bread.

I fell into conversation with a woman who had helped develop Montessori Letter Sounds, an app that teaches preschoolers the Montessori methods of spelling.

She was a former Montessori teacher and a mother of four. I myself have three children who are all fans of the touch screen. What games did her kids like to play?, I asked, hoping for suggestions I could take home.

"They don't play all that much."

Really? Why not?

"Because I don't allow it. We have a rule of no screen time during the week," unless it's clearly educational.

No screen time? None at all? That seems at the outer edge of restrictive, even by the standards of my overcontrolling parenting set.

"On the weekends, they can play. I give them a limit of half an hour and then stop. Enough. It can be too addictive, too stimulating for the brain."

Her answer so surprised me that I decided to ask some of the other developers who were also parents what their domestic ground rules for screen time were. One said only on airplanes and long car rides. Another said Wednesdays and weekends, for half an hour. The most permissive said half an hour a day, which was about my rule at home. At one point I sat with one of the biggest developers of e-book apps for kids, and his family. The toddler was starting to fuss in her high chair, so the mom did what many of us have done at that moment—stuck an iPad in front of her and played a short movie so everyone else could enjoy their lunch. When she saw me watching, she gave me the universal tense look of mothers who feel they are being judged. "At home," she assured me, "I only let her watch movies in Spanish."

By their pinched reactions, these parents illuminated for me the neurosis of our age: as technology becomes ubiquitous in our lives, American parents are becoming more, not less, wary of what it might be doing to their children. Technological competence and sophistication have not, for parents, translated into comfort and ease. They have merely created yet another sphere that parents feel they have to navigate in exactly the right way. On the one hand, parents want their children to swim expertly in the digital stream that they will have to navigate all their lives; on the other hand, they fear that too much digital media, too early, will sink them. Parents end up treating tablets like precision surgical instruments, gadgets that might perform miracles for their child's IQ and help him win some nifty robotics competition—but only if they are used just so. Otherwise, their child could end up one of those sad, pale creatures who can't make eye contact and has an avatar for a girlfriend.

Norman Rockwell never painted *Boy Swiping Finger on Screen,* and our own vision of a perfect childhood has never adjusted to accommodate that now-common tableau. Add to that our modern fear that every parenting decision may have lasting consequences—that every minute of enrichment lost or mindless entertainment indulged will add up to some permanent handicap in the future—and you have deep guilt and confusion. To date, no body of research has definitively proved that the iPad will make your preschooler smarter or teach her to speak Chinese, or alternatively that it will rust her neural circuitry—the device has been out for only three years, not much more than the time it takes some academics to find funding and gather research subjects. So what's a parent to do?

In 2001, the education and technology writer Marc Prensky popularized the term *digital natives* to describe the first generations of children growing up fluent in the language of computers, video games, and other technologies. (The rest of us are *digital immigrants,* struggling to understand.) This term took on a whole new significance in April 2010, when the iPad was released. iPhones had already been tempting young children, but the screens were a little small for pudgy toddler hands to navigate with ease and accuracy. Plus, parents tended to be more possessive of their phones, hiding them in pockets or purses. The iPad was big and bright, and a case could be made that it belonged to the family. Researchers who study children's media immediately recognized it as a game changer.

Previously, young children had to be shown by their parents how to use a mouse or a remote, and the connection between what they were doing with their hand and what was happening on the screen took some time to grasp. But with the iPad, the connection is obvious, even to toddlers. Touch technology follows the same logic as shaking a rattle or knocking down a pile of blocks: the child swipes, and something immediately happens. A "rattle on steroids," is what Buckleitner calls it. "All of a sudden a finger could move a bus or smush an insect or turn into a big wet gloopy paintbrush." To a toddler, this is less magic than intuition. At a very young age, children become capable of what the psychologist Jerome Bruner called "enactive representation"; they classify objects in the world not by using words or symbols but by making gestures—say, holding an imaginary cup to their lips to signify that they want a drink. Their hands are a natural extension of their thoughts.

I have two older children who fit the early idea of a digital native—they learned how to use a mouse or a keyboard with some help from their parents and were well into school before they felt comfortable with a device in their lap. (Now, of course, at ages 9 and 12, they can create a Web site in the time it takes me to slice an onion.) My youngest child is a whole different story. He was not yet 2 when the iPad was released. As soon as he got his hands on it, he located the Talking Baby Hippo app that one of my older children had downloaded. The little purple hippo repeats whatever you say in his own squeaky voice, and responds to other cues. My son said his name ("Giddy!"); Baby Hippo repeated it back. Gideon poked Baby Hippo; Baby Hippo laughed. Over and over, it was funny every time. Pretty soon he discovered other apps. Old MacDonald, by Duck Duck Moose, was a favorite. At first he would get frustrated trying to zoom between screens, or not knowing what to do when a message popped up. But after about two weeks, he figured all that out. I must admit, it was eerie to see a child still in diapers so competent and intent, as if he were forecasting his own adulthood. Technically I was the owner of the iPad, but in some ontological way it felt much more his than mine.

Without seeming to think much about it or resolve how they felt, parents began giving their devices over to their children to mollify, pacify, or otherwise entertain them. By 2010, two-thirds of children ages 4 to 7 had used an iPhone, according to the Joan Ganz Cooney Center, which studies children's media. The vast majority of those phones had been lent by a family member; the center's researchers labeled this the "pass-back effect," a name that captures well the reluctant zone between denying and giving.

The market immediately picked up on the pass-back effect, and the opportunities it presented. In 2008, when Apple opened up its App Store, the games started arriving at the rate of dozens a day, thousands a year. For the first 23 years of his career, Buckleitner had tried to be comprehensive and cover every children's game in his publication, *Children's Technology Review.* Now, by Buckleitner's loose count, more than 40,000 kids' games are available on iTunes, plus thousands more on Google Play. In the iTunes "Education" category, the majority of the top-selling apps target preschool or elementary-age children. By age 3, Gideon would go to preschool and tune in to what was cool in toddler world, then come home, locate the iPad, drop it in my lap, and ask for certain games by their approximate description: "Tea? Spill?" (That's Toca Tea Party.)

As these delights and diversions for young children have proliferated, the pass-back has become more uncomfortable, even unsustainable, for many parents:

> He'd gone to this state where you'd call his name and he wouldn't respond to it, or you could snap your fingers in front of his face . . .
>
> But, you know, we ended up actually taking the iPad away for—from him largely because, you know, this example, this thing we were talking about, about zoning out. Now, he would do that, and my wife and I would stare at him and think, *Oh my God, his brain is going to turn to mush and come oozing out of his ears.* And it concerned us a bit.

This is Ben Worthen, a *Wall Street Journal* reporter, explaining recently to NPR's Diane Rehm why he took the iPad away from his son, even though it was the only thing that could hold the boy's attention for long periods, and it seemed to be sparking an interest in numbers and letters. Most parents can sympathize with the disturbing sight of a toddler, who five minutes earlier had been jumping off the couch, now subdued and staring at a screen, seemingly hypnotized. In the somewhat alarmist *Endangered Minds: Why Children Don't Think—and What We Can Do About It,* author Jane Healy even gives the phenomenon a name, the " 'zombie' effect," and raises the possibility that television might "suppress mental activity by putting viewers in a trance."

Ever since viewing screens entered the home, many observers have worried that they put our brains into a stupor. An early strain of research claimed that when we watch television, our brains mostly exhibit slow alpha waves—indicating a low level of arousal, similar to when we are daydreaming. These findings have been largely discarded by the scientific community, but the myth persists that watching television is the mental equivalent of, as one Web site put it, "staring at a blank wall." These common metaphors are misleading, argues Heather Kirkorian, who studies media and attention at the University of Wisconsin at Madison. A more accurate point of comparison for a TV viewer's physiological state would be that of someone deep in a book, says Kirkorian, because during both activities we are still, undistracted, and mentally active.

Because interactive media are so new, most of the existing research looks at children and television. By now, "there is universal agreement that by at least age 2 and a half, children are very cognitively active when they are watching TV," says Dan Anderson, a children's-media expert at the University of Massachusetts at Amherst. In the 1980s, Anderson put the zombie theory to the test, by subjecting roughly 100 children to a form of TV hell. He showed a group of children ages 2 to 5 a scrambled version of *Sesame Street*: he pieced together scenes in random order, and had the characters speak backwards or in Greek. Then he spliced the doctored segments with unedited ones and noted how well the kids paid attention. The children looked away much more frequently during the scrambled parts of the show, and some complained that the TV was broken. Anderson later repeated the experiment with babies ages 6 months to 24 months, using *Teletubbies.* Once again he had the characters speak backwards and chopped the action sequences into a nonsensical order—showing, say, one of the Teletubbies catching a ball and then, after that, another one throwing it. The 6- and 12-month-olds seemed unable to tell the difference, but by 18 months the babies started looking away, and by 24 months they were turned off by programming that did not make sense.

Anderson's series of experiments provided the first clue that even very young children can be discriminating viewers—that they are not in fact brain-dead, but rather work hard to make sense of what they see and turn it into a coherent narrative that reflects what they already know of the world. Now, 30 years later, we understand that children "can make a lot of inferences and process the information," says Anderson. "And they can learn a lot, both positive and negative." Researchers never abandoned the idea that parental interaction is critical for the development of very young children. But they started to see TV watching in shades of gray. If a child never interacts with adults and always watches TV, well, that is a problem. But if a child is watching TV instead of, say, playing with toys, then that is a tougher comparison, because TV, in the right circumstances, has something to offer.

How do small children actually experience electronic media, and what does that experience do to their development? Since the '80s, researchers have spent more and more time consulting with television programmers to study and shape TV content. By tracking children's reactions, they have identified certain rules that promote engagement: stories have to be linear and easy to follow, cuts and time lapses have to be used very sparingly, and language has to be pared down and repeated. A perfect example of a well-engineered show is Nick Jr.'s *Blue's Clues,* which aired from 1996 to 2006. Each episode features Steve (or Joe, in later seasons) and Blue, a cartoon puppy, solving a mystery. Steve talks slowly and simply; he repeats words and then writes them down in his handy-dandy notebook. There are almost no cuts or unexplained gaps in time. The great innovation of *Blue's Clues* is something called the "pause." Steve asks a question and then pauses for about five seconds to let the viewer shout out an answer. Small children feel much more engaged and invested when they think they have a role to play, when they believe they are actually helping Steve and Blue piece together the clues. A longitudinal study of children older than 2 and a half showed that the ones who watched *Blue's Clues* made measurably larger gains in flexible thinking and problem solving over two years of watching the show.

For toddlers, however, the situation seems slightly different. Children younger than 2 and a half exhibit what researchers call a "video deficit." This means that they have a much easier time processing information delivered by a real person than by a person on videotape. In one series of studies, conducted by Georgene Troseth, a developmental psychologist at Vanderbilt University, children watched on a live video monitor as a person in the next room hid a stuffed dog. Others watched the exact same scene unfold directly, through a window between the rooms. The children were then unleashed into the room to find the toy. Almost all the kids who viewed the hiding through the window found the toy, but the ones who watched on the monitor had a much harder time.

A natural assumption is that toddlers are not yet cognitively equipped to handle symbolic representation. (I remember my older son, when he was 3, asking me if he could go into the TV and pet Blue.) But there is another way to interpret this particular phase of development. Toddlers are skilled at seeking out what researchers call "socially relevant information." They tune in to people and situations that help them make a coherent narrative of the world around them. In the real world, fresh grass smells and popcorn tumbles and grown-ups smile at you or say something back when you ask them a question. On TV, nothing like that happens. A TV is static and lacks one of the most important things to toddlers, which is a "two-way exchange of information," argues Troseth.

A few years after the original puppy-hiding experiment, in 2004, Troseth reran it, only she changed a few things. She turned the puppy into a stuffed Piglet (from the Winnie the Pooh stories). More important, she made the video demonstration explicitly interactive. Toddlers and their parents came into a room where they could see a person—the researcher—on a monitor. The researcher was in the room where Piglet would be hidden, and could in turn see the children on a monitor. Before hiding Piglet, the researcher effectively engaged the children in a form of media training. She asked them questions about their siblings, pets, and toys. She played Simon Says with them and invited them to sing popular songs with her. She told them to look for a sticker under a chair in their room. She gave them the distinct impression that she—this person on the screen—could interact with them, and that what she had to say was relevant to the world they lived in. Then the researcher told the children she was going to hide the toy and, after she did so, came back on the screen to instruct them where to find it. That exchange was enough to nearly erase the video deficit. The majority of the toddlers who participated in the live video demonstration found the toy.

Blue's Clues was on the right track. The pause could trick children into thinking that Steve was responsive to them. But the holy grail would be creating a scenario in which the guy on the screen did actually respond—in which the toddler did something and the character reliably jumped or laughed or started to dance or talk back.

Like, for example, when Gideon said "Giddy" and Talking Baby Hippo said "Giddy" back, without fail, every time. That kind of contingent interaction (I do something, you respond) is what captivates a toddler and can be a significant source of learning for even very young children—learning that researchers hope the children can carry into the real world. It's not exactly the ideal social partner the American Academy of Pediatrics craves. It's certainly not a parent or caregiver. But it's as good an approximation as we've ever come up with on a screen, and it's why children's-media researchers are so excited about the iPad's potential.

A couple researchers from the Children's Media Center at Georgetown University show up at my house, carrying an iPad wrapped in a bright-orange case, the better to tempt Gideon with. They are here at the behest of Sandra Calvert, the center's director, to conduct one of several ongoing studies on toddlers and iPads. Gideon is one of their research subjects. This study is designed to test whether a child is more likely to learn when the information he hears comes from a beloved and trusted source. The researchers put the iPad on a kitchen chair; Gideon immediately notices it, turns it on, and looks for his favorite app. They point him to the one they have invented for the experiment, and he dutifully opens it with his finger.

Onto the screen comes a floppy kangaroo-like puppet, introduced as "DoDo." He is a nobody in the child universe, the puppet equivalent of some random guy on late-night public-access TV. Gideon barely acknowledges him. Then the narrator introduces Elmo. "Hi," says Elmo, waving. Gideon says hi and waves back.

An image pops up on the screen, and the narrator asks, "What is this?" (It's a banana.)

"This is a banana," says DoDo.

"This is a grape," says Elmo.

I smile with the inner glow of a mother who knows her child is about to impress a couple strangers. My little darling knows what a banana is. Of course he does! Gideon presses on Elmo. (The narrator says, "No, not Elmo. Try again.") As far as I know, he's never watched *Sesame Street,* never loved an Elmo doll or even coveted one at the toy store. Nonetheless, he is tuned in to the signals of toddler world and, apparently, has somehow figured out that Elmo is a supreme moral authority. His relationship with Elmo is more important to him than what he knows to be the truth. On and on the game goes, and sometimes Gideon picks Elmo even when Elmo says an orange is a pear. Later, when the characters both give made-up names for exotic fruits that few children would know by their real name, Gideon keeps doubling down on Elmo, even though DoDo has been more reliable.

As it happens, Gideon was not in the majority. This summer, Calvert and her team will release the results of their study, which show that most of the time, children around age 32 months go with the character who is telling the truth, whether it's Elmo or DoDo—and quickly come to trust the one who's been more accurate when the children don't already know the answer. But Calvert says this merely suggests that toddlers have become even more savvy users of technology than we had imagined. She had been working off attachment theory, and thought toddlers might value an emotional bond over the correct answer. But her guess is that something about tapping the screen, about getting feedback and being corrected in real time, is itself instructive, and enables the toddlers to absorb information accurately, regardless of its source.

Calvert takes a balanced view of technology: she works in an office surrounded by hardcover books, and she sometimes edits her drafts with pen and paper. But she is very interested in how the iPad can reach children even before they're old enough to access these traditional media.

"People say we are experimenting with our children," she told me. "But from my perspective, it's already happened, and there's no way to turn it back. Children's lives are filled with media at younger and younger ages, and we need to take advantage of what these technologies have to offer. I'm not a Pollyanna. I'm pretty much a realist. I look at what kids are doing and try to figure out how to make the best of it."

Despite the participation of Elmo, Calvert's research is designed to answer a series of very responsible, high-minded questions: Can toddlers learn from iPads? Can they transfer what they learn to the real world? What effect does interactivity have on learning? What role do familiar characters play in children's learning from iPads? All worthy questions, and important, but also all considered entirely from an adult's point of view. The reason many kids' apps are grouped under "Education" in the iTunes store, I suspect, is to assuage parents' guilt (though I also suspect that in the long run, all those "educational" apps merely perpetuate our neurotic relationship with technology, by reinforcing the idea that they must be sorted vigilantly into "good" or "bad"). If small children had more input, many "Education" apps would logically fall under a category called "Kids" or "Kids' Games." And many more of the games would probably look something like the apps designed by a Swedish game studio named Toca Boca.

The founders, Emil Ovemar and Bjorn Jeffery, work for Bonnier, a Swedish media company. Ovemar, an interactive-design expert, describes himself as someone who never grew up. He is still interested in superheroes, Legos, and animated movies, and says he would rather play stuck-on-an-island with his two kids and their cousins than talk to almost any adult. Jeffery is the company's strategist and front man; I first met him at the conference in California, where he was handing out little temporary tattoos of the Toca Boca logo, a mouth open and grinning, showing off rainbow-colored teeth.

In late 2010, Ovemar and Jeffery began working on a new digital project for Bonnier, and they came up with the idea of entering the app market for kids. Ovemar began by looking into the apps available at the time. Most of them were disappointingly "instructive," he found—"drag the butterfly into the net, that sort of thing. They were missing creativity and imagination." Hunting for inspiration, he came upon Frank and Theresa Caplan's 1973 book *The Power of Play,* a quote from which he later e-mailed to me:

> What is it that often puts the B student ahead of the A student in adult life, especially in business and creative professions? Certainly it is more than verbal skill. To create, one must have a sense of adventure and playfulness. One needs toughness to experiment and hazard the risk of failure. One has to be strong enough to start all over again if need be and alert enough to learn from whatever happens. One needs a strong ego to be propelled forward in one's drive toward an untried goal. Above all, one has to possess the ability to play!

Ovemar and Jeffery hunted down toy catalogs from as early as the 1950s, before the age of exploding brand tie-ins. They made a list of the blockbusters over the decades—the first Tonka trucks, the Frisbee, the Hula-Hoop, the Rubik's Cube. Then they made a list of what these toys had in common: None really involved winning or losing against an opponent. None were part of an effort to create a separate child world that adults were excluded from, and probably hostile toward; they were designed more for family fun. Also, they were not really meant to teach you something specific—they existed mostly in the service of having fun.

In 2011 the two developers launched Toca Tea Party. The game is not all that different from a real tea party. The iPad functions almost like a tea table without legs, and the kids have to invent the rest by, for example, seating their own plushies or dolls, one on each side, and then setting the theater in motion. First, choose one of three tablecloths. Then choose plates, cups, and treats. The treats are not what your mom would feed you. They are chocolate cakes, frosted doughnuts, cookies. It's very easy to spill the tea when you pour or take a sip, a feature added based on kids' suggestions during a test play (kids love spills, but spilling is something you can't do all that often at a real tea party, or you'll get yelled at). At the end, a sink filled with soapy suds appears, and you wash the dishes, which is also part of the fun, and then start again. That's it. The game is either very boring or terrifically exciting, depending on what you make of it. Ovemar and Jeffery knew that some parents wouldn't get it, but for kids, the game would be fun every time, because it's dependent entirely on imagination. Maybe today the stuffed bear will be naughty and do the spilling, while naked Barbie will pile her plate high with sweets. The child can take on the voice of a character or a scolding parent, or both. There's no winning, and there's no reward. Like a game of stuck-on-an-island, it can go on for five minutes or forever.

Soon after the release of Toca Tea Party, the pair introduced Toca Hair Salon, which is still to my mind the most fun game out there. The salon is no Fifth Avenue spa. It's a rundown-looking place with cracks in the wall. The aim is not beauty but subversion. Cutting off hair, like spilling, is on the list of things kids are not supposed to do. You choose one of the odd-looking people or creatures and have your way with its hair, trimming it or dyeing it or growing it out. The blow-dryer is genius; it achieves the same effect as Tadao Cern's Blow Job portraits, which depict people's faces getting wildly distorted by high winds. In August 2011, Toca Boca gave away Hair Salon for free for nearly two weeks. It was downloaded more than 1 million times in the first week, and the company took off. Today, many Toca Boca games show up on lists of the most popular education apps.

Are they educational? "That's the perspective of the parents," Jeffery told me at the back of the grand hall in Monterey. "Is running around on the lawn educational? Every part of a child's life can't be held up to that standard." As we talked, two girls were playing Toca Tea Party on the floor nearby. One had her stuffed dragon at a plate, and he was being especially naughty, grabbing all the chocolate cake and spilling everything. Her friend had taken a little Lego construction man and made him the good guy who ate neatly and helped do the dishes. Should they have been outside at the beach? Maybe, but the day would be long, and they could go outside later.

The more I talked with the developers, the more elusive and unhelpful the "Education" category seemed. (Is *Where the Wild*

Things Are educational? Would you make your child read a textbook at bedtime? Do you watch only educational television? And why don't children deserve high-quality fun?) Buckleitner calls his conference Dust or Magic to teach app developers a more subtle concept than pedagogy. By *magic,* Buckleitner has in mind an app that makes children's fingers move and their eyes light up. By *dust,* he means something that was obviously (and ploddingly) designed by an adult. Some educational apps, I wouldn't wish on the naughtiest toddler. Take, for example, Counting With the Very Hungry Caterpillar, which turns a perfectly cute book into a tedious app that asks you to "please eat 1 piece of chocolate cake" so you can count to one.

Before the conference, Buckleitner had turned me on to Noodle Words, an app created by the California designer and children's-book writer Mark Schlichting. The app is explicitly educational. It teaches you about active verbs—*spin, sparkle, stretch.* It also happens to be fabulous. You tap a box, and a verb pops up and gets acted out by two insect friends who have the slapstick sensibility of the Three Stooges. If the word is *shake,* they shake until their eyeballs rattle. I tracked down Schlichting at the conference, and he turned out to be a little like Maurice Sendak—like many good children's writers, that is: ruled by id and not quite tamed into adulthood. The app, he told me, was inspired by a dream he'd had in which he saw the word *and* floating in the air and sticking to other words like a magnet. He woke up and thought, *What if words were toys?*

During the course of reporting this story, I downloaded dozens of apps and let my children test them out. They didn't much care whether the apps were marketed as educational or not, as long as they were fun. Without my prompting, Gideon fixated on a game called Letter School, which teaches you how to write letters more effectively and with more imagination than any penmanship textbooks I've ever encountered. He loves the Toca Boca games, the Duck Duck Moose games, and random games like Bugs and Buttons. My older kids love The Numberlys, a dark fantasy creation of illustrators who have worked with Pixar that happens to teach the alphabet. And all my kids, including Gideon, play Cut the Rope a lot, which is not exclusively marketed as a kids' game. I could convince myself that the game is teaching them certain principles of physics—it's not easy to know the exact right place to slice the rope. But do I really need that extra convincing? I like playing the game; why shouldn't they?

Every new medium has, within a short time of its introduction, been condemned as a threat to young people. Pulp novels would destroy their morals, TV would wreck their eyesight, video games would make them violent. Each one has been accused of seducing kids into wasting time that would otherwise be spent learning about the presidents, playing with friends, or digging their toes into the sand. In our generation, the worries focus on kids' brainpower, about unused synapses withering as children stare at the screen. People fret about television and ADHD, although that concern is largely based on a single study that has been roundly criticized and doesn't jibe with anything we know about the disorder.

There are legitimate broader questions about how American children spend their time, but all you can do is keep them in mind as you decide what rules to set down for your own child. The statement from the American Academy of Pediatrics assumes a zero-sum game: an hour spent watching TV is an hour not spent with a parent. But parents know this is not how life works. There are enough hours in a day to go to school, play a game, and spend time with a parent, and generally these are different hours. Some people can get so drawn into screens that they want to do nothing else but play games. Experts say excessive video gaming is a real problem, but they debate whether it can be called an addiction and, if so, whether the term can be used for anything but a small portion of the population. If your child shows signs of having an addictive personality, you will probably know it. One of my kids is like that; I set stricter limits for him than for the others, and he seems to understand why.

In her excellent book *Screen Time,* the journalist Lisa Guernsey lays out a useful framework—what she calls the three C's— for thinking about media consumption: content, context, and your child. She poses a series of questions—Do you think the content is appropriate? Is screen time a "relatively small part of your child's interaction with you and the real world?"—and suggests tailoring your rules to the answers, child by child. One of the most interesting points Guernsey makes is about the importance of parents' attitudes toward media. If they treat screen time like junk food, or "like a magazine at the hair salon"—good for passing the time in a frivolous way but nothing more—then the child will fully absorb that attitude, and the neurosis will be passed to the next generation.

"The war is over. The natives won." So says Marc Prensky, the education and technology writer, who has the most extreme parenting philosophy of anyone I encountered in my reporting. Prensky's 7-year-old son has access to books, TV, Legos, Wii—and Prensky treats them all the same. He does not limit access to any of them. Sometimes his son plays with a new app for hours, but then, Prensky told me, he gets tired of it. He lets his son watch TV even when he personally thinks it's a "stupid waste." *SpongeBob SquarePants,* for example, seems like an annoying, pointless show, but Prensky says he used the relationship between SpongeBob and Patrick, his starfish sidekick, to teach his son a lesson about friendship. "We live in a screen age, and to say to a kid, 'I'd love for you to look at a book but I hate it when you look at the screen' is just bizarre. It reflects our own prejudices and comfort zone. It's nothing but fear of change, of being left out."

Prensky's worldview really stuck with me. Are books always, in every situation, inherently better than screens? My daughter, after all, often uses books as a way to avoid social interaction, while my son uses the Wii to bond with friends. I have to admit, I had the exact same experience with *SpongeBob.* For a long time I couldn't stand the show, until one day I got past the fact that the show was so loud and frenetic and paid more attention to the story line, and realized I too could use it to talk with my son about friendship. After I first interviewed Prensky, I decided to conduct an experiment. For six months, I would let my toddler live by the Prensky rules. I would put the iPad in the toy basket, along with the remote-control car and the Legos. Whenever he wanted to play with it, I would let him.

Gideon tested me the very first day. He saw the iPad in his space and asked if he could play. It was 8 A.M. and we had to get ready for school. I said yes. For 45 minutes he sat on a chair and played as I got him dressed, got his backpack ready, and failed to feed him breakfast. This was extremely annoying and obviously untenable. The week went on like this—Gideon grabbing the iPad for two-hour stretches, in the morning, after school, at bedtime. Then, after about 10 days, the iPad fell out of his rotation, just like every other toy does. He dropped it under the bed and never looked for it. It was completely forgotten for about six weeks.

Now he picks it up every once in a while, but not all that often. He has just started learning letters in school, so he's back to playing LetterSchool. A few weeks ago his older brother played with him, helping him get all the way through the uppercase and then lowercase letters. It did not seem beyond the range of possibility that if Norman Rockwell were alive, he would paint the two curly-haired boys bent over the screen, one small finger guiding a smaller one across, down, and across again to make, in their triumphant finale, the small *z*.

Critical Thinking

1. Why did the American Academy of Pediatrics (2011) discourage any passive media use for children younger than age 2?
2. What are the advantages of learning to navigate digital technology in early childhood?

Create Central

www.mhhe.com/createcentral

Internet References

Internet Safety Rules: The Constant Pursuit of Keeping Your Child Safe Online
www.articlesbase.com/parenting-articles/internet-safety-rules

Study: 40 Percent of Kids Use iPads Before They Can Speak
http://nymag.com/thecut/2013

Tech and Young Children
www.techandyoungchildren.org

HANNA ROSIN is a national correspondent for *The Atlantic*.

Article

Prepared by: Claire N. Rubman, *Suffolk County Community College*

Luck of the Draw

Your place in the family pecking order has some surprising influences on how you turn out, finds Lesley Evans Ogden

LESLEY EVANS OGDEN

Learning Outcomes

After reading this article, you will be able to:

- Explain the educational advantages of being the firstborn child within a family.
- Determine which child would be more likely to take risks according to birth order.
- Describe the "morphological repercussions" of birth order.

The psychiatrist Alfred Adler, a contemporary of Sigmund Freud, was convinced that our place among our siblings influences what he termed "style of life." Eldest children, he argued, are more likely to be neurotic and authoritarian as a result of younger siblings displacing them from their king-of-the-castle position and burdening them with extra responsibilities. Youngest children are spoiled and lack empathy; only middle children are even-tempered and successful, albeit more rebellious and independent, he asserted. Perhaps it was no coincidence that Adler himself was the second child of seven.

His thinking struck a chord. Interest in birth order and its possible consequences grew rapidly in the early 20th century, spawning a new field of research. In the 1980s, however, there was a backlash against the idea, and most of the early studies are now discredited. But in recent years, the pendulum has swung back, with compelling research revealing the importance of birth order in animals. Now there is mounting evidence that we, too, are influenced by our position in the family hierarchy. This appears to be linked with all manner of things, from body shape and intelligence to disease susceptibility and sexuality. The reason it has such far-reaching repercussions is also becoming clearer as we untangle the complex web of factors involved.

Historically, the inheritance of firstborns has often extended beyond their genes. Even before Adler came along, Charles Darwin's half-cousin, the eminent anthropologist, geographer, and statistician Francis Galton, had claimed that it was exclusively firstborn males and only sons who went on to become renowned English scientists. It sounds like an outrageous generalisation but, in 1874, when his book *English Men of Science: Their nature and nurture* was published, there may well have been something to it. Back then, firstborn sons were often favoured when inheriting family wealth, giving them greater freedom to pursue the career or interests of their choosing.

In some families, even now, the firstborn may inherit the crown jewels or the family business—but, in general, cultural expectations based on family hierarchy are not as rigid as they once were. Nevertheless, Galton's work is highly relevant to modern researchers because of its emphasis on both "nature and nurture"—a phrase he coined. Distinguishing between biological and environmental factors is vital if we are to understand why someone's place among their siblings might affect his or her life chances. As a result, today's studies, unlike many in Adler's time, take account of factors such as socioeconomic status and family size. What have they found?

One of the most striking discoveries to emerge from animal studies is that birth order can have life-or-death consequences (see "Fatal Pecking Order"). The same appears to be true in humans. A study of more than 600,000 people in Norway, by Hans Gravseth and colleagues at Oslo's National Institute of Occupational Health, found that the more older siblings someone had, the greater that individual's risk of committing suicide. The effect was more pronounced among women, although their suicide rate was one-quarter that of men. "If you are a firstborn, the first few years you are alone, and have full attention from your parents. You may develop your personality in a more robust and stable direction, and develop resilience to stressful conditions later in life," Gravseth speculates. That reasoning is similar to Adler's, although he concedes that it isn't totally clear what the link between suicide rate and birth order might be.

Psychologist Catherine Salmon at the University of Redlands in California has explored how birth order might affect family relationships. She finds that firstborns and last-borns tend to have the closest relationships with their parents, whereas middle children have stronger relationships outside the family. She puts this down to middle children tending to receive less parental attention, which she says helps hone their skills as "friendship specialists" (The Secret Power of Middle Children, Hudson Street Press, 2011).

Who's a Chancer?

Many effects of an individual's place in the family are not a matter of life and death, but to do with behaviour. Mark Mainwaring and Ian Hartley at Lancaster University, UK, found that when zebra finch chicks become adults, the youngest birds from a clutch are more likely to be adventurous than their older siblings when exploring novel surroundings. In humans too, there are hints that birth order is linked to risk-taking. Frank Sulloway and Richard Zweigenhaft at the University of California, Berkeley, found that younger siblings were more likely to participate in dangerous sports. And among 408 brothers who played professional baseball, the younger brothers were 10 times as likely to attempt the high-risk ploy of stealing a base—and three times as successful when they did.

So firstborns may be more cautious, but they may be slightly more intelligent, too. An IQ study involving nearly 250,000 Norwegian male army conscripts found that eldest brothers had, on average, a 2.3-point advantage over second brothers—a trend that continued down the birth ranking. But when the researchers, led by Petter Kristensen at the University of Oslo, looked at males whose elder brother had died—in effect moving the surviving brother up the ranking—they found that these men had a higher IQ than the average for their original slot in the hierarchy. Their results suggest that what matters is one's social position rather than actual order of birth. Although these differences in IQ scores are small, Kristensen suggests they could affect chances of getting a university place.

Birth order may also influence leadership style and potential. When researchers at Leiden University in the Netherlands surveyed 1200 Dutch men and women in public office, they found 36 percent were firstborns and 19 percent were last-borns (Political Psychology, vol. 24, p. 605). The eldest and youngest children in a family each make up about a quarter of the Dutch population, so firstborns are over-represented and last-borns under-represented among the country's politicians. However, when it comes to leadership that challenges the status quo, Sulloway says it is a different story. His research suggests that later-borns are more likely to embrace revolutionary ideas or movements. Darwin, he notes, was the fifth child in his family; firstborns, meanwhile, were vastly over-represented among opponents of his theory of evolution (*Born to Rebel,* Pantheon Books, 1996).

Marked physical differences between siblings are apparent in a variety of animals, and birth order also appears to have morphological repercussions in humans. For a start, firstborns tend to be taller: 2.5cm taller on average than their siblings, according to recent research by Wayne Cutfield and colleagues at the University of Auckland, New Zealand, taking into account socioeconomic status, ethnicity, and parental height. Other research found that firstborn males also have a larger waist size as young adults. Epidemiologist Darren Dahly at the University of Leeds, UK, who co authored this study, suspects these differences arise before birth. "The utero-placental vasculature may not be as well developed in the earlier pregnancies," he says. As a result, the first child is less well nourished in the womb than later ones and tends to be lighter at birth. Individuals whose metabolism develops in an environment of scarcity and who subsequently experience plenty are thought to be at higher risk of obesity in adult life—an idea called the mismatch hypothesis, referring to the mismatch between pre- and postnatal environments. Dahly believes this may help explain his findings.

This could perhaps be linked to another discovery by Cutfield and colleagues. Studying prepubescent children, they found that the ability of the body to respond to insulin was 21 percent lower in firstborns than in later-borns, and their blood pressure was significantly higher. They suggest that this may make firstborns more prone to adult diseases including type 2 diabetes, heart disease, stroke, and hypertension. Birth order may influence our susceptibility to other diseases too, including the types of cancer we are prone to, although the picture is still very unclear.

A link with allergies is well documented, however. Matt Perzanowski of Columbia University in New York studied low-income kids in the U.S. government-funded Head Start program, for example, found that 4- to 5-year-olds with older siblings were almost three times less likely to go to the emergency room with allergic asthma than children without older siblings. According to what is called the hygiene hypothesis, being exposed to more viruses, fungi, and bacteria early in childhood somehow tempers the immune system, making later-borns, whose older siblings might bring pathogens into the home, less prone to allergies than firstborns.

An alternative explanation links allergies and asthma to the fetal environment. The idea is that the mother's body must downgrade its immune response to avoid rejecting the developing child. Perzanowski suggests that if this becomes more effective with each successive pregnancy, then later-borns will develop fewer antibodies against their mother in the womb, making them less likely to overreact to innocuous substances they encounter in the outside world.

But this idea runs counter to another fascinating insight. In 1992, Ray Blanchard at the University of Toronto, Canada, showed that the more older brothers a man has, the more likely he is to be gay. He suggested that male fetuses trigger an immune response in their mother, one that becomes stronger with each pregnancy. A link between homosexuality and being a younger brother has since been found in many populations.

As for the underlying mechanism, Tony Bogaert at Brock University in Hamilton, Canada, suspects that the target of the mother's immune response may be proteins on the surface of male fetal brain cells in the anterior hypothalamus, a brain area linked to sexual orientation. If her antibodies bind to these molecules and alter their role in typical sexual differentiation, that might lead some later-born males to be attracted to men, he suggests. Since blood retains an immunological "memory" of past immune responses, even after many years, Bogaert is now analysing blood samples from mothers of gay and straight sons to test this idea.

Birth order is a flip of the evolutionary coin, and just one component of the multiplicity of factors that make us who we are as individuals. But a decline in fertility rates worldwide means that the proportion of people who are firstborn children is rising, making it more important to understand what impacts birth order may have. It may subtly influence our physical and mental health, our opportunities for education, and our careers. Not all younger siblings will be spoiled and allergy-free, not all middleborns will be social butterflies, and not all older siblings will be tall, intelligent, responsible leaders, but our place in parity provides fascinating insights into the complexity that makes each of us unique.

Fatal Pecking Order

In some birds, birth order is a matter of life or death. Nazca boobies, seabirds that breed on the Galapagos Islands, lay two eggs. The first-hatched nestling always attacks its younger, smaller sibling, finally ejecting it from the pebble-strewn nest. Mother boobies do not intervene, leaving the expelled chick to face certain death from dehydration or predators. In the related blue-footed booby, both chicks may survive when food is plentiful but, if it is scarce, the older chick shows no mercy, attacking and killing its sibling.

Scott Forbes recalls being shocked when he first observed baby ospreys "beating the hell out of each other" during his doctoral research. Now at the University of Winnipeg, Canada, he studies sibling rivalry in red-winged blackbirds. Although not quite as dramatic as in ospreys, it is lethal all the same. In a typical brood of five eggs, he says, "the last-hatched chick has roughly a 10 percent chance of surviving, while the first-hatched chick has a better than 80 percent chance."

Clutches of blackbird's eggs, like those of many birds, do not hatch simultaneously, and this appears to provide a safety valve. When times are good and food is plentiful, even the runts may survive. When times are tough, it is survival of the fittest, and older chicks almost always win.

In one experiment, Forbes manipulated the eggs of yellow-headed blackbirds so that they all hatched simultaneously. It was disastrous for the offspring: in lean years, all the chicks died. He likens the phenomenon to investing money, with blackbird parents dividing their offspring into core and marginal groups (*Oikos,* vol. 118, p. 1561). The older siblings are the "blue chips," the younger ones their more risky holdings that only sometimes pay Darwinian dividends.

It is not just birds that play birth-order politics. The eldest piglets in a litter use their temporary teeth to fight their younger siblings for access to their mother's frontmost teats, which provide most milk. By achieving this position, they are more than twice as likely to survive than siblings further down the milk bar.

In sand tiger sharks, siblicide occurs before birth, with the largest embryo in each of the mother's two uteri breaking out of their egg capsules and engaging in cannibalism of smaller siblings.

"Birth order" even matters in some plants. Indian black plums produce seeds with up to 30 ovules, but the first to be fertilised secretes a toxin that kills off the rest.

Born Leader or Natural Rebel?

Your place within the family has a subtle influence on your tendency to exhibit a variety of characteristics

Firstborn or only child	Middle child	Youngest
Taller	Shorter	Shortest
Higher IQ	Lower IQ than oldest sibling	
Fatter	Less prone to obesity than older sibling	
Allergy prone	Less prone to allergies and asthma	
Conventional leader	Unconventional/revolutionary leader	
Cautious	Friendship specialist	Risk taker

Spot the middle children—they are the friendship specialists

Among Nazca boobies sibling rivalry is a matter of life and death

Critical Thinking

1. Why have earlier studies on birth order been discredited today?
2. What is the relationship between the greatest leaders in the world and their birth order within their own family?

Create Central

www.mhhe.com/createcentral

Internet References

Birth Order and Personality

http://www.parents.com/baby/development/social/birth-order-and-personality

Does Birth Order Really Matter?

http://www.wvu.edu/~exten/infores/pubs/fypubs/WL_237%20Birth%20Order%20Leader.pdf

The Birth Order Effect

https://psychologies.co.uk/family/the-birth-order-effect.html

---

Lesley Evans Ogden is a writer (and firstborn) in Vancouver, Canada, on Twitter @ljevanso

---

Ogden, Lesley Evans. "Luck of the Draw." *New Scientist Magazine* 219. 2933 (September, 7, 2013): 40–43.

Article

Prepared by: Claire N. Rubman, *Suffolk County Community College*

No Child Locked Inside

A Florida department develops a campaign to increase awareness about the dangers of leaving children in hot vehicles.

JORGE ROSSI

Learning Outcomes

After reading this article, you will be able to:

- Explain why the 1998 federal laws regarding airbags relates to an increase child deaths in cars.
- Describe what can happen to items held in memory when one new item is added.

On Sept. 25, 2012, a 6-month-old girl was found dead in a car after being left in it accidentally for as long as 9 hours. The discovery was made at 5:45 P.M. at Doral Academy Preparatory School in West Miami-Dade Florida. Police said the father was supposed to have dropped the baby off at a day care center around 9 A.M., but apparently forgot she was in the car and went about his day. The father told detectives it was not part of his routine to care for the baby.

This is the most recent of the 61 recorded heat-stroke death incidents that have occurred in the state of Florida since 1998. These deaths began to occur in 1998 as the federal government mandated all auto makers to install driver and passenger air bags for frontal impact protection, requiring all children to be placed in the rear seat in a properly restrained child seat. Across the United States, there have been 559 juvenile vehicular hyperthermia deaths due to being left inside of hot vehicles, with an average of 38 deaths per year.

As a result of these incidents, Florida is one of 19 states that have passed laws to address leaving a child unattended in a vehicle. Florida Statute 316.6135 states that no child under 6 years of age shall be left unattended in excess of 15 minutes, or for any period of time if the vehicle is left running or the health of the child is in danger. Violation of the statute can be faced with non criminal traffic infractions, with fines ranging from $50 to $500. Currently, Utah is the only state that has proposed criminal legislation.

Caregivers always should leave their purse or briefcase in the back seat. This forces them to look in the rear seat.

With these alarming trends, fire and EMS organizations must stop being reactionary and must begin taking a proactive approach within their respective communities in an effort to reduce these preventable deaths from occurring.

Survey Says

In early 2012, what began as an applied research project for the Executive Fire Officer program at the National Fire Academy evolved into an active, well-received awareness program in the city of Pompano Beach, Florida In order to establish an effective awareness program, one must first find out what is causing the problem then address how to resolve it.

During the near year-long research, fire-EMS incidents involving children locked in vehicles within the city of Pompano Beach were tracked from May through October to determine cause and outcome. Nearly 50 percent of the incidents occurred due to the caregivers forgetting the child was in the back seat. Luckily, in these cases, it was realized moments later and no serious death or injury occurred during the research period in the city of Pompano Beach. The city of Pompano Beach experienced its first and only hyperthermia death from being left unattended in April 2003.

A five-question random survey also was conducted during the research period to decipher what was causing caregivers to leave children unattended inside of vehicles and also to gauge the current awareness of the dangers of doing so. A total of 400 surveys were completed for the research. The surveys were conducted during child-safety seat events, local charity events, day cares, and schools within the city.

The first question asked participants if they have ever left their child unattended inside the car; 62.8 percent answered "yes." The next question asked participants if there were any laws in Florida making it illegal to leave a child unattended inside of a vehicle. The majority (63 percent) acknowledged being aware of such a law in Florida. Another, revealing question asked participants what they felt was the number one reason for leaving a child unattended inside of a car. Amazingly, 45.7 percent felt that running into the store was the leading reason for leaving a child unattended inside of a car, and only 13.1 percent of the participants felt that forgetting the child was the reason for leaving a child inside of car.

62.8 percentage of survey respondents who admitted to leaving a child in their care in a car unattended. Of those, 45.7 percent said runnning into the grocery store was the No. 1 reason they did so.

What makes these responses so revealing is that out of the 559 deaths that have occurred throughout the United States since 1998, 52 percent of them occurred because of being forgotten by the caregiver. Another interesting fact is that there is no particular high-risk group in this case. These tragic, preventable deaths have occurred in all socioeconomic groups, races, and religions. No one is immune to the fast-paced, multi-tasked society of today. With multiple jobs, and both parents being employed to make ends meet, life of today seems to be a constant juggling act that is one mental mistake away from tragedy.

One could draw the conclusion that caregivers do not want to intentionally harm their child and are in denial that something so terrible could ever happen to them. So then the question is: How can someone forget their child inside of a car? According to an ABC News segment that aired in 2010, it was explained when people are stressed they can get distracted by their problems, especially if there is a break in their normal routine. The segment goes on to explain how the basal ganglia in the human brain can power people through the regular routines, and any change in the routine can be dropped from the thought process.

In one psychology news article researchers discussed how they discovered in their research that most people were able to only hold four items in active memory, and when new items enter the active memory file older items would be forgotten.

Pompano's Action Plan

With the overwhelming problem being that caregivers are forgetting children in the vehicles, several nonprofit organizations have taken action and have begun awareness campaigns. These organizations are include Safe Kids Worldwide, Kids and Cars, NHTSA and Jan Null with Golden Gate Weather Services.

But it's time for fire and EMS agencies to help increase awareness about the dangers of leaving children inside of hot vehicles. Pompano Beach Fire Rescue has embarked on the "No Child Locked Inside: Creating awareness of the dangers of leaving children in hot vehicles" awareness program.

The action plan listed below provides established goals, objectives and tasks that must be completed in order to ensure a successful awareness program and see a reduction in injury and death of children.

The stated goal of the program is to reduce death and injury of children locked inside of vehicles through education, law enforcement, future engineering, and continued emergency response, when called upon.

Final Outcome Objectives

I. Have a 50 percent reduction in fire department responses to children being locked in vehicles in Pompano Beach by Oct. 31, 2013.

II. Have a "No Child Locked Inside" sticker placed at the entrance to all street front businesses in Pompano Beach by Dec. 31, 2013.

III. Provide "No Child Locked Inside" educational and awareness handouts to 20,000 Pompano Beach residents by Dec. 31, 2013.

Process Objectives

I. Objective I will be accomplished through:
   - a. Establish a 501(c)(3) for donations if one is not in place.
   - b. Education: local news media, newspapers, community wide events, public service announcements, city website.
   - c. Local police enforcement of Florida Statue 316.6135

II. Objective II will be accomplished by:
   a. Seeking approval by city commissioners to pass city ordinance for all street front businesses to place a "No Child Locked Inside" sticker at the entrance.
   b. Going door-to-door and requesting store owners to place a "No Child Locked Inside" sticker at the entrance.

III. Objective III will be accomplished by:
   a. Attending community events and passing out No Child Locked Inside handouts.
   b. Providing handouts during all car seat events hosted by Pompano Beach Fire Rescue and teach safety tips/reminders.
   c. Publishing the handouts in the city newspaper and magazine every quarter.
   d. Posting the handout on the city website.

Although new, the program has been well received by those citizens who have had exposure to the surveys and handouts. Many are taken back by the statistics and unaware of the grim realities of what has occurred over the past 14 years. They have expressed extreme appreciation for the newfound awareness.

The hope is that by sharing this research, you will take a comprehensive look at your hometown communities and, if warranted, decide to take a proactive approach to community risk reduction and establish your own awareness program to help spread the word to leave No Child Locked Inside.

Critical Thinking

1. What causes a person to forget a child in the rear of a car?
2. Are there safeguards that can be put in place to help parents and child minders remember about infants and toddlers in their cars?
3. How does multitasking impact memory?

Create Central

www.mhhe.com/createcentral

Internet References

Father arraigned on charges of leaving child in hot car on Long Island

http://7online.com/news/father-arrested-for-leaving-child-in-hot-car-on-long-island/154104

HOW TO; Multitask

http://www.nytimes.com/2001/04/08/magazine/how-to-multitask.html

Kaitlyn's Law: Unattended Child in Motor Vehicle Act

http://www.cityoflagunaniguel.org/DocumentCenter/Home/View/527

Most Are Unaware That Leaving a Child in a Car Is Illegal

http://www.post-gazette.com/news/state/2011/09/29/Most-are-unaware-leaving-a-child-in-car-is-illegal/stories/201109290494

Woman Left Child in 140-Degree Car to Get Nails Done

http://fox2now.com/2014/07/29/child-left-in-car-during-nail-painting

---

Jorge Rossi is a lieutenant and paramedic with Pompano Beach (Fla.) Fire Rescue. He recently received the Nicholas Rosecrans Award for Injury Prevention from Epic Medics.

Rossi, Jorge. "No Child Locked Inside." *Fire Chief* 57. 6 (June, 2013): 34–37.

Unit 3

UNIT

Prepared by: Claire N. Rubman, *Suffolk County Community College*

Development During Childhood: Cognition and Schooling

What does it mean to "educate" a child? Is there a set of facts that all children should know at any given age or is it a less tangible type of knowledge or skill set? How do ethnicity, mental health, socioeconomic status, evaluation, and psychological well-being tie in to our educational paradigm? What problems do we associate with our educational system today and how can we remedy them?

Trubowitz suggests that the educational woes of our nation should be addressed by reading more books. He hypothesizes that test scores will rise and parents will become less fixated on them if more children read more books in a more literary-oriented society. To encourage literacy, Trubowitz recommends numerous ways that a community can come together to promote reading. His recommendations span from prenatal education classes to giving out poems with pizza pies in an attempt to improve literacy!

Regardless of how many books we read, or how literary minded our community is, Yeager, Walton, and Cohen suggest that we have an achievement gap in our society that should be addressed with psychological interventions. They suggest that these interventions will alter how students perceive themselves and their school experience. Using an individually designed "delivery mechanism" will improve results along with early intervention. These mechanisms are not, however, designed to replace educational changes or reforms because they do not address curricular content. They focus on the individual student's sense of belonging, stress reduction and the removal of a closed mindedness or "fixed mindset" that may impede learning.

Whether literacy or psychological intervention is the goal, change takes time. No one knows this better than Michelle Rhee who tried, unsuccessfully, to bulldoze her way through the Washington, DC, educational system in 2007 as the school chancellor. In an attempt to improve a child's educational experience, Rhee tried to reform teacher evaluations, reinvent reading and math programs, and change the prevailing culture of failure. In her article, "What I've Learned," Rhee comments on her own failures. She acknowledges that she could have communicated better, she could have cut spending, and she could have had a more positive approach. Since her resignation, she has spearheaded a movement called "StudentsFirst" to continue her battle toward educational reform. With the United States placing 21st in science among the top 30 nations, 23rd in reading, and 25th in math, she certainly has her work cut out for her.

Taking a closer look at education, there is a multicultural component that could benefit all students. "Visiting Room 501" by Curwen focuses on the influence of middle-class Latino students. Curwen, a former teacher and researcher, noticed that third-generation Latinos have made fewer educational and economic gains than their predecessors. In an attempt to address this issue, Curwen looked at the sociological and anthropological perspectives that affect Latinos in the United States.

Teachers often provide invaluable insight and Schneider and Christison are no exception. In the article, "Are Exams Bad for Children?" these two teachers debate the relative advantages and disadvantages of exams within the school curriculum. They discuss the racial and economic inequalities of our current educational system and the growing discontentment among parents, children, and educators in the current educational climate, and they look for viable options and educational models.

The final article in this unit looks at the individual child and his or her inability to focus inside the classroom. Sroufe evaluates the use of drugs such as Ritalin or Adderall to fix our students' attention deficits. He reports on a large study of 600 students that initially touted the benefits of medication for attention-deficit disorders but later found that any perceived benefits dissipated over time. He suggests that the focus ought to be on brain functioning among children with attentional deficits rather than medicating the behaviors. He advocates a de-emphasis on drug use among this vulnerable population.

Article

Prepared by: Claire N. Rubman, *Suffolk County Community College*

Creating a Country of Readers

SID TRUBOWITZ

Learning Outcomes

After reading this article, you will be able to:

- Identify five ways to get children to read more.
- Explain why book reading and storytelling are considered preferable to talking on a cell phone or watching TV or movies.

When I consider what can be done to create a society in which people read regularly, I recall strolling down a street in Italy and hearing a sanitation worker humming an aria from an opera as he swept debris into his cart. As I sat in a Rome barbershop, I heard strains from a Puccini opera filling the air. In a Milan opera house, I was part of an audience of people from every economic and social stratum.

If the United States is to become a nation of readers, we must do more than just develop programs to increase standardized test scores. If we could create a society where hunger for books is pervasive, there would be less need for concern about scores on standardized tests. If we want reading to permeate our culture and infiltrate every corner of our society in the same way opera is an everyday element in the life of Italy, we must think broadly about how we can accomplish this. Here are a few of my ideas.

Begin each school day with reading as a meditative experience. As students enter a room, they seat themselves, breathe in the surrounding quiet, take out a book, and proceed to read. In this way, a morning of rushing to get to school on time gives way to a time for relaxing and focusing.

Schools, towns, and cities can periodically highlight different writers and encourage residents to read their publications. On a trip to Scotland, I was struck by the fact that the entire country was celebrating the birthday of Robert Burns. Why not a Robert Frost, John Steinbeck, or E.B. White Day in the United States?

Prenatal and postnatal instruction for new mothers ought to include guidance on reading to children. Every new parent on leaving the hospital should be provided with reading kits that include nursery rhymes, books, and lists of appropriate reading material for children at different ages.

Books should be available for sale and casual reading at different locations—at supermarket checkout counters, in hospital emergency rooms, in banks, in post offices.

Extend rather than diminish library hours. Libraries should have children's rooms that are attractive, welcoming areas with games for toddlers, stuffed animals for cuddling, and comfortable corners where youngsters can read, browse, or listen to an adult read.

The President can appoint a Secretary of Cultural Development who is responsible for feeding the soul of the country. This person can promote library funding, invite writers to meet government officials, and arrange reading events such as poetry slams. The President and First Lady can also talk regularly about what they've been reading and why.

Investment in reading in many and varied ways would be required to develop a widespread love of reading in the United States.

Communities can agree to television blackout hours devoted to reading before bedtime. They can sponsor events in which the entire population is encouraged to read a designated book. Iowa City, Iowa, for example, invited local residents to read *The Tortilla Curtain* by T.C. Boyle (Viking 1995) in preparation for his visit to the city. For nearly 10 years, Chicago has been inviting its diverse population to read and discuss a single book in its citywide One Book, One Chicago activity.

Businesses can join this effort to integrate reading into everyday life. One pizza chain distributed a poem along with the pizzas it delivered or had picked up. Marc Kelly Smith, a Midwestern poet supporting this idea, commented, "Poetry is an everyman thing. I wonder if there's a family who's never had pizza." Companies could include brief biographies of such people as Alexander Graham Bell, Samuel Morse, and Thomas Edison along with their monthly bills. Tenants' associations and co-op boards can set aside a room in their buildings as a lending library for residents.

I imagine a country in which people walk down the streets book in hand, rather than a cell phone, a place where book readings prevail over sugarcoated movies, and where storytelling is an integral part of family living.

Critical Thinking

1. When should a child first experience a parent or caregiver reading to him/her? Why?
2. What is the Chicago citywide activity known as "One Book, One Chicago" designed to accomplish?
3. How would you react to a silent reading/meditative experience every school day before your classes begin?
4. Indicate how reading and storytelling are related.

Create Central

www.mhhe.com/createcentral

Internet References

Reach Out and Read
www.reachoutandread.org

10 Reasons Why Reading Is Important (for Kids and Adults)
http://everydayadventure//.blogspot.com

The Importance of Reading
http://esl.fisedu/parents/advice/read.htm

Sid Trubowitz is professor emeritus at Queens College of the City University of New York, N.Y.

Article

Prepared by: Claire N. Rubman, *Suffolk County Community College*

Addressing Achievement Gaps with Psychological Interventions

Carefully devised and delivered psychological interventions catalyze the effects of high-quality educational reforms, but don't replace them.

DAVID YEAGER, GREGORY WALTON, AND GEOFFREY L. COHEN

Learning Outcomes

After reading this article, you will be able to:

- Explain why the "fixed mindset" (intelligence is fixed and cannot change) is detrimental to learning.
- Discuss how a teacher's belief in a student's potential to learn can help a student achieve up to that potential.
- Explain how psychological interventions raise students' achievements.

Besides being researchers, each of us is also a teacher. Like anyone who has taught, we know the feeling of failing to connect with some students. It's disheartening. Before going into research, one of us (Yeager) taught middle school. He wanted to help kids in tough straits get a good education. Yet, looking at his gradebook at the end of his first year teaching 7th-grade English in Tulsa, Okla., he saw large gains for more advantaged students but much smaller gains for less advantaged students, including racial and ethnic minority students. He thought that he'd given these students just as much attention, if not more, and that he'd held them to equally high standards. He'd given them plenty of helpful critical feedback and cared about their success. What had gone wrong? And what could be done differently?

Many teachers have such experiences. Our research investigates why, sometimes, no matter how hard you work to create a good lesson plan or provide high-quality feedback, some students don't stay as motivated or learn as much as teachers would like. We also look at what can be done to improve their outcomes.

Take the Student's Perspective

When confronted with a problem in education—students falling behind in math, for example—we tend to focus on what teachers teach and how they teach it. We tend to prescribe solutions that take the perspective of the teacher, like *How can we teach math differently?*

That is an important perspective. But it can also help to adopt the vantage point of a student. How does the classroom look to a student sitting at a desk in the third row? What is he or she concerned about? How does the student feel about his or her potential? Does the student feel accepted by the teacher and fellow classmates? When you begin with questions like these, a different picture emerges—one that focuses on the psychology of students. This approach suggests that teachers should look beyond how they communicate academic content and try to understand and, where appropriate, change how students experience school. Even when a classroom seems to be the same for all students—for instance, when all students are treated similarly—different students can experience the class very differently. Understanding what school feels like for different students can lead to nonobvious but powerful interventions.

A common problem is that students have beliefs and worries in school that prevent them from taking full advantage of learning opportunities. For example, students who struggle in math may think that they are "dumb" or that teachers or peers could see them as such. Or girls in advanced math or minority students in general may wonder if other people will look at them through the lens of a negative stereotype about their group instead of judging them on their merits.

These beliefs and worries don't reflect low self-esteem, insecurity, or flaws in the student. From the students' viewpoint, they're often reasonable. If students are aware that negative stereotypes exist about their group, it makes sense for them to be alert to the possibility that stereotypes are in play (Steele, Spencer, & Aronson, 2002). Likewise, if a student has learned that many people see math ability as something that you either have or don't, it makes sense for that student to worry about being seen as "dumb" in math. Below we look at some of these beliefs in more detail and describe how they can be addressed.

Growth mindset

Carol Dweck has shown that some students think that people's amount of intelligence is fixed and cannot change (2006). Students who have this belief—called a *fixed mindset*—who then struggle in math may find it hard to stay motivated. They may think, "I'll never get it" and avoid math. But countering this belief can have powerful effects.

Teaching students that intelligence can be developed—that, like a muscle, it grows with hard work and good strategies—can help students view struggles in school not as a threat ("Am I dumb?") but as an opportunity to grow and learn ("This will make my brain stronger!"). In rigorous randomized experiments, even relatively brief messages and exercises designed to reinforce this *growth mindset* improved student achievement over several months, including the achievement of low-income and minority students (Aronson, Fried, & Good, 2002; Blackwell, Trzesniewski & Dweck, 2007).

Buttressing belonging and reducing stress

Worrying about belonging—"Do I belong? Will other students and teachers value me?"—is a chronic stressor. Students from historically marginalized groups, like black and Latino students or women in quantitative fields, may worry more about belonging. When students worry about belonging and something goes wrong—for instance, when a student feels left out, criticized, or disrespected—it can seem like proof that they don't belong. This can increase stress and undermine students' motivation and engagement over time.

Two types of interventions can remedy these worries. First, social-belonging interventions convey the positive message that almost all students worry about belonging at some point ("your concerns are not unique to you") and that these worries fade with time ("things will get better"). Such interventions can require as little as an hour to administer, and, by using persuasive delivery mechanisms that quickly change students' beliefs, they can be successful. One such intervention improved minority college students' grades for three years with no reinforcement from researchers, halving the achievement gap (Walton & Cohen, 2011).

Stealthy approaches don't feel controlling and don't stigmatize students as in need of help, factors that could do more harm than good.

Second, values affirmation interventions give students opportunities to reflect on personal values that bring them a sense of belonging and identity, such as relationships with friends and family, religion, or artistic pursuits. Students reflect on these values through structured in-class writing assignments timed to coincide with stressors throughout the year. These interventions shore up belonging in school and boost the GPAs of students contending with negative stereotypes in both adolescence and college.

High standards and assurance

Many students, but especially students who face negative stereotypes, worry that a teacher could be biased or unfair. They may wonder if critical feedback is a genuine attempt to help them or reflects bias against their group—something understandable given the historical marginalization of their group. Even a little mistrust can harm a student's learning. But when minority students were encouraged to see critical feedback as a sign of their teacher's high standards and his or her belief in their potential to reach those standards, they no longer perceived bias (Cohen, Steele, & Ross, 1999). In rigorous field studies, interventions of this sort boosted urban black youths' GPAs and reduced the black-white achievement gap several months after the intervention (Yeager et al., 2012).

Psychological Interventions aren't "Magic"

Understanding what students worry about in school can help us develop targeted interventions. These interventions can require only one or several class periods and modest resources. Sometimes they can even be delivered over the Internet (see www.perts.net). Yet all of these interventions have been experimentally evaluated and can have powerful effects on students' grades and test scores. But they are not "magic." They are not worksheets or phrases that will universally or automatically raise grades. Psychological interventions will help students only when they are delivered in ways that change how students think and feel in school, and when student performance suffers in part from psychological factors rather than entirely from other problems like poverty or neighborhood trauma. That means interventions depend critically on the school context, as we elaborate below.

How Psychological Interventions Work

Psychological interventions raise student achievement by:

- Changing students' subjective experience in school—what school feels like for them, their *construals* of themselves and the classroom;
- Leveraging powerful but *psychologically wise* tactics that deliver the treatment message effectively without generating problematic side effects like stigmatizing recipients; and
- Tapping into self-reinforcing or *recursive processes* that sustain the effects of early interventions (Garcia & Cohen, 2012; Yeager & Walton, 2011).

Construal

Each psychological intervention began by understanding what school feels like to students. These interventions may seem small to outside observers, and often they are in terms of time and cost relative to other school reforms. But to a student who worries that a poor test score means that she is stupid or could be seen as stupid, learning that the brain can grow and form new connections when challenged, or being told that a teacher believes that she can meet a higher standard, can be powerful. Despite its subtlety—or perhaps *because* of it—the message assuages fears that might stifle learning.

Psychologically wise delivery

Psychological interventions change how students think or feel about school or about themselves in school. If they don't deliver their message in a way that leads to these changes, they won't be effective. Each intervention used a delivery mechanism that drew on research into how to make messages stick. Rather than simply presenting an appeal to a student, each intervention enlisted students to actively generate the intervention itself. For instance, one delivery mechanism involves asking students to write letters to younger students advocating for the intervention message (e.g., "Tell a younger student why the brain can grow"). As research on the "saying-is-believing" effect shows, generating and advocating a persuasive message to a receptive audience is a powerful means of persuasion (Aronson, 1999). Similarly, rather than telling students that they are successfully meeting important values in their lives, values affirmations have students self-generate ways in which this is the case.

Although such delivery mechanisms are psychologically powerful, they are also stealthy, which may increase their effectiveness. None of the interventions expose students to a persuasive appeal (e.g., "You should know that your teachers are not biased") or tell them they are receiving "an intervention" to help them. Stealthy approaches don't feel controlling and don't stigmatize students as in need of help, factors that could do more harm than good (Ross & Nisbett, 1991).

Often psychological interventions are brief—not extensive or repeated. Excessive repetition risks sending the message that students are seen as needing help or may undermine the credibility of a reassuring message (as in "thou doth protest too much"). In this way, delivering psychological interventions differs markedly from teaching academic content. Academic content is complex and taught layer on layer: The more math students are taught, the more math they learn. Changing students' psychology, by contrast, can call for a light touch.

One mistake is to encourage students to give "more effort" when they really need not only to apply more effort but also change strategy.

Recursive processes

What can seem especially mysterious is how a brief or one-shot psychological intervention can generate effects that persist over long periods. For instance, people may assume that an intervention must remain on students' minds to retain its effects. But, like many experiences, a psychological intervention will become less salient as it recedes in time. A key to understanding the long-lasting effects of psychological interventions is to understand how they tap into self-reinforcing processes in schools—like how students make friends and then feel more confident they belong, how they build relationships with teachers who give them more support and encouragement, and how they simply feel more confident in their ability to learn and succeed.

In education, early success begets more success. As students study, learn, and build academic skills, they're better prepared to learn and perform in the future. As students form better relationships in school, these become sources of support and learning that promote feelings of belonging and academic success. When students achieve success beyond what they thought possible, their beliefs about their own agency often improve, leading them to become more invested in school, further improving performance, and reinforcing their belief in their potential for growth. As students perform well, they're placed in higher-level classes—gateways that raise expectations, expose them to high-achieving peers, and put them on a trajectory of success. A well-timed, well-targeted psychological intervention can improve students' relationships, experiences, and performance at a critical stage and thus improve their trajectory through their school careers (Yeager & Walton, 2011). It is thus essential to intervene early, before a negative recursive process has gained momentum, if we are to improve students' outcomes over long periods (Garcia & Cohen, 2012).

Education occurs in a complex system. If students are to succeed, they need both learning opportunities and openness to these opportunities. As a result, it would be absurd to replace traditional educational reforms, like improving curricula, pedagogy, or teacher quality, with psychological interventions. Indeed, making students optimistic about school without actually giving them opportunities to learn could not only be ineffective but counterproductive. Psychological interventions work only because they catalyze the student's potential and the classroom resources for growth.

Use Psychological Interventions Thoughtfully

Excellent teachers already use versions of the techniques discussed here. But, when trying to improve those techniques by applying psychological interventions, practitioners will want to be thoughtful. Psychology is subtle, and you can make many mistakes when trying to change it (believe us—we've made them).

One mistake is to encourage students to give "more effort" when they really need not only apply more effort but also change strategy. Effort is necessary but it is not the sole ingredient for success. When confronted with continued failures despite heightened effort, students might conclude that they can't succeed, sapping their motivation. Effective growth mindset interventions challenge the myth that raw ability matters most by teaching the fuller formula for success: effort + strategies + help from others.

Psychological interventions complement—and do not replace—traditional education reforms.

Second, any psychological intervention can be implemented poorly. The devil is in the details: An intervention to instill belonging, a growth mindset, or a sense of affirmation hinges on subtle and not-so-subtle procedural craft. Classroom activities that promote a rah-rah ethos or that express platitudes ("everyone belongs here") but don't make students feel personally valued and respected will fail. Bolstering a sense of belonging for poor-performing students requires establishing credible norms that worry about belonging are common and tend to fade with time—not rah-rah boosterism. Similarly, values affirmation exercises might backfire if they're delivered in a cursory way or seen as something that the teacher cares little about.

A third example of well-intended but unwise strategies for changing student psychology involves teacher feedback. Many teachers are tempted to overpraise students for mediocre performance, especially students who face negative stereotypes, so as to appear unbiased and boost student self-esteem (Harber, Gorman, Gengaro, & Butisingh, in press). Sometimes, teachers go out of their way to praise student ability on classroom tasks. But such overpraising risks worsening student psychology by conveying low expectations or by sending the message that ability rather than effort and strategy matter the most.

Good teachers often know the importance of belonging, growth, and positive affirmation. But they may not know the best ways to bring these about. Well-intended practices can sometimes even do more harm than good. At the same time, researchers may not always know the best way to make their interventions speak to students in a given class. And many of the interventions developed here were borne of observations of real-world success stories—educators who boosted the performance and life chances of their at-risk youth. This is why, going forward, we believe it is critical for educators and practitioners to work together to develop ways to change students' psychology in school for the better.

Conclusion

Psychological interventions complement—and do not replace—traditional educational reforms. They don't teach students academic content or skills, restructure schools, or improve teaching. A psychological intervention will never teach a student to spell or do fractions. Instead, it will allow students to seize opportunities to learn. Psychological and structural interventions when combined could go a long way toward solving the nation's educational problems.

References

Aronson, E. (1999). The power of self-persuasion. *American Psychologist, 54,* 875–884.

Aronson, J., Fried, C., & Good, C. (2002). Reducing the effects of stereotype threat on African-American college students by shaping theories of intelligence. *Journal of Experimental Social Psychology, 38,* 113–125.

Blackwell, L.A., Trzesniewski, K.H., & Dweck, C.S. (2007). Theories of intelligence and achievement across the junior high school transition: A longitudinal study and an intervention. *Child Development, 78,* 246–263.

Cohen, G.L., Steele, C.M., & Ross, L.D. (1999). The mentor's dilemma: Providing critical feedback across the racial divide. *Personality and Social Psychology Bulletin, 25,* 1302–1318.

Dweck, C.S. (2006). *Mindset.* New York, NY: Random House.

Garcia, J. & Cohen, G.L. (2012). A social-psychological approach to educational intervention. In E. Shafir (Ed.), *Behavioral foundations of policy,* pp. 329–350. Princeton, NJ: Princeton University Press. https://ed.stanford.edu/sites/default/files/social_psych_perspective_education.pdf.

Harber, K.D., Gorman, J.L., Gengaro, F.P., & Butisingh, S. (in press). Students' race and teachers' social support affect the positive feedback bias in public schools. *Journal of Educational Psychology, 104* (4), 1149–1161.

Ross, L. & Nisbett, R.E. (1991). *The person and the situation: Perspectives of social psychology.* New York, NY: McGraw-Hill.

Steele, C.M., Spencer, S.J., & Aronson, J. (2002). Contending with group image: The psychology of stereotype and social identity threat. In M.P. Zanna (Ed.), *Advances in experimental social psychology* (vol. 34), pp. 379–440. San Diego, CA: Academic Press.

Walton, G.M. & Cohen, G.L. (2011). A brief social-belonging intervention improves academic and health outcomes of minority students. *Science, 331,* 1447–1451.

Yeager, D.S., Purdie-Vaughns, V., Garcia, J., Pebley, P., & Cohen, G.L. (2012). *Lifting a barrier of mistrust: "Wise" feedback to racial minorities.* Unpublished manuscript. Austin, TX: University of Texas.

Yeager, D.S. & Walton, G. (2011). Social-psychological interventions in education: They're not magic. *Review of Educational Research, 81,* 267–301.

Critical Thinking

1. What do you see as the greatest challenge in helping students develop a "growth mindset" over a "fixed mindset"?
2. How can social-belonging interventions reduce the stress of marginalized students?
3. Why is it important to help students change strategies rather than give more time and effort to studying?

Create Central

www.mhhe.com/createcentral

Internet References

Support All Students to Close the Achievement Gap
www.wholechildeducation.org

The Achievement Gap
www.achievementfirst.org

The Challenge: Why Are Some Students Unmotivated?
www.perts.net/home/about.php

David Yeager (yeager@psy.utexas.edu) is an assistant professor of developmental psychology at University of Texas, Austin, Texas. **Gregory Walton** (gwalton@stanford.edu) is an assistant professor of psychology and **Geoffrey L. Cohen** (glc@stanford.edu) is a professor of education and psychology at Stanford University, Stanford, Calif.

Article

Prepared by: Claire N. Rubman, *Suffolk County Community College*

What I've Learned

We can't keep politics out of school reform. Why I'm launching a national movement to transform education.

MICHELLE RHEE

Learning Outcomes

After reading this article, you will be able to:

- Explain why a child's relationship with his/her teacher matters in education.
- Describe the changes Michelle Rhee wants to see in public schools.

After my boss, Washington, D.C., mayor Adrian Fenty, lost his primary in September, I was stunned. I had never imagined he wouldn't win the contest, given the progress that was visible throughout the city—the new recreation centers, the turnaround of once struggling neighborhoods, and, yes, the improvements in the schools. Three and a half years ago, when I first met with Fenty about becoming chancellor of the D.C. public-school system, I had warned him that he wouldn't want to hire me. If we did the job right for the city's children, I told him, it would upset the status quo—I was sure I would be a political problem. But Fenty was adamant. He said he would back me—and my changes—100 percent. He never wavered, and I convinced myself the public would see the progress and want it to continue. But now I have no doubt this cost him the election.

The timing couldn't have been more ironic. The new movie *Waiting for Superman*—which aimed to generate public passion for school reform the way *An Inconvenient Truth* had for climate change—premiered in Washington the night after the election. The film championed the progress Fenty and I had been making in the District, and lamented the roadblocks we'd faced from the teachers' union. In the pro-reform crowd, you could feel the shock that voters had just rejected this mayor and, to some extent, the reforms in their schools.

When I started as chancellor in 2007, I never had any illusions about how tough it would be to turn around a failing system like D.C.'s; the city had gone through seven chancellors in the 10 years before me. While I had to make many structural changes—overhauling the system for evaluating teachers and principals, adopting new reading and math programs, making sure textbooks got delivered on time—I believed the hardest thing would be changing the culture. We had to raise the expectations that people had about what was possible for our kids.

I quickly announced a plan to close almost two dozen schools, which provoked community outrage. We cut the central office administration in half. And I also proposed a new contract for teachers that would increase their salaries dramatically if they abandoned the tenure system and agreed to be paid based on their effectiveness.

Though all of these actions caused turmoil in the district, they were long overdue and reaped benefits quickly. In my first two years in office, the D.C. schools went from being the worst performing on the National Assessment of Educational Progress examination, the national test, to leading the nation in gains at both the fourth and eighth grade in reading as well as math. By this school year we reversed a trend of declining enrollment and increased the number of families choosing District schools for the first time in 41 years.

Because of results like these, I have no regrets about moving so fast. So much needed to be fixed, and there were times when I know it must have felt overwhelming to the teachers because we were trying to fix everything at once. But from my point of view, waiting meant that another year was going by when kids were not getting the education they deserved.

My comments about ineffective teachers were often perceived as an attack on all teachers.

I know people say I wasn't good enough at building consensus, but I don't think consensus can be the goal. Take, for example, one of our early boiling points: school closures. We held dozens of community meetings about the issue. But would people really have been happier with the results if we had done it more slowly? I talked to someone from another district that spent a year and a half defining the criteria that outlined which schools would close. But when the results were announced, everyone went nuts. They had seen the criteria. What did they think was going to happen? That's when I realized there is no good way to close a school.

Still, I could have done a better job of communicating. I did a particularly bad job letting the many good teachers know that I considered them to be the most important part of the equation. I should have said to the effective teachers, "You don't have anything to worry about. My job is to make your life better, offer you more support, and pay you more." I totally fell down on doing that. As a result, my comments about ineffective teachers were often perceived as an attack on all teachers. I also underestimated how much teachers would be relying on the blogs, random rumors, and innuendo. Over the last 18 to 24 months, I held teacher-listening sessions a couple of times a week. But fear was already locked in. In the end, the changes that we needed to make meant that some teachers and principals would lose their jobs in a punishing economy. I don't know if there was any good way to do that.

Some people believed I had disdain for the public. I read a quote where a woman said it seemed like I was listening, but I didn't do what she told me to do. There's a big difference there. It's not that I wasn't listening; I just didn't agree and went in a different direction. There's no way you can please everyone.

But it's true that I didn't do enough to bring parents along, either. I saw a poll of people who live in a part of the city where the schools experienced a significant turnaround, and everyone agreed that they were overwhelmingly much better now. But when they were asked, did we need to fire the teachers to see this turnaround, they said no. We didn't connect the dots for them.

After the shock of Fenty's loss, it became clear to me that the best way to keep the reform going in the D.C. schools was for me to leave my job as chancellor. That was tough for me to accept. I called the decision heartbreaking, and I meant it, because there is a piece of my heart in every classroom, and always will be. To this day, I get mail from D.C. parents and kids who say, "Why did you leave us? The job wasn't done. Why did you give up on us?" Those kinds of letters are really hard to read and respond to. I loved that job. But I felt that Mayor-elect Vincent Gray should have the same ability that Fenty had to appoint his own chancellor. And I knew I had become a lightning rod and excuse for the anti-reformers to oppose the changes that had to be made.

After stepping down, I had a chance to reflect on the challenges facing our schools today and the possible solutions. The truth is that despite a handful of successful reforms, the state of American education is pitiful, and getting worse. Spending on schools has more than doubled in the last three decades, but the increased resources haven't produced better results. The U.S. is currently 21st, 23rd, and 25th among 30 developed nations in science, reading, and math, respectively. The children in our schools today will be the first generation of Americans who will be less educated than the previous generation.

When you think about how things happen in our country—how laws get passed or policies are made—they happen through the exertion of influence. From the National Rifle Association to the pharmaceutical industry to the tobacco lobby, powerful interests put pressure on our elected officials and government institutions to sway or stop change.

The truth is, the state of American education is pitiful, and it's getting worse.

Education is no different. We have text-book manufacturers, teachers' unions, and even food vendors that work hard to dictate and determine policy. The public-employee unions in D.C., including the teachers' union, spent huge sums of money to defeat Fenty. In fact, the new chapter president has said his No. 1 priority is job security for teachers, but there is no big organized interest group that defends and promotes the interests of children.

You can see the impact of this dynamic playing out every day. Policymakers, school-district administrators, and school boards who are beholden to special interests have created a bureaucracy that is focused on the adults instead of the students. Go to any public-school-board meeting in the country and you'll rarely hear the words "children," "students," or "kids" uttered. Instead, the focus remains on what jobs, contracts, and departments are getting which cuts, additions, or changes. The rationale for the decisions mostly rests on which grown-ups will be affected, instead of what will benefit or harm children.

The teachers' unions get the blame for much of this. Elected officials, parents, and administrators implore them to "embrace change" and "accept reform." But I don't think the unions can or should change. The purpose of the teachers' union is to protect the privileges, priorities, and pay of their members. And they're doing a great job of that.

What that means is that the reform community has to exert influence as well. That's why I've decided to start StudentsFirst, a national movement to transform public education in our country. We need a new voice to change the balance of power in public education. Our mission is to defend and promote the interests of children so that America has the best education system in the world.

From the moment I resigned, I began hearing from citizens from across this country. I got e-mails, calls, and letters from parents, students, and teachers who said, "Don't give up. We need you to keep fighting!" Usually, they'd then share with me a story about how the education system in their community was not giving students what they need or deserve. I got one e-mail from two people who have been trying to open a charter school in Florida and have been stopped every step of the way by the school district. No voices have moved me more than those of teachers. So many great teachers in this country are frustrated with the schools they are working in, the bureaucratic rules that bind them, and the hostility to excellence that pervades our education system.

We're hoping to sign up 1 million StudentsFirst members and raise $1 billion in our first year.

The common thread in all of these communications was that these courageous people felt alone in battling the bureaucracy. They want help and advocates. There are enough people out there who understand and believe that kids deserve better, but until now, there has been no organization for them. We'll ask people across the country to join StudentsFirst—we're hoping to sign up 1 million members and raise $1 billion in our first year.

StudentsFirst will work so that great teachers can make a tremendous difference for students of every background. We believe every family can choose an excellent school—attending a great school should be a matter of fact, not luck. We'll fight against ineffective instructional programs and bureaucracy so that public dollars go where they make the biggest difference: to effective instructional programs. Parent and family involvement are key to increased student achievement, but the entire community must be engaged in the effort to improve our schools.

Though we'll be nonpartisan, we can't pretend that education reform isn't political. So we'll put pressure on elected officials and press for changes in legislation to make things better for kids. And we'll support and endorse school-board candidates and politicians—in city halls, statehouses, and the U.S. Congress—who want to enact policies around our legislative agenda. We'll support any candidate who's reform-minded, regardless of political party, so reform won't just be a few courageous politicians experimenting in isolated locations; it'll be a powerful, nationwide movement.

Lastly, we can't shy away from conflict. I was at Harvard the other day, and someone asked about a statement that Secretary of Education Arne Duncan and others have made that public-school reform is the civil-rights issue of our generation. Well, during the civil-rights movement they didn't work everything out by sitting down collaboratively and compromising. Conflict was necessary in order to move the agenda forward. There are some fundamental disagreements that exist right now about what kind of progress is possible and what strategies will be most effective. Right now, what we need to do is fight. We can be respectful about it. But this is the time to stand up and say what you believe, not sweep the issues under the rug so that we can feel good about getting along. There's nothing more worthwhile than fighting for children. And I'm not done fighting.

Critical Thinking

1. What role does politics play in public school education?
2. How do you feel about the "last hired, first fired" policy of unionized workers? Why?
3. Why is public school reform needed in the United States?

Create Central

www.mhhe.com/createcentral

Internet References

Is School Reform Making America Less Competitive?
www.washingtonpost.com/blogs/answer-sheet/wp/2013/02/06

School Reform: False Assumptions That Drive School Reform
http://teaching.about.com/od/Parentalinvolvement

StudentsFirst
www.studentsfirst.org

Article

Prepared by: Claire N. Rubman, *Suffolk County Community College*

Visiting Room 501

Middle-class Latino students in the United States negotiate life as transnational citizens, developing an identity and a culture that translate their contemporary, lived experiences and highlight within-group variances.

MARGARET SAUCEDA CURWEN

Learning Outcomes

After reading this article, you will be able to:

- Explain what is meant by "cultural capital."
- Describe how multiple cultural codes lead to a transnational identity.
- Evaluate the unidimensional portrayal of Latino students as marginalized and non-mainstream even if they are U.S.-born, with English as their home language.

"If you are in trouble, if you need money, I will help you. You are my favorite cousin," wrote Sammy as part of a "friendly letter" assignment in Room 501.

Why did Sammy, a 5th grader in an American elementary school, offer such support to his Mexican cousin? "People living in Mexico work hard and there is not very much money," he explained.

Sammy was a student in Room 501, a classroom in an upwardly mobile middle-class Latino community in Southern California where students were primarily from Mexico but differed in generational status.

I spent more than two months observing Room 501 to learn how children with Latino ancestry tap into their lived experiences, history, background knowledge, and language skills—what Paulo Freire and Donaldo Macedo (1987) describe as cultural capital—while engaged in their classroom's literacy activities.

Students in Room 501 were exploring and negotiating their lives as transnational citizens. In a globalized world of instantaneous information and communication, Latino students are shaping, morphing, and evolving into a new generation. This study highlights one group of students who were aspiring toward middle class, which is not the typical perception created when educators and policy makers identify Latino children as "at risk." The tacit and explicit addressing of students' culture through local school practices, curriculum, and pedagogy is intertwined with students' identity and contributes to their academic expectations. This research highlights the educational importance of understanding within-group differences, as well as students' contemporary experiences, to identify and access their strengths.

The vignette above illustrates two key points from my study. The first is the distinction that students, such as Sammy, make between their current middle-class neighborhood and their perceptions of life in Mexico. Now living in the United States, they consider themselves better off financially and therefore able to help relatives who remain in Mexico and whom they perceive as less fortunate.

Second, these students maintain relationships that cross geographic borders through literacy practices that incorporate cultural, social, economic, linguistic, and political domains. In this example, Sammy displays his newly constructed transnational identity, one which he seems to embrace with remarkable ease. He demonstrates not only geographical flexibility, but also an inclination to draw on multiple cultural codes that transcend his personal history and that of his parents.

A startling, and somewhat alarming, finding by sociologists triggered my initial interest in exploring the classroom interactions of young children: The education and economic gains made by first- and second-generation Latinos are not sustained in later generations. Stated another way, the prospects for economic, educational, health, and social viability for Latinos actually decreases by the third generation. This discovery compelled me to rethink my assumptions that Latino immigrants of the late 20th century would follow trajectories similar to those of 19th-century European immigrants. After all, this upward mobility was the "Great American Dream" and part of this country's cultural narrative. My research needed to move beyond pedagogy and interactions between child and teacher. Clearly, there were other issues. Although I am a former classroom teacher and currently focused on research into children's literacy development, my curiosity drew me to a much broader landscape of sociological and anthropological perspectives and readings into critical theory and public policy.

Understanding the Latino Experience

In 2003, there were 37 million Latinos in the United States, making them the "largest minority group" (Darder and Torres 2004). Much has been said about this group's educational achievement, language issues, and identity patterns. However, Latinos are not a monolithic group. As often happens with other ethnic groups, such as Asians and African Americans, a demographic umbrella descriptor subsumes the multifaceted groups within. For Latinos, these within-group variances include such distinguishing characteristics as occupation, place of residence, class, and educational attainment. For Latino immigrants, other contributing aspects include country of origin, reception in this country, availability of an existing support system, language of preference, and generational status (Orellana and Bowman 2003).

Two-thirds of the Latino population in this country have Mexican origins, and an increasing proportion is becoming middle class. However, research has shown that the academic achievement of U.S.-born, English-speaking Latinos lags behind those of their school peers. Of particular concern are U.S.-born Latinos whose home language is English. Because this group is native born and has acquired the necessary language skills, one might expect that they would logically find success in school. However, researchers point out that a disproportionate percentage of English-speaking Latino students is underachieving (Nieto 2001), as are third-generation children (Portes and Rumbaut 2001). Though the high school dropout rate for Latinos is high and might be attributed to the process, difficulties, and complications inherent in immigrating to a new country, Latino immigrants account for only one-third of this group's dropout rate.

Systemic and institutional factors have contributed to the disenfranchisement of Latinos. These include differential school resources, *de facto* school segregation, school tracking into low-level courses, disproportionate numbers in school categorical groups, lack of culturally relevant texts, and reductionist reading programs. In addition, the discourse in the education literature on children from diverse backgrounds also can unintentionally create a negative perception. Education researcher Carol Lee (2003) notes that this happens when educators and policy makers identify Latino children or other children from diverse backgrounds as "minority," "non-mainstream," "marginalized," and "at risk." A tendency is to automatically position certain populations, such as Latinos, in a low niche without considering the experiences of other socioeconomic levels, notably working class and middle-class children.

Educators are focused on the academic success of all children. For some children from diverse backgrounds, this focus is on both their English language acquisition and concerns for those living in poverty. The stark reality is that children from diverse populations disproportionately experience poverty, discrimination, and low-quality education. Without question, these needs are real and need to be part of the conversation in developing policies and programs that will advance the educational achievement of all children. Yet, to fully understand the needs of today's learners, school reform efforts must recognize the particular context and respond to the perceptions and adaptive responses of different groups.

Given this perplexing research on the academic trajectories of multigenerational, English-speaking Latinos, I began to wonder about the conversations that might occur in a well-functioning school in which a caring teacher invites children to display their cultural knowledge while engaged in reading and writing. The teacher in Room 501 was a skilled practitioner who built on students' strengths as learners. He recognized that every child had "little pieces of history." Therefore, I was surprised to discover a mismatch between these students' interests and their teacher's attempts to tap into their experiences.

Looking through New Eyes

Learning is more than a solitary "in-the-head" activity. Learning occurs in social spaces where individuals interact in purposeful activity. In doing so, they're shaped by the cultural, historical, economic, and social contexts in which they live and participate (Rogoff 2003; Vygotsky 1987). Children have fully textured lives and move through a multitude of out-of-school social groups, e.g., family, neighborhoods, friends, and clubs, in which they participate and acquire particular ways of being. This social and cultural knowledge can be a resource for their intellectual growth.

I was eager to discover how children in Room 501 might share such resources in the instructional and social setting of their classroom. I was particularly interested in how children might strategically incorporate their cultural capital, like Sammy did, when they responded to reading school texts, in writing class assignments, and during peer collaboration. Because the children's talk revealed the ever-changing nature of their lives and the instantaneous influence of technology, I was prompted to explore more current perspectives into the adaptations of immigrant groups to this country's values and beliefs.

Sociologist Yossi Shain's view of immigrant groups adopting American creed was a helpful orientation (1999). Shain provides an alternative conception of immigration processes that transcends traditional assimilation and acculturation models. In these processes, the individual subsumes aspects of their identity, culture, and language to the new dominant culture. Shain recounts recent experiences of several ethnic groups who develop transnational identities. He contends that some ethnic diasporas, such as Latinos of Mexican descent, adopt American creed, that is, this country's values of freedom, democracy, equity, justice, and human rights. This distinctive notion describes how ethnic groups simultaneously maintain an identity as a diasporic group member while espousing American values. While these aspects of immigrants' and subsequent generational differences are often explored in related fields of sociology, economics, and public policy, the literature on teaching and learning discusses these aspects less often. Thus, this broader conception of individuals as multifaceted helped provide a framework for Room 501 students' learning and negotiating in their classroom space.

Five Findings

I chose Room 501 as a case study site in part because of the teacher's progressive stance on including cultural and contemporary social issues in daily classroom life and his respect for students' diverse experiences, dual linguistic abilities, and cultural backgrounds. Constructivist literacy practices and multilingual and critical pedagogy were hallmarks of the teacher's instruction.

During the spring semester, the 5th graders in Room 501 read their language arts basal program, trade book literature, social studies, and science texts. Their writing projects were purposeful and authentic, and they included multiple genres. Students participated in the school's science fair and performed a class play. The classroom teacher honored and embraced the 5th-grade students' Latino heritage. He sought to include students' cultural heritage in the curriculum through multicultural texts, incorporation of Spanish language, and literary discussions. Often, he initiated critical class discussions surrounding societal issues of poverty and discrimination. However, a mismatch arose between his instructional overtures and his middle-class students' lived experiences. Given the students' mixed responses, I considered it important to carefully examine the nature in which children engaged, remained silent, or shied away from discussions. These instances could lead to theoretical and practical insights for students' readiness to participate in such activities.

My study led me to five key findings:

Adoption of the American creed

Room 501 students were active participants in multiple communities shaping their identity. They wove in views and beliefs from their everyday interests and concerns. They participated in Little League and tuned into popular "texts," including movies, video games, and TV shows. They were more likely to be energized by pop rock groups, teen celebrities, and Disney movies than to declare affinity for the multicultural 1970s United Farm Workers' leader Cesar Chavez or such former national baseball players as Roberto Clemente. Their response was consistent with education scholar Frederick Erickson's assertions that individuals negotiate through a variety of microcultures every day (2004). This engagement and participation shaped students' interests and formed the basis for academic connections they made to their text readings. Furthermore, Shain (1999) asserts that ethnic diasporas want to transform their outsider status and become part of the American lifestyle. Room 501 students' mainstream knowledge and community participation served social goals of peer affiliation and societal inclusion.

Homogeneity of neighborhood

These 5th graders were influenced by the homogeneity of their community and its comfortable security. Students and their families held an ethnic majority status in their neighborhood. When the teacher focused on differences, students didn't seem compelled to differentiate themselves from other racial and ethnic groups. The students' lack of engagement may have been their unwillingness to believe that being Latino could adversely affect their mainstream inclusion. Also, class discussions of contemporary discrimination and poverty, grounded in their basal program language arts and American history texts, were shadowed by a societal historical and current negative sentiment toward Mexican immigrants. Students would have had to publicly reveal exclusionary experiences that had the potential to be more personally humiliating than educationally illuminating.

Unidimensional portrayals of Latino culture

Students seemed uninspired by the teacher's well-intentioned—albeit, one-dimensional—portrayal of Latino culture. Students and their families' backgrounds and experiences defied a simplified "one-size-fits-all" categorization, as the sociologist Rubén Rumbaut notes (2004, p. 1169). They had varied generational, socioeconomic, familial, and linguistic proficiencies and varying ties to other cultures and countries. While the classroom highlighted unquestionably rich multicultural literature, such as *Esperanza Rising* (Muñoz 2000) and *Lupita Mañana* (Beatty 1981), the texts didn't automatically serve as cultural touchstones for Room 501 students.

This was a particularly perplexing finding because multicultural literature plays a key role in fostering student identity and affiliation. Upon closer inspection, however, an explanation became clearer. Cultural images were frozen in time; contemporary reflections of students' lives were absent. These texts, as well as others used in the classroom, typically portrayed Mexicans as recent immigrants or migrant laborers. They were representations of only a single facet of the ethnic diaspora's experience. Such textual depictions didn't adequately capture the full range of this ethnic diaspora's subsequent generational economic gain, social mobility, educational attainment, varied employment, and interest in participating in American society. Room 501 students' experiences as middle-class with access to a multitude of technological resources underscores the need to refine perceptions of today's students.

In discussions about a social issue such as discrimination, Room 501 students were disinclined to publicly include personal experience. On the surface, students distanced themselves from the salience of discrimination in their lives. In their view, discrimination had been erased through the efforts of Martin Luther King, Jr. and Rosa Parks; two students even said aloud that these individuals "saved our lives and stopped discrimination." Another student noted, "Discrimination doesn't happen here." But in further discussions, children repeatedly cited instances of discrimination in popular movies and TV sitcoms. For example, several students described in detail a recent episode of the teen television show, *That's So Raven,* when a black character wasn't given an opportunity to apply for a job but then overcame the issue. It was problematic that the school's sanctioned texts consisted typically of historical—not contemporary—stories. In popular movies and TV shows, racial and ethnic struggles have been resolved, which helps shape a perception among students that racism and discrimination are merely archival events.

Pursuit of upward mobility

Students and their families were not consigned to one economic class but were aspiring upwards. This was evidenced by parents' and their children's expressed interest in higher education, material attainment, parental career orientations, and English-language acquisition. Children contrasted their single-family homes in their stable suburb to other Southern California communities where recent-entry immigrants live in dense areas of apartments. The lifestyle of these 5th graders and their families symbolized middle-class standing to them.

Gravitating toward English language

English was perceived as a high-status language and was a priority for parents and their children. Families knew about political pressures and societal negative sentiment toward the Spanish language. Since the late 1990s, legislation in California and Arizona, reverberating with a strong anti-immigrant sentiment, promulgated the authority of the English language and all but eliminated bilingual education. Parents in this school were increasingly choosing English-language instruction over bilingual instruction. This finding disrupts popular beliefs that members and children of the Mexican diaspora persist in maintaining their language at the expense of national unity. When these multigenerational children were asked about their interest in speaking Spanish, their responses varied: Evita relished the chance to share a phone conversation after school in Spanish, and Conner recounted translating his school-assigned poems written in English for his Spanish-speaking grandmother. Other students expressed concern about losing their cultural language and "sounding weird" by speaking Spanish among their peers and in their home. Chloe lamented, "I don't know how to pronounce the [Spanish] words anymore," and Geraldo noted, "I can't find the words." They were adept and strategic about choosing which language to use and when. They were linguistically negotiating as transnational citizens as well as among microcultural communities of family, peers, and schools.

Of note were the generational tensions regarding the erosion of Spanish language competency. Parents expressed their desire for their children to be bilingual. This finding was consistent with the findings of anthropologist Sally Merry (2006), who described the contradictions and clashes between group members when some adopt new practices. When culture is recognized for its dynamic, fluid, and porous nature, the eruption of tensions, such as the one between parents and their offspring over language retention, can be expected.

In conclusion, these 5th-grade Latino students circulated in varied cultural worlds. This snapshot of social interaction in Room 501 captures a single point in time of one specific group. This exploration in a classroom, watching and listening closely to children talk, provides insight for educators. Similar to all ethnic diaspora groups, the students' identities were fluid and shifting. In a time of instantaneous information and communication, students were continuously shaping their identity. However, as Michael Olneck contends, "schools rarely recognize the transnational aspects of their immigrant group's identities and lives" (2004, p. 383). Modern conceptions of culture are analogous to a kaleidoscope: With each turn, culture is always shifting and changing.

The perception of culture guides institutional policy and reform efforts. Thus educators need a dynamic, fluid, and evolving conception of culture. Only then can the learning experiences of children of ethnic diasporas be understood and nurtured.

References

Beatty, Patricia. *Lupita Mañana.* New York: Morrow, 1981.

Darder, Antonia, and Rodolfo D. Torres. *After Race: Racism After Multiculturalism.* New York: New York University Press, 2004.

Erickson, Frederick. "Culture in Society and Educational Practices." In *Multicultural Education: Issues and Perspectives,* 5th ed., ed. James A. Banks and Cherry A. McGee Banks, pp. 31–60. Hoboken, N.J.: Wiley, 2004.

Freire, Paulo, and Donaldo Macedo. *Literacy: Reading the Word and the World.* Westport, Conn.: Bergin and Garvey, 1987.

Lee, Carol D. "Why We Need to Re-Think Race and Ethnicity in Educational Research." *Educational Researcher* 32 (June/July 2003): 3–5.

Merry, Sally E. "Introduction: Culture and Transnationalism." In *Human Rights and Gender Violence* (pp. 1–35). Chicago: University of Chicago Press, 2006.

Muñoz Ryan, Pam. *Esperanza Rising.* New York: Scholastic Press, 2000.

Nieto, Sonia. "Foreword." In *The Best for Our Children: Critical Perspectives on Literacy for Latino Students,* ed. Maria de la Luz Reyes and John J. Halcon, pp. ix–xi. New York: Teachers College Press, 2001.

Olneck, Michael. "Immigrants and Education in the United States." In *Handbook of Research on Multicultural Education,* 2nd ed., ed. James A. Banks and Cherry A. McGee Banks, pp. 381–403. San Francisco: Jossey-Bass, 2004.

Orellana, Marjorie Faulstich, and Phillip Bowman. "Cultural Diversity Research on Learning and Development: Conceptual, Methodological, and Strategic Considerations." *Educational Researcher* 32 (June/July 2003): 26–32.

Portes, Alejandro, and Rubén G. Rumbaut. *Legacies: The Story of the Immigrant Second Generation.* Berkeley: University of California Press, 2001.

Rogoff, Barbara. *The Cultural Nature of Human Development.* New York: Oxford University Press, 2003.

Rumbaut, Rubén. "Ages, Life Stages, and Generational Cohorts: Decomposing the Immigrant First and Second Generations in the United States." *International Migration Review* 38, no. 3 (2004): 1160–1205.

Shain, Yossi. *Marketing the American Creed Abroad: Diasporas in the U.S. and Their Homelands.* Cambridge, Mass.: Harvard University Press, 1999.

Vygotsky, Lev S. *The Collected Works of L. S. Vygotsky, Volume 1. Problems of General Psychology,* ed. Robert W. Riber and Aaron S. Carton (1934; reprint, New York: Plenum Press, 1987).

Critical Thinking

1. Why do non-Latinos view the 37+ million Latinos in the U.S. as "all alike"?
2. Support the desire of some parents to have their children be bilingual, even if they are educated in the English language.
3. What contributes to the finding that the educational and economic gains made by first- and second-generation Latinos are not sustained in later generations?

Create Central

www.mhhe.com/createcentral

Internet References

At the Intersection of Transnationalism, Latina/o Immigrants, and Education
http://muse.jhu.edu/journals/hsj/summary/v092/92.4

Latino Identity
www.huffingtonpost.com/tag/latino-identity

When Labels Don't Fit: Hispanics and Their View of Identity
www.pewhispanic.org/2012/04/04

Margaret Sauceda Curwen of Long Beach, California, is the winner of this year's PDK Outstanding Doctoral Dissertation Award.

Her dissertation was titled "The Nature of Middle-Class Latino/a Students' Cultural Capital in a 5th-Grade Classroom's Reading and Writing Activities."

Curwen received her Ph.D. from the Rossier School of Education at the University of Southern California in 2007. She is now an assistant professor of education at Chapman University in Orange, California. She is a member of the University of Southern California Chapter.

Article

Prepared by: Claire N. Rubman, *Suffolk County Community College*

Are Exams Bad for Children?

STEPHANIE SCHNEIDER AND MATT CHRISTISON

Learning Outcomes

After reading this article, you will be able to:

- Describe the misunderstandings that surround standardized tests.
- Explain the benefits of "contextualized assessment."

The most powerful evidence that tests harm children is the emerging resistance of parents, teachers, and students who see the damage first hand.

—Stephanie

Stephanie

A fellow teacher once shared with me this analogy to standardized testing: it's like checking to make sure a plant is growing properly by repeatedly ripping it out of the ground and examining the roots. When that plant is placed back into the soil, it does not remain the same but rather is traumatized by the drastic act.

Just as we know of better ways to grow plants, we know of better ways to assess children. More reliable methods of assessment can provide meaningful information that assist student learning, rather than a test that often serves as a punitive device.

If we are interested in children succeeding in school then we need to provide an education rich in context and relevance, accomplished through quality instructional time. Unfortunately, as the use of standardized tests increases, more classroom time is being dedicated to exam preparation and administration, which only results in a narrowing of the curriculum.

If we are interested in success for ALL children then we need to be clear that the current testing regime does nothing to address racial and economic inequalities and instead reinforces them. Often, we find in the United States that the data of such tests is used to rationalize policy that is damaging to schools in low-income neighbourhoods and in communities of color.

Finally, the most powerful evidence that tests harm children is the emerging resistance of parents, teachers, and students who see the damage first hand and are growing louder in their collective refusal to comply.

Matt

As both a teacher and a gardener, I agree that uprooting plants—and students—serves no purpose. Yet examinations, especially standardized tests, in and of themselves are not bad—any more than examining in detail the growth of a plant is bad. What is bad is how we use examinations and the misunderstandings that surround standardized testing in particular.

For the purpose of simplicity, I will refer to examinations in this discussion as "standardized testing and tests". Well-constructed, thoughtful, standardized tests have integrity in their validity and reliability. They are reliable in that well-constructed tests provide similar performances by the students in the same grade or taking the same course, under the similar or the same parameters (time, format, etc). What standardized testing does well is provide descriptive information for thoughtful use by well-trained and well-prepared teachers.

Yet, as you point out, this does not happen with much of the descriptive information we derive from well-constructed tests. The descriptive information—which can be used in a focused, diagnostic manner to provide the next steps for student learning—is often superseded by the ills of education you have presented: time constraints, justification of rankings and placements, and the reinforcement of inequities.

What we need is the hybrid: standardized testing used for its descriptive and diagnostic purposes without the simplistic and inappropriate agendas of those who wish to sort, restrict, and punish; along with the contextualized, rich and robust ongoing assessment of learning. If we want success for ALL students, then we must use ALL forms of assessment for the purposes they are intended, and neither hijack them for our own agendas nor reject them because they do not fit our preferences and current understandings.

We must use all forms of assessment for the purposes they are intended, and neither hijack them for our own agendas nor reject them because they do not fit our preferences.

— Matt

Stephanie

One could say standardized tests don't kill education; it is only the use of these tests that does. But for me, separating the use and intention is a futile task. It is their current manifestation that I deal with as a classroom teacher and even if the tests were of better quality, I still see the way testing favours certain kinds of skills as problematic.

I am required to give my kindergarten students the MAP (Measures of Academic Progress) test three times a year. Each time I explain this test is very different from what we do in the classroom. It never fails that children will try to help each other and I find myself telling them: "You may not help your friend solve that problem." I am forced to administer this test that prioritizes individual achievement and disallows any collaborative learning.

These tests do not inform my instruction. Since I am not allowed to see the content of the test, any resulting information is worthless.

I disagree that it is idealistic to use contextualized assessments—if there is a lack of training and experience on the part of teachers, then the solution is to redirect resources currently used for standardized tests to implement meaningful professional development on classroom-based assessments.

Any kind of assessment beyond that would have to be low stakes and should be given to a random selection of students only in certain grades. This can still provide valid information and yet limit the amount of resources and instructional time a test can occupy.

Matt

All forms of assessment—standardized testing and teacher-based classroom assessments—are subjective. What is emphasized (creativity, arithmetic proficiency, reading abilities, neatness, cooperation, and risk taking) and what is not emphasized sends a clear and often damaging message to students, parents, and teachers.

I agree with and see your critiques of standardized testing as valid, no pun intended. The politics and inappropriate uses of standardized testing do interfere with the daily work of teachers and learning in schools.

However, to turn against standardized testing and reject it is, in my mind, no better than embracing it as a panacea, as the solution to educational ills and woes, and as a means to sorting, selecting, and valuing students. What we must have is a balance, the complete picture of student learning in school contexts, working with others, working alone, creating, trying and experimenting, assessing processes and products in as many robust, well-thought-out, and well-developed (and open to change and constructive criticisms) assessments as possible.

Standardized testing is unlikely to disappear: and as such, we all need to take from it the insights it can provide while fighting against the political and power-based misuses that overshadow and stifle what standardized testing has to offer: descriptive information to help inform practice and support learning.

Stephanie

Imagining school without standardized testing (or very minimal testing) isn't too difficult because examples already exist. In fact, in some of the most highly regarded private schools, standardized tests are few and far between. Additionally, in the much-lauded example of education innovation, Finland, the standardized test is used infrequently and with low stakes.

I know that both these examples have their own circumstances but I suggest them because I want to demonstrate the possibility. Places do exist where teachers are trusted to educate students without the reliance on a standardized test.

That said, I do appreciate your effort to mitigate the misuse of such tests and I could certainly find a test more palatable if it really did provide valuable information and did not serve to punish and reward. If such a test were to exist I would require a few additional criteria.

First of all, a standardized test should not provide a lucrative profit to some entity. I would trust a test a lot more if I knew that no-one was making money off something that was potentially damaging to my students or school. Second, the test should be clear in its intent and not be used to determine a school's funding, a teacher's livelihood or a student's future. And finally, a test should be thoroughly vetted for bias with continued reflection coinciding with its use.

Matt

Ideally, you and I, as well as other parties, would work collaboratively so that the forms of assessment used would present the most well-rounded, helpful, and bias-free information to support student learning. As such a situation is unlikely to occur in the immediate future, I would add the following to your criteria.

First, standardized testing would be done outside of schools and school settings. It could be done as it is conducted in Finland: students write those tests when they are ready, having completed the requisite courses, and the examinations are held in community sites, with the test questions and answers published the following day for all community members to see, discuss, and review. Thus the standardized testing would be open to all types of scrutiny and transparency in and of its format, structure, and presentation.

Second, standardized testing would be voluntary, with those who wish to utilize the results paying for the costs of administration, creation, and development. Thus those who wish to use it would be known, and their intentions would be clear and connected directly with the testing. Should the results be used for admissions to postsecondary institutions, or ranking schools or other purposes, then those who participate would do so knowing who was to use them and why.

Perhaps this is idealistic, yet I know that open discussion about assessment and standardized testing will lead to improvements for students, learning, teachers, and the community at large.

Critical Thinking

1. Ideally, how could teachers assess student success without the use of standardized tests?
2. Under what circumstances could standardized tests be used more productively?
3. How could parents, teachers, and school districts work together to improve the current climate of testing and assessment?

Create Central

www.mhhe.com/createcentral

Internet References

How Tests Make Us Smarter

http://www.nytimes.com/2014/07/20/opinion/sunday/how-tests-make-us-smarter.html

Opting Out-The National Center for Fair and Open Testing

http://www.fairtest.org/get-involved/opting-out

Pros and Cons of Standardized Testing

http://worklife.columbia.edu/files_worklife/public/Pros_and_Cons_of_Standardized_Testing_1.pdf

Standardized Tests Pros and Cons

http://standardizedtests.procon.org/

Too Much Stress? Parents, Experts Discuss High-Stakes Standardized Test Anxiety

http://news.wjct.org/post/too-much-test-stress-parents-experts-discuss-high-stakes-standardized-test-anxiety

---

Stephanie Schneider teaches three- to six-year-olds at a public Montessori School in Milwaukee, Wisconsin, USA. She is also an active member of the Educators Network for Social Justice, a teacher activist group, and serves on the Executive Board of her local trade union, the Milwaukee Teacher Education Association. **Matt Christison** is a high school principal, sessional instructor in graduate studies at the University of Calgary, Alberta, Canada, and a lifelong questioner of the status quo. He earned a Doctorate of Education in 1996 from the University of Calgary, undertaking an analysis of gender performance differences on standardized testing.

Schneider, Stephanie and Matt Christison. "Are Exams Bad for Children?" *New Internationalist*. 464 (July/August, 2013): 30–32.

Article Prepared by: Claire N. Rubman, *Suffolk County Community College*

Ritalin Gone Wrong

L. Alan Sroufe

Learning Outcomes

After reading this article, you will be able to:

- Describe the initial success for children with attention deficits.
- Explain how stimulants can calm a child down in relation to ADD and medication.
- Explain the term *inborn defects* in relation to neurotransmitters and other brain anomalies.

Three million children in this country take drugs for problems in focusing. Toward the end of last year, many of their parents were deeply alarmed because there was a shortage of drugs like Ritalin and Adderall that they considered absolutely essential to their children's functioning.

But are these drugs really helping children? Should we really keep expanding the number of prescriptions filled?

In 30 years, there has been a 20-fold increase in the consumption of drugs for attention-deficit disorder.

As a psychologist who has been studying the development of troubled children for more than 40 years, I believe we should be asking why we rely so heavily on these drugs.

Attention-deficit drugs increase concentration in the short term, which is why they work so well for college students cramming for exams. But when given to children over long periods of time, they neither improve school achievement nor reduce behavior problems. The drugs can also have serious side effects, including stunting growth.

Sadly, few physicians and parents seem to be aware of what we have been learning about the lack of effectiveness of these drugs.

What gets publicized are short-term results and studies on brain differences among children. Indeed, there are a number of incontrovertible facts that seem at first glance to support medication. It is because of this partial foundation in reality that the problem with the current approach to treating children has been so difficult to see.

Back in the 1960s I, like most psychologists, believed that children with difficulty concentrating were suffering from a brain problem of genetic or otherwise inborn origin. Just as Type I diabetics need insulin to correct problems with their inborn biochemistry, these children were believed to require attention-deficit drugs to correct theirs. It turns out, however, that there is little to no evidence to support this theory.

In 1973, I reviewed the literature on drug treatment of children for *The New England Journal of Medicine.* Dozens of well-controlled studies showed that these drugs immediately improved children's performance on repetitive tasks requiring concentration and diligence. I had conducted one of these studies myself. Teachers and parents also reported improved behavior in almost every short-term study. This spurred an increase in drug treatment and led many to conclude that the "brain deficit" hypothesis had been confirmed.

But questions continued to be raised, especially concerning the drugs' mechanism of action and the durability of effects. Ritalin and Adderall, a combination of dextroamphetamine and amphetamine, are stimulants. So why do they appear to calm children down? Some experts argued that because the brains of children with attention problems were different, the drugs had a mysterious paradoxical effect on them.

However, there really was no paradox. Versions of these drugs had been given to World War II radar operators to help them stay awake and focus on boring, repetitive tasks. And when we reviewed the literature on attention-deficit drugs again in 1990 we found that all children, whether they had attention problems or not, responded to stimulant drugs the same way. Moreover, while the drugs helped children settle down in class, they actually increased activity in the playground. Stimulants generally have the same effects for all children and adults. They enhance the ability to concentrate, especially on tasks that are not inherently interesting or when one is fatigued or bored, but they don't improve broader learning abilities.

And just as in the many dieters who have used and abandoned similar drugs to lose weight, the effects of stimulants on children with attention problems fade after prolonged use. Some experts have argued that children with A.D.D. wouldn't develop such tolerance because their brains were somehow different. But in fact, the loss of appetite and sleeplessness in children first prescribed attention-deficit drugs do fade, and, as we now know, so do the effects on behavior. They apparently develop a tolerance to the drug, and thus its efficacy disappears. Many parents who take their children off the drugs find that behavior worsens, which most likely confirms their belief that the drugs work. But the behavior worsens because the children's bodies have become adapted to the drug. Adults may have similar reactions if they suddenly cut back on coffee, or stop smoking.

To date, no study has found any long-term benefit of attention-deficit medication on academic performance, peer relationships, or behavior problems, the very things we would most want to improve. Until recently, most studies of these drugs had not been properly randomized, and some of them had other methodological flaws.

But in 2009, findings were published from a well-controlled study that had been going on for more than a decade, and the results were very clear. The study randomly assigned almost 600 children with attention problems to four treatment conditions. Some received medication alone, some cognitive-behavior therapy alone, some medication plus therapy, and some were in a community-care control group that received no systematic treatment. At first this study suggested that medication, or medication plus therapy, produced the best results. However, after 3 years, these effects had faded, and by 8 years there was no evidence that medication produced any academic or behavioral benefits.

Indeed, all of the treatment successes faded over time, although the study is continuing. Clearly, these children need a broader base of support than was offered in this medication study, support that begins earlier and lasts longer.

Nevertheless, findings in neuroscience are being used to prop up the argument for drugs to treat the hypothesized "inborn defect." These studies show that children who receive an A.D.D. diagnosis have different patterns of neurotransmitters in their brains and other anomalies. While the technological sophistication of these studies may impress parents and nonprofessionals, they can be misleading. Of course the brains of children with behavior problems will show anomalies on brain scans. It could not be otherwise. Behavior and the brain are intertwined. Depression also waxes and wanes in many people, and as it does so, parallel changes in brain functioning occur, regardless of medication.

Many of the brain studies of children with A.D.D. involve examining participants while they are engaged in an attention task. If these children are not paying attention because of lack of motivation or an underdeveloped capacity to regulate their behavior, their brain scans are certain to be anomalous.

However brain functioning is measured, these studies tell us nothing about whether the observed anomalies were present at birth or whether they resulted from trauma, chronic stress, or other early-childhood experiences. One of the most profound findings in behavioral neuroscience in recent years has been the clear evidence that the developing brain is shaped by experience.

It is certainly true that large numbers of children have problems with attention, self-regulation, and behavior. But are these problems because of some aspect present at birth? Or are they caused by experiences in early childhood? These questions can be answered only by studying children and their surroundings from before birth through childhood and adolescence, as my colleagues at the University of Minnesota and I have been doing for decades.

Since 1975, we have followed 200 children who were born into poverty and were therefore more vulnerable to behavior problems. We enrolled their mothers during pregnancy, and over the course of their lives, we studied their relationships with their caregivers, teachers, and peers. We followed their progress through school and their experiences in early adulthood. At regular intervals we measured their health, behavior, performance on intelligence tests, and other characteristics.

By late adolescence, 50 percent of our sample qualified for some psychiatric diagnosis. Almost half displayed behavior problems at school on at least one occasion, and 24 percent dropped out by 12th grade; 14 percent met criteria for A.D.D. in either first or sixth grade.

Other large-scale epidemiological studies confirm such trends in the general population of disadvantaged children. Among all children, including all socioeconomic groups, the incidence of A.D.D. is estimated at 8 percent. What we found was that the environment of the child predicted development of A.D.D. problems. In stark contrast, measures of neurological anomalies at birth, I.Q. and infant temperament—including infant activity level—did not predict A.D.D.

Plenty of affluent children are also diagnosed with A.D.D. Behavior problems in children have many possible sources. Among them are family stresses like domestic violence, lack of social support from friends or relatives, chaotic living situations, including frequent moves, and, especially, patterns of parental intrusiveness that involve stimulation for which the baby is not prepared. For example, a 6-month-old baby is playing, and the parent picks it up quickly from behind and plunges it in the bath. Or a 3-year-old is becoming frustrated in solving a problem, and a parent taunts or ridicules. Such practices excessively stimulate and also compromise the child's developing capacity for self-regulation.

Putting children on drugs does nothing to change the conditions that derail their development in the first place. Yet those conditions are receiving scant attention. Policy makers are so convinced that children with attention deficits have an organic disease that they have all but called off the search for a comprehensive understanding of the condition. The National Institute of Mental Health finances research aimed largely at physiological and brain components of A.D.D. While there is some research on other treatment approaches, very little is studied regarding the role of experience. Scientists, aware of this orientation, tend to submit only grants aimed at elucidating the biochemistry.

Thus, only one question is asked: are there aspects of brain functioning associated with childhood attention problems? The answer is always yes. Overlooked is the very real possibility that both the brain anomalies and the A.D.D. result from experience.

Our present course poses numerous risks. First, there will never be a single solution for all children with learning and behavior problems. While some smaller number may benefit from short-term drug treatment, large-scale, long-term treatment for millions of children is not the answer.

Second, the large-scale medication of children feeds into a societal view that all of life's problems can be solved with a pill and gives millions of children the impression that there is something inherently defective in them.

Finally, the illusion that children's behavior problems can be cured with drugs prevents us as a society from seeking the more complex solutions that will be necessary. Drugs get everyone—politicians, scientists, teachers, and parents—off the hook. Everyone except the children, that is.

If drugs, which studies show work for 4 to 8 weeks, are not the answer, what is? Many of these children have anxiety or depression; others are showing family stresses. We need to treat them as individuals.

As for shortages, they will continue to wax and wane. Because these drugs are habit forming, Congress decides how much can be produced. The number approved doesn't keep pace with the tidal wave of prescriptions. By the end of this year, there will in all likelihood be another shortage, as we continue to rely on drugs that are not doing what so many well-meaning parents, therapists, and teachers believe they are doing.

Critical Thinking

1. Are parents aware of the research on the long- and short-term effects of attention-deficit medication on their children?
2. Are the side effect of medication for attention deficits, such as sleeplessness and a loss of appetite, worth the benefits of the medication for children?
3. Discuss the relationship between socioeconomic status and behavior problems.

Create Central

www.mhhe.com/createcentral

Internet References

ADD/ADHD Medications-Help Guide

http://www.helpguide.org/mental/adhd_medications.htm

Behavioral Treatments for Kids With ADHD-Helping kids get organized and control problem behaviors

http://www.childmind.org/en/posts/articles/2014-1-21-behavioral-treatment-kids-adhd

How Do ADHD Medications Work?

http://www.sciencedaily.com/releases/2013/10/131016100222.htm

NIMH · Attention Deficit Hyperactivity Disorder

http://www.nimh.nih.gov/health/publications/attention-deficit-hyperactivity-disorder/index.shtml

L. Alan Sroufe is a professor emeritus of psychology at the University of Minnesota's Institute of Child Development.

Sroufe, Alan L. "Ritalin Gone Wrong." *The New York Times*. (January, 28, 2012).

Unit 4

UNIT

Prepared by: Claire N. Rubman, *Suffolk County Community College*

Development During Childhood: Family and Culture

What type of family environment is best for a child? Is the traditional image of a two-parent family a construct of a bygone era or do two parents play a key role in the life of a child? Can single mothers compensate for absentee fathers? Similarly, is the traditional concept of public school the ideal educational environment for children or do other educational paradigms, such as homeschooling work better? Would you homeschool your child? Perhaps the experience you had in elementary, middle, or high school has swayed your opinion in one direction or another. Is that how parents make many of their parenting choices—past experience? Do they look to research, statistics, and psychological theories or do they rely on their own personal experiences to guide their decision-making processes? Do they spoil and overindulge their children instead of disciplining them? Do children today, for example, do household chores? Are today's children more spoiled than in past generations?

What would motivate a parent to homeschool a child? Be it religious grounds, poor educational perceptions, medical conditions, or a fear of the increase in violence in our culture, many parents are opting out of the public school system in favor of educating their children at home. Consider the relative advantages and disadvantages of public school versus homeschooling as you read about the Schreiber family, the Spigels, and educational expert Rebecca Ward. Linda Perlstein sheds light on education from a family's perspective in "Do-It-(All)-Yourself Parents." Homeschooling may satisfy a parent's needs, but is it ideal for the child?

While considering the best interests of the child, what is the role of a mother or a father in child development? "Pop Psychology" by Drevitch focuses on the role of dad as a child develops. What is the value, function, and role of a father in today's society? According to Drevitch, children who grow up with the loving interactions of a father have better language development, fewer behavioral issues, and less delinquent behavior in adolescence. John Bowlby (1907–1990) traced dysfunctional adolescent behavior back to early attachment bonds. This article reinforces the importance of those early childhood bonds with a child's father.

As we continue to think about the child's best interests, what about the toys that children play with? Should children, for example, play with guns? Is rough-and-tumble play a thing of the past since our zero tolerance policies were adopted in light of the Columbine school shooting tragedy in 1999? Since Dylan Klebold and Eric Harris went on their tragic and now infamous shooting rampage, potentially inspired by violent video games, have they changed the way that children play in perpetuity? According to Mildred Parten (1932), rough-and-tumble play is an essential part of cooperation and construction of the imaginary world. Psychologist Lawrence Cohen echoes similar sentiments in the article "Is War Play Bad for Kids?" by Holly Pevzner. This type of rough-and-tumble play allows children to explore and master their fears or aggressive impulses while also building social skills and communication.

Many misguided beliefs relate rough-and-tumble play to aggressive behavior and bullying. While bullying is a pervasive problem in childhood, we need to refocus our attention on the root causes and our approach to the bully and the victim. According to the research, around 25 percent of our children have been bullied with many of the incidences never being reported. Susan Porter describes why our current approach to bullying is inadequate in the article "Why Our Approach to Bullying Is Bad for Kids." The prefrontal cortex of the brain is targeted as poorly developed. This means that impulse control, empathy, and judgment can be limited or impaired in children as they progress toward adolescence. The preadolescent brain also turns inward to focus on the self, which creates egocentric individuals who have a tendency toward oversensitivity as they struggle with their developing sense of self. These developmental constraints, coupled with the zero tolerance policy in place in public schools can, according to Porter, impact a child's delicate self-esteem and developing resilience. Until the brain's executive function matures, how should we address bullying behaviors in our preadolescent population?

Looking at a more global family issue, this article addresses immunizations in poorer communities and the morality of bribing families to immunize their children. In rural regions of India, families are being bribed with the promise of a free kilo of lentils if they had their child immunized. Immunization rates jumped from 2 percent to 18 percent in Rajasthan. This is far below the 90 percent rate in the United States where families are not bribed. Is it ethical to bribe poorer communities even if the authorities believe they are acting in the best interests of the children? Is it true that here in the United States we do not bribe families or children? Children often receive candy or stickers for their participation while families must immunize their children if they want to participate in public school, summer camp, or childcare. Where should we draw the line when we try to act in our children's best interests?

The culture and climate for child development is addressed in Kolbert's article titled "Spoiled Rotten." This article focuses on parenting styles that do not focus on autonomy or good behavior. Rather, they overindulge children and spoil them. Kolbert explores the possibility that more independence and discipline might be beneficial to children. She recommends household chores and saying "no" to children to encourage better development. Is it possible, as Kolbert suggests, that we are raising a generation of children who "can't, or at least wont, tie their own shoes"?

As we consider bullying in our culture, Gottesman suggests that we look to our own homes as the bully can often be a sibling. In her article, "The Bully at Home," Gottesman assesses behaviors that cross the line from sibling rivalry and teasing to sibling abuse. The physical and emotional relationships between siblings can be precarious. Gottesman explores this "hidden epidemic" looking for indicators and possible solutions. She advocates addressing the behavior before it escalates by separating children, letting them cool down, teaching them to speak up without interruption, stating consequences, and reviewing house rules. She cautions that the consequences for sibling bullying range from depression and anxiety to anger and low self-esteem.

Article

Prepared by: Claire N. Rubman, *Suffolk County Community College*

Do-It-(All)-Yourself Parents

They raise chickens. They grow vegetables. They knit. Now a new generation of urban parents is even teaching their own kids.

LINDA PERLSTEIN

Learning Outcomes

After reading this article, you will be able to:

- Contrast reasons for homeschooling today with those in the past.
- Summarize what is meant by "differentiated instruction."

In the beginning, your kids need you—a lot. They're attached to your hip, all the time. It might be a month. It might be five years. Then suddenly you are expected to send them off to school for seven hours a day, where they'll have to cope with life in ways they never had to before. You no longer control what they learn, or how, or with whom.

Unless you decide, like an emerging population of parents in cities across the country, to forgo that age-old rite of passage entirely.

When Tera and Eric Schreiber's oldest child was about to start kindergarten, the couple toured the high-achieving public elementary school a block away from their home in an affluent Seattle neighborhood near the University of Washington. It was "a great neighborhood school," Tera says. They also applied to a private school, and Daisy was accepted. But in the end they chose a third path: no school at all.

Eric, 38, is a manager at Microsoft. Tera, 39, had already traded a career as a lawyer for one as a nonprofit executive, which allowed her more time with her kids. But "more" turned into "all" when she decided that instead of working, she would homeschool her daughters: Daisy, now 9; Ginger, 7; and Violet, 4.

We think of homeschoolers as evangelicals or off-the-gridders who spend a lot of time at kitchen tables in the countryside. And it's true that most homeschooling parents do so for moral or religious reasons. But education observers believe that is changing. You only have to go to a downtown Starbucks or art museum in the middle of a weekday to see that a once-unconventional choice "has become newly fashionable," says Mitchell Stevens, a Stanford professor who wrote *Kingdom of Children*, a history of homeschooling. There are an estimated 300,000 homeschooled children in America's cities, many of them children of secular, highly educated professionals who always figured they'd send their kids to school—until they came to think, *Hey, maybe we could do better*.

When Laurie Block Spigel, a homeschooling consultant, pulled her kids out of school in New York in the mid-1990s, "I had some of my closest friends and relatives telling me I was ruining my children's lives." Now, she says, "the parents that I meet aren't afraid to talk about it. They're doing this proudly."

Many of these parents feel that city schools—or any schools—don't provide the kind of education they want for their kids. Just as much, though, their choice to homeschool is a more extreme example of a larger modern parenting ethos: that children are individuals, each deserving a uniquely curated upbringing. That peer influence can be noxious. (Bullying is no longer seen as a harmless rite of passage.) That DIY—be it gardening, knitting, or raising chickens—is something educated urbanites should embrace. That we might create a sense of security in our kids by practicing "attachment parenting," an increasingly popular approach that involves round-the-clock physical contact with children and immediate responses to all their cues.

Even many attachment adherents, though, may have trouble envisioning spending almost all their time with their kids—for 18 years! For Tera Schreiber, it was a natural transition. When you have kept your kids so close, literally—she breast-fed her youngest till Violet was 4—it can be a shock to send them away.

Tera's kids didn't particularly enjoy day care or preschool. The Schreibers wanted a "gentler system" for Daisy; she was a perfectionist who they thought might worry too much about measuring up. They knew homeschooling families in their neighborhood and envied their easygoing pace and flexibility—late bedtimes, vacations when everyone else is at school or work. Above all, they wanted to preserve, for as long as possible, a certain approach to family.

Several homeschooling moms would first tell me, "I know this sounds selfish," and then say they feared that if their kids were in school, they'd just get the "exhausted leftovers" at the end of the day. Says Rebecca Wald, a Baltimore homeschooler, "Once we had a child and I realized how fun it was to see her discover stuff about the world, I thought, why would I want to let a teacher have all that fun?"

It's 12:30 P.M. on a Thursday, and Tera and her daughters have arrived home from a rehearsal of a homeschoolers' production of *Alice in Wonderland*. Their large green Craftsman is typical Seattle. There are kayaks in the garage, squash in the slow cooker, and the usual paraphernalia of girlhood: board games, dolls, craft kits. Next to the kitchen phone is a printout of the day's responsibilities. Daisy and Ginger spend about two hours daily in formal lessons, including English and math; today they've also got history, piano, and sewing.

Laws, and home-crafted curricula, vary widely. Homeschoolers in Philadelphia, for instance, must submit a plan of study and test scores, while parents in Detroit need not even let officials know they're homeschooling. Some families seek out a more classical curriculum, others a more unconventional one, and "unschoolers" eschew formal academics altogether. There are parents who take on every bit of teaching themselves, and those who outsource subjects to other parents, tutors, or online providers. Advances in digital learning have facilitated homeschooling—you can take an AP math class from a tutor in Israel—and there's a booming market in curriculum materials, the most scripted of which enable parents to teach subjects they haven't studied before.

So far, Tera says, these books have made the teaching itself easy—insofar as anything is easy about mothering three kids nonstop. The girls have started their lessons at the kitchen table, but there are also sandwiches to be assembled, cats who want treats, and girls who want drinks or ChapStick or napkins or, in the youngest's case, attention.

"Violet, Ginger is getting a lesson, so you have to be quiet," Tera says from across the open kitchen, while heating tea and coaching Ginger on sounding out Y words. "The first word: is it two syllables? What does Y say at the beginning of a word?"

"Yuh."

"At the end?"

"Eee? Yucky."

"Yucky is correct."

Tera sits down to eat a bowl of salmon salad while helping Ginger with her reading workbook. Daisy is reading a fantasy book about wild cats. Violet is playing with a big clock.

"Sam has a c-ane and a c-ape," Ginger says. "Sam has a c-ap and a c-an."

"If you use your finger, it will work better," Tera says.

Teaching Daisy to read was a breeze. With Ginger it's been more complicated, and Tera has had to research different approaches. She gives her lots of workbook activities, because Ginger retains information better when she's writing and not just listening. Since hearing about a neurological link between crawling and reading, Tera also has Ginger circle the house on hands and knees 10 times daily.

A school, Tera says, might not have teased out precisely how Ginger learns best. This is something I heard often from urban homeschoolers: the desire to craft an education just right for each child. They worry that formal schooling might dim their children's love of learning (yet there is a flip side: a reduced likelihood of being inspired along the way by the occasional magical teacher, full of passion and skill). They want their children to explore the subjects that interest them, as deeply as they care to go. For Daisy and Ginger, that has meant detours into herbalism, cat shows, musical theater, and deer.

Many parents are happy to sidestep environments that might be too intense, loading kids up with homework, making them feel an undue burden to perform. "The pressure from the reform movement today, from kindergarten on, has been all about 'Let's push, push, push for academic achievement,' " says Michael Petrilli, executive vice president of the Thomas B. Fordham Institute, an education think tank, and the author of a forthcoming book about urban parents' schooling decisions. Some urban homeschooled kids, particularly those with special needs, were previously enrolled in school but not served well there.

In truth, some conventional schools are making strides toward diagnosing and remedying each child's weaknesses. "Differentiated instruction"—the idea that teachers simultaneously address students' individual needs—is a catchphrase these days in public schools. And many elementary classrooms are no longer filled by rows of desks with children working in lockstep. But it is also true that you can never tailor instruction more acutely than when the student-teacher ratio is 1–1.

The Schreiber girls spend most of their time out and about, typically at activities arranged for homeschoolers. There are Girl Scouts and ceramics and book club and enrichment classes and park outings arranged by the Seattle Homeschool Group, a secular organization whose membership has grown from 30 families to 300 over the last decade. In a way, urban homeschooling can feel like an intensified version of the extracurricular madness that is the hallmark of any contemporary middle-class family, or it can feel like one big, awesome field trip.

Institutions throughout the country have discovered a reliable weekday customer in urban homeschoolers. "Everywhere you turn there's a co-op or a class or a special exhibit," says Brian Ray, founder of the National Home Education Research Institute in Oregon. Three years ago, the Museum of Science and Industry in Chicago began to court homeschoolers with free admission, their own newsletters, and courses designed specifically for them. Participation has doubled each year. "The more we offer, the more we sell out," says Andrea Ingram, vice president of education and guest services.

A mini-industry of homeschool consultants has cropped up, especially in New York City, whose homeschooling population has grown 36 percent in eight years, according to the school district. (While states usually require homeschoolers to register, many parents choose not to, so official estimates skew low.) In Seattle, even the public-school system runs a center that offers classes just to homeschoolers.

"My kids actually have to tell me to stop," says Erin McKinney Souster, a mother of three in Minneapolis, whose kids have learned to find an academic lesson in something as mundane as the construction of a roller-rink floor. "Everything is always sounding so cool and so fun."

Still, you can't help but wonder whether there's a cost to all this family togetherness. There are the moms, of course, who for two decades have their lives completely absorbed by their children's. But the mothers I got to know seem quite content with that, and clearly seem to be having fun getting together with each other during their kids' activities.

And the kids? There's concern that having parents at one's side throughout childhood can do more harm than good. Psychologist Wendy Mogel, the author of the bestselling book *The Blessing of a Skinned Knee*, admires the way homeschoolers manage to "give their children a childhood" in an ultracompetitive world. Yet she wonders how kids who spend so much time within a deliberately crafted community will learn to work with people from backgrounds nothing like theirs. She worries, too, about eventual teenage rebellion in families that are so enmeshed.

Typical urban homeschooled kids do tend to find the space they need by the time they reach those teenage years, participating independently in a wealth of activities. That's just as well for their parents, who by that time can often use a breather. And it has made them more appealing to colleges, which have grown more welcoming as they find that homeschoolers do fine academically. In some ways these students may arrive at college more prepared, as they've had practice charting their own intellectual directions, though parents say they sometimes bristle at having to suffer through courses and professors they don't like.

Tera figures that her daughters are out in the world enough to interact with all sorts of people. She feels certain they will be able to be good citizens precisely because of her and Eric's "forever style of parenting," as she calls it, not in spite of it. It's hard for Tera to get too worried when she's just spent the weekend, as the Schreibers often do, hanging out on a trip with homeschooled kids of all ages, including confident, competent teenagers who were happy playing cards with their parents all evening, with no electronics in sight.

Milo, my 3-year-old, never wants to go to preschool. So the more I hung out with homeschoolers, the more I found myself picking him up from school early, to squeeze in some of the fun these families were having. I began to think, why not homeschool? Really, there's something of the homeschooler in all of us: we stuff our kids with knowledge, we interact with them more than our parents did with us. I am resourceful enough to make pickles and playdough; why couldn't I create an interdisciplinary curriculum around Milo's obsession with London Bridge? I calculated what we'd have to give up if I cut back on work (though some homeschooling moms work full time or at least occasionally—like Tera, who writes parenting articles).

But my husband and I are loyal to what we call "detachment parenting": we figure we are doing a good job if Milo is just as confident and comfortable without us as he is with us. Family for us is more a condition—a joyous one, for sure—than a project, one of several throughlines of our lives.

For many of the homeschoolers I met, family is more: the very focus of their lives. And they wouldn't want it any other way. One comfort Tera and Eric Schreiber held on to when they started homeschooling was that if it wasn't working out, they could enroll the girls in school, literally the next day. That developed into an annual reassessment. By now their rhythms are deeply their own; they are embedded in a community they love. And at the college up the road there are plenty of calculus tutors, should they need them one day.

Critical Thinking

1. Why is homeschooling "newly fashionable"?
2. Identify some of the pros of homeschooling.
3. Identify some of the cons of homeschooling.
4. Defend the proposition that an educator should be able to address each student's individual needs.
5. Is there a happy medium between too much and not enough family togetherness? Should family togetherness increase or decrease as children age?

Create Central

www.mhhe.com/createcentral

Internet References

Homeschool Laws and Regulations
http://homeschooling.about.com/od/legal

How to Homeschool: Homeschooling Requirements and Information
www.motherearthnews.com/how-to-home-school.aspx

You Can Homeschool—Introduction
www.youcanhomeschool.org

Linda Perlstein, a freelance writer and editor based in Seattle, is the author of two books about schools and children, *Tested* and *Not Much Just Chillin'*.

Article

Prepared by: Claire N. Rubman, *Suffolk County Community College*

Pop Psychology

Fathers have long been seen as the less important parent. In *do fathers matter?,* Paul Raeburn marshals a slew of evidence against this misconception, proving that dads deliver even more than many of us imagined.

GARY DREVITCH

Learning Outcomes

After reading this article, you will be able to:

- Identify the linguistic benefits for children whose fathers are actively involved during early childhood.
- Explain why adolescents with absentee fathers have higher rates of teenage pregnancy.

As recently as the 1970s, psychologists and parenting experts had a ready answer to the question of how much fathers contributed to, children's development: Not much.

Admittedly, science journalist Paul Raeburn writes' in his new book, *Do Fathers Matter?,* researchers at the time had little data to prove the value of fathers—but that was because few had taken the time to look into it. "When we bother to look for the father's impact, we find it—always," Yale psychiatrist and fatherhood research pioneer Kyle Pruett told Raeburn. Ignoring dads, Pruett says, produced a field of research with "staggering blind spots."

Today we know better. The body of work that psychologists, biologists, sociologists, and neuroscientists have begun to produce on fatherhood is "one of the most important developments in the study of children and families," Raeburn believes, even though many findings have yet to receive wide attention.

As for his own family, Raeburn, a father of five, writes, "I'm glad to know my involvement is a good thing. But that's not why I spend time with my kids. I do it because I like it."

Following are seven discoveries about paternal influence Raeburn shares in his book, covering life from conception through adulthood:

1. At Conception: A Battle in the Womb

Harvard University biologist David Haig has detected that some "imprinted" genes—those that can be identified as coming from the male or female parent—compete for resources within the womb. Some paternal genes push the fetus to extract as much nourishment and energy from the mother as possible, even to the detriment of her health, while some maternal genes seek to deliver the fetus only as much as it needs. Haig's explanation is that "maternal genes have a substantial interest in the mother's well-being and survival," while "paternal genes favor greater allocation of maternal time and effort to their particular child."

2. In Pregnancy: The Power of Presence

During a woman's pregnancy, there would appear to be little a father could do to affect the child. A recent University of South Florida study shows that's not the case. Infants whose fathers were absent during pregnancy were more likely to be born prematurely or with lower birth weights than those whose fathers were present. Such babies were also four times more likely to die within their first year. Even in mothers, complications of pregnancy that would seem to have no connection to male involvement, including anemia and high blood pressure, were more common when fathers were absent.

3. At Birth: Men Deliver Relief

Old sitcoms showing fathers anxiously pacing in waiting rooms while their wives delivered their children were no exaggeration: From the 1930s, when most U.S. births had moved from the home to the hospital, until the late 1960s, when more men had successfully agitated to gain a place by their wives' bedsides, delivery was a women-and-professionals only affair, to the apparent detriment of everyone involved. As more men took their place in the maternity ward, women reported feeling less pain, and requests for pain medication declined. Mothers were even less likely to cry. What's more, men present for their children's birth report being more attached to their infants and more involved in their care. Letting dads in, Raeburn writes, "pays off in ways no one anticipated."

4. Postpartum: An Underreported Risk

How can we gauge the importance of paternal companionship in a child's early months? In part by observing what happens when infants are deprived of it. One in 10 men experience some form of postpartum depression, Raeburn reports, limiting their ability to emotionally connect with their babies. Children of fathers with major episodes of postpartum depression appear to be eight times as likely as others to have behavior problems as they grow and 36 times as likely to have difficulty getting along with peers.

In at least one aspect of childhood—acquiring language—fathers simply matter more than mothers.

5. Toddlerhood: Dads as Bullyproofers

University of Oxford researchers visiting families beginning in babies' first year found that when fathers maintained a remote relationship with their infants, those children later had higher rates of aggressive behavior, no matter how their mothers had interacted with them. In a related meta-analysis of 24 studies of paternal involvement, Swedish researchers found that kids whose fathers helped care for them, played with them, and took them on outings had fewer behavioral problems in early childhood and a lower likelihood of delinquency as adolescents.

6. Early Childhood: Look Who Gets You Talking

In at least one aspect of childhood—acquiring language—fathers simply matter more than mothers. For example, researchers studying parental roles in language development among poor, rural children found that a father's use of vocabulary when reading to kids at 6 months of age predicted their expressiveness at 15 months and their use of advanced language at age—three regardless of the mother's educational level or how she spoke to the children. The hypothesis: Since mothers spend more time with children, they're more likely to use words with which kids are most familiar, while fathers, less attuned to their children's linguistic comfort zone, introduce a wider vocabulary.

7. The Teen Years: The Scent of a Father

For years, evolutionary biologists have puzzled over why girls with absent or departed fathers tend to reach sexual maturation earlier and have higher rates of teen pregnancy. Bruce Ellis of the University of Arizona studied families with divorced parents, and daughters who were at least 5 years apart, in which the older daughter would have had several more early years of "exposure" to a present father. He found that the younger sisters had their first periods about 11 months earlier than their older siblings did. Psychologist Sarah Hill of Texas Christian University told Raeburn that she believes a father's absence delivers girls a subconscious cue about "the mating system they are born into": Men will not stick around, so they need to find mates quickly. Their genes then effectively push the girls into early puberty. (This effect is more pronounced in families in which the absent fathers had not been a positive presence while in the home.) What's the source of this phenomenon? Ellis believes it could be a father's scent. In animal experiments, there is evidence that sustained exposure to a father's pheromones can slow down puberty, although that hypothesis remains largely untested in humans.

Critical Thinking

1. How could fathers be made more aware of their importance in their child's development?
2. What could our society (mothers, employers, schools, etc.) do to be more supportive of fathers in their parenting endeavors?

Create Central

www.mhhe.com/createcentral

Internet References

Child Welfare.gov The Importance of Fathers in the Healthy Development of Children

https://www.childwelfare.gov/pubs/usermanuals/fatherhood/chaptertwo.cfm

New York Times When Children Are Better Off Fatherless

http://www.nytimes.com/roomfordebate/2013/06/03/what-are-fathers-for/when-children-are-better-off-fatherless

pewsocialtrends.org The Rise of Single Fathers

http://www.pewsocialtrends.org/2013/07/02/the-rise-of-single-fathers

---

Drevitch, Gary. "Pop Psychology." *Psychology Today* 47. 3 (May/June, 2014): 40–41.

Article

Prepared by: Claire N. Rubman, *Suffolk County Community College*

Use the Science of What Works to Change the Odds for Children at Risk

The federal government should heed seven essential principles when it invests in breaking the cycle of disadvantage.

SUSAN B. NEUMAN

Learning Outcomes

After reading this article, you will be able to:

- Discuss cost-effective strategies to improve the lives of at-risk children.
- Propose tactics to recruit at-risk families into compensatory programs.

Dating back to President Lyndon Johnson's War on Poverty, Americans have relied on federal dollars to tackle our most intractable issues in education. For example, the federal government helped support school integration, recognize the needs of handicapped and challenged children, and provide for the "least restrictive environments" in classrooms. The federal push for early education led to Head Start, a program targeted to the preschool years. Federal funds also helped to defray the costs of college, allowing even the poorest student to get a high-quality college degree. In these and other cases, federal funds have provided a safety net, a kind of "emergency response system," a means of filling in the gaps when critical national priorities and needs arise that go beyond the means of individual states and local supports for education.

The federal government must once again step up to the challenge. Today, despite the great wealth for some in this nation, nearly one out of every five American children lives in poverty—one of the highest poverty rates in the developed world (Neuman 2008*b*). And even though our schools are in the midst of the most major and costly education reform in their history and are grappling with the federal mandates to leave no child behind, any influence a school might have is trumped by this reality. The single best determinant of a school's likely output is a single input—the characteristics of the entering children. The painful truth is that we have done almost nothing to raise or change the trajectory of achievement for our disadvantaged children.

The single best determinant of a school's likely output is a single input—the characteristics of the entering children.

The idea that schools, by themselves, can't cure educational inequity is hardly astonishing, but much of our political discourse is implicitly predicated on the notion that schools can do it alone. The national conversation has almost exclusively targeted schools as if they were the source of the problem, as well as the sole solution. The fact that 6.7% of our country's population lives in the very poorest and most vulnerable census tracts with higher proportions of very young children and higher rates of single parenting and less-educated adults, and that it is in these very same census tracts where schools supposedly are failing miserably to close the achievement gap has seemed to be lost in the ongoing conversation (Browning 2003). Expecting teachers to overcome a 30-million-word gap between high- and low-income children (Hart and Risley 2003) in kindergarten alone is beyond optimistic. It is nonsensical. Regardless of what political aisle you stand on, fixing schools has become the cure to everything but the common cold,

Research over the last 30 years has pointed to seven essential principles for breaking the cycle of disadvantage:

- Target interventions to children who need help the most;
- Begin early;
- Engage highly trained professionals;
- Provide intensive interventions;
- Coordinate health, education, and social services;
- Provide compensatory instructional benefits; and
- Be accountable.

erasing all debate about the devastating effects of entrenched poverty and what to do about it.

Good schools can go a long way toward helping poor children achieve more, but the fact remains that educational inequity is rooted in economic problems and social pathologies too deep to be overcome by school alone. Even as we work to reform schools as if there were no limits to their powers, our only hope to break the cycle of disadvantage lies outside their influence.

Ending the cycle of disadvantage requires prevention and early intervention programs that help families who are desperately struggling to do the best for their children. Childcare, family support, and community-based programs working in public settings and social service agencies are a critical part of the "closing the gap" equation. But they are not nearly enough. If we're truly serious about breaking cycles of poverty, inequality, and limited opportunity that place enormous constraints on our nation's resources, we need to recognize and appropriately support education whether it is delivered in clinics, childcare centers, community-based organizations, libraries, church basements, or storefronts. By using the science of what works, we can change the odds, helping create a more promising future for millions of children growing up in vulnerable circumstances.

How We Can Change the Odds

There is the story of 86 young children growing up in a small rural town in the Southeast in the 1960s. The families were black and poor. Isolated both geographically and socially from the larger community and the beginning stirrings of the civil rights movement, these children were about to attend segregated schools. They seemed destined to follow in their parents' footsteps—a life of poverty, discrimination, and disadvantage.

But here the predictable trajectory for what we might expect for these children took on a different, more positive twist. By age 20, these children were neither on welfare nor delinquent or indigent. Instead, most had completed high school, and a few had gone on to college. Tracking their progress, Susan Gray and her colleagues (1982) tell the story of these children's lives, their schooling, and their experiences as participants in an early intervention program, a preschool program fashioned to help children advance through school with greater success.

During the turbulent years of the late 1950s and early 1960s, a group of academics, psychologists, and social scientists began to challenge the prevailing view that ability and achievement were immutable. Recognizing the all-too-consistent correlation between poverty and achievement, these researchers realized that intellectual development couldn't possibly relate solely to the child's inherent ability. Intellectual ability had to relate to the environment. To explore this notion of "intellectual plasticity," a series of experimental early intervention programs began throughout the country, all sharing the presumption that environmental factors must play an important role in children's cognitive and social-emotional development and that early intervention could have significant, positive, long-term effects.

Susan Gray and her colleagues at Vanderbilt University took up the challenge in what became known as the Early Training Project. Identifying characteristics of early experience that related to educability, she developed an intervention designed to offset the cumulative deficits for these three-year-olds, targeting language, concept development, and motivation. Setting up an intensive summer camp program, highly experienced expert teachers worked with children in small groups, supporting their perceptual and cognitive skills and attitudes related to achievement.

Nevertheless, soon it became clear that even 10 weeks in the highest quality program could hardly overcome the economic hardships that children had accumulated, even at three years old. So she developed a home visiting program, enlisting mature women with certified experience in early education to make weekly hour-long visits with the children and parents in an effort to bridge what had been learned from one summer to the next. These home visits weren't just about teaching, but about enlisting the mothers' emotional support for helping their children learn, explore, and communicate, with the goal of eventually meeting school requirements. Over the next 2½ years, children from ages 3 to 6 and their families participated in these summer programs and winter visits.

Yet the resolute Gray and her colleagues charted children's progress far beyond these years. In fact, at regular intervals, she continued to measure their development until they were 20 years old. And strikingly, many of the gains that Gray and her colleagues reported were enduring, some for long periods of time. Children were able to meet school requirements, fewer were placed in special education, fewer were likely to be retained or drop out of high school. Even those who became pregnant as teens were more likely to return to school. As one mother remarked, "I wasn't going to let a little old baby keep me from graduatin' from high school."

There is another story, this time in the heart of the Rust Belt—Ypsilanti, Michigan, home to automobile manufacturing—where local school administrators, despite entreaties from local families, refused to adjust the curriculum to better serve their high-risk children. With high special education referrals and high school dropout rates soaring, 123 of the poorest children in the neighborhood were about to enter these settings with all the odds against their success.

However, David Weikart and his special service staff took things into their own hands (Weikart, Bond, and McNeil 1978). Checking the local census for who might be entering from the Perry School neighborhood, Weikart and his team walked door-to-door, identifying children most likely at risk for school failure. He found them in crowded residences with over twice the number of people you might expect in a typical household, their children's intelligence bordering only on educability (79 I.Q.), the parents unskilled and too beaten down to provide much encouragement for learning. Working against all odds, Weikart was determined to change those odds by developing what was unheard of at the time, a daily preschool program starting with three-year-olds along with regular visits to their families in homes. Over a period of either one or two years, specialists in early childhood involved small groups of children—no more than five or six at a time—to actively learn, think, plan, and express their ideas in language. Recognizing that children learn best through hands-on activities, such as sand and water play, teachers encouraged them to experiment with materials and talk about what they'd learned. They would ask "why" questions, like "Why might the cork float in water?" helping the children to discover new concepts on their own. In addition to turning around these children's lives, the enormous return on investment would be hard for an economist to ignore: 65% of these children graduated from high school, compared to only 45% of those not in the program; 61% got good jobs, compared to just 38% in the nonprogram group. The findings have remained stable some 27 years later.

Garber recognized that risk is a caution and not a condemnation, essentially proving that early intervention had the power to change children's lives.

Then there is another story that completely blows away the myth of equal opportunity for all children. In this case, the story is about 20 infants in Milwaukee, Wisconsin, born to severely low-functioning mothers. Each family's poverty conditions only exacerbated any hope for stimulation or learning. Examining surveys that yielded the likely trajectory for these children, all evidence amassed by Herb Garber (1988) suggested that by the time they entered school, these children would likely succumb to what was described as "induced retardation," declining functioning and cognitive processing skills.

Recognizing, perhaps for the first time, that disorganized multi-risk families face a level of disadvantage far different from poor but stable working families, Garber devised a two-generation program, foreshadowing others that would come later. Starting at about three months, infant caregivers helped prepare mothers and children, first visiting them for three to five hours three times a week, then transitioning them to center-based care, where the infants received seven hours of stimulating activities each day until they were four years old. At the same time, caregivers helped mothers learn basic home-management skills and got them enrolled in vocational education programs so that they could get jobs and responsibly take care of their children.

Garber's intervention effectively stopped the decline in children's cognitive development. He prevented the intergenerational transfer of risk and disadvantage. In fact, all experimental children whose mothers were mentally retarded performed at least 20 points higher than their mothers and averaged 32 points higher than did their own mothers. By providing an intensive program designed to compensate for what children were lacking in the home, Garber was able to offset the negative influences of an impoverished learning environment. By focusing on the single most important environmental influence—the intimate interaction between child and caregiver—he was able to help severely at-risk children avoid significant cognitive delays. He recognized that risk is a caution and not a condemnation, essentially proving that early intervention had the power to change children's lives.

Despite differences in location, population, and risk categories, each of these stories—backed by the solid scientific evidence that accompanies them (Consortium for Longitudinal Studies 1983; Shonkoff and Phillips 2000)—share some striking commonalities. Each recognized the extraordinary role that environment plays in children's development. Acknowledging its malleability, each modified the environment to maximize children's potential. Involving the primary caregivers in their children's education, each regarded the family as a learning unit that is a critical part of the solution.

Weaving these accounts together, however, illuminates an even more powerful story. Across these richly detailed programs is a set of principles for what is required to make a difference in the lives of highly vulnerable children. Recognizing the sense of urgency, these programs *targeted their efforts to children and families at greatest risk.* They *began early* in the child's development, engaging *highly trained professionals* to provide *intensive interventions,* operationally defining intensity as more hours, longer-term, and greater focus according to the family's needs. Together, these programs reached children and families where they were located, both psychologically and physically, through *comprehensive services,* realizing that a child who is suffering from Otis media (ear infections) and other illnesses can't possibly be successful in learning without relief from continuing pain. Furthermore, they recognized that the problem was not children's ability to learn, but the opportunities to learn, so they provided *compensatory instructional benefits* to make up for the cognitively and socially stimulating activities that many of these children lacked. Finally, all were *accountable,* using tangible, quantitative evidence and evaluations to examine whether they were achieving desired effects, adjusting when necessary in order to make that happen.

In essence, evident throughout these programs, and subsequently validated through research over the last 30 years (Bowman, Donovan, and Burns 2000; Farren 2000; Shonkoff and Phillips 2000), are seven essential principles for breaking the cycle of disadvantage:

- Target interventions to children who need help the most;
- Begin early;
- Engage highly trained professionals;
- Provide intensive interventions;
- Coordinate health, education, and social services;
- Provide compensatory instructional benefits; and
- Be accountable.

These stories, each better known by their project names and illustrative leaders—Susan Gray's Early Learning Project, David Weikart's Perry Preschool Project, and Herb Garber's Milwaukee Project—were originally conceived as research and demonstration projects and, as such, designed to examine the extent to which interventions, given adequate resources, a fully engaged and highly talented staff, and continuous and ongoing monitoring of progress, might affect the cognitive and social development of disadvantaged children. Capturing the public's attention even more than skill achievements, however, were the real life measures used in these reports, such as employment histories and declines in delinquency that, when combined with cost-benefit analysis, led to dramatic claims that early intervention was a highly sound investment, saving citizens an average of $7 for every dollar spent.

Together, they set a benchmark for what was possible, making a compelling case in public policy for early intervention and for the ways in which resources might be allocated for improving achievement for highly disadvantaged children.

The science of intervention has come a long way since these projects. Yet the principles remain the same. Programs that serve our most vulnerable children are tied to seven essentials and have a coherent and self consistent vision of pedagogy, curriculum, and structure. Interventions like the Nurse-Family Partnership, Early Head Start, and Avance provide critical parent supports early on; Reach Out and Read and Books Aloud give important access to books in community wide programs in libraries and clinics; Core Knowledge and Bright Beginnings have programs that help children develop content-rich learning in developmentally appropriate ways (Neuman 2008*a*).

These programs and others like them provide demonstrable evidence that we can remove some of the most significant risk factors through systematic intervention and support. And this new knowledge can become the foundation of a broader, bolder new effort in education to change the odds of our most at risk children, reorienting the federal role in education to become the emergency response system it was designed to be.

References

Bowman, Barbara, Suzanne Donovan, and M. Susan Burns. *Eager to Learn: Educating Our Preschoolers.* Washington, D.C.: National Academy Press, 2000.

Browning, Lynnley. "U.S. Income Gap Widening." *The New York Times,* September 25, 2003, p. 10.

Consortium for Longitudinal Studies. *As the Twig Is Bent.* Hillsdale, N.J.: Lawrence Erlbaum Associates, 1983.

Farren, Dale C. "Another Decade of Intervention for Children Who Are Low Income or Disabled: What Do We Do Now?" In *Handbook of Early Childhood Intervention,* ed. Jack P. Shonkoff and Sam Meisels. New York: Cambridge University Press, 2000.

Garber, Herb. *The Milwaukee Project.* Washington, D.C.: American Association on Mental Retardation, 1988.

Gray, Susan W., Barbara K. Ramsey, and Rupert A. Klaus. *From 3 to 20: The Early Training Project.* Baltimore, Md.: University Park Press, 1982.

Hart, Betty, and Todd Risley. "The Early Catastrophe." *American Educator* 27 (Spring 2003): 4, 6–9.

Neuman, Susan B. *Changing the Odds for Children at Risk: Seven Essential Principles of Educational Programs That Break the Cycle of Poverty.* Westport, Conn.: Praeger, 2008a.

Neuman, Susan B., ed. *Educating the Other America: Top Experts Tackle Poverty, Literacy, and Achievement in Our Schools.* Baltimore, Md.: Brookes, 2008b.

Shonkoff, Jack P., and Deborah Phillips, eds. *From Neurons to Neighborhoods.* Washington, D.C.: National Academy Press, 2000.

Weikart, David, James T. Bond, and J.T. McNeil. *The Ypsilanti Perry Preschool Project.* Ypsilanti, Mich.: High/Scope, 1978.

Critical Thinking

1. Give examples of activities of daily life for children living in poverty.
2. Explain why children at-risk affect the school achievement of all students.
3. Suggest research-based solutions for high-low income inequality.

Create Central

www.mhhe.com/createcentral

Internet References

Effects of Poverty, Hunger, and Homelessness on Children and Youth
www.apa.org/pi/families/poverty.aspx

Families and Work Institute
www.familiesandwork.org/index.html

Harborview Injury Prevention and Research Center
http://depts.washington.edu/hiprc

Susan B. Neuman is a professor of educational studies at the University of Michigan, Ann Arbor, Michigan.

Article

Prepared by: Claire N. Rubman, *Suffolk County Community College*

Why Our Approach to Bullying Is Bad for Kids

SUSAN PORTER

Learning Outcomes

After reading this article, you will be able to:

- Describe how the development of the brain's prefrontal cortex and executive functions contributes to bullying behaviors.
- Account for the wide range of statistics that are reported on bullying behaviors.
- Define the "expanded definition of bullying" and its effect on development.

It's hard to avoid the topic of bullying these days. From parents chatting about it on the soccer field sidelines, to op-ed pieces calling for police presence on school campuses, to the President and First Lady hosting webcasts on the subject—just about everyone with a soapbox, real or virtual, is talking about how to deal with the bullying scourge that is sweeping the nation's schools. And, boy, is it bad.

The next time you've got a spare moment, Google "statistics on bullying" and see for yourself. When I last looked, this is what popped up:

- One in five kids is bullied.
- Twenty-three percent of students say they been bullied several times.
- One in four kids is bullied.
- Fifty percent of kids are bullied, and 10 percent are bullied on a regular basis.
- Seventy-four percent of 8- to 11-year-olds said teasing and bullying occurs at their schools.
- Seventy-seven percent of students say they've been bullied recently.
- It is estimated that *more than half* [emphasis added] of school bullying incidents are never reported.

Despite the fact that the statistics are wildly inconsistent, even the lowest percentages are scary, and they suggest that our kids aren't safe in schools because they're hurting one another at alarmingly high rates. At best, the data suggest that we've got a serious problem on our hands.

Or do we?

Parents often ask me what's behind the rise of bullying among children, and whether or not kids today are different from those of previous generations. As a school counselor, with almost 25 years of experience, I tell parents that kids haven't changed much over the years, but something significant *has* changed recently, and that's how our culture thinks about, talks about, and deals with aggressive childhood behavior. And the change is profound.

A Shift in Definition

A few years ago, a K-12 school asked me to consult on the subject of bullying. This was about the time many schools were implementing "Zero Tolerance Anti-Bullying" policies. In preparation for my presentation, I researched the topic by reviewing local and regional policies on bullying, and articles in the professional literature. I was stunned by what I learned.

First, I discovered that bullying was everywhere. The statistics were as disturbing and wide ranging then as they are today. Admittedly, I was shocked. Here I was, a school counselor with years of experience as both a mental health clinician in schools and a consultant to schools, and somehow I had missed all of this. Of course, I had dealt with cases of bullying in my own work, but the sweeping nature of the phenomenon, as suggested by my research, had eluded me. The ground under my professional feet started to shake. As I digested the information I felt horrible. *How could I have been so blind?*

But then, as I researched further, I learned another important thing about bullying. According to the many definitions I read, the term had come to include not only the classic forms of harassment between children, behaviors such as shaking down a kid for lunch money, beating up a smaller kid in the schoolyard, or repeated hate speech. Now, it also included behaviors such as social exclusion, name-calling, teasing, sarcasm, and being unfriendly. I also noted a corresponding shift in the telltale signs expressed by the victims of bullying, which in addition to extreme symptoms, such as *school phobia* and *depression,* now included symptoms such as *feeling upset* and *being sad.*

As I considered all of this, I realized what I'd missed in my work was not a rise in incidents of classic bullying, but rather the creeping expansion of the definition of bullying, which according to the average anti bullying policy was now a catch-all term for the routine—albeit nasty—selfishness, meanness, and other social misfires that characterize childhood and adolescence. I call this the *expanded definition of bullying.*

As I completed my research, I sensed that this expanded definition of bullying was doing more than just attempting to protect kids. It was also making a lot of normal childhood behaviors seem pathological and dangerous. Many of the behaviors described in the bullying literature were almost inevitable, given brain development, but this didn't seem to matter. What mattered instead was setting unrealistic guidelines for children's behavior in the hopes of preventing them from feeling pain. Lost, it seemed, was the intention of helping kids learn from their mistakes and developing resilience in the face of adversity.

The Preadolescent and Adolescent Brains and Development

The preadolescent and adolescent brains can be characterized in many ways, the most important of which, when it comes to the expanded definition of bullying, is that they are *not yet fully developed.* And the most important part of the brain that has not yet developed is the prefrontal cortex, the part of the brain that deals with functions such as impulse control, judgment, and empathy. These functions are often referred to as *executive functions,* and researchers believe we continue to develop these functions well into our 20s.

This means children, even older teenagers, have brains that are not yet capable of being consistently in control of themselves, even when they try *really, really* hard. As children age, however, the executive functions start to kick in more predictably, and therefore older teenagers can be entrusted, for example, to drive a car or babysit a younger child or do their homework without a nightly battle. That said, the key is *consistency,* and even the best-behaved and seemingly mature teenager can have lapses in judgment and behave without the benefit of fully formed executive functions.

If you consider the expanded definition of bullying in light of brain development, and think about behaviors such as teasing, name-calling, and social exclusion, you can see why kids and teenagers might exhibit these behaviors, given the fact that their brains simply aren't fully formed yet. Being polite, keeping their hands to themselves, not saying everything that pops into their heads, staying on task, and being thoughtful—these are the things kids work on every day, and their brains won't master these tasks for years. The brain constantly makes mistakes as it develops these capacities, and often these mistakes come at the expense of another person's feelings.

Add to this various aspects of development, such as the marked self-consciousness that characterizes adolescence, and you have a recipe for insensitive behavior. When kids walk down school hallways, they aren't thinking about other people's feelings; they're thinking *me, me, me.* This is normal. But this leaves them vulnerable to making big mistakes when it comes to attending to the needs of others, and acting with these needs in mind.

So, regardless of what we'd like, we can't expect kids to sail through childhood and adolescence without blundering—especially given that the average adolescent brain, still under construction, is hardwired to behave in ways that are irritating and selfish at times. This explains, in part, the prevalence of bullying (the expanded version) these days.

There are other reasons why the milder bullying behaviors are rampant (and always have been), and why we can't eradicate them.

First, brains at this age are prone to misinterpreting facial cues, a fact that has huge implications when it comes to social interactions. For example, the teenage brain might interpret a classmate's frown to mean, "She really hates me! She doesn't want to be my friend," when, in fact, it probably means something completely different. A missed cue of this kind, coupled with the self-absorption of the age, can turn a nonsituation into an emotional drama, as the teenager imagines her classmate's expression to be both (A) extremely negative and (B) necessarily about her.

Second, brains at this stage tend to respond very emotionally to social situations. For example, Cathy looks at Susie the wrong way. Unlike an adult, Susie isn't unaffected by Cathy's expression, or simply annoyed by it. Susie takes it personally. She may feel overwrought. This is especially true if Susie believes Cathy's expression indicates that she (Cathy) wishes to exclude her (Susie). Research has shown that the threat of social exclusion is one of the scariest things for a preteen girl's brain to deal with, so Susie's response to Cathy's expression could conceivably cause Susie's brain to initiate a fight-or-flight response, sending Susie on an emotional roller-coaster ride that terrifies her.

An important point to understand about a situation like Susie's is that her reactions and feelings are real *to her,* but that doesn't mean they are an accurate gauge of the outside situation. Our current approach to bullying places so much emphasis on a child's inner experience that I often deal with children (supported by their parents) who believe that their feelings are facts. In today's social climate, Susie's very real, albeit internal and emotional response to Cathy's frown can be sufficient evidence to Susie that Cathy has done something really bad. And, if Susie claimed that Cathy had repeatedly acted this way, and if Susie had some very wounded feelings as evidence, then Cathy could be in big trouble. At the very least, she'd probably get a stern talking-to from a teacher or school administrator. And for what, making a face? But with our expanded definition of bullying, Susie's pain is the trump card.

Finally, bullying is widespread because kids at this age tend to see the world in black and white terms. Their brains are just developing the capacity for abstract thought, and while they may have glimpses of it here and there, for the most part, and especially when it comes to social situations, the world to them is pretty cut and dried. As such, there is little room for a nuanced interpretation of painful situations, so a perceived social attack is usually interpreted in dire terms.

Unfortunately, in our desire to protect perceived victims, we downplay or ignore these essential truths about development such that, over the past decade or so, we have succeeded in redefining many unpleasant childhood behaviors as bullying, and thus the epidemic. With this expanded definition of bullying in place, the average child, behaving in an average way, is statistically likely to be branded a bully at some point, and to become a victim of bullying—and this troubles me.

None of this means that we should ignore children's bad behavior or pain. But our current approach to bullying, which superimposes on the childhood brain an adult-like capacity for intent and self-control, gives little encouragement for growth and change. It also ignores children's capacity for resilience, and it does both through its use of labels.

Code of Conduct for XYZ Academy

Middle School (or High School) is a time of tremendous physical, psychological, and emotional growth and change, and the expectations for XYZ Academy students reflect the capabilities of adolescents (or children) at this developmental stage and the aspirations the community has for them.

All XYZ Academy students are expected to behave in ways that support the well-being, health, and safety of themselves and others. To this end, students should be respectful in their interactions and relationships and learn to recognize how their actions, including their speech, affect others. XYZ students should aim to be courteous, kind, and inclusive, and accept constructive feedback and criticism as being essential parts of learning and membership within the community.

As an educational community, XYZ recognizes that social-emotional development, as any other subject, takes time to master, and involves mistakes and missteps. As such, adults are charged to help students reflect upon their behavioral choices, especially when these choices hurt or deny the rights of others. In cases of severe or repeated negative behavior that falls short of expected conduct, disciplinary action may be taken.

Fixed Mindsets and the Problem with Labels

Labels are everywhere when it comes to bullying, and they are an important part of how antibullying rhetoric aims to educate kids about aggression. Go to any antibullying website, or review antibullying curricula, and you will see what I mean. The labels are ubiquitous: active bully, passive bully, lieutenant, henchman, bystander, ally, hero, and, of course, victim. They constitute the *dramatis personae* of the bully play. In learning about bullying, students are instructed to identify the players, imagine what roles they play, and clearly distinguish between the wrongdoer and the wronged. It's all fixed, perhaps in an effort to simplify what is usually an inherently complicated situation. And with these labels, the painful dynamics that occur among children become carved in stone.

By now, most educators are familiar with the work of Stanford University psychologist Carol Dweck. In *Mindset: The New Psychology of Success,* she describes the two lenses through which we make sense of the world: the fixed mindset and the growth mindset. The fixed mindset is characterized by a belief that personality and intelligence are static qualities, and that they can't be developed. A growth mindset, on the other hand, is characterized by a belief that these qualities *can* change and develop, and that effort leads to learning and therefore growth.

Our approach to bullying is problematic, if for no other reason, because it provides kids (and adults) with little conceptual room to maneuver. When a child misbehaves and is labeled a bully, the label declares something about his character, not just about his behavior. For adults, the bully label affixed to a child sticks in our minds, and encourages us to view the child's behavior—past, present, and future—through this lens. If we consider that children don't develop the capacity for abstract thought until early adolescence (if then), we see how problematic labels are. Children can't see beyond the concrete, so they will take labels like bully or victim and run with them, usually to their own detriment. But adults should know better. Our goal is to facilitate growth and change.

I encourage readers to carefully examine their own schools' and states' antibullying policies and curricula to bring this point home. I have yet to come across a policy that approaches the issue of problematic childhood and adolescent behavior from a growth mindset. These policies, in their presumed effort to protect kids and shape behavior, do little more than make us view children and their behavior in a fixed framework. The formulaic ways in which aggression among kids is described, and a general indifference to context through the use of easy-to-apply labels, let us off the hook for approaching problematic situations between children with compassion for all parties involved.

The use of labels, and the accompanying fixed mindset they engender, does nothing to help us help kids. Children need us to understand their social lives and behavior in dynamic, not static, terms, and to separate their behavior from their characters. Children should be allowed to make mistakes, and these mistakes, even if egregious, should not result in the children receiving labels that limit our ability (and possibly our desire) to help them develop into responsible adults.

But labels aren't bad for just the bullies; they're bad for the victims, too. Remember, mindsets are about whether we see the world through fixed or growth lenses, and the victim label is as fixed and inflexible as the bully one. Both discourage self-exploration and faith in change. The bully has no incentive to change as long as the adults (and children) around him see him in wholly negative terms, while the victim has no incentive to develop resilience if he is continually identified with and reminded of his wounds. In my experience, victims are often the biggest losers when it comes to labeling because, as victims, they are encouraged to identify with their vulnerability, and as a result, their sense of agency often derives from their feelings of helplessness and pain.

The other labels used in the bully rhetoric—such as bystander, ally, and hero—are also problematic. For starters, they give children, and especially young children, the incorrect impression that they are responsible for preventing other people's pain. In addition, they lead children to believe that they must be vigilant at all times, and know when and how to intervene in complex social situations. Sure, kids should be encouraged to help out other kids, but it is neither their role nor their duty to assume this much responsibility for situations beyond their control, and yet this is the impression our use of labels gives them.

If nothing else, we should abandon labels and the fixed mindset around bullying because they alienate parents, and we need to work closely with parents if we want to help children change their behavior. I routinely tell parents to stop listening if someone (let's say a teacher or another parent) calls their child a bully. Why? Because when adults use the term bully, they have stopped seeing a child's potential, and they aren't focused on helping that child grow. Using the term bully is an easy way out, and it allows adults to avoid the very hard work of helping children change their behavior. This is not just an issue of semantics, as any parent of an accused child can attest. It's about believing in growth or not.

Using the term bully is an easy way out, and it allows adults to avoid the very hard work of helping children change their behavior. This is not just an issue of semantics, as any parent of an accused child can attest. It's about believing in growth or not.

An Alternative Approach

In order to do right by our students, we must first understand brain and psychological development and set reasonable expectations for student behavior. We must recognize that the brain doesn't fully develop for years, and that it makes plenty of mistakes along the way, whether in mathematics or history or relationships. We succeed as educators when we help students solve academic problems. Likewise, we succeed when we help students solve behavioral problems. And just as we avoid labels when it comes to students as academic learners, we should avoid labels when it comes to students as social-emotional learners.

We must also abandon the conceptual frameworks and rhetoric that encourage us to understand childhood aggression in simple and formulaic ways, and we should adopt policies that reflect a growth mindset. To this end, I have included a Code of Conduct statement that approaches behavior and expectations from a growth mindset. You will note that it does not specify certain behaviors or reactions to behaviors, as do most antibullying policies. It is aspirational, open-ended, and doesn't dictate how a school should respond to complex social situations among students.

As educators, it is our job to lead the way. When we stop seeing the potential for growth and change in children, it's time for us to retire.

Critical Thinking

1. How should a parent simultaneously help a child combat bullying while also supporting resilience and autonomy?
2. How does the development of the brain's prefrontal cortex and emerging executive functions contribute to our understanding of solutions to bullying and antisocial behaviors in adolescents and preadolescents?
3. What can parents and teachers do to reduce "labeling" among bullies and victims?

Create Central

www.mhhe.com/createcentral

Internet References

Bullying Statistics.org Bullying Statistics
http://www.bullyingstatistics.org

gov.uk What is Bullying?
http://www.stopbullying.gov/what-is-bullying

Psychology Today.com Sticks and Stones—Hurtful Words Damage the Brain–Verbal abuse in childhood inflicts lasting physical effects on brain structure
http://www.psychologytoday.com/blog/the-new-brain/201010/sticks-and-stones-hurtful-words-damage-the-brain

Reform of anti-social behaviour powers—Bullying—What is the issue?
https://www.gov.uk/government/uploads/system/uploads/attachment_data/file/248751/01_BULLYING_WEB.PDF

Sydney.edu Bullying, Harassment, Discrimination or Antisocial Behaviour
http://sydney.edu.au/student_affairs/complaints/how/harrassment_discrimination.shtml

---

SUSAN PORTER is dean of students at The Branson School (California). Her hook, Bully Nation: Why America's Approach to Bullying Is Bad for Everyone, is scheduled to be released by Paragon Press in the spring of 2013.

Porter, Susan. "Why Our Approach to Bullying is Bad for Kids." *Independent School* 72. 2 (Winter, 2013): 72–78.

Article Prepared by: Claire N. Rubman, *Suffolk County Community College*

Bribing the Poor

Good ideas that work aren't always as "nice" as we'd like.

ANYA KAMENETZ

Learning Outcomes

After reading this article, you will be able to:

- Compare parental bribing in the United States (e.g., candy) with the bag of lentils that is being offered to Indian families.
- Evaluate the success of this philanthropic "incentive" program in India.

Rajasthan is India's desert state, an often inhospitable place where per capita income averages around $1.77 per day. Poverty like that—understanding it and imagining ways to fix it—is what Esther Duflo lives for. Since 2003, her Abdul Latif Jameel Poverty Action Lab (named for a wealthy Saudi donor), or J-PAL, has conducted 240 randomized, controlled trials of specific ways to help the poor. She tests poverty solutions the way medical researchers test new drugs, which can violate the pieties of the philanthropic community. But she has earned a lot of respect along the way: In 2009, the MIT economist won a MacArthur "genius award" for bringing the scientific method to development work.

In Rajasthan, Duflo has been exploring whether incentives might help get more young children vaccinated. In countries like the United States, more than 90 percent of children are immunized. But that's not the case in the developing world. Some 27 million children around the globe fail to get the shots they need each year; 2 to 3 million people die as a result. In India, 44 percent of children get them, but in Rajasthan the official number drops to 22 percent; in Duflo's study area near the city of Udaipur, it was less than 2 percent.

There are several reasons for the low numbers. While the Indian government offers free basic medical care at rural subcenters, government nurses in the area were chronically absent, resulting in clinics pad locked nearly half the time. According to Duflo's recent book *Poor Economics* (written with Abhijit Banerjee), there is a cultural resistance to immunization. Superstitions play a powerful role—the "evil eye" is believed to cause illness, and babies are traditionally kept inside for the first year to protect them from it. Furthermore, immunizations have an image problem. When they work, the effect is invisible. When they don't seem to work, however, the effects are extremely visible and frightening: The sight of a child made sick by vaccination is terrible, at least in part because it emphasizes how powerless the average person feels in the hands of modern medicine. Rumors of links to autism drove vaccination rates down among rich, educated Americans; not surprisingly, J-PAL found that irrational fears held sway among poor Indians as well.

To combat all this, Duflo's team attempted some simple solutions. "First," she says, "we wanted to make it easy." Seva Mandir, a local not-for-profit that partnered with J-PAL, set up monthly immunization camps in 60 villages, each well publicized in the local area and each with a nurse—who was paid only when her attendance was verified. "Second," Duflo adds, "we wanted to give them a reason to act today, as opposed to waiting one more day." And that's where the incentive came in. At half of the immunization camps, researchers gave families a free kilo of lentils every time they brought their child in for shots. If they completed a full series of shots, the family got a set of plates. At the other camps, families only got the shots.

The results were compelling. Simply making shots more available increased the immunization rate from 2 percent to 18 percent, according to a survey of households with children aged 1 to 3 years old. But in villages with incentives, the rate jumped to 38 percent. That's a great result, of course, but it came with an added benefit. Since so many children showed up, the total cost per immunized child fell by half, despite the $1 bags of lentils that were handed out. Since the nurses were paid by the hour, the busier camps made more efficient use of their time.

So there you have it: A classic win-win, right? Healthier children at cheaper rates. What could be better?

Unfortunately, empirical evidence doesn't have instant power to convince. "There has been resistance on the left and on the right to the idea of paying people to do the right thing," says Duflo. "On the left, people say, 'How can you be so patronizing?' On the right, they insist that the poor have to be responsible, so we shouldn't give a handout." Priyanka Singh, Seva Mandir's chief executive, says that the approach was initially controversial even within her organization, and points out that other NGOs have also been divided on the issue. The Rajasthani government, after 5 years of Seva Mandir's continued success with the model, is still resisting linking immunization to an incentive—even though it offers incentives for family planning and sterilization.

Duflo remains undaunted. "I'm not giving up," she says. "My day job is to identify good ideas; my night job is to convince policy makers that they *are* good ideas. That makes for long days!"

Bribing the poor is a notion that could offend just about anyone. We all like our philanthropy pure: Give the money, volunteer at the shelter, act with good intentions, and things will just get better. That's not a mode of thinking that allows the less fortunate to have human motivations, and it's certainly not a mode of thinking that encourages us to reflect on our own flaws. But be honest—you'd probably offer your own child a piece of candy as a reward for taking her shots. If we really want to make change, we have to discard what Duflo calls our "cartoon visions" of the poor. Doing good means engaging with what people really need and getting it to them by any means necessary.

Critical Thinking

1. Is operant conditioning an effective technique to modify behavior?
2. Should we bribe adults and children with food in an attempt to change their behavior?
3. Does the end justify the means for this vaccination project?

Create Central

www.mhhe.com/createcentral

Internet References

ruralpovertyportal.org Rural Poverty in India
http://www.ruralpovertyportal.org/country/home/tags/india

Simply Psychology Kohlberg
http://www.simplypsychology.org/kohlberg.html

SJDM.org The Psychology of Moral Reasoning
http://journal.sjdm.org/8105/jdm8105.html

Statistics India UNICEF
http://www.unicef.org/infobycountry/india_statistics.html

Vaccineindia.org Vaccine India
http://vaccineindia.org/

Kamenetz, Anya. "Bribing the Poor." *Fast Company*. 158 (September, 2011): 52–53.

Article Prepared by: Claire N. Rubman, *Suffolk County Community College*

Spoiled Rotten

ELIZABETH KOLBERT

Learning Outcomes

After reading this article, you will be able to:

- Explain why saying "no" is beneficial to a child's development.
- Articulate the benefit of household chores.
- Explain the term *helicopter parent.*

In 2004, Carolina Izquierdo, an anthropologist at the University of California, Los Angeles, spent several months with the Matsigenka, a tribe of about 12,000 people who live in the Peruvian Amazon. The Matsigenka hunt for monkeys and parrots, grow yucca and bananas, and build houses that they roof with the leaves of a particular kind of palm tree, known as a kapashi. At one point, Izquierdo decided to accompany a local family on a leaf-gathering expedition down the Urubamba River.

A member of another family, Yanira, asked if she could come along. Izquierdo and the others spent 5 days on the river. Although Yanira had no clear role in the group, she quickly found ways to make herself useful. Twice a day, she swept the sand off the sleeping mats, and she helped stack the kapashi leaves for transport back to the village. In the evening, she fished for crustaceans, which she cleaned, boiled, and served to the others. Calm and self-possessed, Yanira "asked for nothing," Izquierdo later recalled. The girl's behavior made a strong impression on the anthropologist because at the time of the trip Yanira was just 6 years old.

While Izquierdo was doing field work among the Matsigenka, she was also involved in an anthropological study closer to home. A colleague of hers, Elinor Ochs, had recruited 32 middle-class families for a study of life in twenty-first-century Los Angeles. Ochs had arranged to have the families filmed as they ate, fought, made up, and did the dishes.

Izquierdo and Ochs shared an interest in many ethnographic issues, including child rearing. How did parents in different cultures train young people to assume adult responsibilities? In the case of the Angelenos, they mostly didn't. In the L.A. families observed, no child routinely performed household chores without being instructed to. Often, the kids had to be begged to attempt the simplest tasks; often, they still refused. In one fairly typical encounter, a father asked his 8-year-old son five times to please go take a bath or a shower. After the fifth plea went unheeded, the father picked the boy up and carried him into the bathroom. A few minutes later, the kid, still unwashed, wandered into another room to play a video game.

In another representative encounter, an 8-year-old girl sat down at the dining table. Finding that no silverware had been laid out for her, she demanded, "How am I supposed to eat?" Although the girl clearly knew where the silverware was kept, her father got up to get it for her.

In a third episode captured on tape, a boy named Ben was supposed to leave the house with his parents. But he couldn't get his feet into his sneakers, because the laces were tied. He handed one of the shoes to his father: "Untie it!" His father suggested that he ask nicely.

"Can you untie it?" Ben replied. After more back-and-forth, his father untied Ben's sneakers. Ben put them on, then asked his father to retie them. "You tie your shoes and let's go," his father finally exploded. Ben was unfazed. "I'm just asking," he said.

A few years ago, Izquierdo and Ochs wrote an article for *Ethos,* the journal of the Society of Psychological Anthropology, in which they described Yanira's conduct during the trip down the river and Ben's exchange with his dad. "Juxtaposition of these developmental stories begs for an account of responsibility in childhood," they wrote. Why do Matsigenka children "help their families at home more than L.A. children?" And "Why do L.A. adult family members help their children at home more than do Matsigenka?" Though not phrased in exactly such terms, questions like these are being asked—silently, imploringly, despairingly—every single day by parents from Anchorage to Miami. Why, why, why?

With the exception of the imperial offspring of the Ming dynasty and the dauphins of pre-Revolutionary France, contemporary American kids may represent the most indulged young people in the history of the world. It's not just that they've been given unprecedented amounts of stuff—clothes, toys, cameras, skis, computers, televisions, cell phones, PlayStations, iPods. (The market for Burberry Baby and other forms of kiddie "couture" has reportedly been growing by 10 percent a year.) They've also been granted unprecedented authority. "Parents want their kids' approval, a reversal of the past ideal of children striving for their parents' approval," Jean Twenge and W. Keith Campbell, both professors of psychology, have written. In many middle-class families, children have one, two, sometimes three adults at their beck and call. This is a social experiment on a grand scale, and a growing number of adults fear that it isn't working out so well: according to one poll, commissioned by Time and CNN, two-thirds of American parents think that their children are spoiled.

The notion that we may be raising a generation of kids who can't, or at least won't, tie their own shoes has given rise to a new genre of parenting books. Their titles tend to be either dolorous (*The Price of Privilege*) or downright hostile (*The Narcissism Epidemic, Mean Moms Rule, A Nation of Wimps*). The books are less how-to guides than how-not-to's: how not to give in to your toddler, how not to intervene whenever your teen-ager looks bored, how not to spend two hundred thousand dollars on tuition only to find your twenty-something graduate back at home, drinking all your beer.

Not long ago, Sally Koslow, a former editor-in-chief of *McCall's,* discovered herself in this last situation. After 4 years in college and two on the West Coast, her son Jed moved back to Manhattan and settled into his old room in the family's apartment, together with 34 boxes of vinyl LPs. Unemployed, Jed liked to stay out late, sleep until noon, and wander around in his boxers. Koslow set out to try to understand why he and so many of his peers seemed stuck in what she regarded as permanent "adultescence." She concluded that one of the reasons is the lousy economy. Another is parents like her.

"Our offspring have simply leveraged our braggadocio, good intentions, and overinvestment," Koslow writes in her new book, *Slouching Toward Adulthood: Observations from the Not-So-**Empty** Nest* (Viking). They inhabit "a broad savannah of entitlement that we've watered, landscaped, and hired gardeners to maintain." She recommends letting the grasslands revert to forest: "The best way for a lot of us to show our love would be to learn to un-mother and un-father." One practical tip that she offers is to do nothing when your adult child finally decides to move out. In the process of schlepping Jed's stuff to an apartment in Carroll Gardens, Koslow's husband tore a tendon and ended up in emergency surgery.

Madeline Levine, a psychologist who lives outside San Francisco, specializes in treating young adults. In *Teach Your Children Well: Parenting for Authentic Success* (HarperCollins), she argues that we do too much for our kids because we overestimate our influence. "Never before have parents been so (mistakenly) convinced that their every move has a ripple effect into their child's future success," she writes. Paradoxically, Levine maintains, by working so hard to help our kids we end up holding them back.

"Most parents today were brought up in a culture that put a strong emphasis on being special," she observes. "Being special takes hard work and can't be trusted to children. Hence the exhausting cycle of constantly monitoring their work and performance, which in turn makes children feel less competent and confident, so that they need even more oversight."

Pamela Druckerman, a former reporter for the *Wall Street Journal,* moved to Paris after losing her job. She married a British expatriate and not long after that gave birth to a daughter. Less out of conviction than inexperience, Druckerman began raising her daughter, nicknamed Bean, à l'Américaine. The result, as she recounts in *Bringing Up Bébé* (Penguin Press), was that Bean was invariably the most ill-behaved child in every Paris restaurant and park she visited. French children could sit calmly through a three-course meal; Bean was throwing food by the time the apéritifs arrived.

Druckerman talked to a lot of French mothers, all of them svelte and most apparently well rested. She learned that the French believe ignoring children is good for them. "French parents don't worry that they're going to damage their kids by frustrating them," she writes. "To the contrary, they think their kids will be damaged if they can't cope with frustration." One mother, Martine, tells Druckerman that she always waited 5 minutes before picking up her infant daughter when she cried. While Druckerman and Martine are talking, in Martine's suburban home, the daughter, now 3, is baking cupcakes by herself. Bean is roughly the same age, "but it wouldn't have occurred to me to let her do a complicated task like this all on her own," Druckerman observes. "I'd be supervising, and she'd be resisting my supervision."

Also key, Druckerman discovered, is just saying non. In contrast to American parents, French parents, when they say it, actually mean it. They "view learning to cope with 'no' as a crucial step in a child's evolution," Druckerman writes. "It forces them to understand that there are other people in the world, with needs as powerful as their own."

Not long ago, in the hope that our sons might become a little more Matsigenka, my husband and I gave them a new job:

unloading the grocery bags from the car. One evening when I came home from the store, it was raining. Carrying two or three bags, the youngest, Aaron, who is 13, tried to jump over a puddle. There was a loud crash. After I'd retrieved what food could be salvaged from a Molotov cocktail of broken glass and mango juice, I decided that Aaron needed another, more vigorous lesson in responsibility. Now, in addition to unloading groceries, he would also have the task of taking out the garbage. On one of his first forays, he neglected to close the lid on the pail tightly enough, and it attracted a bear. The next morning, as I was gathering up the used tissues, ant-filled raisin boxes, and slimy Saran Wrap scattered across the yard, I decided that I didn't have time to let my kids help out around the house. (My husband informed me that I'd just been "kiddie-whipped.")

Ochs and Izquierdo noted, in their paper on the differences between the family lives of the Matsigenka and the Angelenos, how early the Matsigenka begin encouraging their children to be useful. Toddlers routinely heat their own food over an open fire, they observed, while "3-year-olds frequently practice cutting wood and grass with machetes and knives." Boys, when they are 6 or 7, start to accompany their fathers on fishing and hunting trips, and girls learn to help their mothers with the cooking. As a consequence, by the time they reach puberty Matsigenka kids have mastered most of the skills necessary for survival. Their competence encourages autonomy, which fosters further competence—a virtuous cycle that continues to adulthood.

The cycle in American households seems mostly to run in the opposite direction. So little is expected of kids that even adolescents may not know how to operate the many labor-saving devices their homes are filled with. Their incompetence begets exasperation, which results in still less being asked of them (which leaves them more time for video games). Referring to the Los Angeles families, Ochs and Izquierdo wrote, "Many parents remarked that it takes more effort to get children to collaborate than to do the tasks themselves."

One way to interpret these contrary cycles is to infer that Americans have a lower opinion of their kids' capacities. And, in a certain sense, this is probably true: how many parents in Park Slope or Brentwood would trust their 3-year-olds to cut the grass with a machete? But in another sense, of course, it's ridiculous. Contemporary American parents—particularly the upscale sort that "unparenting" books are aimed at—tend to take a highly expansive view of their kids' abilities. Little Ben may not be able to tie his shoes, but that shouldn't preclude his going to Brown.

In *A Nation of Wimps: The High Cost of Invasive Parenting* (Broadway), Hara Estroff Marano argues that college rankings are ultimately to blame for what ails the American family. Her argument runs more or less as follows: high-powered parents worry that the economic opportunities for their children are shrinking. They see a degree from a top-tier school as one of the few ways to give their kids a jump on the competition. In order to secure this advantage, they will do pretty much anything, which means not just taking care of all the cooking and cleaning but also helping their children with math homework, hiring them S.A.T. tutors, and, if necessary, suing their high school. Marano, an editor-at-large at *Psychology Today,* tells about a high school in Washington State that required students to write an eight-page paper and present a 10-minute oral report before graduating. When one senior got a failing grade on his project, his parents hired a lawyer.

Today's parents are not just "helicopter parents," a former school principal complains to Marano. "They are a jet-powered turbo attack model." Other educators gripe about "snowplow parents," who try to clear every obstacle from their children's paths. The products of all this hovering, meanwhile, worry that they may not be able to manage college in the absence of household help. According to research conducted by sociologists at Boston College, today's incoming freshmen are less likely to be concerned about the rigors of higher education than "about how they will handle the logistics of everyday life."

One of the offshoots of the L.A. family study is a new book, *Life at Home in the Twenty-First Century* (Cotsen Institute of Archaeology), which its authors—the anthropologists Jeanne Arnold, of U.C.L.A., Anthony Graesch, of Connecticut College, and Elinor Ochs—describe as a "visual ethnography of middle-class American households." Lavishly illustrated with photographs (by Enzo Ragazzini) of the families' houses and yards, the book offers an intimate glimpse into the crap-strewn core of American culture.

"After a few short years," the text notes, many families amass more objects "than their houses can hold." The result is garages given over to old furniture and unused sports equipment, home offices given over to boxes of stuff that haven't yet been stuck in the garage, and, in one particularly jam-packed house, a shower stall given over to storing dirty laundry.

Children, according to *Life at Home,* are disproportionate generators of clutter: "Each new child in a household leads to a 30 percent increase in a family's inventory of possessions during the preschool years alone." Many of the kids' rooms pictured are so crowded with clothes and toys, so many of which have been tossed on the floor, that there is no path to the bed. (One little girl's room contains, by the authors' count, 248 dolls, including a 165 Beanie Babies.) The kids' possessions, not to mention their dioramas and their T-ball trophies, spill out into other rooms, giving the houses what the authors call "a very child-centered look."

When anthropologists study cultures like the Matsigenkas', they tend to see patterns. The Matsigenka prize hard work and self-sufficiency. Their daily rituals, their child-rearing practices, and even their folktales reinforce these values, which have an obvious utility for subsistence farmers. Matsigenka stories often feature characters undone by laziness; kids who still don't get the message are rubbed with an itch-inducing plant.

In contemporary American culture, the patterns are more elusive. What values do we convey by turning our homes into warehouses for dolls? By assigning our kids chores and then rewarding them when they screw up? By untying and then retying their shoes for them? It almost seems as if we're actively trying to raise a nation of "adultescents." And, perhaps without realizing it, we are.

As Melvin Konner, a psychiatrist and anthropologist at Emory University, points out in *The Evolution of Childhood* (Belknap), one of the defining characteristics of *Homo sapiens* is its "prolonged juvenile period." Compared with other apes, humans are "altricial," which is to say immature at birth. Chimpanzees, for instance, are born with brains half their adult size; the brains of human babies are only a third of their adult size. Chimps reach puberty shortly after they're weaned; humans take another decade or so. No one knows when exactly in the process of hominid evolution juvenile development began to slow down, but even *Homo ergaster,* who evolved some 1.8 million years ago, seems to have enjoyed—if that's the right word—a protracted childhood. It's often argued by anthropologists that the drawn-out timetable is what made humans human in the first place. It's the fact that we grow up slowly that makes acquiring language and building complicated social structures possible.

The same trend that appears in human prehistory shows up in history as well. The farther back you look, the faster kids grew up. In medieval Europe, children from seven on were initiated into adult work. Compulsory schooling, introduced in the nineteenth century, pushed back the age of maturity to 16 or so. By the middle of the twentieth century, college graduation seemed, at least in this country, to be the new dividing line. Now, if Judd Apatow is to be trusted, it's possible to close in on 40 without coming of age.

Evolutionarily speaking, this added delay makes a certain amount of sense. In an increasingly complex and unstable world, it may be adaptive to put off maturity as long as possible. According to this way of thinking, staying forever young means always being ready for the next big thing (whatever that might be).

Or adultesence might be just the opposite: not evidence of progress but another sign of a generalized regression. Letting things slide is always the easiest thing to do, in parenting no less than in banking, public education, and environmental protection. A lack of discipline is apparent these days in just about every aspect of American society. Why this should be is a much larger question, one to ponder as we take out the garbage and tie our kids' shoes.

Critical Thinking

1. Under what circumstances would it be considered appropriate for a 6-year-old child to fish, cook, and serve dinner in the United States?
2. What accounts for cultural nuances in childrearing practices?
3. What are the perceived benefits of discipline from a cultural and historical perspective?

Create Central

www.mhhe.com/createcentral

Internet References

alfiekohn.org The Myth of Spoiled Children
http://www.alfiekohn.org/books/msc.htm

DevPsy.Org Diana Baumrind & Parenting Styles
http://www.devpsy.org/teaching/parent/baumrind_styles.html

Forbes.com Father's Day Advice from Billionaires: How to Not Raise Spoiled Kids
http://www.forbes.com/sites/erincarlyle/2012/06/15/billionaire-advice-how-to-not-raise-spoiled-kids/2/

NASPCenter.org Teenagers and Chores Guidelines for Parents
http://www.naspcenter.org/adol_chores2.html

Psychology Today.com Parenting: Raise Independent Children
http://www.psychologytoday.com/blog/the-power-prime/201011/parenting-raise-independent-children

Kolbert, Elizabeth. "Spoiled Rotten." The New Yorker 88. 19 (July, 2, 2012): 76–79.

Part 5

UNIT

Prepared by: Claire N. Rubman, *Suffolk County Community College*

Development During Adolescence and Young Adulthood

The period of development between childhood and adulthood appears to be changing. What is causing those changes and how do they impact early adulthood? Is it possible that we are becoming more self-centered and more self-indulged than ever before? How does this potential change impact our careers, our marriages, and our lives? This unit looks at a diverse range of topics from early puberty to marriage and college cheats and adolescent crime.

Perhaps it's the additives in the food that we eat, or it may be the healthier diets that our wealthy societies maintain, but whatever the reason, children are reaching puberty earlier than preceding generations. "The Incredible Shrinking Childhood" by Weil examines "precocious puberty" through the life of Ainsley Sioux, who began to show signs of early puberty at age 6. Experts such as Marcia Herman-Giddens and endocrinologist Louise Greenspan chronicled these early maturing cases. They discuss bone loss, emotional development, and "the process of normalizing" or accepting maturation. Weil compares children of divorce, noting that their maturation rates are younger, suggesting the possibility that stress might be related to early puberty. Weil also notes the relationship between mental health issues such as depression and early puberty. Parents discussed failed methods that they have tried to forestall puberty such as marathon running, additive- and hormone-free diets, or removing plastics from their homes.

While some families are trying to delay puberty, others are focused on maintaining the status quo. Foster's article "Will Your Marriage Last?" addresses the problems associated with maintaining a marriage after the honeymoon phase has ended. Psychologist John Gottman recommends "the magic ratio" of five positive interactions for every negative one between couples. Gottman applied his theory to 700 newly weds with a 94 percent accuracy rate. Other contributing factors also appear to include whether you are a product of divorce, the age you marry, money, mutual respect, and perceptions about your spouse.

Perhaps some marriages fail to thrive due to the self-obsessed nature ascribed to "Generation Y." Laura Spinney discusses the inflated sense of self, the heightened self-esteem, and the narcissistic tendencies of this generation. Her article "All about Me" focuses on the implications for this generation who appear to have developed an overinflated sense of self. She discusses the increased rates of cheating, plastic surgery, and an increased use of antidepressants.

Continuing this trend toward a changing generation, let's look to women and their career choices. "The Retro Wife" by Lisa Miller discusses the decline of feminist values and the desire of many women today to focus on one job within the home, that is, raising their children. Miller suggests that "feminism has fizzled, its promise only half fulfilled." In 2011, only 19 percent of men did housework or laundry. Families with children under 6 reported that men spent 26 minutes on "physical care" such as feeding, dressing, or bathing their children.

"Kids Are Not Adults" looks at the juvenile justice system in light of research on the brain that suggests that maturity occurs around age 25. The idea that adolescents act on the basis of short-term consequences suggests that perhaps our justice system is not set up to adequately address this concept. Sarah Alice Brown highlights the difference between treating adolescents as adults or children within the judicial system. Brown discusses crime rates, the economy, and recent findings in brain development to present the case that adolescents should not be treated like adults in the judicial system. She compares policies and trends in states around the country including Arizona, California, Ohio, and Texas. She advocates effective programs, such as family functional therapy and aggression-replacement training.

Along with the disillusion of feminism is the disappointment that some parents experience with the concept of parenting. Jennifer Senior explores this dissatisfaction in "All Joy and No Fun: Why Parents Hate Parenting." Senior reports that parents do not report being any happier than their childless peers. In the hierarchy of discontentment, mothers are less happy than fathers, and single parents are the least content. What contributes to this disillusion and what can we do differently? Does a parent need to be happy or is that not a prerequisite for successful parenting?

Another key topic in adolescence is the prevalence of cyberbullying. In her article "High-Tech Bullies," Ingrid Sturgis discusses bullying at the college level. Problems on college campuses include cyberstalking, gossiping, and masquerading as another person. Tyler Clemente's tragic cyberbullying case brought this issue to light in 2010 as his Rutgers roommate videotaped him in a sexual encounter that he played on the Internet for all to witness. Unable to withstand the humiliation, Clemente committed suicide by jumping off the George Washington Bridge. Sturgis explores why college students use this perceived anonymity to bully and humiliate their peers. She also explores what college campuses are doing to combat this high-tech bullying.

Technology is blamed for yet another deficit in our adolescent and young adult population according to Schnoebelen in her article "Many Professors Say Their Students Lack Professional Qualities for Future Jobs." According to recent surveys, this lack of preparedness for the workforce is a result of a combination of an inflated sense of entitlement and etiquette problems associated with technology. This brief but poignant article should be a wakeup call to many students who hope to enter the workforce.

Returning to the topic of the developing brain in adolescence and young adulthood, Catherine Sebastian in her article, "Don't Leave Me Out," explores peer rejection in relation to emerging data on the adolescent brain. Sebastian defines social rejection both as the deliberate exclusion of an individual by a group and as a type of relational aggression. She considers the social environment, the theory of the mind, and emotional development. She acknowledges the pain and emotional sensitivity associated with peer rejection.

Another legal issue involving adolescents and young adults is highlighted in the final article in this unit titled "Cheating in the Age of Facebook" by Steven Schlozman. This article discusses the cheating scandal at the prestigious Harvard University in Massachusetts. Schlozman details the pervasiveness of cheating on college campuses with 60 percent of students admitting that they cheated in 2007 compared to 20 percent in the 1940s. Schlozman suggests strategies for professors including clearer instructions and a rethinking of the "old world rules."

Article

Prepared by: Claire N. Rubman, *Suffolk County Community College*

The Incredible Shrinking Childhood

How Early Is Too Early for Puberty?

ELIZABETH WEIL

Learning Outcomes

After reading this article, you will be able to:

- Appraise some of the reasons for precocious puberty.
- Suggest several ways that parents can deal with girls who experience early puberty.

One day last year when her daughter, Ainsley, was 9, Tracee Sioux pulled her out of her elementary school in Fort Collins, Colo., and drove her an hour south, to Longmont, in hopes of finding a satisfying reason that Ainsley began growing pubic hair at age 6. Ainsley was the tallest child in her third-grade class. She had a thick, enviable blond-streaked ponytail and big feet, like a puppy's. The curves of her Levi's matched her mother's.

"How was your day?" Tracee asked Ainsley as she climbed in the car.

"Pretty good."

"What did you do at a recess?"

"I played on the slide with my friends."

In the back seat, Ainsley wiggled out of her pink parka and looked in her backpack for her Harry Potter book. Over the past three years, Tracee—pretty and well-put-together, wearing a burnt orange blouse that matched her necklace and her bag—had taken Ainsley to see several doctors. They ordered blood tests and bone-age X-rays and turned up nothing unusual. "The doctors always come back with these blank looks on their faces, and then they start redefining what normal is," Tracee said as we drove down Interstate 25, a ribbon of asphalt that runs close to where the Great Plains bump up against the Rockies. "And I always just sit there thinking, What are you talking about, normal? Who gets pubic hair in first grade?"

Fed up with mainstream physicians, Tracee began pursuing less conventional options. She tried giving Ainsley diindolylmethane, or DIM, a supplement that may or may not help a body balance its hormones. She also started a blog, the Girl Revolution, with a mission to "revolutionize the way we think about, treat and raise girls," and the accompanying T.G.R. Body line of sunscreens and lotions marketed to tweens and described by Tracee as "natural, organic, craptastic-free products" containing "no estrogens, phytoestrogens, endocrine disrupters."

None of this stopped Ainsley's body from maturing ahead of its time. That afternoon, Tracee and Ainsley visited the office of Jared Allomong, an applied kinesiologist. Applied kinesiology is a "healing art" sort of like chiropractic. Practitioners test muscle strength in order to diagnose health problems; it's a refuge for those skeptical and weary of mainstream medicine.

"So, what brings you here today?" Allomong asked mother and daughter. Tracee stroked Ainsley's arm and said, wistfully, "Precocious puberty."

Allomong nodded. "What are the symptoms?"

"Pubic hair, armpit hair, a few pimples around the nose. Some budding." Tracee gestured with her hands, implying breasts. "The emotional stuff is getting worse, too. Ainsley's been getting super upset about little things, crying, and she doesn't know why. I think she's cycling with me."

Ainsley closed her eyes, as if to shut out the embarrassment. The ongoing quest to understand why her young body was turning into a woman's was not one of Ainsley's favorite pastimes. She preferred torturing her 6-year-old brother and playing school with the neighborhood kids. (Ainsley was always the teacher, and she was very strict.)

"Have you seen Western doctors for this?" Allomong asked.

Tracee laughed. "Yes, many," she said. "None suggested any course of action. They left us hanging." She repeated for

Allomong what she told me in the car: "They seem to have changed the definition of 'normal.' "

For many parents of early-developing girls, "normal" is a crazy-making word, especially when uttered by a doctor; it implies that the patient, or patient's mother, should quit being neurotic and accept that not much can be done. Allomong listened intently. He nodded and took notes, asking Tracee detailed questions about her birth-control history and validating her worst fears by mentioning the "extremely high levels" of estrogen-mimicking chemicals in the food and water supply. After about 20 minutes he asked Ainsley to lie on a table. There he performed a lengthy physical exam that involved testing the strength in Ainsley's arms and legs while she held small glass vials filled with compounds like cortisol, estrogen and sugar. (Kinesiologists believe that weak muscles indicate illness, and that a patient's muscles will test as weaker when he or she is holding a substance that contributes to health problems.)

Finally, he asked Ainsley to sit up. "It doesn't test like it's her own estrogens," Allomong reported to Tracee, meaning he didn't think Ainsley's ovaries were producing too many hormones on their own. "I think it's xeno-estrogens, from the environment," he explained. "And I think it's stress and insulin and sugar."

"You can't be more specific?" Tracee asked, pleading. "Like tell me what crap in my house I can get rid of?" Allomong shook his head.

On the ride back to Fort Collins, Tracee tried to cheer herself up thinking about the teenage suffering that Ainsley would avoid. "You know, I was one of those flat-chested girls at age 14, reading, 'Are You There God? It's Me, Margaret,' just praying to get my period. Ainsley won't have to go through that! When she gets her period, we're going to have a big old party. And then I'm going to go in the bathroom and cry."

In the late 1980s, Marcia Herman-Giddens, then a physician's associate in the pediatric department of the Duke University Medical Center, started noticing that an awful lot of 8- and 9-year-olds in her clinic had sprouted pubic hair and breasts. The medical wisdom, at that time, based on a landmark 1960 study of institutionalized British children, was that puberty began, on average, for girls at age 11. But that was not what Herman-Giddens was seeing. So she started collecting data, eventually leading a study with the American Academy of Pediatrics that sampled 17,000 girls, finding that among white girls, the average age of breast budding was 9.96. Among black girls, it was 8.87.

When Herman-Giddens published these numbers, in 1997 in Pediatrics, she set off a social and endocrinological firestorm. "I had no idea it would be so huge," Herman-Giddens told me recently. "The Lolita syndrome"—the prurient fascination with the sexuality of young girls—"created a lot of emotional interest. As a feminist, I wish it didn't." Along with medical professionals, mothers, worried about their daughters, flocked to Herman-Giddens's slide shows, gasping as she flashed images of possible culprits: obesity, processed foods, plastics.

Meanwhile, doctors wrote letters to journals criticizing the sample in Herman-Giddens's study. (She collected data from girls at physicians' offices, leaving her open to the accusation that it wasn't random.) Was the age of puberty really dropping? Parents said yes. Leading pediatric endocrinologists said no. The stalemate lasted a dozen years. Then in August 2010, the conflict seemed to resolve. Well-respected researchers at three big institutions—Cincinnati Children's Hospital, Kaiser Permanente of Northern California and Mount Sinai School of Medicine in New York—published another study in Pediatrics, finding that by age 7, 10 percent of white girls, 23 percent of black girls, 15 percent of Hispanic girls and 2 percent of Asian girls had started developing breasts.

Now most researchers seem to agree on one thing: Breast budding in girls is starting earlier. The debate has shifted to what this means. Puberty, in girls, involves three events: the growth of breasts, the growth of pubic hair and a first period. Typically the changes unfold in that order, and the process takes about two years. But the data show a confounding pattern. While studies have shown that the average age of breast budding has fallen significantly since the 1970s, the average age of first period, or menarche, has remained fairly constant, dropping to only 12.5 from 12.8 years. Why would puberty be starting earlier yet ending more or less at the same time?

To endocrinologists, girls who go through puberty early fall into two camps: girls with diagnosable disorders like central precocious puberty, and girls who simply develop on the early side of the normal curve. But the line between the groups is blurring. "There used to be a discrete gap between normal and abnormal, and there isn't anymore," Louise Greenspan, a pediatric endocrinologist and co-author of the August 2010 Pediatrics paper, told me one morning in her office at Kaiser Permanente in San Francisco. Among the few tools available to help distinguish between so-called "normal" and "precocious" puberty are bone-age X-rays. To illustrate how they work, Greenspan pulled out a beautiful old book, Greulich and Pyle's "Radiographic Atlas of Skeletal Development of the Hand and Wrist," a standard text for pediatric endocrinologists. Each page showed an X-ray of a hand illustrating "bone age." The smallest hand was from a newborn baby, the oldest from an adult female. "When a baby is born, there's all this cartilage," Greenspan said, pointing to large black gaps surrounding an array of delicate white bones. As the body grows, the pattern of black and white changes. The white bones lengthen, and the black interstices between them, some of which is cartilage, shrink. This process stops at the end of puberty, when the growth plates fuse.

One main risk for girls with true precocious puberty is advanced bone age. Puberty includes a final growth spurt, after which girls mostly stop growing. If that growth spurt starts too early in life, it ends at an early age too, meaning a child will have fewer growing years total. A girl who has her first period at age 10 will stop growing younger and end up shorter than a genetically identical girl who gets her first period at age 13.

That morning one of Greenspan's patients was a 6 ½-year-old girl with a bone age of 9. She was the tallest girl in her class at school. She started growing pubic hair at age 4. No one thought her growth curve was normal, not even her doctors. (Eight used to be the age cutoff for normal pubic-hair growth in girls; now it's as early as 7.) For this girl, Greenspan prescribed a once-a-month shot of the hormone Leuprolide, to halt puberty's progress. The girl hated the shot. Yet nobody second-guessed the treatment plan. The mismatch between her sexual maturation and her age—and the discomfort that created, for everybody—was just too great.

By contrast, Ainsley was older, and her puberty was progressing more slowly, meaning she wasn't at much of an increased risk for short stature or breast cancer. (Early periods are associated with breast cancer, though researchers don't know if the risk stems from greater lifetime exposure to estrogen or a higher lifetime number of menstrual cycles, or perhaps something else, like the age at which a girl has her growth spurt.) In cases of girls Ainsley's age, Greenspan has been asked by parents to prescribe Leuprolide. But Greenspan says this is a bad idea, because Leuprolide's possible side effects—including an increased risk of osteoporosis—outweigh the benefits for girls that age. "If you have a normal girl, a girl who's 8 or 9, there's a big ethical issue of giving them medicine. Giving them medicine says, 'Something is wrong with your body,' as opposed to, 'This is your body, and let's all find a way to accept it.'"

"'Giving them medicine says, Something is wrong with your body, as opposed to, This is your body, and let's all find a way to accept it.'"

"I would have a long conversation with her family, show them all the data," Greenspan continues. Once she has gone through what she calls "the process of normalizing"—a process intended to replace anxiety with statistics—she has rarely had a family continue to insist on puberty-arresting drugs. Indeed, most parents learn to cope with the changes and help their daughters adjust too. One mother described for me buying a drawer full of football shirts, at her third-grade daughter's request, to hide her maturing body. Another reminded her daughter that it's O.K. to act her age. "It's like when you have a really big toddler and people expect the kid to talk in full sentences. People look at my daughter and say, 'Look at those cheekbones!' We have to remind her: 'You may look 12, but you're 9. It's O.K. to lose your cool and stomp your feet.'"

"We still have a lot to learn about how early puberty affects girls psychologically," says Paul Kaplowitz, chief of endocrinology at Children's National Medical Center. "We do know that some girls who start maturing by age 8 progress rapidly and have their first period before age 10, and many parents prefer that we use medications to slow things down. However, many girls do fine if they are simply monitored and their parents are reassured that they will get through it without major problems."

In some ways early puberty is most straightforward for families like those of the kindergartner on Leuprolide. She has a diagnosis, a treatment plan. In Greenspan's office, I asked the girl's father at what age he might choose to take his child off the drugs and let her puberty proceed. He laughed. Then he spoke for most parents when he said, "Would it be bad to say 22?"

So why are so many girls with no medical disorder growing breasts early? Doctors don't know exactly why, but they have identified several contributing factors.

Girls who are overweight are more likely to enter puberty early than thinner girls, and the ties between obesity and puberty start at a very young age. As Emily Walvoord of the Indiana University School of Medicine points out in her paper "The Timing of Puberty: Is It Changing? Does It Matter?" body-mass index and pubertal timing are associated at age 5, age 3, even age 9 months. This fact has shifted pediatric endocrinologists away from what used to be known as the critical-weight theory of puberty—the idea that once a girl's body reaches a certain mass, puberty inevitably starts—to a critical-fat theory of puberty. Researchers now believe that fat tissue, not poundage, sets off a feedback loop that can cause a body to mature. As Robert Lustig, a professor of clinical pediatrics at the University of California, San Francisco's Benioff Children's Hospital, explains, fatter girls have higher levels of the hormone leptin, which can lead to early puberty, which leads to higher estrogen levels, which leads to greater insulin resistance, causing girls to have yet more fat tissue, more leptin and more estrogen, the cycle feeding on itself, until their bodies physically mature.

In addition, animal studies show that the exposure to some environmental chemicals can cause bodies to mature early. Of particular concern are endocrine-disrupters, like "xeno-estrogens" or estrogen mimics. These compounds behave like steroid hormones and can alter puberty timing. For obvious ethical reasons, scientists cannot perform controlled studies proving the direct impact of these chemicals on children, so researchers instead look for so-called "natural experiments," one of which occurred in 1973 in Michigan, when cattle were accidentally fed grain contaminated with an estrogen-mimicking chemical, the flame retardant PBB. The daughters born to the pregnant women who ate the PBB-laced meat and drank the PBB-laced milk started menstruating significantly earlier than their peers.

One concern, among parents and researchers, is the effect of simultaneous exposures to many estrogen-mimics, including the compound BPA, which is ubiquitous. Ninety-three percent of Americans have traces of BPA in their bodies. BPA was first made in 1891 and used as a synthetic estrogen in the 1930s. In the 1950s commercial manufacturers started putting BPA in hard plastics. Since then BPA has been found in many common products, including dental sealants and cash-register receipts. More than a million pounds of the substance are released into the environment each year.

Family stress can disrupt puberty timing as well. Girls who from an early age grow up in homes without their biological fathers are twice as likely to go into puberty younger as girls who grow up with both parents. Some studies show that the presence of a stepfather in the house also correlates with early puberty. Evidence links maternal depression with developing early. Children adopted from poorer countries who have experienced significant early-childhood stress are also at greater risk for early puberty once they're ensconced in Western families.

Bruce Ellis, a professor of Family Studies and Human Development at the University of Arizona, discovered along with his colleagues a pattern of early puberty in girls whose parents divorced when those girls were between 3 and 8 years old and whose fathers were considered socially deviant (meaning they abused drugs or alcohol, were violent, attempted suicide or did prison time). In another study, published in 2011, Ellis and his colleagues showed that first graders who are most reactive to stress—kids whose pulse, respiratory rate and cortisol levels fluctuate most in response to environmental challenges—entered puberty earliest when raised in difficult homes. Evolutionary psychology offers a theory: A stressful childhood inclines a body toward early reproduction; if life is hard, best to mature young. But such theories are tough to prove.

Evolutionary psychology offers a theory: A stressful childhood inclines a body toward early reproduction; if life is hard, best to mature young.

Social problems don't just increase the risk for early puberty; early puberty increases the risk for social problems as well. We know that girls who develop ahead of their peers tend to have lower self-esteem, more depression and more eating disorders. They start drinking and lose their virginity sooner. They have more sexual partners and more sexually transmitted diseases. "You can almost predict it"—that early maturing teenagers will take part in more high-risk behaviors, says Tonya Chaffee, associate clinical professor of pediatrics at University of California, San Francisco, who oversees the Teen and Young Adult Health Center at San Francisco General Hospital. Half of the patients in her clinic are or have been in the foster system. She sees in the outlines of their early-developing bodies the stresses of their lives—single parent or no parent, little or no money, too much exposure to violence.

Some of this may stem from the same social stresses that contribute to early puberty in the first place, and some of it may stem from other factors, including the common nightmare of adolescence: being different. As Julia Graber, associate chairwoman of psychology at the University of Florida, has shown, all "off-time" developers—early as well as late—have more depression during puberty than typically-developing girls. But for the late bloomers, the negative effect wears off once puberty ends. For early bloomers, the effect persists, causing higher levels of depression and anxiety through at least age 30, perhaps all through life. "Some early-maturing girls have very serious problems," Graber told me. "More than I expected when I started looking for clinical significance. I was surprised that it was so severe."

Researchers know there's a relationship between pubertal timing and depression, but they don't know exactly how that relationship works. One theory is that going through puberty early, relative to other kinds of cognitive development, causes changes in the brain that make it more susceptible to depression. As Elizabeth Sowell, director of the Developmental Cognitive Neuroimaging Laboratory at Children's Hospital Los Angeles, points out, girls in general tend to go through puberty earlier than boys, and starting around puberty, girls, as a group, also experience more anxiety and depression than boys do. Graber offers a broader hypothesis, perhaps the best understanding of the puberty-depression connection we have for now. "It may be that early maturers do not have as much time as other girls to accomplish the developmental tasks of childhood. They face new challenges while everybody else is still dealing with the usual development of childhood. This might be causing them to make less successful transitions into adolescence and beyond."

Over the past year, I talked to mothers who tried to forestall their daughters' puberty in many different ways. Some trained with them for 5K runs (exercise is one of the few interventions known to help prevent early puberty); others trimmed milk and meat containing hormones from their daughters' diets; some purged from their homes plastics, pesticides and soy. Yet sooner rather than later, most threw up their hands. "I'm empathetic with parents in despair and wanting a sense of agency," says Sandra Steingraber, an ecologist and the author of *Raising Elijah: Protecting Our Children in an Age of*

Environmental Crisis. "But this idea that we, as parents, should be scrutinizing labels and vetting birthday party goody bags—the idea that all of us in our homes should be acting as our own Environmental Protection Agencies and Departments of Interior—is just nuts. Even if we could read every label and scrutinize every product, our kids are in schools and running in and out of other people's homes where there are brominated flame retardants on the furniture and pesticides used in the backyard."

Adding to the anxiety is the fact that we know so little about how early puberty works. A few researchers, including Robert Lustig, of Benioff Children's Hospital, are beginning to wonder if many of those girls with early breast growth are in puberty at all. Lustig is a man prone to big, inflammatory ideas. (He believes that sugar is a poison, as he has argued in this magazine.) To make the case that some girls with early breast growth may not be in puberty, he starts with basic science. True puberty starts in the brain, he explains, with the production of gonadotropin-releasing hormone, or GnRH. "There is no puberty without GnRH," Lustig told me. GnRH is like the ball that rolls down the ramp that knocks over the book that flips the stereo switch. Specifically, GnRH trips the pituitary, which signals the ovaries. The ovaries then produce estrogen, and the estrogen causes the breasts to grow. But as Lustig points out, the estrogen that is causing that growth in young girls may have a different origin. It may come from the girls' fat tissue (postmenopausal women produce estrogen in their fat tissue) or from an environmental source. "And if that estrogen didn't start with GnRH, it's not puberty, end of story," Lustig says. "Breast development doesn't automatically mean early puberty. It might, but it doesn't have to." Don't even get him started on the relationship between pubic-hair growth and puberty. "Any paper linking pubic hair with early puberty is garbage. Garbage. Pubic hair just means androgens, or male hormones. The first sign of puberty in girls is estrogen. Androgen is not even on the menu."

Frank Biro, lead author of the August 2010 Pediatrics paper and director of adolescent medicine at Cincinnati Children's Hospital, began having similar suspicions last spring after he flew to Denmark to give a lecture. Following his talk, Biro looked over the published data on puberty of his colleague Anders Juul. In Juul's study, some of the girls with early breast development had unexpectedly low levels of estradiol, the predominant form of estrogen in women's bodies from the onset of puberty through menopause. Biro had seen a pattern like this in his data, suggesting to him that the early breast growth might be coming from nonovarian estrogens. That is to say, the headwaters for the pubertal changes might not be in the girls' brains. He is now running models on his own data to see if he can determine where the nonovarian estrogens are coming from.

The possibility that these early "normal" girls are reacting to estrogens that are not coming from their ovaries is compelling. Part of the comfort is that a girl who is not yet in puberty may not have developed an adolescent brain. This means she would not yet feel the acute tug of her own sexual urges. She would not seek thrills and risk. Still, the idea that there are enough toxins or fat cells in a child's body to cause breast development is hardly consoling. Besides, some of the psychosocial problems of early puberty derive from what's happening inside a girl's body; others, from how people react to her. "If a girl is 10 and she looks 15, it doesn't make any difference if her pituitary is turned on or if something else caused her breast growth," Biro says. "She looks like a middle adolescent. People are going to treat her that way. Maybe she's not interested in reciprocal sex, but she might be pressured into sex nonetheless, and her social skills will be those of a 10-year-old."

So what are families of early bloomers to do? Doctors urge parents to focus on their daughters' emotional and physical health rather than on stopping or slowing development. In this way, the concept of a new normal is not just a brushoff but an encouragement to support a girl who is vulnerable.

"I know they can't change the fact that their daughter started developing early, but they can change what happens downstream," Louise Greenspan, the pediatric endocrinologist at Kaiser Permanente, told me. Parents can keep their daughters active and at healthy body weights. They can treat them the age they are, not the age they look. They can defend against a culture that sells push-up bikinis for 7-year-olds and otherwise sexualizes young girls. "Most of the psychological issues associated with early puberty are related to risk-taking behaviors," Greenspan continued, and parents can mitigate those. "I know it sounds corny and old-fashioned, but if you're in a supportive family environment, where you are eating family meals and reading books together, you actually do have control." Early breast growth may be just that—early breast growth: disconcerting, poorly understood, but not a guarantee of our worst fears. "You don't go directly from the first signs of early puberty to anorexia, depression, drinking and early sexual debut."

In Fort Collins, Tracee, Ainsley's mother, tried to stay focused on the positive. At one point during my visit, she disappeared into her basement, the headquarters for her company, T.G.R. Body, and returned with a pink hat box filled with chemical-free samples of Peppermint Pimple Popper and Bad Hair Day Miracle Powder. "I just want to be part of the solution," Tracee said, rubbing a sample of silver hair-streaking gel on my wrist. "I'm so tired of running away. I need to have something Ainsley is moving toward."

Mothers who have been through it urge candor. "Be honest with her, and by honest I mean brutally honest"—about what's going to happen to her body—"while still being kind," says the mother of a girl who recently turned 10 but who first showed signs of developing what she calls "a shape" at age 3. "You don't want your daughter experiencing something for which she's unprepared."

Patience and perspective may be the greatest palliatives. "The thing with puberty is that everybody is going to go through it at some point," another mother told me. Three years ago this woman was installing small trash cans in her third-grade girl's school bathroom stalls so that her daughter could discreetly throw away menstrual pads. But now that daughter is 12, in the sixth grade; her body seems less strange. "I feel so much better, and so does she. By another two or three years down the road, all the other girls will have caught up."

Critical Thinking

1. Why do some researchers insist that there is no puberty without the production of gonadotropin-releasing hormone (GnRH)?
2. Identify sources of environmental estrogens that may cause breast development in preadolescents.
3. How are cognitive development and depression correlated in females who experience early puberty? What might explain this correlation?

Create Central

www.mhhe.com/createcentral

Internet References

Link between Body Fat and the Timing of Puberty
http://pediatrics.aapublications.org/content/121

Lolita Syndrome
www.hindustantimes.com/Entertainment/Wellness

Onset of Puberty in Girls Has Fallen
www.theguardian.com/society/2012/oct/21/puberty

Physical Development in Girls: What to Expect
www.healthychildren.org/English/ages-stages/gradeschool

Article

Prepared by: Claire N. Rubman, *Suffolk County Community College*

Will Your Marriage Last?

What social scientists have learned from putting couples under the microscope.

BROOKE LEA FOSTER

Learning Outcomes

After reading this article, you will be able to:

- Identify three things that make some couples more likely to divorce than other couples.
- Describe three things that make some couples less likely to divorce than other couples, and explain why.
- Explain the paradox of less, then more, happiness in a marriage with children.

My husband, John, and I lived together for four years before we got engaged. He's Filipino; I'm white. And we have a two-year-old. Can you guess which of these things makes us more likely to divorce than other couples?

The answer: all of the above.

People who live together before marriage are more likely to divorce than those who move in together after their engagement. Mixed-race couples don't fare as well as couples of the same race or ethnicity: According to the National Center for Health Statistics, 41 percent of couples who intermarry will divorce before the ten-year mark. And as for kids, let's just say the research doesn't paint a rosy picture of marriage post-baby.

Psychologists have been trying for decades to figure out why some marriages last while others fail. It's easy to be cynical about marriage. With the conventional wisdom saying about half of all couples will divorce, it's hard to go to a wedding without wondering if a couple will make it. At age 36, I already know several people who split up within a few years of getting married. I've got bets on others.

The secret to long-lasting relationships is particularly confounding considering that most couples start in the same place: madly in love. What happens after the wedding that alters the course of so many relationships?

It turns out that the initial years of marriage are particularly telling. Once the honeymoon is over and the fairy dust settles, the work of merging two lives begins. Talking gas bills and car payments can kill the mood. Sometimes one partner might feel disappointed in the relationship, and bad habits can form.

"The first two years are supposed to be a honeymoon," says Barry McCarthy, a professor of psychology at American University and coauthor of *Sexual Awareness: Your Guide to Healthy Couple Sexuality.* "But research says they're quite difficult. You're figuring out sexually and emotionally how to be a couple."

Most divorces happen within the first several years of marriage in part because, McCarthy says, "many couples just can't figure these things out and they end up fighting all of the time." Those who make it through aren't exactly in the clear—racking up marital years isn't the same as having a happy and fulfilling marriage.

Last December, the University of Virginia's National Marriage Project analyzed a survey of more than 1,400 couples between ages 18 and 46 about the key to a happy marriage. The project found that couples who reported higher levels of generosity toward each other also reported happier marriages. The study defined generosity as "being affectionate and forgiving of your spouse."

Is the key to marital happiness as easy as making your partner breakfast each morning—or simply saying "I love you"?

"It's not that simple," laughs the study's lead author, W. Bradford Wilcox, director of the National Marriage Project. But the study did reveal that playing nice improves your sex life, another key factor in a couple's happiness. Respondents who reported high levels of generosity, commitment, religious faith, and quality time together also said they had increased sexual satisfaction. Interestingly, women were more sexually satisfied when husbands shared the housework. Says Wilcox: "It seems that what happens outside of the bedroom has a lot to do with what happens inside the bedroom."

Pioneering marriage researcher John Gottman, a psychology professor at the University of Washington, has been trying to figure out the secret to a happy marriage for decades. He calls one of his most famous theories "the magic ratio." Gottman believes that couples who have at least five positive interactions for every negative one are more likely to make it.

In 1992, Gottman did a study of 700 newlywed couples, inviting them in for a 15-minute videotaped conversation. He counted how many positive and negative interactions they had during the interview. Based on his 5-to-1 ratio, he predicted which couples would be together ten years later and which would be divorced. In a 2002 follow-up study, his findings were astounding: He had a 94-percent accuracy rate, which means he could predict marital happiness for strangers in a quarter of an hour.

A clue to how happy your marriage is may lie in the way you talk about it. Last year, researchers at the University of California at Berkeley found that middle-aged and older couples who used words such as "we," "our," and "us" tended to treat each other better and were better at resolving conflicts. Couples who emphasized their "separateness"—using pronouns such as "I," "me," and "you"—tended to be less happy.

Do you have couple friends? If not, you should get some. Professor Geoffrey Greif and associate professor Kathleen Holtz Deal of the University of Maryland's School of Social Work recently authored a book, *Two Plus Two: Couples and Their Couple Friendships*. After interviewing 123 couples, they found that those who had a social network of couple friends reported higher levels of marital happiness. The researchers said that having couple friends promotes marital satisfaction because it increases attraction to each other and allows couples to observe how other couples interact and resolve differences.

Everyone brings some baggage to a relationship, but a parent's divorce greatly affects marital quality. If your parents split up when you were a kid, you have a 50-percent greater chance of getting divorced yourself. If you and your spouse are both children of divorce, you have a 200-percent higher risk of divorce, says Nicholas Wolfinger, an associate professor of family and consumer studies at the University of Utah and author of a book called *Understanding the Divorce Cycle: The Children of Divorce in Their Own Marriages*.

People who live together before getting engaged tend to "slide" into a lifelong commitment.

Children of divorce are also more likely to live together before marriage or to marry young—both of which increase the chance of divorce. You'd think cohabiting partners would have lower divorce rates—isn't the whole point of moving in together to test the waters, to give couples a chance to try each other on as life partners?

Apparently, it doesn't work. Researchers say that people who live together before getting engaged tend to "slide" into a lifelong commitment rather than choose it. In other words, they've already got the house, the patio furniture, and someone to split the bills with—why wouldn't they take the next step?

Experts say this inertia doesn't bode well for lasting happiness. Scott Stanley, a psychologist at the University of Denver, found that 19 percent of couples who lived together before their engagement suggested divorce at least once over the course of the five-year study, compared with only 10 percent who moved in together after the big day.

But cohabitation doesn't always spell doom: Couples who move in together after their engagement—but before marriage—appear to fare just as well as couples who moved in together after saying "I do."

As for having kids, the jury is out on whether they strain or enrich a marriage. "There's a dip in marital happiness after the birth of your first child," says the Marriage Project's W. Bradford Wilcox. A study by Texas A&M University and the University of Denver of 218 couples in their mid-twenties—roughly two-thirds of whom welcomed their first child within eight years of marrying and a third of whom had no children—showed that couples with kids were less happy than childless couples. While the study showed that overall marital happiness decreased over time for both those with kids and those without, the couples with children reported a more sudden drop in marital dissatisfaction; the childless couples' happiness levels decreased more slowly over time.

Still, Wilcox says that couples with kids often rebound and report higher levels of happiness later in life. Longitudinal data show that marital satisfaction increases as children get older and leave home. In other words, while individuals love their children and glean much happiness from them, their marriages benefit when their kids enter college and they're able to spend more quality time together.

There doesn't seem to be a magic age for getting married. Even so, couples who wed later tend to report higher levels of education, leading to greater affluence and greater marital satisfaction. If you have a college degree, you're 66 percent less likely to divorce. "It's partly because people with college degrees make more money and do better in the professional world," says Wilcox, "but it's also because many have the social skills needed to navigate married life more successfully."

Money makes a big difference in a couple's life. Research cited in a 2009 article by Jeffrey Drew of the National Marriage Project found that wives with higher incomes and assets are happier in their marriages; they're also less likely to get a divorce. Couples who reported fighting about money once a week were 30 percent more likely to split up than couples who argued about finances a few times a month. And couples with no assets at the beginning of a three-year period were 70 percent likelier to divorce than couples with at least $10,000 in assets.

But while having money can help, it's not a good sign if either spouse is too motivated by it. A Brigham Young University study of 1,734 married couples found that those who said money wasn't important scored 10 to 15 percent better on marriage stability than couples in which one or both said they highly valued "having money and lots of things."

"Couples where both spouses are materialistic were worse off on nearly every measure we looked at," says Jason Carroll, a BYU professor of family life.

A second study cited in Drew's National Marriage Project article found that perceptions of how well one's spouse handles money can also cause strain. If you feel your husband or wife doesn't handle money well, you probably have a lower level of marital happiness. "In one study, feeling that one's spouse spent money foolishly increased the likelihood of divorce by 45 percent for both men and women. Only extramarital affairs and alcohol/drug abuse were stronger predictors of divorce," Drew writes.

What do happy couples have incommon?

They respect each other. They don't nitpick, criticize, or put each other down. And yes, they go out of their way to be nice. Says Wilcox: "Being an affectionate and engaging spouse is going to make both of you happier."

My husband and I may be of different ethnicities and we may have a kid, but I think we're going to make it. Here's why: When my feet are cold in winter, he'll always let me warm them up on his legs. I kiss him hello every day when he gets home. He encourages me to take time for myself when he sees I'm feeling drained. In other words, we're kind to each other—and as the studies show, that counts for a lot.

Critical Thinking

1. Why does "playing nice" improve a couple's sex life?
2. What are some of the positive interactions that contribute to the 5-to-1 ratio of positive-to-negative interactions that predict marital success?
3. How does the desire for money and lots of things decrease the chances of marital success?

Create Central

www.mhhe.com/createcentral

Internet References

Child Out of Wedlock: Huffington Post
www.huffingtonpost.com/tag/child-out-of-wedlock

Does Living Together before Marriage Increase Chances of Divorce?
www.eharmony.com/blog/2013/07/24/does-living-together-before-marriage-increase-chances-of-divorce

The Downside of Cohabitating before Marriage
www.nytimes.com/2012/04/15/opinion/Sunday

U.S. Rate of Interracial Marriage Hits Record High
http://usatoday30/usatoday.com/health/news/2012-02-16

Article

Prepared by: Claire N. Rubman, *Suffolk County Community College*

All About Me

LAURA SPINNEY

Learning Outcomes

After reading this article, you will be able to:

- Define *generation me.*
- Address the question of a "self-esteem gene."

"Young people are coddled long after they should start learning that they aren't perfect." That was the conclusion of HS, a blogger commenting on an article in *The New York Times* lamenting the state of today's youth. The trouble with kids, he went on, is that they have an overinflated opinion of themselves because they have been brought up to believe that everything they do is valuable and important. This was no grumpy old codger, but a young man writing **about** his own generation, those people born between **about** 1980 and 2000 who have been labeled Generation Y, or Generation **Me.**

As its name suggests, Generation **Me** has drawn some flak. Its members stand accused of being spoiled, arrogant, and narcissistic, with an undeserved sense of entitlement. College professors complain that today's students demand constant attention. Employers find it hard to stomach the overblown egos of their young recruits, and therapists say they are seeing a new generation of patients depressed because they are unable to live up to their own excessive expectations. Critics argue that the blame lies with the parents, teachers, and other adults who have gone out of their way to inflate children's opinions of themselves from an early age.

These are damning allegations that reflect badly not just on Generation Y but also a philosophy **about** child-rearing that began in the 1980s and is still going strong. If correct, we would need to revise the view that boosting children's self-esteem is the best way to ensure they reach their full potential. So what is the evidence? Are today's young people really more egotistical than past generations? If so, is that a problem? And if the modern western cult of building self-esteem is to blame, what can we do **about** it?

One of the most vocal critics of today's youth is Jean Twenge, a psychologist at San Diego State University, California, and author of *Generation **Me*** (Free Press, 2006). For evidence of Generation Y's inflated ego we need look no further than the annual American Freshman survey of 9 million college students, she says. It reveals that 52 percent of the 2009 cohort rated themselves as having a level of social self-confidence higher than the average for the general population, compared with 30 percent of students questioned in 1966. Today's students also rate their intellectual self-confidence, public speaking skills, and leadership ability around 50 percent higher than their 1966 counterparts (*Self and Identity,* DOI: 10.1080/15298868.2011.576820).

The overriding importance of self-esteem to Generation Y was highlighted in an experiment in 2010. A team led by Brad Bushman at Ohio State University in Columbus found that college students valued a boost to their self-esteem—for example, receiving a grade hike or a compliment—more highly than the rewards that have motivated humanity since the dawn of time, such as eating a favourite food or engaging in a sexual activity.

Students also rated that boost more highly than getting paid, drinking alcohol, and seeing a best friend (*Journal of Personality,* DOI: 10.1111/j.1467-6494.2010.00712.x). Exploring further, the researchers asked the students to rate how much they wanted each of these rewards versus the pleasure they gained from them. Wanting something more than liking it is considered an indication of addiction. In **all** cases, they liked the reward more than they wanted it, but the difference between the two was smallest for boosts to self-esteem.

Yet the picture is not quite that simple. Mark Leary, a social psychologist at Duke University in Durham, North Carolina, cautions that colleges are not as elitist as they were in the 1960s, so the demographic profile of students has changed, making past and present cohorts not entirely comparable. "We don't know if this is a real change, or if it has to do with a change in the people who are being tested," he says.

Indeed, Kali Trzesniewski at the University of California, Davis, has looked at a survey of 400,000 U.S. high-school students over the 30 years from 1976, and found no evidence for increasing egotism in this slightly younger group. "Self-esteem scores have not changed at **all,**" she says (*Perspectives on Psychological Science,* vol 5, p 58). She suspects that some, generally older, researchers have fallen foul of an age-old prejudice: "We critique the next generation. That's just what we do," she says. It is possible, she notes, that everyone, not just Generation Y, has gradually become more egocentric—but with limited data **about** other age groups it is difficult to test this idea.

The generous generation?

More sceptical still is Jeffrey Arnett, a psychologist who studies adolescence at Clark University in Worcester, Massachusetts. He points out that young people are volunteering for charity work in greater numbers than ever before, and are more concerned **about** social inequalities than their parents were. He has gone so far as to rename Generation **Me,** the "Generous Generation."

Nevertheless, most researchers acknowledge that there has been a real increase in self-esteem—at least in the United States, where the phenomenon has been studied most. That still leaves the question of whether this is a problem. When American psychologist William James coined the term self-esteem in 1890, he defined it as the ratio of a person's successes to their "pretensions" or goals. In other words, self-esteem is a subjective measure of your own value that increases as you achieve your goals. This matches the dictionary definition: "respect for or a favourable opinion of oneself." Surely there can be nothing wrong with that?

These days, however, self-esteem has acquired a second meaning: "an unduly high opinion of oneself; vanity." It is this definition that best fits Generation Y, according to Twenge. And that is the source of the problem. For a start, inflated egos leave many young people with unrealistic expectations, and their inability to achieve these can lead to depression. It is no coincidence, she says, that the U.S. Centers for Disease Control and Prevention in Atlanta, Georgia, reported last October that 1 in 9 Americans over the age of 12 now takes antidepressants—a quadrupling of the rate since the late 1980s.

Twenge sees another sign of dangerously overblown self-esteem in rising levels of narcissism. She found that twice as many college students had high levels of narcissism in 2006 compared with the early 1980s. Narcissists tend to be intolerant of criticism and prone to cheating and aggression. "These are the people who wind up in your office arguing over a grade," she says. They are also more concerned **about** their physical appearance, and as she points out, Americans are resorting to plastic surgery in greater numbers than ever before. In her latest book, *The Narcissism Epidemic,* written with W. Keith Campbell (Free Press, 2009), she recounts anecdotes of people hiring fake paparazzi to make themselves look famous, and buying "McMansions" on credit, as evidence of the United States's overblown ego.

"We have taken individualism too far," says Twenge, and popular culture reflects this. She has worked with University of Kentucky social psychologist Nathan DeWall and others to chart an increase in the frequency of the word "I" in the lyrics of hit U.S. pop songs from 1980 to 2007. In the same time frame words related to other people, social interaction, and positive emotions have decreased in frequency (*Psychology of Aesthetics, Creativity, and the Arts,* vol 5, p 200). Twenge blames four factors: changes in parenting styles, the cult of celebrity, the internet and easy credit. "**All** of these things allow people to have an inflated sense of self in which the appearance of performance is more important than the actual performance," she says.

Others blame the self-esteem movement that began in California in the 1980s. Unfortunately, says Leary, the movement was born of a misunderstanding. Studies had shown a correlation between high self-esteem and positive life events. "People jumped to the conclusion that self-esteem was the cause of those other things, and it's not really," he says. Three decades and many self-esteem-boosting programmes later, the view persists that the best way to rear children is to build their self-esteem through a constant stream of praise and positive feedback. The evidence is equivocal at best.

In 2003, a team led by Roy Baumeister at Florida State University in Tallahassee conducted a review of the literature. A complicated picture emerged. They found that high self-esteem was generally associated with greater happiness and initiative-taking and low self-esteem was linked to depression. However, contrary to expectation, people with high self-esteem became more depressed in stressful times, while those with low self-esteem were more resilient when faced with life's ups and downs. It also emerged that attempts to boost schoolchildren's self-esteem did not improve their academic performance and could sometimes be counterproductive. High self-esteem seemed to protect girls from bulimia, but it did not prevent children from smoking, drinking, taking drugs, or having sex—if anything it prompted them to try these things. Performing well in the workplace was sometimes linked to high self-esteem, but the correlation was variable and the direction of causality unclear. Self-esteem could predict neither the quality nor the duration of relationships. The overall picture was so mixed that Baumeister and his team felt unable to endorse programmes that boosted self-esteem (*Psychological Science in the Public Interest,* vol 4, p 1).

The consensus among psychologists today is that high self-esteem is more often a consequence of positive life events than a cause—a message that has failed to reach most parents and teachers. Leary goes so far as to assert that self-esteem that is boosted artificially, without reference to achievements, has no intrinsic value. Meanwhile, educational psychologist Herbert Marsh at the University of Oxford argues that we should think of self-esteem as just one part of the broader notion of something called self-concept, which also incorporates ideas **about** one's ethnic and academic identities, and gender. He believes that a good self-concept and high educational achievement are cause and effect of each other. "That's what makes schoolteachers' jobs so difficult," he says. "They not only have to teach skills, they also have to build self-belief, and then they have to link the two."

Baumeister argues that instead of building up children's egos we should build their self-control. In his new book, written with journalist John Tierney, he points to amassing evidence that willpower, not self-esteem is the essential ingredient for a successful life (*Willpower: Rediscovering Our Greatest Strength,* Allen Lane, 2012). He proposes that kids should learn to control their impulses and persevere at difficult tasks so that they can achieve their goals, which will naturally boost their self-esteem. Parents and teachers can help foster self-discipline by encouraging children to acquire good habits. And instead of giving constant and therefore meaningless praise, they should encourage real achievement.

If Baumeister's approach seems too draconian, Leary is more pragmatic. The message parents should be sending their children, he says, is that they are loved even though they are not perfect, and that they can improve. "Give them honest feedback." Above **all,** don't tell your child that he or she is the greatest kid in the world, "because no kid is."

Within a generation narcissism has doubled among college students

The cult of celebrity is making youth culture more self-obsessed

If everyone's a winner, kids get an overinflated opinion of their abilities You're so vain/Me, myself, my/All about me

All About Others

An overinflated opinion of oneself can lead to problems (see main story) but so too can low self-esteem. During adolescence children become vulnerable, as the seamless egocentrism of their younger self rapidly acquires cracks, says Sander Thomaes, a developmental psychologist at Utrecht University in the Netherlands. Girls experience a greater decline in self-esteem than boys, but for both sexes the change is permanent. Another problem is that young people's self-esteem may be high but unstable, plummeting at the first criticism, for example. Parents understandably want to protect their teenagers' self-opinion from sinking too low at this critical time, but showering them with unfounded praise is not the answer. A better tactic is to encourage them to think **about** others.

Among several researchers whose work points in this direction are Jennifer Crocker and Amy Canevello from Ohio State University in Columbus. In their study of around 200 pairs of college students they found that those who sought to boost their self-esteem by getting their roommate to acknowledge their good points failed. Their own self-esteem and their roommate's opinion of them both dropped off over the 3 months of the study. "The thing that did work was actually caring **about** the well-being of the other person," says Crocker (*European Journal of Social Psychology,* vol 41, p 422).

Parents should help their kids acquire the social and other skills they need to perform well, says Thomaes. "If they succeed in that, their children will develop a reasonable sense of self-esteem."

A Self-Esteem Gene

Some people deal with stress better than others. This ability has been linked with optimism, mastery, and, more controversially, high self-esteem. Although such psychological resources are known to run in families, their genetic basis has remained obscure. But last September, Shimon Saphire-Bernstein and colleagues at the University of California, Los Angeles, announced they had identified a gene that influences self-esteem (*Proceedings of the National Academy of Sciences,* vol 108, p 15118).

OXTR codes for a receptor for oxytocin, a hormone that plays a role in behaviours including social recognition, bonding and also aggression (*New Scientist,* 11 February 2012, p 39). At a particular location in its DNA sequence, the gene can have either an adenine (A) or a guanine (G) nucleotide. Everybody carries two copies of OXTR, and Saphire-Bernstein's team found that people with one or two copies of the A variant reported lower levels of self-esteem than those with two copies of the G variant. The A group also reported more depressive symptoms.

Sander Thomaes at Utrecht University in the Netherlands thinks genetic influences probably account for between 30 and 50 percent of individual differences in self-esteem. Saphire-Bernstein's group emphasises that OXTR is likely to be one of many genes that affect self-esteem. Nevertheless, the finding underlines the importance of biology in human psychology.

Critical Thinking

1. What contributing factors led to the perceived generosity of Generation Y?
2. How can an adolescent in the 21st century develop a realistic and positive sense of self?
3. Under what circumstances would you allow your adolescent to use plastic surgery or anti-depressants to improve his or her self-esteem?

Create Central

www.mhhe.com/createcentral

Internet References

Naspoline.org Self-Concept and Self-Esteem in Adolescents
http://www.nasponline.org/families/selfconcept.pdf

New York Times.com Seeking Self-Esteem Through Surgery
http://www.nytimes.com/2009/01/15/fashion/15skin.html?pagewanted=all

Psychology Today.com Low Self-esteem What is it? What to do about it.
http://www.psychologytoday.com/blog/fighting-fear/201304/low-self-esteem

therapistaid.com Self-Esteem Worksheets for Adolescents
http://www.therapistaid.com/therapy-worksheets/selfesteem/adolescents

LAURA SPINNEY is a writer based in Lausanne, Switzerland.

Spinney, Laura. "All About Me." *New Scientist Magazine* 214. 2862 (April, 28, 2012): 44–47.

Article Prepared by: Claire N. Rubman, *Suffolk County Community College*

The Retro Wife

Feminists who say they're having it all—by choosing to stay home.

LISA MILLER

Learning Outcomes

After reading this article, you will be able to:

- Contrast traditional women's roles (stay home and nurture husband/children) with the liberated women's roles (independence, career).
- Explain why women who expect their husbands to fully share housework, child care, and money-making in careers are frequently disappointed.

When Kelly Makino was a little girl, she loved to go orienteering—to explore the wilderness near her rural Pennsylvania home, finding her way back with a compass and a map—and the future she imagined for herself was equally adventuresome. Until she was about 16, she wanted to be a CIA operative, a spy, she says, "like La Femme Nikita." She put herself through college at Georgia State working in bars and slinging burgers, planning that with her degree in social work, she would move abroad, to India or Africa, to do humanitarian work for a couple of years. Her husband would be nerdy-hip, and they'd settle down someplace like Williamsburg; when she eventually had children, she would continue working full time, like her mother did, moving up the nonprofit ladder to finally "run a United Way chapter or be the CEO." Kelly graduated from college magna cum laude and got an M.S.W. from Penn, again with honors, receiving an award for her negotiating skills.

Now Kelly is 33, and if dreams were winds, you might say that hers have shifted. She believes that every household needs one primary caretaker, that women are, broadly speaking, better at that job than men, and that no amount of professional success could possibly console her if she felt her two young children—Connor, 5, and Lillie, 4—were not being looked after the right way. The maternal instinct is a real thing, Kelly argues: Girls play with dolls from childhood, so "women are raised from the get-go to raise children successfully. When we are moms, we have a better toolbox." Women, she believes, are conditioned to be more patient with children, to be better multitaskers, to be more tolerant of the quotidian grind of playdates and temper tantrums; "women," she says, "keep it together better than guys do." So last summer, when her husband, Alvin, a management consultant, took a new position requiring more travel, she made a decision. They would live off his low-six-figure income, and she would quit her job running a program for at-risk kids in a public school to stay home full time.

Kelly is not a Martha Stewart spawn in pursuit of the perfectly engineered domestic stage set. On the day I met her, she was wearing an orange hoodie, plum-colored Converse low-tops, and a tiny silver stud in her nose. In the family's modest New Jersey home, the bedroom looked like a laundry explosion, and the morning's breakfast dishes were piled in the sink. But Kelly's priorities are nothing if not retrograde. She has given herself over entirely to the care and feeding of her family. Undistracted by office politics and unfettered by meetings or a nerve-fraying commute, she spends hours upon hours doing things that would make another kind of woman scream with boredom, chanting nursery rhymes and eating pretend cake beneath a giant *Transformers* poster. Her sacrifice of a salary tightened the Makinos' upper-middle-class budget, but the subversion of her personal drive pays them back in ways Kelly believes are priceless; she is now able to be there for her kids no matter what, cooking healthy meals, taking them hiking and to museums, helping patiently with homework, and devoting herself to teaching the life lessons—on littering, on manners, on good habits—that she believes every child should know. She introduces me as "Miss Lisa," and that's what the kids call me all day long.

Alvin benefits no less from his wife's domestic reign. Kelly keeps a list of his clothing sizes in her iPhone and, devoted to his cuteness, surprises him regularly with new items, like the dark-washed jeans he was wearing on the day I visited. She tracks down his favorite recipes online, recently discovering one for pineapple fried rice that he remembered from his childhood in Hawaii. A couple of times a month, Kelly suggests that they go to bed early and she soothes his work-stiffened muscles with a therapeutic massage. "I love him so much, I just want to spoil him," she says.

Kelly calls herself "a flaming liberal" and a feminist, too. "I want my daughter to be able to do anything she wants," she says. "But I also want to say, 'Have a career that you can walk away from at the drop of a hat.' " And she is not alone. Far from the Bible Belt's conservative territories, in blue-state cities and suburbs, young, educated, married mothers find themselves not uninterested in the metaconversation about "having it all" but untouched by it. They are too busy mining their grandmothers' old-fashioned lives for values they can appropriate like heirlooms, then wear proudly as their own.

Feminism has fizzled, its promise only half-fulfilled. This is the revelation of the moment, hashed and rehashed on blogs and talk shows, a cause of grief for some, fury for others. American women are better educated than they've ever been, better educated now than men, but they get distracted during their prime earning years by the urge to procreate. As they mature, they earn less than men and are granted fewer responsibilities at work. Fifty years after the publication of *The Feminine Mystique,* women represent only a tiny fraction of corporate and government leaders, and they still earn only 77 cents on the male dollar.

What to do? One solution is to deny the need for broader solutions or for any kind of sisterly help. It's every woman for herself, and may the best one win. "I don't, I think, have, sort of, the militant drive and, sort of, the chip on the shoulder that sometimes comes with that," said Yahoo CEO Marissa Mayer in an interview with PBS, in which she declined to label herself a "feminist." "I think it's too bad, but I do think that *feminism* has become in many ways a more negative word." (*I went to Stanford, worked at Google, got pregnant, and still became the chief executive of a Fortune 500 company,* she seemed to say. *If you're smart enough, so can you.*) But others, as you may have read, believe it's time for women to resume the good fight. In her much-discussed *Atlantic* piece, Anne-Marie Slaughter, by profession a policy wonk (now at Princeton, formerly at the State Department), calls for better workplace programs: more parental leave, more part-time and flextime options. Facebook COO Sheryl Sandberg, in her new book, *Lean In,* acknowledges the need for better policies, but argues that the new revolution needs to start with women themselves, that what's needed to equalize U.S. workplaces is a generation of women tougher, stronger, wilier, more honest about their ambition, more strategic, and more determined to win than American women currently are.

But what if all the fighting is just too much? That is, what if a woman isn't earning Facebook money but the salary of a social worker? Or what if her husband works 80 hours a week, and her kid is acting out at school, and she's sick of the perpetual disarray in the closets and the endless battles over who's going to buy the milk and oversee the homework? Maybe most important, what if a woman doesn't have Sandberg-Slaughter-Mayer-level ambition but a more modest amount that neither drives nor defines her?

Reading *The Feminine Mystique* now, one is struck by the white-hot flame of Betty Friedan's professional hunger, which made her into a prophet and a pioneer. But it blinded her as well: She presumed that all her suburban-housewife sisters felt as imprisoned as she did and that the gratification she found in her work was attainable for all. That was never true, of course; the revolution that Friedan helped to spark both liberated women and allowed countless numbers of them to experience financial pressure and the profound dissatisfactions of the workaday grind. More women than ever earn some or all of the money their family lives on. But today, in the tumultuous 21st-century economy, depending on a career as a path to self-actualization can seem like a sucker's bet.

Meanwhile, what was once feminist blasphemy is now conventional wisdom: Generally speaking, mothers instinctively want to devote themselves to home more than fathers do. (Even Sandberg admits it. "Are there characteristics inherent in sex differences that make women more nurturing and men more assertive?" she asks. "Quite possibly.") If feminism is not only about creating an equitable society but also a means to fulfillment for individual women, and if the rewards of working are insufficient and uncertain, while the tug of motherhood is inexorable, then a new calculus can take hold: For some women, the solution to resolving the long-running tensions between work and life is not more parent-friendly offices or savvier career moves but the full embrace of domesticity. "The feminist revolution started in the workplace, and now it's happening at home," says Makino. "I feel like in today's society, women who don't work are bucking the convention we were raised with . . . Why can't we just be girls? Why do we have to be boys and girls at the same time?" She and the legions like her offer a silent rejoinder to Sandberg's manifesto, raising the possibility that the best way for some mothers (and their loved ones) to have a happy life is to make home their highest achievement.

"What these women feel is that the trade-offs now between working and not working are becoming more and more unsustainable," says Stacy Morrison, editor-in-chief of BlogHer, a network of 3,000 blogs for and by women. "The conversation we hear over and over again is this: 'The sense of calm and control that we feel over our lives is so much better than what is currently on offer in our culture.' And they're not wrong." The number of stay-at-home mothers rose incrementally between 2010 and 2011, for the first time since the downturn of 2008. While staying home with children remains largely a privilege of the affluent (the greatest number of America's SAHMs live in families with incomes of $100,000 a year or more), some of the biggest increases have been among younger mothers, ages 25 to 35, and those whose family incomes range from $75,000 to $100,000 a year.

This is not the retreat from high-pressure workplaces of a previous generation but rather a more active awakening to the virtues of the way things used to be. Patricia Ireland, who lives on the Upper West Side, left her job as a wealth adviser in 2010 after her third child was born. Now, even though her husband, also in finance, has seen his income drop since the recession, she has no plans to go back to work. She feels it's a privilege to manage her children's lives—"not just what they do, but what they believe, how they talk to other children, what kind of story we read together. That's all dictated by me. Not by my nanny or my babysitter." Her husband's part of the arrangement is to go to work and deposit his paycheck in the joint account. "I'm really grateful that my husband and I have fallen into traditional gender roles without conflict," says Ireland. "I'm not bitter that I'm the one home and he goes to work. And he's very happy that he goes to work."

A lot of the new neo-traditionalists watched their own mothers strain under the second shift, and they regard Sandberg's lower-wattage mini-mes, rushing off to Big Jobs and back home with a wad of cash for the nanny, with something like pity. They don't want a return to the confines of the fifties; they treasure their freedoms, but see a third way. When Slaughter tours the lecture circuit, she is often approached, she says, by women younger than 30 who say, "I don't see a senior person in my world whose life I want." In researching her 2010 book *The Unfinished Revolution: Coming of Age in a New Era of Gender, Work and Family,* New York University sociologist Kathleen Gerson found that, in spite of all the gains young women have made, about a quarter say they would choose a traditional domestic arrangement over the independence that comes with a career, believing not just "that only a parent can provide an acceptable level of care" but also that "they are the only parent available for the job."

The harried, stressed, multiarmed Kali goddess, with a laptop in one hand and homemade organic baby food in the other, has been replaced with a domestic Madonna, content with her choices and placid in her sphere. "I was . . . blessed," wrote one woman on the UrbanBaby message boards recently, "with the patience to truly enjoy being home with my kids and know that in the end family is what is important in life—not pushing papers at some crap job." When the UB community fired back with a fusillade of snark, the poster remained serene. "It's sacred work but not for everyone," she wrote. "I will never have regrets." In season three of *The Good Wife,* Caitlin D'arcy, the law firm's ambitious and strategically minded female associate, unexpectedly quits her job when she becomes pregnant, saying she wants to be a full-time wife and mother. Her mentor, Alicia Florrick—separated from her husband and a mother of two—tries to dissuade her. "You're smart and clever," she says. "If you give this up for someone, even someone important to you, you'll regret it."

"I'm not giving it up for my fiancé," says Caitlin. "I'm giving it up for myself. I like the law, but I love my fiancé."

"But you don't need to choose," protests Alicia. "There's no reason why you can't work, be a wife and a mother."

"But I want to choose," says Caitlin. "Maybe it's different for my generation, but I don't have to prove anything. Or if I have to, I don't want to. I'm in love."

In Friedan's day, housewives used novel technologies such as the automatic washing machine to ease the burden of their domestic work; today, technology helps them to avoid the isolation of their grandmothers and to show off the fruits of their labor. Across the Internet, on a million mommy blogs and Pinterest pages, these women—conceptual cousins of the bearded and suspendered artisanal bakers and brewers who reside in gentrified neighborhoods—are elevating homemaking to an art, crocheting baby hats, slow-roasting strawberries for after-school snacks ("taste like Twizzlers!"), and making their own laundry soap from scratch. Young mothers fill the daytime upholstery and pattern-making courses at Third Ward, a craftspace in Williamsburg, and take knitting classes at the Brooklyn Yarn Café in Bushwick while their kids are in school.

Home, to these women, is more than a place to watch TV at the end of the day and motherhood more than a partial identity. It is a demanding, full-time endeavor, requiring all of their creativity, energy, and ingenuity. Kelly Makino set up a giant mothers' group in northern Jersey, using her M.S.W. to help other parents pool time and resources. (Such "side projects," she says, have the added benefit of "keeping us sane.") Homeschooling, once the province of Christian conservatives, is now increasingly chosen by lefty families; in New York City, the number of children being taught in their apartments rose by nearly 10 percent over the past year.

For Rebecca Woolf, maternal ambition led to the creation of her website, Girl's Gone Child, in 2005, when she was 23 and had just given birth to her son Archer. She has since had three more children (a girl, Fable, and twins named Reverie and Boheme), and every day she posts staged photos of her kids that make her family life look like one big, wholesome-but-funky romp. Here are the twins wearing adorable handmade animal hats with ears! Here is a lesson in at-home bang trimming! Woolf, who lives in Los Angeles and whose husband is a television producer, points out that as the founder of a thriving blog, she does have a job. But the image of home life she presents for popular consumption is as glossy and idealized as the mythical feminine perfection Friedan rebelled against. It is perhaps no wonder that in the world of mommy blogs, tattooed Fort Greeners and Mormons unknowingly collide, trafficking the same sites and trading recipes on the same message boards. They may vote different tickets, but on the centrality of home and family to a satisfying life, their interests are aligned.

Before they marry, college students of both genders almost universally tell social scientists that they want marriages in which housework, child care, professional ambition, and moneymaking will be respectfully negotiated and fully shared. According to a 2008 report by the Families and Work Institute, two thirds of people younger than 29 imagine for themselves partnerships not defined by traditional gender roles. Maybe she'll change the lightbulbs; maybe he'll go part time for a while after the birth of the baby. Seventy-four percent of American employees say they believe that women who work outside the home can be as good at mothering as those who don't. The institute's data also indicates that "men today view the 'ideal' man as someone who is not only successful . . . but also involved as a father, husband/partner, and son." Once married, the research shows, men are more contented over the long term, and women are happiest in an egalitarian union—so long as both parties agree about what egalitarian means.

That, of course, is where things get tricky. Despite their stated position, men still do far less housework than their spouses. In 2011, only 19 percent spent any time during the average day cleaning or doing laundry; among couples with kids younger than 6, men spent just 26 minutes a day doing what the Bureau of Labor Statistics calls "physical care," which is to say bathing, feeding, or dressing children. (Women did more than twice as much.) In her research, Gerson found that in times of stress men overwhelmingly revert to the traditional provider role, allowing them to justify punting on the dishes. "All [men]," she says, "agree that no matter what the gender revolution prescribes, it is still paramount for men to earn a living and support their families, which also implies taking a backseat as caregiver." As a romantic college student, a man may imagine he will request an extended paternity leave, but it's very likely that he won't. The average amount of time a man takes off after the birth of a child is five days. "That's exactly what happened to me!" exclaimed Kelly Makino when I relayed that stat to her. Alvin had planned on taking a two-week leave after Lillie was born but was back at the office after half that time.

All those bachelors' vows of future bathroom cleanings, it turns out, may be no more than a contemporary mating call. "People espouse equality because they conform to the current normative values of our culture," says University of Texas evolutionary psychologist David Buss. "Any man who did not do so would alienate many women—yes, espousing values is partly a mating tactic, and this is just one example." At least in one area, there's scant penalty for this bait and switch. Last year, sociologists at the University of Washington found that the less cooking, cleaning, and laundry a married man does, the more frequently he gets laid.

Feminism has never fully relieved women from feeling that the domestic domain is theirs to manage, no matter what else they're juggling. There is a story, possibly apocryphal yet also believable, of an observer looking over Secretary of State Madeleine Albright's shoulder during a Cabinet meeting in the late nineties. On the pad before her, the secretary had written not "paths to peace in the Middle East" but "buy cottage cheese." (Albright declined to comment for this story, but while promoting a book in 2009, she told an audience that all her life she made it a point always to answer phone calls from her children, no matter what else she was doing. "Every woman's middle name is guilt," she said.) Those choices have a different tenor now, one that upholds the special importance of the maternal role. "My sense," says Buss, "is that younger women are more open to the idea that there might exist evolved psychological gender differences." Among my friends, many women behave as though the evolutionary imperative extends not just to birthing and breast-feeding but to administrative household tasks as well, as if only they can properly plan birthday parties, make doctors' appointments, wrap presents, communicate with the teacher, buy the new school shoes. A number of those I spoke to for this article reminded me of a 2010 British study showing that men lack the same mental bandwidth for multitasking as women. Male and female subjects were asked how they'd find a lost key, while also being given a number of unrelated chores to do—talk on the phone, read a map, complete a math problem. The women universally approached the hunt more efficiently. Joanna Goddard, who runs the women's lifestyle blog A Cup of Jo, says she hears this refrain among her friends. "I'll just do it. It'll be easier. I'll just do it. It'll be faster. I'll do the dishes. I know where everything goes."

Psychologists suggest that perhaps American women are heirs and slaves to some atavistic need to prove their worth through domestic perfectionism: "So many women want to control their husbands' parenting," says Barbara Kass, a therapist with a private practice in Brooklyn. "'Oh, do you have the this? Did you do the that? Don't forget that she needs this. And make sure she naps.' Sexism is internalized." Perhaps this mentality explains the baffling result of a survey that the Families and Work Institute conducted last spring for *Real Simple* magazine. Women said they yearned for more free time and that they hated doing most housework. But when they got free time, they used it to do housework—convinced that no one else could do it as well.

If women and men are at odds with themselves over what they value most, if a woman says she wants a big job but also needs to be home by 5:30 to oversee homework, and her husband promises to pick up the kids from chess club but goes instead to the meeting with the boss, how can marriages with two working parents not wind up conflict-ridden? From Kelly Makino's perspective, it was a no-brainer. "Some days I just have to pinch myself," she says. "It's so easy, it's so rewarding to live this way."

Kelly and Alvin decided to change their lives one night last spring during a mini-vacation to Washington, D.C. They were there to see the cherry blossoms, and Kelly was aware, all weekend long, of the ebbing of her anxiety. "I didn't have to worry about 500 people's lives. I had to worry about four people's lives."

Connor had been in a fight at school. Lillie had been having nightmares. After the kids were in bed, the Makinos retired to the bathroom of their hotel room. "We realized that neither one of us were happy. We were sleep deprived and stressed out all the time," says Kelly. If they scaled back, they reasoned, they could live on Alvin's salary. But first Kelly had to come to terms with her unfulfilled ambition—"I knew I had it in me to be the best"—and the disapproval of her parents. Her father worried that she'd be bored out of her mind. Her mother accused her of "mooching." It took Kelly three months to quit her job.

Sitting at their kitchen table, littered with the detritus from a birthday-party goody bag, the Makinos retrace how their relationship turned out the way it has. They met at a biker bar where Kelly was waitressing, and at first, when Alvin envisioned their collective future, he thought, "*Oh, it's totally not going to be like my parents. We're going to do things equally. Both of us are working, and we'll take care of the kids together.* It just seemed so simple in my mind."

"I remember you said you wanted us to be a power couple," says Kelly.

But there was tension. Alvin earned a lot more money. Kelly felt that her job contributed more good to the world, that its emergencies were more urgent. One time, she remembers, she was just leaving work when she found herself face-to-face with an anguished child. "It's 4:30, this 12-year-old girl tells me she has been raped." Kelly attended to the girl and contacted the school authorities; after she got home, she put her own kids to bed and then was on the phone making a report to protective services until midnight. It was exhausting work but gratifying. "Honestly, before I had kids," she says, "I kind of looked down on stay-at-home moms a little. I thought, *You can't hack it.* It was a prejudice that was wrong. I thought, *Why can't you do it? You must've sucked at your job if you stay home.*"

Kelly's commitment to her career "put a lot more pressure on me to make sure I could pick up the kids and I could feed the kids," says Alvin. "As much as I tried to be really supportive, there were conflicts with schedule, with availability, with resource time. We would get home at 6:30 or 7:00, then we'd have to think about dinner. It's a rush to get the kids to bed. The time either of us had with the kids was short, hectic, stressful. Day to day, managing our schedules—sometimes my meeting would last two hours instead of twenty minutes—it put a lot of strain on our relationship." They got fat on takeout. At bedtime, they talked about "bills, plans, schedules, the next day, everything but spending time together," says Alvin. They never had sex, remembers Kelly. They rarely had any fun at all.

In 2006, British researchers studied work–life conflict in five European countries. They found a lot of strife in France, despite a high percentage of women in the workforce and widespread government policies aimed at helping women remain employed when their children are young: subsidized nursery schools, day-care collectives, and the like. What's more, the French expressed progressive, optimistic ideals about gender roles. Seventy-four percent of full-time employees in France disagreed with the following statement: "A man's job is to earn money, a woman's job is to look after the home and family."

The explanation for the disconnect, the researchers surmised, was that French people, like Americans, lie to themselves about what they want. French women (like their American counterparts) do the bulk of the domestic work, and the majority also work full time. Quoting from colleagues' earlier work, the sociologists showed that sexism in France is as much a part of the culture as great bread, wine, and a long lunch hour. In France, "there were numerous men who were available to look after children during the week when their partner was employed . . . but nevertheless did not take responsibility for child care even when they were free." They were saying one thing and doing another, which in marriage, says the historian Stephanie Coontz, is "a recipe for instability and unhappiness."

That same year, an American sociologist published a paper describing similar results. Predictors of marital unhappiness, found Bradford Wilcox at the University of Virginia, included wives who earned a large share of household income and wives who perceived the division of labor at home as unfair. Predictors of marital happiness were couples who shared a commitment to the institutional idea of marriage and couples who went to religious services together. "Our findings suggest," he wrote, "that increased departures from a male-breadwinning-female-homemaking model may also account for declines in marital quality, insofar as men and women continue to tacitly value gendered patterns of behavior in marriage." It's an idea that thrives especially in conservative religious circles: The things that specific men and women may selfishly want for themselves (sex, money, status, notoriety) must for the good of the family be put aside. Feminists widely critiqued Wilcox's findings, saying it puts the onus on women to suck it up in marriage, when men should be under more pressure to change. But these days you'll find echoes of Wilcox's thesis in unlikely places. "We look at straight people," a gay friend said to me recently as we were comparing anecdotes about husbands, "and we think marriage must be so much easier for them."

When I look at Kelly and Alvin Makino, I feel the same way. I have worked full time for almost all my daughter's nine years, and only very rarely have I ever felt that nature required anything else of me. I love my job and have found work to be gratifying and even calming during periods when other parts of my life are far less so. Like 65 percent of American couples, my husband and I both work to pay our bills, but my commitment to my career extends way beyond financial necessity. My self-sufficiency sets a good example for my daughter (or so we tell ourselves), which is one reason why even if we were to win the lotto, staying at home would not likely be a course I'd choose.

And yet. I am not immune to the notion that I have powers and responsibilities as a mother that my husband does not have. I prepare our daughter's lunch box every morning with ritualistic care, as if sending her off to school with a bologna sandwich made by me can work as an amulet against all the pain of my irregular, inevitable absences. I believe that I have a special gift for arranging playdates, pediatrician appointments, and piano lessons, and I yearn sometimes for the vast swaths of time Kelly Makino has given herself to keep her family's affairs in order. In an egalitarian marriage, every aspect of home life is open to renegotiation. When two people need to leave the house at 6 A.M., who gets the children ready for school? When two people have to work late, who will meet that inflexible daycare pickup time? And who, finally, has the energy for those constant transactions?

Two of the fastest-growing religious movements in America are Mormonism and Orthodox Judaism, which clearly define gender roles along traditional lines. It's difficult not to see the appeal—if only as a fleeting fantasy. How delicious might our weeknight dinners be, how straight the part in our daughter's hair, how much more carefree my marriage, if only I spent a fraction of the time cultivating our domestic landscape that I do at work.

This veneration of motherhood is fed by popular culture. On critically praised TV shows, ambitious women are nutty and single (Claire Danes in *Homeland,* Tina Fey on *30 Rock*), while good mothers are chopping veggies with a big glass of Chardonnay at their elbow. Beyoncé and Marissa Mayer never explain how they do it all, I suspect, because they have teams of nannies and housekeepers on the payroll—and realize that outing themselves as women who rely on servants will taint them, somehow, as bad parents. (Sandberg places this feeling within "the holy trinity of fear: the fear of being a bad mother/wife/daughter.") In my Facebook feed, Michelle Obama is an object of obsession not for the causes she's pursued as First Lady but for her child-rearing tactics: two mandatory sports (one chosen by them and one chosen by her) and no screen time on weeknights. When her husband first ran for president, he delivered speeches proclaiming the heroism of the working mother: "I don't accept an America that makes women choose between their kids and their careers." Four years later, against an opponent whose home life looked like a Disney production, Obama took a sanctity-of-motherhood tack: There is "no tougher job than being a mom."

Even Anne-Marie Slaughter would say that her maternal drive ultimately superseded her professional one, which is why she was unable to achieve more in her huge State Department job. She had a troubled kid at home. Thus the policy solutions she proposes do not dispel the mind-sets that continue to haunt American couples: In a world where men still run things and women still feel drawn to the kitchen and the nursery, an army of flextime females might lock in a second-class tier of workers who will never be able to compete with men for the top jobs. "That's the criticism of my piece that I worry most about," Slaughter says. "If that turns out to be true, I'll have to live with it forever."

Even as she enjoys her new life, Kelly Makino misses certain things about her old one. She misses getting dressed for work in clothes that have buttons and hems and sexy shoes to match. She misses "eating lunch with chopsticks," a euphemism for a universe of cuisine beyond chopped fruit and yogurt cups. She acknowledges the little luxuries of an office: a desk, a quiet cup of coffee, sick days. She misses her work friends—it is vexing trying to find the same hours free—and the validation that bosses and colleagues offer for a job well done. "There is no way my wonderful, loving family can fill that need," she says. In February, a few months after I met the Makinos at their home in New Jersey, they moved to the suburbs of Washington, D.C., for Alvin's job. Out of her element and detached from her old network, she is, for the first time since quitting work, bored.

Kelly loved her old profession and does not want to be painted as betraying the goals of feminism. She prefers to see herself as reaching beyond conventional ideas about what women should do. "I feel like we are evolving into something that is not defined by those who came before us," she says. By making domesticity her career, she and the other stay-at-home mothers she knows are standing up for values, such as patience, and kindness, and respectful attention to the needs of others, that have little currency in the world of work. Professional status is not the only sign of importance, she says, and financial independence is not the only measure of success.

I press her on this point. What if Alvin dies or leaves her? What if, as her children grow up, she finds herself resenting the fact that all the public accolades accrue to her husband? Kelly wrestles with these questions all the time, but for now she's convinced she's chosen the right path. "I know this investment in my family will be paid back when the time is right." When her kids don't need her anymore, she'll figure out what she wants to pursue next. Someday, she's sure, she'll have the chance to "play leapfrog" with Alvin; she'll wind up with a brilliant career, or be a writer, or go back to school. "You have to live in the now. I will deal with later when later comes. I'll find a way," she says. "Who knows? Maybe I will be home for ever and ever. Maybe I will have the best-kept lawn on the block for the rest of my life."

Critical Thinking

1. If a woman is benign in her confrontations, yet assertive, will her husband fully share housework and child care in a dual-career marriage? Why or why not?
2. Why are women more nurturing and men more assertive? Are these traits biological or learned?
3. What attributes foster creativity, energy, and ingenuity in child caregiving?

Create Central

www.mhhe.com/createcentral

Internet References

Genderless Child-Rearing
www.feminagination.com/1365/genderless-childrearing

How Involved Are Fathers in Raising Children?
www.prb.org/Publications/Articles/2000

Is Aggression Genetic?
www.salon.com/2012/05/28/is_aggression_genetic

Is There a Genetic Contribution to Cultural Differences?
http://scan.oxfordjournals.org/content/5/2-3/203.long

Article

Prepared by: Claire N. Rubman, *Suffolk County Community College*

Kids Are Not Adults

Brain research is providing new insights into what drives teenage behavior, moving lawmakers to rethink policies that treat them like adults.

SARAH ALICE BROWN

Learning Outcomes

After reading this article, you will be able to:

- Detail why adolescents differ from adults in their decision-making processes.
- Explain the RECLAIM program.
- Discuss why 19 is a critical age in relation to violence.

Juvenile justice policy is at a crossroads. Juvenile crime has decreased. Recent brain and behavioral science research has revealed new insights into how and when adolescents develop. And state budgets remain tight. Together, these factors have led many lawmakers to focus on which approaches can save money, yet keep the public safe and treat young offenders more effectively.

Why Now?

When youth violence reached a peak more than 20 years ago, the country lost confidence in its ability to rehabilitate juveniles. Legislatures responded by passing laws allowing more young offenders to be tried as adults. Since then, however, juvenile crime has steadily declined.

Between 1994 and 2010, violent crime arrest rates decreased for all age groups, but more for juveniles than for adults. More specifically, the rates dropped an average of 54 percent for teenagers 15 to 17, compared to 38 percent for those between 18 and 39. And while arrest rates for violent crimes were higher in 2010 than in 1980 for all ages over 24, the rates for juveniles ages 15 to 17 were down from 1980.

With the steady decline in juvenile violence, the current state of the economy and new information on how brain development shapes teens' behavior, some lawmakers are reconsidering past assumptions.

Legislatures across the country are working on their juvenile justice policies, from passing individual measures to revamping entire codes. Arkansas revised its juvenile justice code in 2009; Georgia and Kentucky are considering doing so, and many other states are at various stages of making changes in juvenile justice.

"It's time to bring the juvenile code back to current times and find methods that work by looking at best practices nationally," says Georgia Representative Wendell Willard (R), who introduced a bill to revise the code this session. "We need to incorporate key items, such as instruments to assess risks, and put interventions in place within communities for young people involved in the system," says Willard.

Last year, lawmakers in Kentucky formed a task force to study juvenile justice issues. The group will recommend whether to amend any of the state's current juvenile code in 2013. "Frankly, our juvenile code is out of date, but this task force will give the legislature the foundation to change that and reflect best practices nationwide," says Representative John Tilley (D), co-chair of the task force.

Changes are not always easily made, and states are at different stages of reform. Among the various viewpoints and depths of changes, however, is the generally agreed-upon belief that juveniles are different from adults.

For Adults Only

Research distinguishing adolescents from adults has led states to re-establish boundaries between the criminal and juvenile justice systems. New policies reflect the growing body of research on how the brain develops, which has discovered teens' brains do not fully develop until about age 25, according to the John D. & Catherine T. MacArthur Foundation's

Research Network on Adolescent Development and Juvenile Justice. Other social science and behavioral science also shows that kids focus on short-term payoffs rather than long-term consequences of their actions and engage in immature, emotional, risky, aggressive and impulsive behavior, and delinquent acts.

Dr. David Fassler, a psychiatry professor at the University of Vermont College of Medicine, has testified before legislative committees on brain development. He says the research helps explain—not excuse—teenage behavior.

"It doesn't mean adolescents can't make rational decisions or appreciate the difference between right and wrong. But it does mean that, particularly when confronted with stressful or emotional circumstances, they are more likely to act impulsively, on instinct, without fully understanding or considering the consequences of their actions."

"Every single adult has been a teenager, and many have also raised them. We all know firsthand the mistakes teens can make simply without thinking. Now we have the science that backs this up," says North Carolina Representative Marilyn Avila (R). She is working to increase the age at which teenagers can be tried as adults from 16 to 18 in her state.

Other states are considering similar changes. Lawmakers in Colorado passed significant changes in 2012, barring district attorneys from charging juveniles as adults for many low- and mid-level felonies. For serious crimes, they raised the age at which offenders can be tried as adults from 14 to 16.

In Nevada, Mississippi and Utah, lawmakers now leave it up to the juvenile courts to decide whether to transfer a juvenile to adult court. The Oklahoma Legislature upped the age limit at which offenders can be tried as adults for misdemeanors to 18 and one-half. And Ohio now requires a judicial review before transferring anyone under age 21 to an adult jail.

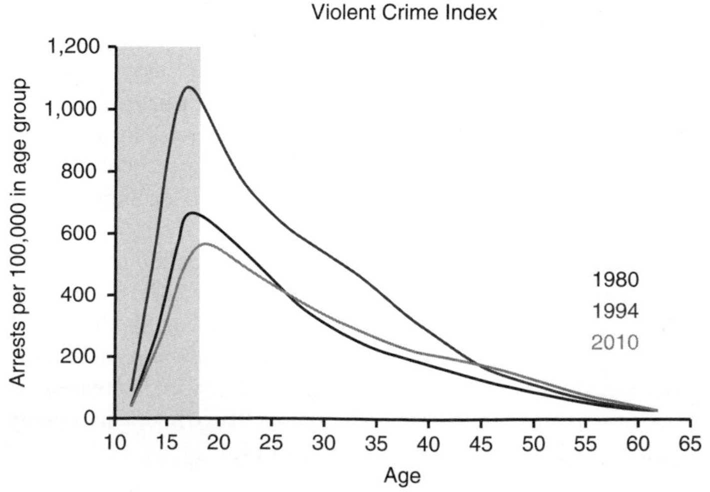

Counsel Is Key

A related trend in the past decade is to increase due process protections to preserve the constitutional rights of young offenders to ensure that youths understand the court process, make reasonable decisions regarding their case, and have adequate counsel. At least 10 states now have laws requiring qualified counsel to accompany juveniles at various stages of youth court proceedings. For juveniles appealing their cases, Utah created an expedited process. And two new laws in Pennsylvania require that all juvenile defendants be represented by counsel and that juvenile court judges state in court the reasoning behind their sentences.

To protect the constitutional rights of young offenders, Massachusetts Senator Karen Spilka (D) says "it is important for states to ensure that juveniles have access to quality counsel." The Bay State created juvenile defense resource centers that provide leadership, training and support to the entire Massachusetts juvenile defense bar.

Legislators are also enacting laws on determining the competency of juvenile offenders to stand trial. At least 16 states—Arizona, California, Colorado, Delaware, Florida, Georgia, Idaho, Kansas, Louisiana, Maine, Michigan, Minnesota, Nebraska, Ohio, Texas, and Virginia—and the District of

Supreme Court Rulings Set Stage

Significant rulings by the U.S. Supreme Court have also reshaped juvenile justice policies. The high court abolished the death penalty for juveniles in 2005 in *Roper v. Simmons,* citing findings by the MacArthur Research Network that adolescents can be less culpable than adults for their crimes.

Its 2010 ruling in *Graham v. Florida* ended life sentences without parole for crimes other than homicide committed by juveniles. Then last summer, in *Miller v. Alabama,* the court ruled that imposing mandatory life sentences without the possibility of parole for juveniles violates the Eighth Amendment of cruel and unusual punishment. Justice Anthony Kennedy wrote that juveniles have less culpability and, as a result, are "less deserving of the most severe punishments."

The Court went on to state in the ruling that life without parole for juveniles is especially harsh because it removes all hope. It makes it so "that good behavior and character improvement are immaterial. When compared with the reality that juveniles are more likely to change than are adults, juveniles who have demonstrated substantial improvement should be given the opportunity for parole."

Columbia, now specifically address competency in statute. For example, Idaho lawmakers established standards for evaluating a juvenile's competency to proceed. Maine passed a similar measure that defines "chronological immaturity," "mental illness," and "mental retardation" for use in determining juvenile competency.

Between 65 percent and 70 percent of the 2 million young people arrested each year in the United States have some type of mental health disorder. Newer policies focus on providing more effective evaluations and interventions for youths who come into contact with the juvenile justice system. This includes proper screening, assessment, and treatment services for young offenders. Some states have special mental health courts to provide intensive case management as well.

New mental health assessments in Louisiana and Pennsylvania give a wide range of professionals the means to reliably ascertain youths' needs. And other states such as Colorado, Connecticut, Ohio, and Texas have passed comprehensive juvenile mental health reform laws.

Family Matters

"Show me it will work, and then I am all for it!" says North Carolina's Avila. "As a legislator, I am very much in favor of evidence-based programming, because I want to invest in what will work." She cites the effectiveness of three kinds of programs that have passed the evaluation test and are being used in at least 10 states. They include the families in the treatments young offenders receive to address specific behaviors to improve positive results for the whole family.

- Multi-systemic therapy teaches parents how to effectively handle the high-risk "acting out" behaviors of teenagers.
- Family functional therapy focuses on teaching communication and problem-solving skills to the whole family.
- Aggression-replacement training teaches positive ways to express anger as well as anger control and moral reasoning.

Massachusetts Senator Spilka believes these kinds of programs are important because "instead of simply focusing on the child's behavior, they look to effectively treat and help the entire family."

Communities Are Key

Policymakers across the country are searching for ways to keep the public safe while reducing costs. Many are looking at effective policies that divert young offenders away from expensive, secure correctional facilities and into local community programs. According to the U.S. Office of Juvenile Justice and Delinquency Prevention, incarceration is a costly and ineffective way to keep delinquent juveniles from committing more serious crimes. Researchers suggest, instead, in investing in successful and cost-effective programs that have undergone rigorous evaluations.

For example, RECLAIM Ohio is a national model for funding reform that channels the money saved from fewer juvenile commitments into local courts to be used in treating and rehabilitating young people. The program not only has reduced juvenile commitments to detention facilities and saved money, but also has cut down on the number of young people re-entering the justice system. The cost of housing 10 young people in a Department of Youth Services' facility is $571,940 a year versus $85,390 a year for RECLAIM Ohio programs.

Realignment shifts responsibility for managing young offenders from states to the counties. Such strategies are based on the premise that local communities are in the best position to provide extensive and cost-effective supervision and treatment services for juvenile offenders, and that youth are more successful when supervised and treated closer to their homes and families.

Illinois lawmakers, for example, passed major changes in 2004 that created Redeploy Illinois, which encourages counties to develop community programs for juveniles rather than confine them in state correctional facilities.

The program gives counties financial support to provide comprehensive services in their home communities to delinquent youths who might otherwise be sent to the Illinois Department of Juvenile Justice. The program has been so successful that it is expanding statewide and has become a model for other states.

Several other states, from California and Georgia, to New York and Texas, are also looking at ways to effectively and safely redirect fiscal resources from state institutions to community services.

"Getting kids out of the correctional centers and treated in the community is obviously the best practice," says Georgia's Willard. "You have to close these large infrastructures and the overhead that goes with it, so you can redirect that money to treating youth in the community. When you go about such an exercise in your own communities, you will accomplish the goal of saving money."

States also are shortening the time juveniles are confined in detention centers, usually while they wait for a court appearance or disposition. A recent Mississippi law, for example, limits it to 10 days for first-time nonviolent youth offenders. And Georgia decreased it from 60 to 30 days. Illinois lawmakers increased the age of kids who can be detained for more than 6 hours in a county jail or municipal lockup from age 12 to 17.

Texas Moves Away from Youth Detention

Texas lawmakers responded quickly to reports of physical and sexual abuse by staff at juvenile detention facilities in 2006. During the following session, the Legislature passed laws to address these incidents and improve the overall administration of juvenile justice. The changes included creating the Independent Ombudsman's office to investigate and review allegations of misconduct, monitoring detention facilities with cameras and on-site officials, and barring juveniles from serving time in detention facilities for committing misdemeanors.

Legislators continued to focus on juvenile justice during the next two sessions, passing laws in 2009 that strengthened support and funding for local and county programs that monitor juveniles closer to their homes. And in 2011, to consolidate oversight of young offenders and improve communication among different levels of government, lawmakers merged the Probation Commission, and the Youth Commission to create the Texas Juvenile Justice Department.

The laws appear to be making a difference. The number of juveniles in state-run detention facilities dropped from nearly 5,000 in 2006 to around 1,200 in 2012, with more participating in county and local programs. The state has closed nine facilities and may close more during the coming biennium. In addition, verified complaints of abuse dropped 69.5 percent from 2008 to 2011.

Challenges with safety within facilities, however, persist. Early in 2012, the Independent Ombudsman reported incidents of youth-on-youth violence in the state's largest remaining detention facility. Executive Director Mike Griffiths, on the job since September 2012, believes that "there needs to be a foundation of safety and security to be effective. We are light years ahead of where we were in 2007, and the success of the community-based programs is encouraging, but safety needs to be a continued focus." Subsequent reports indicate improvements in the culture of the facilities.

One way Texas is tackling violence in its facilities is by placing the most challenging juveniles in The Phoenix Program, which focuses on preventing high-risk youth from becoming reoffenders. It holds the kids in the program "accountable for the actions of each individual, and provides a staffing ratio of one to four, as opposed to the regular one to 12," says Griffiths.

Texas continues to work on improving its juvenile justice system. "My challenge moving forward is to find additional dollars for local community programs, while making sure the overall system is secure," says Griffiths. "It's important to give the staff the support they need, while letting them know that they are accountable."

—Richard Williams, NCSL

Young Offenders Grow Up

Violence toward others tends to peak in adolescence, beginning most often around age 16, according to Emory University psychiatrist Peter Ash. However, if a teenager hasn't committed a violent crime by age 19, he's unlikely to become violent later, Ash says. The promising news is that 66 to 75 percent of violent young people grow out of it. "They get more self-controlled."

Realizing that teens who commit delinquent acts don't always turn into adult criminals, more states are protecting the confidentiality of juvenile records for future educational and employment opportunities to help them make successful transitions into adulthood.

In 2011, Delaware lawmakers passed legislation allowing juvenile criminal cases that are dismissed, acquitted or not prosecuted to be expunged from a young person's record. "Children who are charged with minor crimes that are dismissed or dropped should not have these charges following them around for the rest of their lives," says Representative Michael A. Barbieri (D), sponsor of the bill.

And in 2012, eight states—California, Colorado, Hawaii, Louisiana, Ohio, Oregon, Vermont, and Washington—enacted laws vacating or expunging any prostitution charges juvenile victims of sex trafficking may have received.

A Bipartisan Issue

These recent legislative trends reflect a new understanding of adolescent development. Investing in alternative programs in the community instead of incarceration and adopting only proven intervention programs are among the examples of how state legislators hope to better serve youth and prevent juvenile crime.

"Reforming juvenile justice is definitely a bipartisan issue that all legislators can get behind. It is the right time. All the research says it makes sense and will save money," says Representative Avila from North Carolina.

Critical Thinking

1. Should the adolescent judicial system differ from the adult system? If adolescents under the age of 25 act on the bases of short-term consequences, then should we offer short-term punishments for them rather than adult sentences?
2. If the adolescent brain is still growing, how can we protect our adolescent population and prevent them from committing serious crimes?
3. Why don't all adolescents commit crimes—is there a profile?

Create Central

www.mhhe.com/createcentral

Internet References

aspe.hhs.gov What Challenges Are Boys Facing, and What Opportunities Exist To Address Those Challenges? Fact Sheet

http://aspe.hhs.gov/hsp/08/boys/factsheets/jd/report.pdf

multiplying connections.org The Amazing Adolescent Brain: What Every Educator, Youth Serving Professional, and Healthcare Provider Needs to Know

http://www.multiplyingconnections.org/sites/default/files/Teen%20Provider%20article%20(2)_0.pdf

news.discovery.com The Teen Brain on Rage: How It's Different

http://news.discovery.com/human/teen-brain-rage-violence-120229.htm

NJJN.org National Juvenile Justice Network

http://www.njjn.org/library/search-results?subject=7

Yale.edu Juvenile Delinquency Cause and Effect

http://www.yale.edu/ynhti/curriculum/units/2000/2/00.02.05.x.html

Brown, Sarah Alice. "Kids Are Not Adults." *Juvenile Justice Bulletin* 39. 4 (April, 2013): 20–23.

Article

Prepared by: Claire N. Rubman, *Suffolk County Community College*

All Joy and No Fun

Why Parents Hate Parenting

JENNIFER SENIOR

Learning Outcomes

After reading this article, you will be able to:

- Explain why children tend to reduce marital happiness.
- Summarize the reasons that money does not make parenting easier.

There was a day a few weeks ago when I found my 2½-year-old son sitting on our building doorstep, waiting for me to come home. He spotted me as I was rounding the corner, and the scene that followed was one of inexpressible loveliness, right out of the movie I'd played to myself before actually having a child, with him popping out of his babysitter's arms and barreling down the street to greet me. This happy moment, though, was about to be cut short, and in retrospect felt more like a tranquil lull in a slasher film. When I opened our apartment door, I discovered that my son had broken part of the wooden parking garage I'd spent about an hour assembling that morning. This wouldn't have been a problem per se, except that as I attempted to fix it, he grew impatient and began throwing its various parts at the walls, with one plank very narrowly missing my eye. I recited the rules of the house (no throwing, no hitting). He picked up another large wooden plank. I ducked. He reached for the screwdriver. The scene ended with a time-out in his crib.

As I shuffled back to the living room, I thought of something a friend once said about the Children's Museum of Manhattan—"a nice place, but what it *really* needs is a bar"—and rued how, at that moment, the same thing could be said of my apartment. Two hundred and 40 seconds earlier, I'd been in a state of pair-bonded bliss; now I was guided by nerves, trawling the cabinets for alcohol. My emotional life looks a lot like this these days. I suspect it does for many parents—a high-amplitude, high-frequency sine curve along which we get the privilege of doing hourly surfs. Yet it's something most of us choose. Indeed, it's something most of us would say we'd be miserable without.

From the perspective of the species, it's perfectly unmysterious why people have children. From the perspective of the individual, however, it's more of a mystery than one might think. Most people assume that having children will make them happier. Yet a wide variety of academic research shows that parents are not happier than their childless peers, and in many cases are less so. This finding is surprisingly consistent, showing up across a range of disciplines. Perhaps the most oft-cited datum comes from a 2004 study by Daniel Kahneman, a Nobel Prize–winning behavioral economist, who surveyed 909 working Texas women and found that child care ranked sixteenth in pleasurability out of nineteen activities. (Among the endeavors they preferred: preparing food, watching TV, exercising, talking on the phone, napping, shopping, *housework.*) This result also shows up regularly in relationship research, with children invariably reducing marital satisfaction. The economist Andrew Oswald, who's compared tens of thousands of Britons with children to those without, is at least inclined to view his data in a more positive light: "The broad message is not that children make you less happy; it's just that children don't make you *more* happy." That is, he tells me, unless you have more than one. "Then the studies show a more negative impact." As a rule, most studies show that mothers are less happy than fathers, that single parents are less happy still, that babies and toddlers are the hardest, and that each successive child produces diminishing returns. But some of the studies are grimmer than others. Robin Simon, a sociologist at Wake Forest University, says parents are more depressed than nonparents no matter what their circumstances—whether they're single or married, whether they have one child or four.

Mothers are less happy than fathers, single parents are less happy still.

The idea that parents are less happy than nonparents has become so commonplace in academia that it was big news last year when the *Journal of Happiness Studies* published a Scottish paper declaring the opposite was true. "Contrary to much of the literature," said the introduction, "our results are consistent with an effect of children on life satisfaction that is positive, large and increasing in the number of children." Alas, the euphoria was short-lived. A few months later, the poor author discovered a coding error in his data, and the publication ran an erratum. "After correcting the problem," it read, "the main results of the paper no longer hold. The effect of children on the life satisfaction of married individuals is small, often negative, and never statistically significant."

Yet one can see why people were rooting for that paper. The results of almost all the others violate a parent's deepest intuition. Daniel Gilbert, the Harvard psychologist and host of *This Emotional Life* on PBS, wrote fewer than three pages about compromised parental well-being in *Stumbling on Happiness.* But whenever he goes on the lecture circuit, skeptical questions about those pages come up more frequently than anything else. "I've never met anyone who didn't argue with me about this," he says. "Even people who believe the data say they feel sorry for those for whom it's true."

So what, precisely, is going on here? Why is this finding duplicated over and over again despite the fact that most parents believe it to be wrong?

One answer could simply be that parents are deluded, in the grip of some false consciousness that's good for mankind but not for men and women in particular. Gilbert, a proud father and grandfather, would argue as much. He's made a name for himself showing that we humans are pretty sorry predictors of what will make us happy, and to his mind, the yearning for children, the literal mother of all aspirations for so many, is a very good case in point—what children *really* do, he suspects, is offer moments of transcendence, not an overall improvement in well-being.

Perhaps. But there are less fatalistic explanations, too. And high among them is the possibility that parents don't much enjoy parenting because the experience of raising children has fundamentally changed.

"I'm going to count to three."

It's a weekday evening, and the mother in this videotape, a trim brunette with her hair in a bun and glasses propped up on her head, has already worked a full day and made dinner. Now she is approaching her 8-year-old son, the oldest of two, who's seated at the computer in the den, absorbed in a movie. At issue is his homework, which he still hasn't done.

"One. Two . . ."

This clip is from a study conducted by UCLA's Center on Everyday Lives of Families, which earned a front-page story in the Sunday *Times* this May and generated plenty of discussion among parents. In it, researchers collected 1,540 hours of footage of 32 middle-class, dual-earner families with at least two children, all of them going about their regular business in their Los Angeles homes. The intention of this study was in no way to make the case that parents were unhappy. But one of the postdoctoral fellows who worked on it, himself a father of two, nevertheless described the video data to the *Times* as "the very purest form of birth control ever devised. Ever."

"I have to get it to the part and then pause it," says the boy.

"No," says his mother. "You do that *after* you do your homework."

Tamar Kremer-Sadlik, the director of research in this study, has watched this scene many times. The reason she believes it's so powerful is because it shows how painfully parents experience the pressure of making their children do their schoolwork. They seem to feel this pressure even more acutely than their children feel it themselves.

The boy starts to shout. "It's not going to take that long!"

His mother stops the movie. "I'm telling you no," she says. "You're not hearing me. I will *not* let you watch this now."

He starts up the movie again.

"No," she repeats, her voice rising. She places her hand firmly under her son's arm and starts to yank. "I *will not* have this—"

Before urbanization, children were viewed as economic assets to their parents. If you had a farm, they toiled alongside you to maintain its upkeep; if you had a family business, the kids helped mind the store. But all of this dramatically changed with the moral and technological revolutions of modernity. As we gained in prosperity, childhood came increasingly to be viewed as a protected, privileged time, and once college degrees became essential to getting ahead, children became not only a great expense but subjects to be sculpted, stimulated, instructed, groomed. (The Princeton sociologist Viviana Zelizer describes this transformation of a child's value in five ruthless words: "Economically worthless but emotionally priceless.") Kids, in short, went from being our staffs to being our bosses.

"Did you see *Babies*?" asks Lois Nachamie, a couples counselor who for years has run parenting workshops and support groups on the Upper West Side. She's referring to the recent documentary that compares the lives of four newborns—one in Japan, one in Namibia, one in Mongolia, and one in the United States (San Francisco). "I don't mean to idealize the lives of the Namibian women," she says. "But it was hard not to notice how *calm* they were. They were beading their children's ankles and decorating them with sienna, clearly enjoying just sitting and playing with them, and we're here often thinking of all of this stuff as labor."

This is especially true in middle- and upper-income families, which are far more apt than their working-class counterparts to see their children as projects to be perfected. (Children of women with bachelor degrees spend almost five hours on "organized activities" per week, as opposed to children of high-school dropouts, who spend two.) Annette Lareau, the sociologist who coined the term "concerted cultivation" to describe the aggressive nurturing of economically advantaged children, puts it this way: "Middle-class parents spend much more time talking to children, answering questions with questions, and treating each child's thought as a special contribution. And this is very tiring *work*." Yet it's work few parents feel that they can in good conscience neglect, says Lareau, "lest they put their children at risk by not giving them every advantage."

But the intensification of family time is not confined to the privileged classes alone. According to *Changing Rhythms of American Family Life*—a compendium of data about time use and family statistics, compiled by a trio of sociologists named Suzanne M. Bianchi, John P. Robinson, and Melissa A. Milkie—*all* parents spend more time today with their children than they did in 1975, including mothers, in spite of the great rush of women into the American workforce. Today's married mothers also have less leisure time (5.4 fewer hours per week); 71 percent say they crave more time for themselves (as do 57 percent of married fathers). Yet 85 percent of all parents still—still!—think they don't spend enough time with their children.

These self-contradictory statistics reminded me of a conversation I had with a woman who had been in one of Nachamie's parenting groups, a professional who had her children later in life. "I have two really great kids"—ages 9 and 11—"and I enjoy doing a lot of things with them," she told me. "It's the drudgery that's so hard: *Crap, you don't have any pants that fit?* There are just So. Many. Chores." This woman, it should be said, is divorced. But even if her responsibilities were shared with a partner, the churn of school and gymnastics and piano and sports and homework would still require an awful lot of administration. "The crazy thing," she continues, "is that by New York standards, I'm not even overscheduling them."

I ask what she does on the weekends her ex-husband has custody. "I work," she replies. "And get my nails done."

A few generations ago, people weren't stopping to contemplate whether having a child would make them happy. Having children was simply what you did. And we are lucky, today, to have choices about these matters. But the abundance of choices—whether to have kids, when, how many—may be one of the reasons parents are less happy.

That was at least partly the conclusion of psychologists W. Keith Campbell and Jean Twenge, who, in 2003, did a meta-analysis of 97 children-and-marital-satisfaction studies stretching back to the seventies. Not only did they find that couples' overall marital satisfaction went down if they had kids; they found that every successive generation was more put out by having them than the last—our current one most of all. Even more surprisingly, they found that parents' dissatisfaction only grew the more money they had, even though they had the purchasing power to buy more child care. "And my hypothesis about why this is, in both cases, is the same," says Twenge. "They become parents later in life. There's a loss of freedom, a loss of autonomy. It's totally different from going from your parents' house to immediately having a baby. Now you know what you're giving up." (Or, as a fellow psychologist told Gilbert when he finally got around to having a child: "They're a huge source of joy, but they turn every other source of joy to shit.")

Studies have found that parents' dissatisfaction only grew the more money they had, even though they could buy more child care.

It wouldn't be a particularly bold inference to say that the longer we put off having kids, the greater our expectations. "There's all this buildup—as soon as I get this done, I'm going to have a baby, and it's going to be a great reward!" says Ada Calhoun, the author of *Instinctive Parenting* and founding editor-in-chief of Babble, the online parenting site. "And then you're like, 'Wait, *this* is my reward? This nineteen-year grind?'"

When people wait to have children, they're also bringing different sensibilities to the enterprise. They've spent their adult lives as professionals, believing there's a right way and a wrong way of doing things; now they're applying the same logic to the family-expansion business, and they're surrounded by a marketplace that only affirms and reinforces this idea. "And what's confusing about that," says Alex Barzvi, a professor of child and adolescent psychiatry at NYU medical school, "is that there *are* a lot of things that parents can do to nurture social and cognitive development. There *are* right and wrong ways to discipline a child. But you can't fall into the trap of comparing yourself to others and constantly concluding you're doing the wrong thing."

Yet that's precisely what modern parents do. "It was especially bad in the beginning," said a woman who recently attended a parents' group led by Barzvi at the 92nd Street Y. "When I'd hear other moms saying, 'Oh, so-and-so sleeps for twelve hours and naps for three,' I'd think, *Oh, shit, I screwed up the sleep training.*" Her parents—immigrants from huge families—couldn't exactly relate to her distress. "They had no academic reference books for *sleeping,*" she says. (She's read three.) "To my parents, it is what it is."

So how do they explain your anguish? I ask.

"They just think that Americans are a little too complicated about everything."

One hates to invoke Scandinavia in stories about child-rearing, but it can't be an accident that the one superbly designed study that said, unambiguously, that having kids makes you happier was done with Danish subjects. The researcher, Hans-Peter Kohler, a sociology professor at the University of Pennsylvania, says he originally studied this question because he was intrigued by the declining fertility rates in Europe. One of the things he noticed is that countries with stronger welfare systems produce more children—and happier parents.

Of course, this should not be a surprise. If you are no longer fretting about spending too little time with your children after they're born (because you have a year of paid maternity leave), if you're no longer anxious about finding affordable child care once you go back to work (because the state subsidizes it), if you're no longer wondering how to pay for your children's education and health care (because they're free)—well, it stands to reason that your own mental health would improve. When Kahneman and his colleagues did another version of his survey of working women, this time comparing those in Columbus, Ohio, to those in Rennes, France, the French sample enjoyed child care a good deal more than its American counterpart. "We've put all this energy into being perfect parents," says Judith Warner, author of *Perfect Madness: Motherhood in the Age of Anxiety,* "instead of political change that would make family life better."

MOMS: Ever feel alone in how you perceive this role? I swear I feel like I'm surrounded by women who were once smart & interesting but have become zombies who only talk about soccer and coupons.

This was an opening gambit on UrbanBaby this past April. It could have devolved into a sanctimommy pile-on. It didn't.

I totally feel this way.

I am a f/t wohm—Work Outside the Home Mom—*have a career, and I don't feel smart or interesting anymore! I don't talk about soccer or coupons, but just feel too tired to talk about anything that interesting.*

I freely admit that I have gained "more" than I have lost by becoming a parent, but I still miss aspects of my old life.

More generous government policies, a sounder economy, a less pressured culture that values good rather than perfect kids—all of these would certainly make parents happier. But even under the most favorable circumstances, parenting is an extraordinary activity, in both senses of the word *extra:* beyond ordinary and *especially* ordinary. While children deepen your emotional life, they shrink your outer world to the size of a teacup, at least for a while. ("All joy and no fun," as an old friend with two young kids likes to say.) Lori Leibovich, the executive editor of Babble and the anthology *Maybe Baby,* a collection of 28 essays by writers debating whether to have children, says she was particularly struck by the female contributors who'd made the deliberate choice to remain childless. It enabled them to travel or live abroad for their work; to take physical risks; to, in the case of a novelist, inhabit her fictional characters without being pulled away by the demands of a real one. "There was a richness and texture to their work lives that was so, so enviable," she says. (Leibovich has two children.)

Fathers, it turns out, feel like they've made some serious compromises too, though of a different sort. They feel like they don't see their kids *enough.* "In our studies, it's the men, by a long shot, who have more work–life conflict than women," says Ellen Galinsky, president of the Families and Work Institute. "They don't want to be stick figures in their children's lives."

And couples probably pay the dearest price of all. Healthy relationships definitely make people happier. But children adversely affect relationships. As Thomas Bradbury, a father of two and professor of psychology at UCLA, likes to say: "Being in a good relationship is a risk factor for becoming a parent." He directs me to one of the more inspired studies in the field, by psychologists Lauren Papp and E. Mark Cummings. They asked 100 long-married couples to spend two weeks meticulously documenting their disagreements. Nearly 40 percent of them were about their kids.

"And that 40 percent is merely the number that was explicitly about kids, I'm guessing, right?" This is a former patient of Nachamie's, an entrepreneur and father of two. "How many other arguments were those couples having because everyone was on a short fuse, or tired, or stressed out?" This man is very frank about the strain his children put on his marriage, especially his firstborn. "I already felt neglected," he says. "In my mind, anyway. And once we had the kid, it became so pronounced; it went from zero to negative 50. And I was like, *I can deal with zero. But not negative 50.*"

This is the brutal reality about children—they're such powerful stressors that small perforations in relationships can turn into deep fault lines. "And my wife became more demanding," he continues. "'You don't do this, you don't do that.' There was this idea we had about how things were supposed to be: *The family should be dot dot dot, the man should be dot dot dot the woman should be dot dot dot.*"

This is another brutal reality about children: They expose the gulf between our fantasies about family and its spikier realities.

They also mean parting with an old way of life, one with more freewheeling rhythms and richer opportunities for romance. "There's nothing sexy or intimate between us, based on the old model," he says. "The new model, which I've certainly come to adopt, is that our energy has shifted toward the kids. One of the reasons I love being with my wife is because I love the family we have."

Most studies show that marriages improve once children enter latency, or the ages between 6 and 12, though they take another sharp dive during the war zone of adolescence. (As a friend with grown children once told me: "Teenagers can be casually brutal.") But one of the most sobering declines documented in *Changing Rhythms of American Family Life* is the amount of time married parents spend alone together each week: Nine hours today versus twelve in 1975. Bradbury, who was involved in the UCLA study of those 32 families, says the husbands and wives spent less than 10 percent of their home time alone together. "And do you think they were saying, "Gee honey, you look lovely. I just wanted to pick up on that fascinating conversation we were having earlier about the Obama administration'?" he asks. "Nope. They were exhausted and staring at the television."

"I'm not watching it," insists the boy. We're back to the videotape now, and that den in Los Angeles. Mother and son are still arguing—tensely, angrily—and she's still pulling on his arm. The boy reaches for the keyboard. "I'm putting it on pause!"

"I want you to do your homework," his mother repeats. "You are not—"

"I know," the son whines. "I'm going to pause it!"

His mother's not buying it. What she sees is him stalling. She pulls him off the chair.

"No, you're *not,*" says his mother. "You're still not listening!"

"Yes I am!"

"No, you're not!"

Children may provide unrivaled moments of joy. But they also provide unrivaled moments of frustration, tedium, anxiety, heartbreak. This scene, which isn't even all that awful or uncommon, makes it perfectly clear why parenting may be regarded as less fun than having dinner with friends or baking a cake. Loving one's children and loving the act of parenting are not the same thing.

Yet that's where things get tricky. Obviously, this clip shows how difficult and unpleasant parenting can be. What it doesn't show is the love this mother feels for her son, which we can pretty much bet has no equal. Nor does it convey that this unpleasant task she's undertaking is part of a larger project, one that pays off in subtler dividends than simply having fun. Kremer-Sadlik says that she and her fellow researchers were highly conscious of these missing pieces when they gathered each week to discuss their data collection. "We'd all remember the negative things," she says. "Whereas everything else was between the lines. So it became our moral dilemma: How can we talk about the good moments?" She pauses, and then asks the question that, to a parent (she herself has two children), is probably most relevant of all: "And why were the good moments so elusive?"

The answer to that may hinge on how we define "good." Or more to the point, "happy." Is happiness something you *experience*? Or is it something you *think*?

When Kahneman surveyed those Texas women, he was measuring moment-to-moment happiness. It was a feeling, a mood, a state. The technique he pioneered for measuring it—the Daily Reconstruction Method—was designed to make people reexperience their feelings over the course of a day. Oswald, when looking at British households, was looking at a condensed version of the General Health Questionnaire, which is best described as a basic gauge of mood: *Have you recently felt you could not overcome your difficulties? Felt constantly under strain? Lost much sleep over worry?* (What parent hasn't answered, yes, yes, and God yes to these questions?) As a matter of mood, there does seem to be little question that kids make our lives more stressful.

But when studies take into consideration how *rewarding* parenting is, the outcomes tend to be different. Last year, Mathew P. White and Paul Dolan, professors at the University of Plymouth and Imperial College, London, respectively, designed a study that tried to untangle these two different ideas. They asked participants to rate their daily activities both in terms of pleasure and in terms of reward, then plotted the results on a four-quadrant graph. What emerged was a much more commonsense map of our feelings. In the quadrant of things people found both pleasurable *and* rewarding, people chose volunteering first, prayer second, and time with children third (though time with children barely made it into the "pleasurable" category). Work was the most rewarding not-so-pleasurable activity. Everyone thought commuting was both unrewarding and unfun. And watching television was considered one of the most pleasurable unrewarding activities, as was eating, though the least rewarding of all was plain old "relaxing." (Which probably says something about the abiding power of the Protestant work ethic.)

Seven years ago, the sociologists Kei Nomaguchi and Melissa A. Milkie did a study in which they followed couples for five to seven years, some of whom had children and some of whom did not. And what they found was that, yes, those couples who became parents did more housework and felt less in control and quarreled more (actually, only the women thought they quarreled more, but anyway). On the other hand, the married women were *less depressed* after they'd had kids than their childless peers. And perhaps this is because the study sought to understand not just the moment-to-moment moods of its participants, but more existential matters, like how connected they felt, and how motivated, and how much despair they were in (as opposed to how much stress they were under): *Do you not feel like eating? Do you feel like you can't shake the blues? Do you feel lonely? Like you can't get going?* Parents, who live in a clamorous, perpetual-forward-motion machine almost all of the time, seemed to have different answers than their childless cohorts.

The authors also found that the most depressed people were single fathers, and Milkie speculates that perhaps it's because they wanted to be involved in their children's lives but weren't. Robin Simon finds something similar: The least depressed parents are those whose underage children are in the house, and the most are those whose aren't.

This finding seems significant. Technically, if parenting makes you unhappy, you should feel *better* if you're spared the task of doing it. But if happiness is measured by our own sense of agency and meaning, then noncustodial parents lose. They're robbed of something that gives purpose and reward.

When I mention this to Daniel Gilbert, he hardly disputes that meaning is important. But he does wonder how prominently it should figure into people's decisions to have kids. "When you pause to *think* what children mean to you, of course they make you feel good," he says. "The problem is, 95 percent of the time, you're not thinking about what they mean to you. You're thinking that you have to take them to piano lessons. So you have to think about which kind of happiness you'll be consuming most often. Do you want to maximize the one you experience almost all the time"—moment-to-moment happiness—"or the one you experience rarely?"

Which is fair enough. But for many of us, purpose *is* happiness—particularly those of us who find moment-to-moment happiness a bit elusive to begin with. Martin Seligman, the positive-psychology pioneer who is, famously, not a natural optimist, has always taken the view that happiness is best defined in the ancient Greek sense: leading a productive, purposeful life. And the way we take stock of that life, in the end, isn't by how much fun we had, but what we did with it. (Seligman has seven children.)

About twenty years ago, Tom Gilovich, a psychologist at Cornell, made a striking contribution to the field of psychology, showing that people are far more apt to regret things they *haven't* done than things they have. In one instance, he followed up on the men and women from the Terman study, the famous collection of high-IQ students from California who were singled out in 1921 for a life of greatness. Not one told him of regretting having children, but ten told him they regretted not having a family.

"I think this boils down to a philosophical question, rather than a psychological one," says Gilovich. "Should you value moment-to-moment happiness more than retrospective evaluations of your life?" He says he has no answer for this, but the example he offers suggests a bias. He recalls watching TV with his children at three in the morning when they were sick. "I wouldn't have said it was too fun at the time," he says. "But now I look back on it and say, 'Ah, remember the time we used to wake up and watch cartoons?'" The very things that in the moment dampen our moods can later be sources of intense gratification, nostalgia, delight.

It's a lovely magic trick of the memory, this gilding of hard times. Perhaps it's just the necessary alchemy we need to keep the species going. But for parents, this sleight of the mind and spell on the heart is the very definition of enchantment.

Critical Thinking

1. Recognize that love for children and dislike of child care can co-exist.
2. Identify several factors that make child care an emotional roller coaster.
3. Report which of the following make parenting easier: money, age of parent, age of children, being single, knowledge of child development.

Create Central

www.mhhe.com/createcentral

Internet References

Does Having Children Make You Unhappy?
http://parenting.blogs.nytimes/2009/04/01/why-does-anyone

How to Raise a Happy Child
www.babycenter.co/0_how-to-raise-a-happy-child

Marital Satisfaction When Raising Teenagers
http://technorati.com/women/article/marital-satisfaction

Parents Who Hate Parenting: The Latest Trend?
http://shine.yahoo.com/parenting

Article Prepared by: Claire N. Rubman, *Suffolk County Community College*

High-Tech Bullies

Suicides have made administrators aware that acts of aggression in the wireless, viral world of the Internet demand action to protect targeted students.

INGRID STURGIS

Learning Outcomes

After reading this article, you will be able to:

- Identify the most vulnerable members of our society who are most prone to bullying.
- Describe what colleges and universities are doing to combat cyberbullying.

Cases of cyberbullying have made headlines over the past decade, raising awareness about the number of young people who have committed suicide or otherwise been harmed as a result of being on the receiving end of constant Internet harassment or shaming.

Bullying that started in email and chat rooms in the early days of the Internet has evolved into other forms—mostly social networking sites and instant messaging, as well as video and pictures, Justin W. Patchin, PhD, co-director of the Cyberbullying Research Center at the University of Wisconsin-Eau Claire, agrees.

"It's constantly changing," he said. "The bullies are pretty creative. Now there is a level of permanence that is not evident in traditional bullying. Early adopters are most likely to use new technology. It's amazing how creative some can be to cause harm."

Patchin, author of *Words Wound: Delete Cyberbullying and Make Kindness Go Viral* (Free Spirit Publishing, December 2013), has been studying cyberbullying among secondary students for more than a decade, starting in 2001. He has surveyed nearly 15,000 students across the United States.

Most cases seem to involve middle school or high school students, whom experts say, are in the primary age group for such behavior.

However, as social media continues its pervasive intrusion into everyday lives, cyberbullying is trickling up to college campuses and even into the workplace. Researchers, law-enforcement lawyers, college officials, and students say there are more reported incidents of acts of cyberbullying cropping up on campus and a rise in incidents of teenage suicide has coincided with the rise in incidents of cyberbullying. In fact, the suicide of Rutgers University freshman Tyler Clementi in 2010, who was the target of a campaign of intimidation by his roommate, put universities on notice that what might have once been treated as a college prank could lead to suicide for vulnerable students. Clementi jumped off the George Washington Bridge after learning that his roommate spied on him during a romantic encounter with a man using a webcam. Clementi also learned that his roommate conspired to "out" him by alerting Twitter followers to a second viewing.

Attacking the Vulnerable

Cyberbullies often target gays, women or people of color. Students who are different in some way (race, ethnicity, sexual orientation, religion, or appearance) or high-profile students (athletes, student government officers) are often the most vulnerable.

Jiyoon Yoon, associate professor and director of the elementary education program at University of Texas at Arlington, said via email that while nearly anyone can be a victim, most victims are targeted because of perceived differences from a group and weaknesses.

"Students who do not fit in may become the prime targets of cyberbullying," she said. "In many contexts, students of minority status and/or lower economic privilege may be more susceptible to the abuse."

Yoon said victims of such bullying are more likely to report feelings of depression than other groups of students, which interfere with their scholastic achievement, social skills, and sense of well-being. She has conducted research with Dr. Julie Smith on cyberbullying among college students and says it is increasing. According to survey responses conducted by Yoon and Smith within a Midwestern university system, 10.1 percent of the students said they experienced cyberbullying by another student; 2.9 percent of the students had been cyberbullied by instructors, and 27.5 percent of the students witnessed cyberbullying behavior by a student toward another student.

This is consistent with other studies on cyberbullying. In one study conducted at Indiana State University, 22 percent of college students reported being cyberbullied, and 9 percent reported cyberbullying someone.

"People thought cyberbullying happened mostly among teenagers who are familiar with and willingly use electronic technology," Yoon said. "However, as portability and accessibility of technology for distance learning increases daily in higher education, incidents of cyberbullying are rising on college campuses."

Dawn Harner, a training coordinator and counselor at Salisbury University, said a potent mix of 24/7, always-on communication lends itself to abuses. She cited the pervasive use of connected mobile devices, multiple social media profiles from Facebook to Twitter to Instagram, growth in text messaging and decline in phone conversations, the illusion of anonymity and the international reach of the Internet, coupled with students' immaturity and newly found freedom.

"It is much more common for students to be connected to social media," Harner said. "Now, as opposed to seven years ago, phones connect to Internet as well."

Researchers are just starting to examine the rise in university-level bullying. Today, universities are obligated to face the problem before another student is hurt. First, they must define cyberbullying.

"A lot of times as academics, we debate definitions," said Patchin. "What's the difference between hazing, bullying and harassing? All could be the same behaviors. We don't focus on it until something happens. We have to focus on behaviors that repeatedly cause harm to another person." Although definitions vary, cyberbullying can be defined as acts of aggression and subterfuge against someone that gain power through digital technology.

The problems can range from the use of gossip sites like JuicyCampus, College Anonymous Confessions Board or College Wall of Shame to "revenge porn sites," in which former lovers upload photos of ex-girl friends and to stalking by emails and text messages. Some of the most popular vehicles for cyberbullying, said Yoon, are Facebook texting, email, Twitter, and YouTube. Other technologies or applications and online gaming technologies, such as AOL Instant Messenger, MSN Messenger MySpace and League of Legends, as well as online forums, message boards, blogs, are also used. Researchers have identified several types of aggression, which include online stalking, flaming, fights, and arguments; posting embarrassing or incriminating photos of a victim; outing, revealing secrets; exclusion and masquerading as someone else.

Aggressors may send mean text messages or emails, spread rumors by email or social networking sites, and they may post videos, put up embarrassing websites, or create fake profiles of a victim. The use of technology means that victims can be exposed to an audience of millions and may be unable to escape scrutiny.

Students also face dangers from impersonation, fraud and trickery online. In one infamous incident, Manti Te'o, the Notre Dame star linebacker and a finalist for the Heisman Trophy, became a victim of "catfishing." He met someone online who pretended to become his "girlfriend" even though they had never met. The ruse was uncovered by a sports website after she was reported to have died. Similarly, MTV's reality TV show called "Catfish" focuses on deceptions in online dating and is popular among college students.

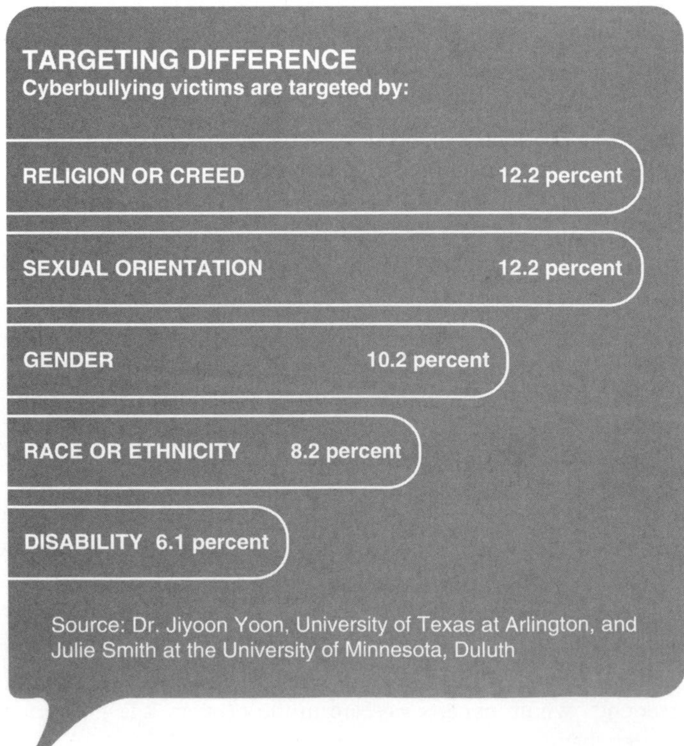

TARGETING DIFFERENCE
Cyberbullying victims are targeted by:
RELIGION OR CREED 12.2 percent
SEXUAL ORIENTATION 12.2 percent
GENDER 10.2 percent
RACE OR ETHNICITY 8.2 percent
DISABILITY 6.1 percent
Source: Dr. Jiyoon Yoon, University of Texas at Arlington, and Julie Smith at the University of Minnesota, Duluth

Handling the Cyberbully

Colleges and universities are developing courses, starting anti-bully campaigns and offering mentoring relationships and other tools to deal with the emerging social issue of cyberbullying. Rutgers University opened the Tyler Clementi Center to help students adjust to college life. Other colleges and universities are developing anti-bullying policies and taking other actions to combat problems of cyberbullying and "online incivility."

In many states, schools are required to address cyberbullying in their anti-bullying policy. Some state laws also cover off-campus behavior that creates a hostile school environment. Some universities also address direct punishment of the cyberbullying and provide special reporting tools when cyberbullying is exhibited.

University instructors/faculty are also required to report cyberbullying incidents. University IT staffs record and track incidences and courses on college campuses contain "netiquette" rules in syllabi. As most colleges and universities realize the seriousness of cyberbullying on campus, said Dr. Jiyoon Yoon, associate professor and director of the elementary education program at University of Texas at Arlington, they start to incorporate anti-cyberbullying policies into the student handbook or student code of conduct and employment standards for faculty and staff. These policies are clear about what constitutes cyberbullying and what the penalties may be.

Dawn Harner, a training coordinator and counselor at Salisbury University, said the university has a program training first-year students as leaders and asking them to refer students to a counseling center if they are experiencing anxiety or depression as related to bullying.

Whitney Gibson, head of the Internet crises group for Vorys, Sater, Seymour, and Pease LLP, s said victims should tell someone at school or get help by talking to police or school officials or an expert to get screen shots of the offending posts, chats, messages, videos, or emails.

Yoon recommends that victims:

- Take immediate action but do not respond or forward cyberbullying messages.
- Keep evidence of cyberbullying.
- Learn how to use privacy settings to block the bully.
- Report cyberbullying to the social media site, law enforcement officials, the school and online service providers.
- Review the terms and conditions of service at social media sites and Internet service providers.

—Ingrid Sturgis

One of the main characteristics of the cyberbullying is that bullies believe they can act anonymously, said Yoon. "They can harass their victims without the victims ever knowing who or why they are being cyberbullied," she said. "The various forms of current professional technology on campus allow the victims to be continually victimized without identifying the perpetrators." Experts can determine the identities of the abusers, however. The pervasiveness of social media, said Elaine Heath, PhD, dean for Student Services at Howard University, and the fact that the reasoning capabilities in adolescents do not fully mature until age 25, makes students emotionally ill equipped to handle the consequences of being a bully or being bullied.

"They are not mature enough to pick up social cues to determine this is inappropriate behavior," Heath said. "They are shocked when you tell them. Young people don't understand the boundaries and the appropriateness of how to use it."

Heath said bullying often reveals a degree of anger and deep-seated emotions. "It will start within the person and then triggers an outward manifestation," she said. "Anger or emotional problems will be acted out. They will continue the conversation with social media. It's a lack of impulse control."

When Heath asks students why they do it, she said many have given no thought to their actions. "Bottom line, people don't think about it," she said. "They are angry and want to get their story and their say out. These children live in reality TV."

"It's about power and control to instill fear," she said. "People don't fear the consequences. There is a lack of empathy, lack of control, and immaturity around relationships. A lot people don't know how to have healthy relationships."

Patchin of the Cyberbullying Research Center said parents and teachers who may not use social media sometimes underestimate the seriousness of the issue. He said some adults ask cyberbullied students questions like, "Why can't you turn it off?"

"For high school and college students, it's a big part of their social lives," he said. "If you don't know anything about it, it's not a big problem."

Cyberbullying can have implications beyond the campus and maybe even have long-lasting legal ramifications for students. Whitney Gibson, a partner at Vorys, Sater, Seymour, and Pease LLP and head of the firm's Internet crises group, works with schools to help them educate students about the unintended consequences of Internet use.

"What I see is a lot of students using technology," he said. "A lot of students don't think what they are doing is a big deal . . . They don't understand how quickly that goes viral, and they can never get it down. There is a rise of serious damage being done to people on the Internet. People are dying. Kids are getting arrested for felony."

Gibson said students often don't realize that their online behavior, including posting pictures while drinking or using marijuana, as well as acts of bullying, can affect their scholarships or job prospects as more recruiters check social media sites. In addition, Gibson said, college students think they can conceal their identities with fake names.

"They don't realize that it is very hard to remain anonymous on the Internet," he said. "They end up getting in big trouble."

Critical Thinking

1. How much supervision and monitoring is appropriate at the college level?
2. Where do we draw the line between teasing and cyberbullying?
3. How does technology like instagram, vine, and flikr contribute to cyberbullying?

Create Central

www.mhhe.com/createcentral

Internet References

buzzfeed.com 9 Teenage Suicides In The Last Year Were Linked to Cyber-Bullying on Social Network Ask.fm

http://www.buzzfeed.com/ryanhatesthis/a-ninth-teenager-since-last-september-has-committed-suicide

cyberpsychology.eu Cyberbullying in Adolescent Victims: Perception and Coping

http://www.cyberpsychology.eu/view.php?cisloclanku=2011121901

Huffingtonpost.com 8 Scary Social Networking Sites Every Parent Should Know

http://www.huffingtonpost.com/michael-gregg/8-scary-social-network-sites-every-parents-should-know_b_4178055.html

thementalelf.net Bullying and Cyberbullying Increase the Risk of Suicidal Ideation and Suicide Attempts in Adolescents

http://www.thementalelf.net/populations-and-settings/child-and-adolescent/bullying-and-cyberbullying-increase-the-risk-of-suicidal-ideation-and-suicide-attempts-in-adolescents

tylerclementi.org The Tyler Clementi Foundation

http://www.tylerclementi.org/

Ingrid Sturgis is an author, journalist, and assistant professor specializing in new media in the Department of Media, Journalism and Film at Howard University.

Sturgis, Ingrid. "High-Tech Bullies." *Diverse: Issues in Higher Education, Convergence Supplement.* (February, 27, 2014): 19–23.

Article Prepared by: Claire N. Rubman, *Suffolk County Community College*

Many Professors Say Their Students Lack Professional Qualities for Future Jobs

ANN SCHNOEBELEN

Learning Outcomes

After reading this article, you will be able to:

- Describe the relationship between technology use among students and poor professional skills.
- Explain how a sense of entitlement relates to a lack of professional qualities.

In a recent survey of college and university professors, more than one-third (38.3 percent) said they felt that fewer than half of their upper-level students exhibited qualities associated with being professional in the workplace, and nearly as many (37.5 percent) reported a drop over the past 5 years in the percentage of students demonstrating professionalism.

The survey was conducted by the Center for Professional Excellence at York College of Pennsylvania, which over the past four years has conducted an annual study of employers' views of the professionalism of recent college graduates in the workplace.

This year the study was expanded to include a survey of faculty views of the state of professionalism on campuses. More than 400 professors in various disciplines at more than 330 2- and 4-year institutions across the country participated in the survey.

According to a report describing the survey's findings, "2012 Professionalism on Campus," the qualities the respondents most strongly associated with being professional included having good interpersonal skills, being focused and attentive, being dependable in completing tasks on schedule, and displaying a work ethic.

Of those who viewed their students as failing to exhibit professionalism, almost 30 percent blamed that view on a heightened sense of entitlement among students. Entitlement was defined in the survey as "expecting rewards without putting in the work or effort to merit the rewards."

"In unaided questioning," the report says, "22.2 percent of the respondents included a sense of entitlement in their description of unprofessional qualities in students," and nearly two-thirds said they believed there had been an increase in students' sense of entitlement.

"There is obviously something happening on college campuses when it comes to students exhibiting a sense of entitlement," the report states.

Multitasking Blamed

Technology was blamed by 75.6 percent of those surveyed for interrupting student focus, and many said the problem was getting worse. According to 96.7 percent of respondents, information-technology etiquette problems and abuses—such as texting or inappropriate use of the Internet and cellphones during class, poorly written e-mails, and substituting digital communication for in-person communication—had increased or stayed the same over the past 5 years. More than half of respondents also saw students' attempts at multitasking as a factor contributing to a lack of focus.

The faculty survey's findings mirror results the Center for Professional Excellence has consistently seen in its survey of employers about the professionalism of their first-year employees who are recent college graduates.

According to a report describing the findings of the latest employer survey, "2013 Professionalism in the Workplace," 35.9 percent of the employers said the percentage of new employees exhibiting professionalism had fallen.

Deborah D. Ricker, dean of academic services at York College and a coauthor of the report on the faculty survey, said the center decided to poll professors this year after seeing no significant improvement over the past four years in employers' views of the level of professionalism in the workplace among newly hired college graduates.

"Seeing that," Ms. Ricker said in an e-mail message, "we chose to turn back the clock, if you will, to explore their level of professionalism in college before they graduate and enter their career."

The researchers hypothesized that "professional behaviors that are honed in college would be similar to those professional behaviors new graduates take into the workplace," she said, and they found that, "indeed, there were a number of consistencies."

"The overarching consistency," she wrote, "was that declining professionalism among both current college students and newly hired college graduates in the workplace was attributed to a heightened sense of entitlement, a change in culture/values, declining communication skills, and a lack of motivation and focus."

Asked if she expected that trend to continue, Ms. Ricker said, "In the workplace, yes."

Critical Thinking

1. What constitutes professional conduct in the workplace and which skills are most valued by employers?
2. How have today's students developed this "sense of entitlement"?
3. Which skills do our students lack and is this a cross-cultural phenomenon?

Create Central

www.mhhe.com/createcentral

Internet References

CNN.com Generation Y: Too demanding at work?
http://www.cnn.com/2007/LIVING/worklife/12/26/cb.generation

facultyfocus.com Student Entitlement: Six Ways to Respond
http://www.facultyfocus.com/articles/teaching-and-learning/student-entitlement-six-ways-to-respond/

quintcareers.com What Do Employers *Really* Want? Top Skills and Values Employers Seek from Job-Seekers
http://www.quintcareers.com/job_skills_values.html

timeshighereducation.co Students' Sense of Entitlement Angers Academics
http://www.timeshighereducation.co.uk/news/students-sense-of-entitlement-angers-academics/405460.article

Schnoebelen, Ann, "Many Professors Say Their Students Lack Professional Qualities for Future Jobs." *The Chronicle of Higher Education* 59. 29 (March, 29, 2013): A21–A21.

Article Prepared by: Claire N. Rubman, *Suffolk County Community College*

Don't Leave Me Out!

Adolescents are anecdotally sensitive to peer rejection. Many people can vividly recall, even as adults, instances during their teenage years in which they were excluded by a particular clique or left 'out of the loop' about parties or social plans. Rejection is undoubtedly part of the social landscape in adolescence, but why do young people find it quite so distressing? One possibility is that ongoing brain development in regions involved in emotional processing, emotion regulation, and social cognition may contribute to this phenomenon. This development could have far-reaching implications, not just for how adolescents respond to rejection, but for mental health during this crucial and formative stage of development.

Catherine Sebastian

Learning Outcomes

After reading this article, you will be able to:

- Explain how the amygdala, ventral striatum, and prefrontal cortex contribute to adolescent thought and behavior.
- Describe how the author used the "cyberball" paradigm to explore adolescent rejection.

The idea that the brain continues to develop during adolescence has now entered popular consciousness. For example, the excellent *Blame My Brain* by Nicola Morgan (2005) describes for teenagers and their parents alike how changes going on in the brain may at least partially underlie stereotypically 'teenage' behaviours, such as risk-taking in the presence of peers, mood swings, sleeping late, and thrill-seeking. In the equally fascinating *Teenagers: A Natural History,* David Bainbridge (2010) suggests that this protracted period of brain development and plasticity is what allows the human brain to achieve adult levels of abstract thinking and social complexity. This positive spin on adolescence is a welcome antidote to the often negative portrayal of young people in the media, for example during coverage of the recent riots in England.

Thinking about adolescence seems to involve striking a balance: recognising that there are certain features of adolescent biology and cognition that need to be understood, without falling into the trap of stigmatising or patronising young people. In my PhD, I was interested in the link between ongoing brain development and social and emotional behaviour; in particular, how do young people respond to social rejection, and might ongoing brain development contribute to this response? And conversely, what do differences in behaviour and cognition tell us about how the brain develops?

"How do young people respond to social rejection?"

The Teenage Brain

The last decade or so has seen an upsurge in the study and understanding of adolescence. The availability of safe and non-invasive neuroimaging techniques means we now have access to a wealth of data showing that the brain continues to develop well into the second decade of life, and likely into the mid-twenties as well. Particularly influential has been data suggesting that different brain regions mature at different rates and with differing trajectories. For example, Shaw et al. (2008) showed that evolutionarily older parts of the brain, such as the limbic system, mature in a simpler linear trajectory than regions that evolved more recently, such as the neocortex. There is additional evidence that the dopaminergic system, involved in the processing of reward signals, undergoes substantial remodelling during adolescence (Steinberg, 2008).

These data have led to the development of a number of models of how ongoing brain development may help paint the picture of a 'typical' teenager. Several models have been proposed (Nelson et al., 2005; Steinberg, 2008; Casey et al., 2008), with all having in common the idea of a 'developmental mismatch' between parts of the brain involved in processing emotional and reward signals (including brain regions such as the amygdala and ventral striatum), and those responsible for regulating these responses (e.g., parts of the prefrontal cortex). During adolescence, the development of the latter lags behind the former, leaving the adolescent brain in a similar state to a 'fast car with poor brakes'.

Is There More to It Than That?

Of course, adolescents don't develop in a vacuum, and the social environment is vitally important in shaping the adolescent brain (Blakemore, 2008). Adolescence is a time of social transition: early adolescents spend more time with parents than peers, but by mid-late adolescence, this pattern is reversed (Steinberg & Silverberg, 1986). Adolescents' ability to think abstractly about themselves and other people means they have a much more sophisticated understanding of complex social phenomena such as reputation, social hierarchy, personality traits, and how others see them (the 'looking glass self') than do younger children (Harter, 1990; Parker et al., 2006; Sebastian et al., 2008).

Indeed, while until recently it was assumed that theory of mind (understanding others' thoughts, beliefs, and intentions) develops by around age four, evidence now suggests that some aspects of theory of mind continue to develop until late adolescence. For example, Dumontheil et al. (2009) found that the ability to automatically use what we know about another person's point of view during social interaction is still improving between late adolescence (14–17 years) and adulthood. The idea that social cognitive abilities undergo substantial development in adolescence is also supported by neuroimaging studies. In a recent review, Blakemore (2008) noted that across four recent functional magnetic resonance imaging (fMRI) studies using a range of social cognition tasks, all showed a reduction in brain activity between adolescence and adulthood in a region of the brain called medial prefrontal cortex. While the meaning of this reduction in computational terms is unclear (e.g., Does it relate to ongoing anatomical development? Could it index increasing efficiency of processing between adolescence and adulthood?), it does seem that important social cognitive development is ongoing in adolescence.

One of the things I aimed to do in my PhD was to reconcile models of adolescent emotional and social development into a single framework. For example, in Sebastian, Viding et al. (2010), I discussed how 'developmental mismatch' between emotion processing and regulation mechanisms could interact with ongoing social cognitive development to account for social behaviours specific to adolescence; in particular, sensitivity to social rejection.

Adolescent Social Rejection

Social rejection, or ostracism, refers to being deliberately ignored or excluded by an individual or a group (Williams, 2007). In adolescence, social rejection is often used as a form of relational aggression or bullying, with one recent study (Wang et al., 2009), reporting that 27.4 percent of adolescent girls had been excluded or ignored by a group of peers while at school. (Although boys do use relational aggression, there is evidence that girls are both more likely to use it as a bullying tactic and to be more upset by its consequences (Crick et al., 2002, Wang et al., 2009)). Several self-report studies had also shown that adolescents might be more sensitive to social rejection than both adults and younger children in everyday life (Kloep, 1999; O'Brien & Bierman, 1988). However, when I started my PhD, the processes underlying these effects were unclear.

In Sebastian, Viding et al. (2010), I investigated whether adolescent sensitivity to social rejection could be replicated under laboratory conditions. If so, this would suggest that the phenomenon could not be explained as an artefact of the adolescent social environment (e.g., strict social hierarchies at school, or the transition to secondary school). I used the Cyberball paradigm (Williams et al., 2000), in which participants think they are playing a game of 'catch' over the internet with two other players, whereas in fact the actions of the other players can be pre-programmed to either include or exclude the participant.

Relative to adult females, both young (11–13 years) and mid (14–15 years) adolescents reported lower overall mood following the rejection condition, with the young adolescents also reporting greater anxiety. The mid-adolescents did report high anxiety following rejection, but anxiety was also high following inclusion (relative to a baseline condition before they had played either game). This led to the intriguing possibility that social interaction in general can be anxiety-provoking at this age. Indeed evidence suggests that the mean age of onset for social phobia occurs in mid-adolescence at age 15 (Mancini et al., 2005). In contrast, all groups (young adolescents, mid-adolescents, and adults) reported that they had been excluded by the other players to a similar degree, and reported the experience as feeling equally real. This suggests increased emotional responsivity to rejection in the adolescents, in the absence of objective differences in the perception of the rejection episode.

The Rejected Brain

Given that sensitivity to rejection in adolescence could be elicited in a brief online encounter when there were no lasting consequences for social reputation, I investigated whether this phenomenon might be associated with differences in how the brain processes social rejection between adolescence and adulthood. Work by Naomi Eisenberger and colleagues (2003) suggested that the adult brain processes social pain in a similar way to physical pain, and that a brain region called right ventrolateral prefrontal cortex may be involved in regulating or controlling distress associated with social rejection. This was followed up by the same laboratory with an fMRI study using Cyberball with 23 adolescents aged 12–13 (Masten et al., 2009). This study suggested some intriguing differences in the adolescent neural response to rejection, compared with previous studies in adults. However, this study did not compare adults and adolescents directly.

In Sebastian et al. (2011), we used a modified version of the Cyberball paradigm in an fMRI study directly comparing 19 adolescents (aged 14–16), and 16 adults. Regardless of age, all participants activated a network of regions involved in social evaluation and negative emotion. Of most interest was a group difference in right ventrolateral prefrontal cortex, with the adult group showing a greater response in this region during rejection than during inclusion, but the adolescent group showing no difference between conditions.

In the same fMRI session, we also gave participants a rejection emotional Stroop task, in which they indicated the ink colour of rejection-, acceptance-, and neutral-themed words. By using this task, we aimed to look at the way the brain processes rejection-related information implicitly, as opposed to the very overt and explicit social rejection scenario in the Cyberball game. Despite these important differences between the tasks, we again found a reduced response in ventrolateral prefrontal cortex in adolescents relative to adults during the processing of rejection-related words compared with neutral and acceptance words (Sebastian, Roiser et al., 2010).

It seems that across both tasks, the regulatory response of the ventrolateral prefrontal cortex was attenuated in adolescents relative to adults. While speculative, it may be that poor regulation of distress associated with social rejection contributes to adolescent sensitivity to this phenomenon.

However, it is still unclear why this brain region should be responding suboptimally in adolescence. Is it due to ongoing anatomical maturation of the prefrontal cortex? What about connections between ventrolateral prefrontal cortex and other brain regions involved in generating feelings of rejection-related distress? Can differences between groups be explained by adults having more experience over time in dealing with rejection effectively? While there are unanswered questions, our research suggests that there should be a greater focus on training adolescents to regulate their emotions effectively, particularly within the social context.

Social Rejection and the Autism Spectrum

While most people are likely to experience social rejection at some point during adolescence, it can be an unfortunately common occurrence for individuals whose social skills may not keep pace with those of their peers; for example, adolescents with high-functioning autism or Asperger's syndrome. There is evidence that adolescents with autism spectrum conditions (ASC) perceive themselves to hold lower peer approval than their typically developing peers, while placing the same emphasis on its importance (Williamson et al., 2008). At the same time, individuals with ASC often report a desire for friendship (Frith, 2004), while experiencing greater levels of loneliness (Bauminger & Kasari, 2000) and bullying (Van Roekel et al., 2010) than their peers. Given this picture, it is surprising that very little research has addressed the question of how individuals with ASC experience and process social rejection.

Using the Cyberball paradigm, we found that adolescent males with ASC and matched controls (mean age 16.9) reported very similar reactions to social rejection (Sebastian et al., 2009). According to Williams' (1997) need-threat model, social rejection threatens four fundamental social needs: self-esteem, belonging, control, and a sense of meaningful existence. These needs are threatened reflexively, and are not necessarily modulated by context; for example, Zadro et al. (2004) showed that these needs are threatened even when we know that the Cyberball game is controlled by a computer. Adolescents with ASC reported similar or greater levels of need-threat across all four needs compared with controls; and also showed similar modulation of anxiety levels between inclusion and rejection conditions. The only difference between groups was seen for self-reported mood, for which controls showed a greater reduction in mood following exclusion than did individuals with ASC.

While this study explored responses to social rejection behaviourally, three recent follow-up studies have used neuroimaging techniques to investigate responses to social rejection in adolescents with ASC (Bolling et al., 2011; Masten, Colich et al., 2011; McPartland et al., 2011). All found a similar picture of preserved self-reported responses to rejection, but reduced responses in brain regions activated by social rejection, relative to control groups. This is interesting, as it suggests that the picture is more complex than a case of responses to rejection being either "preserved" or "deficient" in ASC. It is clear, however, that adolescents with ASC find social rejection distressing.

Since data suggest that this group are more likely to experience social rejection than are their peers, it makes sense to focus on bullying prevention in this group, as well as on helping these individuals to develop effective coping strategies for dealing with social rejection in everyday life.

Conclusions

Social rejection is painful at any age, but it seems that adolescents may be particularly sensitive to the emotional consequences of social rejection, possibly due to a mismatch in the timing of development of regions involved in emotion processing versus emotion regulation. While for most adolescents, social rejection will have no more than a transitory impact, some will experience more prolonged relational bullying (including rejection), which can feed into feelings of low self-esteem, depression and even, in extreme cases, to suicide. But even responses to a single rejection episode can be informative. One recent fMRI study showed that the way in which the adolescent brain responds to rejection can be used to predict depressive symptoms one year later (Masten, Eisenberger et al., 2011). Future research should focus on the processes by which responses to negative social experiences in adolescence feed into adverse mental health outcomes. With adolescence being a key time for the onset of both internalising and externalising conditions (Kessler et al., 2005; Paus et al., 2008), efforts focused on understanding and prevention at this early stage are likely to be particularly effective.

Questions

1. How do negative social experiences feed into the development of mental illness in adolescence?
2. Why do some young people cope with rejection and bullying better than others?

Resources

Williams, K.D. (2007). Ostracism. *Annual Review of Psychology, 58,* 425–452.

www.kidscape.org.uk (anti-bullying charity)

http://teenagebrain.blogspot.co.uk (blog about teenage brain development)

References

Bainbridge, D. (2010). *Teenagers: A natural history.* London: Portobello Books.

Bauminger, N. & Kasari, C. (2000). Loneliness and friendship in high-functioning children with autism. *Child Development, 71,* 447–456.

Blakemore, S.J. (2008). The social brain in adolescence. *Nature Reviews Neuroscience, 9*(4), 267–277.

Bolling, D.Z., Pitskel, N.B., Deen, B. et al. (2011). Enhanced neural responses to rule violation in children with autism. *Developmental Cognitive Neuroscience, 1*(3), 280–294.

Casey, B., Jones, R.M. & Hare, T.A. (2008). The adolescent brain. *Annals of the New York Academy of Sciences, 1124*(1), 111–126.

Crick, N.R. & Nelson, D.A. (2002). Relational and physical victimization within friendships. *Journal of Abnormal Child Psychology, 30*(6), 599–607.

Dumontheil, I., Apperly, I.A. & Blakemore, S.J. (2009). Online usage of theory of mind continues to develop in late adolescence. *Developmental Science, 13*(2), 331–338.

Eisenberger, N.I., Lieberman, M.D. & Williams, K.D. (2003). Does rejection hurt? *Science, 302*(5643), 290.

Frith, U. (2004). Emanuel Miller Lecture: Confusions and controversies about Asperger syndrome. *Journal of Child Psychology and Psychiatry, 45,* 672–686.

Harter, S. (1990). Developmental differences in the nature of self-representations. *Cognitive Therapy & Research, 14*(2), 113–142.

Kessler, R.C., Berglund, P., Demler, O. et al. (2005). Lifetime prevalence and age-of-onset distributions of DSM-IV disorders in the National Comorbidity Survey Replication. *Archives of General Psychiatry, 62*(6), 593–602.

Kloep, M. (1999). Love is all you need? Focusing on adolescents' life concerns from an ecological point of view. *Journal of Adolescence, 22,* 49–63.

Mancini, C., Van Ameringen, M., Bennett, M. et al. (2005). Emerging treatments for child and adolescent social phobia: A review. *Journal of Child and Adolescent Psychopharmacology, 15*(4), 589–607.

Masten, C.L., Colich, N.L., Rudie, J.D. et al. (2011). An fMRI investigation of responses to peer rejection in adolescents with autism spectrum disorders. *Developmental Cognitive Neuroscience, 1*(3), 260–270.

Masten, C.L., Eisenberger, N.I., Borofsky, L.A. et al. (2009). Neural correlates of social exclusion during adolescence: Understanding the distress of peer rejection. *Social Cognitive and Affective Neuroscience, 4*(2),143–157.

Masten, C.L., Eisenberger, N.I., Borofsky, L.A. et al. (2011). Subgenual anterior cingulate responses to peer rejection. *Development and Psychopathology, 23*(1), 283–892.

McPartland, J.C., Crowley, M.J., Perszyk, D.R. et al. (2011). Temporal dynamics reveal atypical brain response to social exclusion in autism. *Developmental Cognitive Neuroscience,* 1(3), 271–279.

Morgan, N. (2005). *Blame my brain.* London: Walker Books.

Nelson, E.E., Leibenluft, E., McClure, E.B. & Pine, D.S. (2005). The social reorientation of adolescence. *Psychological Medicine, 35*(2), 163–174.

O'Brien, S.F. & Bierman, K.L. (1988). Conceptions and perceived influence of peer groups: Interviews with preadolescents and adolescents. *Child Development, 59*(5), 1360–1365.

Parker, J.G., Rubin, K.H., Erath, S.A. et al. (2006). Peer relationships, child development, and adjustment. In D. Cicchetti & D.J. Cohen (Eds.) *Developmental psychopathology. Vol. 1: Theory and Methods* (2nd edn, pp. 96–161). New York: Wiley.

Paus, T., Keshavan, M. & Giedd, J.N. (2008). Why do many psychiatric disorders emerge during adolescence? *Nature Reviews Neuroscience, 9*(12), 947–957.

Sebastian, C., Blakemore, S.J. & Charman, T. (2009). Reactions to ostracism in adolescents with autism spectrum conditions. *Journal of Autism and Developmental Disorders, 39,* 1122–1130.

Sebastian, C., Burnett, S. & Blakemore, S.J. (2008). Development of the self concept during adolescence. *Trends in Cognitive Sciences, 12*(11), 441–446.

Sebastian, C.L., Roiser, J.P., Tan, G.C. et al. (2010). Effects of age and MAOA genotype on the neural processing of social rejection. *Genes Brain & Behavior, 9,* 628–637.

Sebastian, C.L., Tan, G.C.Y., Roiser, J.P. et al. (2011). Developmental influences on the neural bases of responses to social rejection: Implications of social neuroscience for education. *NeuroImage, 57*(3), 686–694.

Sebastian, C., Viding, E., Williams, K.D. & Blakemore, S.J. (2010). Social brain development and the affective consequences of ostracism in adolescence. *Brain and Cognition, 72,* 134–145.

Shaw, P., Kabani, N.J., Lerch, J.P. et al. (2008). Neurodevelopmental trajectories of the human cerebral cortex. *Journal of Neuroscience, 28*(14), 3586–3594.

Steinberg, L. (2008). A social neuroscience perspective on adolescent risk-taking. *Developmental Review, 28*(1), 78–106.

Steinberg, L. & Silverberg, S.B. (1986). The vicissitudes of autonomy in early adolescence. *Child Development 57,* 841–851.

Van Roekel, E., Scholte, R.H. & Didden, R. (2010). Bullying among adolescents with autism spectrum disorders. *Journal of Autism and Developmental Disorders, 40,* 63–73.

Wang, J., Iannotti, R.J. & Nansel, T.R. (2009). School bullying among adolescents in the United States. *Journal of Adolescent Health, 45,* 368–375.

Williams, K.D. (1997). Social ostracism. In R.M. Kowalski (Ed.) *Aversive interpersonal behaviors* (pp.133–170). New York: Plenum.

Williams, K.D. (2007). Ostracism. *Annual Review of Psychology, 58,* 425–452.

Williams, K.D., Cheung, C.K. & Choi, W. (2000). Cyberostracism: Effects of being ignored over the internet. *Journal of Personality and Social Psychology, 79*(5), 748–762.

Williamson, S., Craig, J. & Slinger, R. (2008). Exploring the relationship between measures of self-esteem and psychological adjustment among adolescents with Asperger syndrome. *Autism, 14*(4), 391–402.

Zadro, L., Williams, K.D. & Richardson, R. (2004). How low can you go? Ostracism by a computer is sufficient to lower self-reported levels of belonging, control, self-esteem, and meaningful existence. *Journal of Experimental Social Psychology, 40,* 560–567.

Critical Thinking

1. Why do adolescents respond differently than adults to emotions such as rejection?
2. What could the reduced role of the medial prefrontal cortex as adolescents shift into adulthood mean in terms of development?
3. How can we help adolescents to cope with rejection and other emotions while their brains are still maturing?

Create Central

www.mhhe.com/createcentral

Internet References

academia.edu The Social Brain in Adolescence: Evidence from Functional Magnetic Resonance Imaging and Behavioural Studies

http://www.academia.edu/415376/The_social_brain_in_adolescence_Evidence_from_functional_magnetic_resonance_imaging_and_behavioural_studies

apa.org Grantee Spotlight: Studying Social Rejection in Adolescence

http://www.apa.org/monitor/2013/12/grantee-spotlight.aspx

Medscape.com Social Cognitive and Affective Neuroscience Adolescent Social Cognitive and Affective Neuroscience Past, Present, and Future

http://www.medscape.com/viewarticle/757839

NCBI.MLN.NIH.gov Special issue on the teenage brain: Sensitivity to social evaluation

http://www.ncbi.nlm.nih.gov/pmc/articles/PMC3992953/

Psychologytoday.com 10 Surprising Facts About Rejection Research Finds that Rejection Affects Intelligence, Reason, and More

http://www.psychologytoday.com/blog/the-squeaky-wheel/201307/10-surprising-facts-about-rejection

---

Catherine Sebastian is a Lecturer in the Department of Psychology, Royal Holloway, University of London catherine.sebastian@rhul.ac.uk

Sebastian, Catherine. "Don't leave me out!" *The Psychologist* 25. 11 (November, 2012): 820–823.

Article

Prepared by: Claire N. Rubman, *Suffolk County Community College*

Cheating in the Age of Facebook

Are we having the right discussion about academic cheating in this era of social media?

STEVEN SCHLOZMAN

Learning Outcomes

After reading this article, you will be able to:

- Articulate the difference between plagiarism and cheating.
- Define cheating in the Internet age.
- Explain the term *digital immigrant.*

LAST YEAR, 125 Students in the Introduction to Congress course at Harvard University appeared to have cheated on a take-home exam by collaborating with one another on essay-form answers—although a no-collaboration policy was printed on the exam itself. A graduate student noticed the similarity among test responses and brought the discovery to the professor's attention. That move triggered a long and painful investigation. The episode even prompted the dean of Yale to email that school's professors, urging them to consider in-class examinations. The incident is now infamously known as the Harvard Cheating Scandal.

This event should make us pause and think. Not because I condone cheating. I do not. We could devote an entirely different discussion to the steady erosion of how we define right and wrong in the classroom. However, many of their peers likely do not view what these students allegedly did as cheating.

What makes the Harvard episode different from all other cheating? Actually, a lot. Most important, the collaboration took place on Facebook.

I simply can't imagine a template for social media in any fashion. I didn't grow up with "likes" and "tweets" and "tags," and I don't cross the boundaries of that medium with even an ounce of the dexterity with which young people do; these tools are part of their routine and everyday lives. Therefore, I am at a loss as I consider how one might feel about using these tools to share ideas and information.

We have some 40 years of curricula stressing collaboration, and now we have technology that makes collaboration unimaginably easy.

To complicate matters even more, when kids talk about these issues, I don't feel that we're all talking about the same thing. I think we're talking about cheating, but many kids and young adults do not. Students aren't being defiant. They just see the use of social modalities in ways that are starkly different from ways many educators expect them to.

We have a generation coming of age with a technology so new that the older generation is probably not able to adequately discuss its ethical strengths and weaknesses. The press offers one horrific story after another involving Facebook, Twitter, and other digital tools, and we all shake our heads and say "tsk, tsk." And then we try to make sense of what our world has become.

Consider the kid who is accused of cheating by finding information on the Internet, or of swapping ideas on Facebook that then show up in exam answers. Perhaps someone has collaborated with a complete stranger to solve a calculus problem by utilizing a series of abbreviated tweets. We tell our students that this is cheating, and they look at us with sad, even dumbfounded faces. They don't look like kids who think they've done wrong.

They look hurt and frightened. They look like they legitimately feel falsely accused. In fact, they look lost.

This is why the issue of what allegedly happened at Harvard is so complicated, We have at least 40 or so years of curricula stressing collaboration and cooperation, and we now have a technology that makes collaboration, even with complete strangers, unimaginably easy. And yet we yell at our students when they use one solve problems.

The Cold, Hard Facts About Cheating

- In a 2007 poll, 60.8 percent of college students admitted to cheating.
- The same poll revealed that 16.5 percent didn't regret it.
- Only 20 percent of college students admitted to cheating in the 1940s.
- Cheaters have higher GPAs.
- Cheating college students likely start in high school.
- The majority of students who cheat think it's essential for success.
- 95 percent of cheaters don't get caught.
- According to *nocheating.org,* cheating carries less and less social stigma. Competition for college admissions makes students more willing to cheat.
- 55 percent of college presidents say plagiarism has increased.
- Most college presidents believe digital tools play a major role in plagiarism.

Source: oedb.org and Pew Research Center

We educators may, during this time of grand technological transition, need to be very, very specific in our warnings. First, any policy addressing the use of social media in academic settings should begin with the acknowledgment that teachers are in over their heads with regard to these modalities.

Of course, if part of the educational goal is to assess whether students can another, via these new modalities, to independently solve complex problems, then the impetus rests with teachers to be explicit about this goal. We should tell students in these instances, very directly, that they cannot use any form of online discussion to complete the assignment. To them, that is not the same thing as being told: "You can't get together and discuss your answers." Yes, that sounds crazy. But there are students, good kids, who say that they didn't understand that Facebook was off-limits even though they were fully aware that sharing their answers in person is wrong.

Most teachers these days are still digital immigrants. We call our students cheaters and they tell US they know what cheating is—yet they remain adamant, appropriately indignant even, that they have not cheated.

We need to find a way to protect the drive toward using these tools to collaboratively innovate and solve problems and at the same time continue with the academic discipline that allows us to move forward in our competitive world.

It is, after all, a new world. The old-world rules might need a little rethinking.

Critical Thinking

1. What would motivate a student to cheat?
2. What could college professors do to discourage cheating?
3. Are the motivating forces for cheating different among Ivy League students?

Create Central

www.mhhe.com/createcentral

Internet References

bostongloble.com How College Classes Encourage Cheating. Our Universities Motivate Students to Be Dishonest. Here's How to Fix Them.

http://www.bostonglobe.com/ideas/2013/08/03/how-college-classes-encourage-cheating/3Q34x5ysYcplWNA3yO2eLK/story.html

faculty.mwsu.edu Academic Dishonesty: Are More Students Cheating?

http://faculty.mwsu.edu/psychology/dave.carlston/Writing%20in%20Psychology/Academic%20Dishonesty/new/adprev.pdf

hub.jhu.edu Why College Students Cheat Academic Dishonesty Is Arguably as Old as School Itself. But the Authors of A New Book Argue That Many Students Today Don't Think of Things Like Plagiarism and Collaborating on Tests as Cheating at All

http://hub.jhu.edu/gazette/2013/january/cheating-in-school-no-easy-answers

Nytimes.com Students Disciplined in Harvard Scandal

http://www.nytimes.com/2013/02/02/education/harvard-forced-dozens-to-leave-in-cheating-scandal.html

westga.edu Cheating in the Digital Age: Do Students Cheat More in Online Courses?

http://www.westga.edu/~distance/ojdla/spring131/watson131.html

Steven Schlozman, M.D., is an associate director of Medical Student Education in Psychiatry for Harvard Medical School. He is also the author of the novel *The Zombie Autopsies: Secret Notebooks from the Apocalypse.*

Schlozman, Steven. "Cheating in the Age of Facebook." *Psychology Today* 46. 2 (March/April, 2013): 47–48.

Unit 6

UNIT

Prepared by: Claire N. Rubman, *Suffolk County Community College*

Development During Middle and Late Adulthood

Do you know anyone who has ever struggled with a weight problem, a mental health issue such as depression or dementia, or a life-threatening illness such as cancer? The articles in this unit focus on overcoming depression, losing weight, life after cancer, and the declines in our brain as we age. What can we do to delay that decline in our brains and how can we enjoy living in our own homes as we age? Finally, how can we identify and prevent the abuse of the elderly in our society?

Kathleen McGowan explores the debilitating effects of depression in the article "Good Morning, Heartache." Through the life of Pata Suyemoto, she personalizes how depression impacts life. McGowan discusses the therapeutic interventions, drug options, and lifestyle choices that can reduce the effects of depression. The physical impact, the mental despair, and the narcissistic thoughts are discussed.

Another possible cure for severe mental illness is suggested in "The Switched-On Brain" by Amy Barth. Barth explores the potential for optogenetics as a cure for severe depression. Optogenetics involes the "switching on and off" of neural pathways in the brain. Optogenetics founder Deisseroth worked on mice and addiction, but his paradigm has inspired researchers around the world.

Still discussing cures, "The New Survivors" assesses the 11 million Americans who have survived a cancer diagnosis. Pamela Weintraub personalizes the fight to beat cancer and live on by describing Jason Zimmerman's battle during and after his disease. He had to overcome his fear and rage over a repeat diagnosis at each checkup. He became a motivational speaker and shared his success with other survivors. Weintraub discusses the inner meaning and added dimension that a cancer diagnosis can bring to a person and the strength that a cure can add to his or her life.

Thinking about obesity, Freedman evaluates three major components in our battle against obesity—the brain, our metabolism, and our genes. In his article "How to Fix the Obesity Crisis," Freedman advocates four steps: initial assessment, behavior shifts, self-monitoring, and support groups. Freedman focuses on behavior therapy but acknowledges the costs may prevent many from utilizing this therapy.

During the normal course of development our brain will age along with our body. Robert Epstein discusses the particulars of what we can expect as we age. Our brain will shrink, we lose dopamine, and our dendrites lose their connectivity. We also face a deterioration in the myelin sheath that insulates our neural pathways. The four domains of decline, according to Epstein in his article "Brutal Truths About the Aging Brain," include our senses, our memory, our knowledge base, and our intelligence.

On a more upbeat note, Beth Howard outlines "10 easy ways to stay sharp forever" in the article titled "Age-Proof Your Brains." Howard's recommendations range from proper vitamin intake to finding a purpose and a social life!

Fishman focuses on the new reality that the world's population is aging. In his article "The Old World" he looks at the future of our society as we age. In China, for example, the working population will begin to shrink in 2015. Fishman posits that one issue that our aging population must grapple with is how to keep older people productively employed for longer. This aging population is a long-term trend, so Fishman recommends that we embrace it!

"The Real Social Network" does not relate to the Internet but is, rather, an account of an elderly community's attempt to stay connected and help each other during poor weather conditions. This "village movement" is an attempt by many elderly people to avoid moving into a retirement community. Thomas describes communities such as Mount Monadnock and Beacon Hill. She also describes the "Village to Village network" that helps communities to get started.

This unit ends with a discussion on the tragic subject of elder abuse. Sorenson discusses ways that the elderly are abused in the final article titled "Elder Abuse Identification: A Public Health Issue." She also discusses warning signs that elder abuse is occurring. She discusses the federal law passed in 2011 on elder abuse prevention and acknowledges that elder abuse is a difficult topic to discuss but emphasizes the importance of the conversation. She offers a myriad of resources for the reader.

Article Prepared by: Claire N. Rubman, *Suffolk County Community College*

Good Morning, Heartache

For millions, depression is a daily reality against which they must struggle to function. The many strategies now available provide what we all might envy—the knowledge that it's possible to get through the worst of times.

KATHLEEN MCGOWAN

Learning Outcomes

After reading this article, you will be able to:

- Explain why each person with depression is different from all others.
- Identify some of the types of therapies available for persons who are depressed.

Last summer, Pata Suyemoto rode her bike from Boston to Cape Cod, 125 miles in one day. An educator who has taught everything from art to English to Reiki, she's funny, she's intense, and she's passionate. Never a jock, three years ago she became a relentless road warrior, riding more than 6,000 miles the first year she took up cycling.

But she would not say that she has conquered depression. Instead, like many people who experience major depression—and there are roughly 15 million Americans who do—she has achieved a kind of delicate détente with it. She manages to live with the disorder, or in spite of it. She thinks of her depression as a recurrent illness; getting it under control demands time, creativity, and an open mind. It keeps her on her toes.

Untamed, her depression is truly ferocious. Suyemoto, 47, has been in and out of psychiatric hospitals since age 17. Ten years ago, there came a time she now refers to as the bottom of the abyss. She could hardly do her job. Mustering the energy to stand in front of a class took all her strength. After class, she'd shut the door to her office and crawl under her desk. She had a young daughter, and she was trying to write her dissertation. Then, her mother died. "I'd write a page, and cry for an hour, then write another page, and cry for another hour," she says now.

Eventually she found cracks of light in the darkness. Antidepressants didn't help much. Glimmers of hope came more from things she did. She wrote in a journal daily, even when she had to prop herself up in bed to do it. She finally found a therapist who knew how to deal with severe depression and trauma. "It was gradual, working things into my life," she says. "It was like weaving a net."

A decade later, she now cherishes a whole a list of things that help, her own personal portfolio of antidepressants. Artistic self-expression in the form of collage gives her a way to communicate the darkest feelings without getting stuck in them. Acupuncture—as often as five times a week—helps. She finally found a medication that works. She volunteers with the Massachusetts group Families for Depression Awareness, leveraging her own experience to help other people who are struggling with depression. Self-help books and tapes offer a reality check, as does a sense of spirituality that puts her troubles in context.

And then there's the bike. It's not just good exercise. It's also a way to test limits and learn when to push herself and when to play it cool.

Is she cured? No. But she has her life back.

"I still have dark times, but they don't consume me in the same way," says Suyemoto. She expects that she may have other bad times; for her as for many people, major depression comes in cycles. She is ready for it. "It's not that I'm free and clear," she says. "But in doing all these things, and weaving them into my life, I've created a much stronger net."

A lot of the news about depression these days is good: An arsenal of treatments now available allows many to lead a normal life in spite of the disorder. The best estimate is that 80 percent of people find substantial relief from their worst symptoms, which typically include persistent sadness, guilt or

Combination Therapy Still Best

Finding the best treatment for depression ***today*** means wading through lots of options. There are 39 antidepressant drugs on the market. And for some people, cognitive therapy works just as well, or better. Other treatments range from light therapy to the implantation of electrodes in the brain.

A major test of drugs and talk therapy, the 2006 STAR*D trial, treated 4,000 participants who are highly typical of patients with major depression: Their disorder had not responded to the first drug they took, and most also had anxiety or an eating disorder.

The study found that no one drug or therapy was clearly best. Adding either a second drug or cognitive therapy worked equally well. Only about a third of subjects saw symptoms vanish with the first drug tried. But most—67 percent—eventually found substantial relief. The bottom line: Hang in there. It may take time to find the right treatments.

"The combination with psychotherapy is very useful," says psychiatrist Dennis Charney. "It's like hand and glove." Psychotherapy can take longer to start working, but it may have the edge in preventing relapses.

What causes depression is still basically a mystery. The altered brain chemistry goes far beyond serotonin, the neurotransmitter targeted by many antidepressant drugs. Dopamine-sensitive brain circuits, which influence pleasure and reward, are off-kilter and may underlie feelings of numbness or despair. Such circuits also influence mood, which may be why people prone to depression struggle to prevent disappointments and setbacks from spiraling into full-blown depressive episodes.

Stress also plays a role, especially in early life. Prolonged childhood stress, such as neglect or abuse, may influence neurochemistry and the responsiveness of the body's alarm system, setting the stage for depression in adulthood.

No one gene causes depression, and only about one-third of the risk of depression is inherited. But genetics might one day improve upon the current trial-and-error process of choosing a drug. A gene scan may predict which antidepressant will work best for you.

For the time being, the best approach is to seek out a depression specialist. Most people rely on their family doctor. But a depression expert has more experience with the range of options—and many more tricks up his or her sleeve.

irritability, sleep and appetite disruption, and the absence of pleasure. "People do recover from depression," says Michael Yapko, a clinical psychologist in California who specializes in treating depression. "There are many pathways in, and there are many pathways out."

Getting there, however, is rarely easy. Few people find simple cures. Instead, they patch together many measures. "I hate it when people say, 'Just go exercise.' Or, 'Just take medication,' or 'Just' anything," says Suyemoto. "Everybody has to find their own path, Healing from depression is a not a universal thing. Everybody's going to be different."

Major depression is so common because a lot of different biological and psychological roads lead to the same place. A variety of switches get tripped—whether by genetic vulnerability, trauma in early life, chronic stress, disturbance of neurochemistry, or guilt-prone tendencies—and the end result is depression.

To successfully cope with depression, most people stumble onto their own combination of lifestyle adaptations, therapeutic techniques, medications, and mental adjustments.

Given the diversity of causes, antidepressant medications alone are rarely enough. To successfully cope with depression, most people stumble onto their own idiosyncratic combination of lifestyle adaptations, therapeutic techniques, medications, and mental adjustments. But the most successful approaches for the long term, says Yapko, all encourage you to take action in the face of a disorder that saps your resolve. "Eventually, if you're persistent, there's a high probability you'll find something."

The most successful approaches for the long term all encourage you to take action in the face of a disorder that saps your resolve.

First, It's Physical

For many people the process of gaining control over depression begins with physical changes. Researchers now know that depression is not just a mental disorder. It affects the immune system, the heart, and basic body functions such as sleep and appetite as well. So it only makes sense that a lot of people who successfully manage their depression are careful about what they eat and drink, how much they sleep, and how active they are.

Former Massachusetts state senator and attorney Bob Antonioni, for example, always makes time for hockey, bike riding, or swimming. "In the past if I was struggling I'd curl up on the couch—that's not good, because you become more isolated, and the isolation feeds the depression," he says. "Very often I find, if I go out and exercise, I'm better for it."

Now 50, he's been dealing with depression since his mid-30s. After his brother's suicide in 1999, it got worse. He was profoundly sad, and the depression also settled into his body. His chest constantly ached. Sometimes it seemed like his body was going into panic mode. At the same time, as a politician, he had a public image to maintain. "I'm supposed to be out and about, smiling," he says now. "I just wasn't able to. I'd go into withdrawal."

He now has a comprehensive strategy; Antonioni goes for regular therapy and takes an antidepressant. But other physical interventions are equally important. He doesn't drink anymore, except on rare occasions—not that he ever had a drinking problem, but the depressant effects of alcohol worsened his symptoms.

Sleep is his number one secret weapon. "Sleep makes all the difference in the world to me," he says. It's not always easy to explain to his aides and colleagues why he won't arrange early-morning meetings. So be it. "The adjustments come," he adds. "People are a lot more willing to be flexible than I might originally have given them credit for."

Mood and sleep share basic biological mechanisms, and, according to Yapko, the single most common symptom of depression is some form of sleep disturbance. Getting lots of sleep is crucial. The challenge is in admitting that you just may not be able to do as much as you want to—and then sticking to your guns, even when life throws drama or excitement your way.

Getting through Despair

"I've found that I have to be careful or I crash," says Kathryn Goetzke, a 37-year-old entrepreneur who battles major depression. "You have to be pretty disciplined about it," Goetzke has her own business, Mood-Lites, which develops decorative lighting. She also founded a nonprofit, the International Foundation for Research and Education on Depression (iFred). Then her husband ran for Congress in 2006. Of course, she got involved in the campaign. "I thought I had it all under control," she says now. "I just took on way, way, way too much."

He lost, and for maybe six months afterward she struggled to do anything at all. The marriage ended, and sometimes money was very tight—two other major sources of stress. "I learned the hard way," she says. "I have to listen to my body. I can't be ashamed. The consequences are much worse, in the long run, if I ignore it."

Goetzke reached out to her mother and brothers, who "moved mountains" to help her through the worst times. When she was closest to the brink, they pulled her back. She found a good therapist and, when she couldn't afford therapy, she turned to support groups, augmented by long walks outside.

Now, she says, she feels pretty good. "I'm happy to be around" is how she puts it. But it still takes a lot of work. She quit drinking entirely, avoids eating too much sugar, gets plenty of sleep, and hikes, plays tennis, does yoga, or bikes almost every day. She relies on her dogs, and the encouragement of a weekly women's support group. She, too, takes medication.

What might have made the biggest difference, though, was inside her own head—a major psychological shift. Before she started grappling with depression, Goetzke was an escapist. Her father, also depressed, committed suicide when she was in college, and she was eventually diagnosed with posttraumatic stress disorder. She drank, and she had an eating disorder, two ways of blunting the bleakness that only made things worse.

Finally, in her 30s, she began to confront how bad she felt and actually learned to live with her feelings of despair. "I sit through my feelings of awfulness," she says. "I let myself fully experience the bad feelings, and then move it toward something positive." Mindfulness meditation, which derails the obsessive thinking that typically intensifies negative feelings, is also useful. In these ways, she has learned to accept herself—and that includes accepting the sorrow.

Being able to withstand feeling lousy has been important to her success. As a businesswoman, she has to endure constant rejection. Once, the head of product development for a major lighting company told her that she would never get her product into a store. Her Mood-Lites are now on the shelves of hundreds of Wal-Marts, as well as in spas and chiropractors' offices across the country.

Cognitive tricks and techniques may seem insubstantial against such a formidable foe as depression, but they work. Cognitive behavioral therapy and interpersonal therapy both focus on the future, teaching mental and emotional skills that challenge negative thought patterns and counteract feelings of helplessness and self-loathing.

"Psychotherapy gives you a toolbox of approaches to handle stress, which can elicit depression," says noted mood disorder researcher Dennis Charney, dean of the Mt. Sinai School of Medicine in New York. "Part of it is getting the right treatment, the right doctor, the right psychotherapist." The important question to ask a therapist, says Charney, is whether she or he is experienced in teaching techniques that work.

"The Narcissism of Depression"

Learning how to step away from your own thoughts and see them objectively is a technique that can short-circuit the downward spiral of despair. In her 20s, Gina Barreca was drowning in sadness and emotional turmoil. Small setbacks and difficulties regularly turned into huge cataclysms that took over her life. She cried constantly, for just about any reason. "I really think of myself in those early days as somebody blindfolded, walking underneath an emotional piñata with a bat," she says now.

Now a professor of English at the University of Connecticut, Barreca, too, eventually found a medication that helped. But she got better mostly because she learned to stop torturing herself. She fills up journals with feelings of self-loathing and misery—but that is where they stay. Over time, with the help of a smart, committed therapist, she figured out how to step around emotional chaos rather than stir it up.

Barreca rejects what she calls "the narcissism of depression," the mental habit of taking wretched feelings seriously and burrowing into them. Instead, she thinks of depression and sorrow as familiar demons who arrive as unwelcome visitors. They're nasty, and they wreck the place, but eventually they move on. Enduring them is part of life. "The hardest thing in the world to learn is a sense of humility in the face of this, that these things are going to pass," says Barreca.

Now 52, she doesn't sink into sadness, but she doesn't shy away from it, either. "I'm not bubble-wrapped," she says. "I still get furious. I still get incredibly sad." But when the tormented feelings well up, she does her best to go on with her life. She shops. She talks to friends. She goes for coffee or has a nice meal. "I do those things that actually make me feel better," she says.

Barreca has written seven humor books; her latest, *It's Not That I'm Bitter,* will be out this month. She is a brilliant and witty writer. That's actually not as unlikely as it might seem. Finding the humor in things requires seeing them from an unexpected angle, a cognitive trick that is key to dispelling depression. "Pain plus time equals humor," says Barreca. "I've had both pain and time."

Making Light of the Darkness

There are many routes out of the isolation of depression. Both Bob Antonioni and Kathryn Goetzke turn to advocacy, going public to reach out to others and to cast off the shame. Pata Suyemoto creates artworks that express her emotional tumult. But there's something especially powerful about humor. It can connect through the terrifying darkness of the disorder, not in spite of it. Humor creates sparks of instantaneous intimacy, a rare gift for anyone—but particularly for those who feel hopelessly alone.

This unique power is the fuel for Victoria Maxwell's one-woman shows, *Crazy for Life* and *Funny, You Don't Look Crazy.* In her performances, often to mental health workers, psychiatrists, and patients, she tells the epic story of her experiences with bipolar disorder. The details are hair-raising. But in her telling, they are also hilarious.

Maxwell's bouts of depression began shortly after she graduated from college, although at first neither she nor her therapist realized quite what they were dealing with. She was binge eating and oversleeping, had trouble concentrating, and was consumed with self-hatred.

At the same time, she embarked upon a spiritual quest. On a three-day meditation retreat, a lack of sleep and food, combined with the silence and stillness, pitched her into mania. During a manic episode, some people become aggressive and others feel unstoppable; her euphoria took on a powerfully spiritual tone. She felt rapturous, like a limitless being composed only of love. But when, convinced she had transcended her earthly body, she began having visions of her grave, her parents took her to the hospital.

Maxwell left with a prescription, but soon quit taking her pills. She thought she was having a spiritual struggle, not mentally ill. During the next couple of years, she went through several more manic episodes, interspersed with horrendous depressions. Finally, one night she went running through the streets of Vancouver naked, looking for God, and got picked up by the police. A wise psychiatric nurse who recognized both Maxwell's spiritual hunger and her mental illness introduced her to a sympathetic psychiatrist who finally convinced her to seek help.

Medication quickly tamed her manic upswings, but the depressions took much longer to manage. At the age of 42, Maxwell now feels pretty stable. She is careful to sleep at least eight hours a night. Intense workouts kick-start her body when she feels slow. And she practices a version of the same technique that Barreca and Goetzke use. Following Buddhist writer Pema Chodron's counsel, she treats her depressions with "compassionate witnessing": recognition and tolerance. "I'm comfortable enough to invite those demons to come in," she says. "I don't resist them."

Performing also helps. She can connect with strangers, rather than feel ashamed of her mental illness. And the sense of love and joy that she felt during her manias still resonates. "It's really liberating to tell people you ran down the street naked, and were tied to a gurney," she says. "At the time, it was terrifying. But to be able to say that to an audience is freeing. To have people laugh with you because they relate is really powerful."

Maxwell considers her bipolar disorder "in remission," but she doesn't take her health for granted. If she's overwhelmed, she takes a day off. She still sees her psychiatrist. But it's no longer a constant struggle: "My life is more about my life than my illness, which is a godsend."

Barreca, Suyemoto, and Maxwell all say they wouldn't wish what they've been through on anyone else. But they're not altogether sorry it happened. Depression required them to learn what many people, depressed or not, never find out: the knowledge that they can get through the worst of times. And after the worst times were over, they found out, it is possible to have a sense of perspective about it all—even to laugh. "Laughter is survival," says Barreca. "It's not because life is easy. It's something you wring out of life. You make joy."

Critical Thinking

1. Identify how depressed persons get through the worst of times.
2. Review the different types of therapy for depression.
3. Explain why most people differ in terms of what relieves their depression.

Create Central

www.mhhe.com/createcentral

Internet References

Acupuncture, Anxiety, and Depression
http://psychcentral.com/lib/acupuncture-anxiety-depression

Depression Symptoms and Warning Signs
www.helpguide.org/mental/depression_signs_types

Depression Traps: Social Withdrawal, Rumination, and More
www.webmd.com/ahrq/depression-traps-and-pitfalls

Depression Treatment: Therapy, Medication, and Lifestyle Changes
www.helpguide.org/mental/treatment_strategies_depression.htm

NIMH: Depression
www.nimh.nih.gov/health/publications/depression

KATHLEEN MCGOWAN is a freelance writer in New York.

Article

Prepared by: Claire N. Rubman, Suffolk *County Community College*

The Switched-On Brain

AMY BARTH

Learning Outcomes

After reading this article, you will be able to:

- Evaluate the research on optogenetics and defeating mental illness.
- Predict what illnesses may be abbreviated or alleviated in the near future with more knowledge about opsins and light therapy.

Stopped at a red light on his drive home from work, Karl Deisseroth contemplates one of his patients, a woman with depression so entrenched that she had been unresponsive to drugs and electroshock therapy for years. The red turns to green and Deisseroth accelerates, navigating roads and intersections with one part of his mind while another part considers a very different set of pathways that also can be regulated by a system of lights. In his lab at Stanford University's Clark Center, Deisseroth is developing a remarkable way to switch brain cells off and on by exposing them to targeted green, yellow, or blue flashes. With that ability, he is learning how to regulate the flow of information in the brain.

Deisseroth's technique, known broadly as optogenetics, could bring new hope to his most desperate patients. In a series of provocative experiments, he has already cured the symptoms of psychiatric disease in mice. Optogenetics also shows promise for defeating drug addiction. When Deisseroth exposed a set of test mice to cocaine and then flipped a switch, pulsing bright yellow light into their brains, the expected rush of euphoria—the prelude to addiction—was instantly blocked. Almost miraculously, they were immune to the cocaine high; the mice left the drug den as uninterested as if they had never been exposed.

Today, those breakthroughs have been demonstrated in only a small number of test animals. But as Deisseroth pulls into his driveway he is optimistic about what tomorrow's work could bring: Human applications, and the relief they could deliver, may not be far off.

For all its complexity, the brain in some ways is a surprisingly simple device. Neurons switch off and on, causing signals to stop or go. Using optogenetics, Deisseroth can do that switching himself. He inserts light-sensitive proteins into brain cells. Those proteins let him turn a set of cells on or off just by shining the right kind of laser beam at the cells.

That in turn makes it possible to highlight the exact neural pathways involved in the various forms of psychiatric disease. A disruption of one particular pathway, for instance, might cause anxiety. To test the possibility, Deisseroth engineers an animal with light-sensitive proteins in the brain cells lying along the suspected pathway. Then he illuminates those cells with a laser. If the animal begins cowering in a corner, he knows he is in the right place. And as Deisseroth and his colleagues illuminate more neural pathways, other researchers will be able to design increasingly targeted drugs and minimally invasive brain implants to treat psychiatric disease.

Optogenetics originally emerged from Bio-X, a multidisciplinary project spearheaded in part by Stephen Chu, then a Stanford physicist and now the U.S. Secretary of Energy. Bio-X takes some of Stanford's best engineers, computer scientists, physicists, chemists, and clinicians and throws them together in the Clark Center, where an open, glass-clad structure makes communication unavoidable. Deisseroth, whose beat-up jeans and T-shirt practically define the universal academic wardrobe, proved a natural at working across disciplines. Over the past decade, his omnivorous quest has filtered far beyond Bio-X into a thousand institutions around the world.

Although his Bio-X work involves esoteric genetics and animal experiments, Deisseroth has never forgotten the human needs that motivated him in the first place. He still divides his time between his basement lab and the psychiatry patients who desperately need his research to pay off.

Psychiatry's Core Dilemma

Karl Deisseroth was 27 when he first brushed past the curtains of the psychiatry ward at Palo Alto's VA hospital in northern California. It was 1998 and he had just completed his first two years of Stanford Medical School, where he had earned a PhD in brain cell physiology, exploring the electrical language of neuron communication. As part of his medical training, he was required to complete a rotation in psychiatry—a hazy specialty, he felt, much less compelling than the brain surgery that was his career goal.

Several patients in the ward lay in narrow beds lined up before him, awaiting a treatment called electroconvulsive therapy (ECT). After the anesthesiologist on duty put them under, the attending psychiatrist placed pads on the patients' temples and walked from bed to bed, pressing a small button on each person's control box, sending volts of electricity into their brains. Their bodies tensed and their brains rattled with seizures for a full minute. The recipients risked losing large swaths of memory, but if things went well, the current would reset their neurons, purging their depression and providing months of relief.

From that experience, Deisseroth determined that he would spend his life solving a core puzzle of psychiatric disease: A brain could appear undamaged, with no dead tissue or anatomical deformities, yet something could be so wrong it destroyed patients' lives. Perhaps because the damage was invisible, the available therapies were shockingly crude. ECT was lifesaving but usually temporary; although it was likely that just a small set of cells caused the patient's troubles, the shock jolted neurons throughout the brain. Psychoactive drugs, targeting general brain regions and cell types, were too broad as well. And scientists were so uncertain about what chemical imbalances impacted which neural circuits that one-third of people with major depression did not respond to drugs at all.

Deisseroth pondered the problem through a subsequent psychiatry residency, where he oversaw more than 200 ECT procedures over four years. Then, in 2004, he became a principal investigator at Stanford and was given his own lab. As a clinician treating patients, his arsenal was limited. But with his scientific imagination roaming free and a brand-new lab sparkling with empty chairs and beakers to fill, he began to envision elegant new strategies. One stood out: a concept first suggested by Francis Crick, the legendary genetics and consciousness researcher.

Crick's idea was that light, with its unparalleled speed and precision, could be the ideal tool for controlling neurons and mapping the brain. "The idea of an energy interface instead of a physical interface to work with the brain was what was so exciting," Deisseroth says. He thought creating a light-sensitive brain was probably impossible, but then an idea floated up: What about tapping the power of light-sensitive microbes, single-celled creatures that drift in water, turning toward or away from the sun to regulate energy intake? Such brainless creatures rely on signals from light-sensitive proteins called opsins. When sunlight hits the opsin, it instantly sends an electric signal through the microbe's cell membrane, telling the tiny critter which way to turn in relation to the sun.

Deisseroth wondered if he could insert these opsins into targeted mammalian brain cells in order to make them light-sensitive too. If so, he could learn to control their behavior using light. Shining light into the brain could then become the tool Crick imagined, providing a way to control neurons without electric shocks or slow-acting, unfocused drugs.

Lighting the Brain

The necessary tools were already out there. The first opsin—the light-sensitive protein made by microbes—had been identified in 1971, the same year Deisseroth was born. Bacteriorhodopsin, as it was called, responded to green light, and scientists have since found it in microbes living in saltwater all over the world. The next opsin, halorhodopsin, which responds to yellow light, was discovered in 1977. Like bacteriorhodopsin, it was found in bacteria living in salty lakes and seas.

Deisseroth, who read everything he could about opsins, realized that light-sensitive microbes speak the same basic language as neurons: When light hits the opsin, gates in the cell membrane open, allowing charged particles called ions to flow in and out. In microbes, ion flow tells the organism which way to turn. In neurons, ions flowing through the cell wall initiate action, setting off a string of communications that tell organisms like us how to feel and behave. This similarity suggested to Deisseroth that opsins could be manipulated to switch brain cells on and off.

Deisseroth was still mulling this over in 2003, when German biologists Georg Nagel and Peter Hegemann announced a new light-sensitive microbe, a green alga called *Chlamydomonas reinhardtii.* The 10-micrometer-wide microbe has a small eyespot, which Deisseroth describes as "kind of cute," that spins around to detect light. It makes a protein called channelrhodopsin-2 (ChR2) that acts as an antenna to receive blue light and convert it to an ion flow. When a light shines on ChR2, the cell becomes active and tells the microbe where to turn.

Deisseroth immediately wanted ChR2. The other opsins might do the trick, but because his goal—putting them into a brain and getting that brain to respond—was so tricky and success so improbable, he needed to try as many options as possible. He wrote to Nagel in the spring of 2004, requesting a copy of the gene and explaining he planned to try inserting it into neurons. "I was realistic enough to know it was worth testing but probably a long ways away from being useful," he says. "If I'd told him I was going to cure depression with it, I'm sure he would have thought I was crazy."

Deisseroth realized that even the first step of his plan—inserting the microbial opsin molecule into a mammalian neuron and getting the two to sync up—was a long shot. For one thing, there was a good chance the mammalian immune system would reject the foreign protein. Even if the opsin was tolerated, there was no way to know whether it could toggle mammalian cells in the same way it controlled algae. The opsin's electric signals would need to fire and shut down within milliseconds of the stimulus to communicate as quickly as neurons; Deisseroth doubted that the simple biology of algae required such speed.

To run the necessary tests, Deisseroth had to hire staff for his lab, and fast. Someone would have to provide expertise in handling viruses—specifically, a virus to serve as a vector, or Trojan horse, to cart algal genes into mammalian cells. The gene for the opsin would need to be inserted into the virus, which would infect the neurons, transferring the opsin gene to them. If all went as planned, mammalian neurons would then produce light-sensitive microbial opsins as if they were proteins of their own.

A Team Is Born

Luck was on Deisseroth's side that summer of 2004. As a new Stanford faculty member, he had moved into an office that had been occupied by Steven Chu, who had recently left Stanford to become director of the Lawrence Berkeley National Laboratory. Deisseroth's door still had Chu's name on it. One afternoon, a disoriented young chemistry student named Feng Zhang wandered in, looking for Chu. "I can still remember looking at him—he was a little surprised to see me," Deisseroth says. But the two started talking. Zhang wanted to understand the chemical imbalances underlying depression. He also had the skills to help Deisseroth with viruses: At age 15 he had started working with viral vectors, a project that won him the top prize at the Intel International Science and Engineering Fair. Now an aspiring Stanford PhD, he decided to join Deisseroth's team.

Next, Deisseroth required someone skilled at patch clamping, a technique that uses an electrode to record ions passing through cells. This would allow him to record when neurons fired or shut down, indicating whether they were responding to light. For this he hired Ed Boyden, a newly minted neuroscience PhD at Stanford. Boyden was brilliant and energetic, with an aggressiveness that was sometimes off-putting but was ideal for tackling nearly impossible experiments and getting them published. He also had expertise in electrophysiology, another skill required for Deisseroth's nascent optogenetics project.

That fall Deisseroth set to work with his new team. First they inserted the ChR2 opsin into a harmless retrovirus that Zhang had harvested. Then they added the engineered virus to a culture of rat neurons in a petri dish. As hoped, Zhang's virus penetrated the neurons and delivered the light-sensitive gene. The final step was observing whether the cell actually fired quickly in response to light. Boyden hooked up one neuron to a glass electrode that could also deliver light. The other end of the electrode was attached to a computer. When the cell was quiet, a steady line appeared on the computer screen; when it was active, the line jumped up in a spike.

To Deisseroth's elation, the effort was a success: As Boyden poked the electrode into the cell, Deisseroth saw pulses of bright blue light in the culture dish and spikes precisely matching those pulses on the computer screen. "For the next nine months we worked frenetically to publish it. We wanted to move quickly," Deisseroth says. The paper, published in *Nature Neuroscience* in August 2005, chronicled the first time anyone had managed to control brain cells with light.

The cell cultures still did not prove whether optogenetics would apply to brain cells inside living, freely moving mammals, however. The effort to find out required expanding the team. By 2006 Deisseroth had a tight-knit group of 15 who took frequent excursions to local Indian buffets and In-N-Out Burger when they were not working intensely side by side.

Cracking the Animal Code

In cell culture, only a small number of mild virus particles were needed to deliver the opsin gene to targeted neurons. But inserting genes into mammalian neurons inside an intact brain required a larger number of more virulent viruses. Zhang worked tirelessly on this challenge, developing a highly concentrated but still-safe retrovirus derived from HIV; in essence, he removed HIV's toxic genes and replaced them with a version of ChR2. He could brew the virus from scratch in just three days.

Deisseroth also needed a miniature flashlight that could be surgically inserted in the brain to turn cells on and off at close range. Mice weigh only about 20 grams, less than two tablespoons of sugar, so the device could not be big or heavy. And although the light needed to be 100 times as bright as room light, the system could not heat the brain as it delivered the beam. The team's solution was to implant a fiber-optic cable in the brain and connect it to a miniature laser affixed to the animal's head. The contraption was small and light enough to travel with the mouse wherever it went.

Finally, Deisseroth needed a way to tag the specific neurons he wanted to study so that only those cells would become activated in response to the light. Other brain researchers had identified certain cell types and areas of the brain associated with fear, reward, addiction, and depression. But they had no way of knowing exactly which neurons within these regions were driving a particular behavior. Deisseroth strove to find out. He used snippets of DNA called promoters to link ChR2 genes with DNA found only in the specific neurons he wanted to study. When he shined his light, it would not disturb the entire region but just the relevant cells.

Only then was Deisseroth ready to test optogenetics in a living animal. He charged Zhang with conducting a study of hypocretin neurons, sleep-related cells located deep in the brain's hypothalamus. The cells are crucial for arousal during sleep–wake cycles and are thought to play a key role in narcolepsy.

Zhang did the research at Stanford Sleep Center, where he could record brain waves of snoozing mice. He targeted ChR2 to the sleep cells and then, using optical fiber, delivered light directly to the mice's brains. In early 2007 his team placed a ChR2-altered mouse in a sleeping chamber with two implants in its skull. One was the optical fiber; the other consisted of four wires that measured the animal's brain waves.

Deisseroth vividly remembers the moment when an excited postdoc summoned him to the room. "I walked in and he whispered to me, 'Be quiet.'" A mouse was peacefully dreaming in his chamber. But when the laser was turned on, they saw a slight change on the brain-wave monitor and the animal began to twitch. It was waking up in response to a light signal inside its brain. For the first time ever, Deisseroth's team had used optogenetics to control behavior in a living animal.

Soon after, in March 2007, their results were more dramatic still. Deisseroth implanted an optical fiber in the cortex of a mouse with ChR2 in its motor neurons. When he flashed blue light through the cable, a meandering mouse began running to the left. When the laser was switched off, the mouse resumed wandering aimlessly. "You can turn it on and off and the animal isn't distressed. It's comfortable. You're just reaching in there with the fiber-optic, controlling the cells, and you're causing its behavior," Deisseroth says. "That was the moment I knew this would be amazing."

In the five years since, the Deisseroth lab, dubbed the D-lab, has expanded into an entire brain-control research center, with more than 40 scientists on the job. Molecular biologists, neuroscientists, engineers, and physicists from all over the world rush through his cavernous laboratories, tinkering with microscopes, lasers, viral soups, electrodes, and rodent brains. Located in the heart of Silicon Valley, the D-lab feels like an entrepreneurial start-up. Members enthusiastically talk among themselves, build and invent together—there is a palpable sense of enthusiasm and urgency.

One of the team's greatest accomplishments was spearheaded by Kay Tye, a former postdoc who now works at MIT. In a lab near Deisseroth's office, Tye inserted a fiber-optic cable into a mouse's little brain at just the right spot, leaving enough slack for the animal to run around. Tye was studying anxiety circuits and needed to put the cable into a specific part of the amygdala. For decades, researchers have known that the amygdala is associated with fear and anxiety but did not know exactly which neurons in what part of the amygdala played a role. Tye used data from previous studies to home in on a likely circuit, then carefully positioned the cable to deliver light right there. As the targeted neurons were stimulated, she watched to see how the mouse's behavior changed. If it suddenly became bolder, that would be a good sign that she had found a neuron set involved in anxiety.

Mice are naturally fearful of exploring open spaces, where they are vulnerable to predators. When placed in Tye's four-armed maze, they would spend most of their time in the two arms protected by high walls, occasionally poking a nose out to explore. But when Tye switched on the light and activated the circuit in her subject's brain, the mouse ventured out, exploring the open part of the maze with no visible anxiety. The results suggested that Tye had located an anxiety circuit in the brain that could someday be targeted by drugs.

Breaking the cycle of addictive behavior was another goal for the D-team. Again working with mice, they built a three-chamber cage in which one room became a designated drug den. Mice in that room received a shot of cocaine. Animals typically formed a positive association between the effects of the cocaine and the room, just as a person addicted to alcohol might form an association between feeling good and the pop of a cork. Left to their own devices, the mice hung around the room long after the cocaine wore off, even when they were free to wander elsewhere.

But when mice were injected with cocaine and also treated with halorhodopsins and light—in this case a yellow pulse sent directly to the brain's reward center—the rush of euphoria was blocked. Those mice never formed a positive association between cocaine and the room and roamed freely around the cage.

Later in 2010, Deisseroth teamed with neuroscientist Anatol Kreitzer at the University of California, San Francisco, to investigate Parkinson's disease—an important step toward using optogenetics to target a neurodegenerative disease. The ultimate cause of Parkinson's is unknown but clearly involves the loss of a set of neurons that control voluntary movement.

The basal ganglia are the brain's action control center. One pathway there sends signals to "go," as in go ahead and perform this action, and one sends "stop" signals. In Parkinson's the pathways are thought to be out of balance, with interrupted motor cells causing the debilitating tremors and loss of movement control symptomatic of the disease.

Although this theory of Parkinson's had been widely considered since the 1980s, there was no way to probe the circuit directly until optogenetics came along. Working with mice, Deisseroth and Kreitzer activated the "go" and "stop" circuits with light, confirming that one in fact facilitates movement while the other inhibits it. Next they tested a more nuanced hypothesis: Might Parkinson's result from an overactive stop circuit? Deisseroth and Kreitzer tagged that circuit with ChR2 and delivered blue light directly into the brains of mice. When the light turned on, movement slowed and the mice had trouble walking, both symptoms of Parkinson's.

What the researchers really wanted, though, was insight into how to treat the disease. They thought activating the go pathway could rebalance the overactive stop network. When they targeted the go circuit, that approach worked even better than expected. The mice began walking normally again, their movement indistinguishable from the way they had moved in their healthy state. Today's leading treatment for Parkinson's—deep brain stimulation—involves inserting a large electrode deep within the patient's brain and zapping all surrounding tissue. Deisseroth hopes that his findings will bring a more targeted treatment soon.

Indeed, by combining opsins, including ChR2, which turns cells on, and halorhodopsin and bacteriorhodopsin, which turn cells off, Deisseroth can ask ever more nuanced questions about complex diseases: Epilepsy, autism, sleep disorders, and schizophrenia may all require this combination approach.

Turning cells on and off efficiently allows a whole range of new, more detailed experiments: Now Deisseroth can tell neurons to fire and shut down quickly, so they can be ready to receive the next signal telling them what to do. Using multiple opsins as well as blue, yellow, and green light, he can experiment with various combinations of activation in hopes of eliminating symptoms of disease.

Pacing the Heart with Light

Despite the fact that Deisseroth has focused on animal brains, the first optogenetic implants—which could be ready for human trials in as little as a decade—will almost surely focus on other organs, where applications are less risky. Early therapies could take the form of a heart pacemaker that uses light to activate heart cells and keep them firing on time. There has been talk of optogenetics for the blind, implanting opsins in vision cells and developing special glasses that shine light into them.

In the fall of 2011, Deisseroth cofounded a company in Menlo Park, around the corner from Stanford, dedicated to translating optogenetics research into therapies. One focus is peripheral nerve disorder, in which messages between the brain and the rest of the body are interrupted. It is often caused by spinal cord injuries, multiple sclerosis, and other nervous system disorders.

"It's not very glamorous, but there's a very large population of people who have peripheral nerve defects that keep them from having good bowel and bladder control," Deisseroth says. "And what's interesting is, if you ask the people who have paralysis if they could choose one thing, to be able to walk or to have bowel and bladder control, they essentially all pick bowel and bladder control, because it's the most limiting for them. It is a problem well suited to optogenetics." Bladder control requires both a contraction of the bladder and a relaxation of the sphincter, and optogenetics can both stimulate and inhibit those different neurons at the same time. Deisseroth hopes to introduce opsins to the crucial peripheral nerves outside the brain and then use simple LED implants to switch function back on.

Once someone has figured out how to get opsins inside the brains of primates and humans—Zhang at MIT is working on the problem now—optogenetic therapies targeting the brain can begin. The possibility also opens the door to Orwellian fears. If Deisseroth can control the brains of mice with light, what is to stop human mind control? The most cogent answer is this: Creating transgenic people by sending a retrovirus into healthy brains will never be allowed. Besides, the potential for healing is too great to ignore—starting with a better implant for those who suffer from Parkinson's, a neurodegenerative disease already treated with electrodes in the brain.

Getting into the Human Brain

Deisseroth's great insight has spawned research around the world. Every two weeks, scientists come from universities in the United States and abroad to spend a week at the D-lab learning the secrets of optogenetics, mastering everything from mouse surgery to cooking up viruses. At the end of the week they present their plans for research of their own. Deisseroth slouches in his seat, wearing coffee-stained jeans, clogs, and a short-sleeve button-down shirt that he has not tucked in. The laissez-faire demeanor is deceptive: Deisseroth is fully engaged and always on, often jumping in during a presentation to ask questions or offer suggestions. The waiting list to attend his workshop is more than a dozen labs long.

One notable alumna is Ana Domingos, who flew in from New York's Rockefeller University a few years back. She was investigating weight loss and wanted to use optogenetics to trigger dopamine, a mood-enhancing neurotransmitter, whenever mice drank water laced with an artificial sweetener, causing them to ignore their usual preference, a sugar-spiked drink. Domingos hopes to use her findings to develop weight loss therapies. "The first time I saw the mouse bingeing on water with sweetener, I got goosebumps," Domingos says. "I couldn't sleep. Karl gave me the tools to play god."

Following these presentations, Deisseroth grabs lunch before attending his weekly patient psychiatry sessions. He picks an outdoor seat at a nearby café swarming with people on a sunny, 75-degree day in mid-January. It's a rare moment of downtime for Deisseroth, who readily admits he needs to relax more.

Even with his lab in high gear, Deisseroth is constantly busy trying to help his psychiatry patients. One of them, Alicia A, has tried nearly every medication, ECT, and various electrical implants to keep her depression under control. She drives seven hours once a month to visit Deisseroth, and together they have found a successful combination of electrical nerve stimulation and antidepressant drugs that has allowed her to return to work and enjoy life. Yet she intently follows Deisseroth's optogenetics work and is adamant that if he ever starts human trials, she will be the first in line.

As much as Alicia A's life has improved from sessions with Deisseroth, the electrical stimulation is often uncomfortable, and her treatment requires constant monitoring. Deisseroth has an entirely different therapy possibility in mind for her. From his experience with ECT, he knows inducing a seizure with electricity resets individual neurons in the brain just like rebooting a computer, so those neurons fire all at once in a different order than before. But something peculiar and fascinating happens to the patient: When the therapy is over everything about the person—memories, priorities, the sense of self—comes back. Apparently these things are not generated by neurons but arise from the brain's physical structure and wiring. The wires are like superhighways, roads of activity where circuits of neurons constantly communicate, but sometimes the road might be gridlocked or icy, and the messenger can't get through.

At one level, optogenetics is nothing more than using light to control a targeted population of cells. But how these cells are wired up is a huge puzzle in itself and, to Deisseroth, one that lies at the true root of future psychiatric cures. To turn his wiring insights into therapy, he wants to use optogenetics to narrow down which circuits dictate which specific behaviors. Then, if he can determine whether the circuits are somehow impeded or blocked, he can try to physically shift them and normalize activity flow.

The Magnetic Cure

Deisseroth isn't certain which tools will allow him to study these connections—it's a capability beyond the reach of optogenetics—so he is once again on the edge of something big and unprecedented. A type of brain imaging, called diffusion tensor imaging, allows doctors to scan patients and produce vibrantly colored images of the brain's wiring. These connections vary from individual to individual. When abnormalities are detected, a machine therapy called transcranial magnetic stimulation (TMS) can send into the brain magnetic pulses powerful enough to shift and rewire those connections so their function is improved. TMS is already used to treat ailments like Parkinson's disease, migraines, and depression.

Years ago as a psychiatry resident, Deisseroth assisted with the clinical trial that got the therapy FDA-approved. He plans to continue using optogenetics to pin down circuits of brain cells responsible for disease and to combine that knowledge with the colorful circuit images to home in on which wires need to go where to establish normal communication. Then TMS can move the wires precisely where they need to go to cure any particular illness. If it works, scientists would have a complete understanding of an individual patient's brain.

The concept may sound extraordinary, too grand to work, but this is the type of challenge Deisseroth loves most. "I want to come up with totally new things, so I don't want to be affected by too many preconceptions," he says. Conveniently, Deisseroth's own brain is wired to generate its best ideas in moments of isolation. "I can remember a couple key insights just driving in my car. For me, that's meditative. I rarely solve a problem by thinking about it. The insights usually come from out of the blue, like a bolt."

Critical Thinking

1. Why do you think people with peripheral nerve defects would rather have good bowel and bladder control than be able to walk again?
2. Do you think the science of optogenetics will allow people to control others (e.g., mind control)? Why or why not?
3. Do you think great insights come "out of the blue" like a bolt, or from meditating on a problem? Why for either choice?

Create Central

www.mhhe.com/createcentral

Internet References

The Primary Structure of a Halorhodopsin
www.jbc.org/content/265/3/1253.abstract

Transcranial Magnetic Stimulation-Scholarpedia
www.scholarpedia.org/article/Transcranial_magnetic_stimulation

What Is Optogenetics?
http://optogenetics.weebly.com/what-is-it.html

Amy Barth is an associate editor at *Discover*.

Article

Prepared by: Claire N. Rubman, *Suffolk County Community College*

The New Survivors

For over 11 million Americans, cancer is no longer a definite death sentence. The dreaded disease has instead become a crucible, often remaking personality and endowing survivors with qualities not even they knew they had.

Pamela Weintraub

Learning Outcomes

After reading this article, you will be able to:

- Examine how "learning to hope" can prolong the lives of cancer patients.
- Explain what is meant by posttraumatic growth and why it is reaped long after the trauma of cancer.

Jasan Zimmerman was 6 months old when he was diagnosed with neuroblastoma of the left neck in 1976. First the cancer was surgically removed, then he was treated with radiation. Perhaps it was exposure to all that radiation that caused the thyroid cancer when he was 15. More surgery, more radiation. But this time, old enough to grasp the situation, he was terrified. "I didn't want to die" recalls Zimmerman, who grit his teeth through the grueling treatment. Almost as difficult was the aftermath: Traumatized by the experience, he spent his teen years sullen and depressed, without quite knowing why.

He tried to put it all out of his mind—until cancer appeared for a third time in 1997. He was 21 and had just graduated from college. Again Zimmerman was successfully treated. He pursued life goals, including a master's degree in microbiology, but his inner turmoil remained.

The literature on survivorship indicates that between 30 and 90 percent of patients became hardier and more upbeat after the diagnosis of cancer was made.

For 11 more years, he went for checkups, always fearing a return of the dread disease. "I'd get road rage on the way to the doctor. Even the smell of clinical antiseptic could piss me off," he reports. Despite some scares, the cancer never came back, but living with his history itself became a burden. How soon into a new relationship would he need to confess his medical past? Would he ever be free of the threat? By 2003, he was so angry that he punched a wall and broke his hand.

Today, Zimmerman is able to turn his back on the ordeal. He's done it only by embracing his role as a survivor and speaking out to many of the 1.4 million Americans diagnosed with the disease each year. His message is about the ability to *overcome,* and he openly describes his own experience. "Each time I share my story people feel hopeful," he says. And he does, too. "I was living under a thundercloud. It's taken me decades to grow from the experience, but the ability to inspire people has turned a negative into a positive and opened me up."

In the past, the very word *cancer* summoned images of hopelessness, pain, and death; little thought was given to life after cancer because it was considered brief. The cancer "victim" was seen as the passive recipient of ill fate and terrible luck. No more.

Survivorship is increasingly common; some 11.4 million Americans are alive today after treatment and are ever more vocal about their experiences. Emboldened by effective diagnosis and treatment strategies, celebrities such as Melissa Etheridge and Fran Drescher have made public disclosure of the disease increasingly routine and the fight definitely important and profound. Tour de France champion Lance Armstrong, determined to train for the world-class athletic event on the heels of treatment for advanced testicular cancer, turned his achievement into advocacy through his LiveStrong movement.

Many cancer survivors are travelers to a highly intense edge world where they battle death and return transformed. They leave as ordinary and burdened mortals and come back empowered and invigorated. In coming closer to fear, risk, and death than most of us, they wind up marshaling qualities not even they knew they had.

As more patients have lived longer, a body of research on their experiences has developed. It demonstrates that many cancer patients muster enormous grit for highly aggressive treatments and endure considerable pain to accrue small gains in the fight for survival. Despite therapies that weaken them physically, they can be especially psychologically hardy, harnessing and growing from their stress. Even the most narrow-minded or inflexible people may come to love art, beauty, and philosophical truth as a way of getting through the ordeal. Those who survive often come out of the experience with bravery, curiosity, fairness, forgiveness, gratitude, humor, kindness, and an enhanced sense of meaning.

Is there something about cancer itself that is transformative and growth-inspiring? Do we literally need to face death to go beyond the often petty limits of our workaday lives? William Breitbart, chief of the psychiatry service at Memorial Sloan-Kettering Cancer Center in New York City and an international leader in psycho-ontology, says we just might.

"It is in our nature to transcend our limitations, but too often we get distracted by everyday life. If life is always smooth, we're never challenged," he says. "Suffering is probably necessary to make us grow." The ultimate tool may be a brush with death. "The need to find meaning is a primary force," adds Breitbart, himself a cancer survivor, "but we may need to be confronted with our own mortality for that to occur." In the school of hard knocks, cancer amounts to earning a PhD.

Learning to Hope

Carol Farran, an eldercare expert from Rush University Medical Center in Chicago, sought to understand why some nursing home residents thrived despite adversity and isolation while others just withered away. The difference between the two groups, she found, was hope—not the blind or rigid optimism that usually passes for hope, but an open sense of possibility, acceptance of risk, and a willingness to work things out. Hopeful people face reality in a clear-eyed fashion, doing the best they can. One woman too sick to go outdoors, for instance, maintained an upbeat attitude by remembering the emotional riches of her past. "The hopeful person looked at reality and then arrived at solutions. If a hoped-for outcome became impossible, the hopeful person would find something else to hope for," Farran found.

The role of hope in cancer has also come under scrutiny. Psychologists at the Royal Marsden Hospital in London and Sutton studied women with early-stage breast cancer and found that risk of recurrence or death increased significantly among those who lacked hope. There was nothing mysterious or mystical about it: Hopeful patients managed their illness themselves instead of letting outsiders pull the strings. They often chose the most aggressive treatments. And envisioning the light at the end of the tunnel helped provide the strength they needed to get through each difficult day.

Yet hope was not a given for them; it was an attitude they wrested from despair. Despite being an expert on hope, Farran could not muster any when she herself was diagnosed with breast cancer. She met the news with anger, grief, and fear of death. Panic propelled her through treatment, in a total daze. Only when she went in for breast reconstruction was a wise nurse able to penetrate her panic: "A year from now you'll be where you want to be, but there is no way to get there except by going through this experience, now."

As despair loosened its hold on Farran, she tried to embrace the flexibility she had studied in others. "I told myself to get a grip." she says. Finally she thought of her love of playing piano and decided to buy a metronome, a symbol of what she called "slow time." It was a palpable reminder to calm down, confront her fear of death, and think things through. "You can start in despair but arrive at hope," says Farran, 18 years later. Hope can be learned.

True Grit

Once empowered by hope, cancer patients have been known to search out cures in the face of daunting odds. Jerome Groopman, a Harvard cancer specialist and author of *Anatomy of Hope,* tells the story of a patient, a pathologist with advanced metastatic stomach cancer that was considered fatal. Soon word spread around the hospital that the pathologist intended to do something "mad." Without any evidence that his cancer was survivable, he insisted on doses of chemotherapy and radiation so toxic they were, by themselves, probably lethal. To Groopman and other cancer doctors on staff at the time, the effort seemed "like a desperate, wrongheaded, ultimately futile effort to resist the inevitable." Surely the treatment would deprive the pathologist of a peaceful end at home. Indeed, Groopman, stopping by the man's bedside, found him bleeding as tissues were literally burned away by the strong treatment he had engineered.

Twenty-five years later, while researching his book on hope, Groopman found that the pathologist was still going strong. "If I'd been treating him, I wouldn't have authorized the therapy and he would have died."

Similar tenacity gripped Sean Patrick, a business strategist and extreme sports enthusiast from Aspen, Colorado, whose rare form of ovarian cancer was diagnosed in 1998. Instead of simply agreeing to follow her doctor's treatment advice, she hired a research firm to comb the scientific literature and come up with a list of experts studying her specific disease. She quickly learned that her doctor had recommended the wrong treatment and if she followed through she might not survive the year.

So she fired her oncologist and hired a medical team known for experimental use of drugs. The side effects of her radical treatment were devastating. "Flu symptoms magnified a thousand times," Patrick said. There was nausea, vomiting, disabling body aches, extreme weakness, chills, and diarrhea. "I would shake so hard my teeth would knock and then have a fever so high I would sweat through my clothes." She nicknamed the side effects "shake and bake." Still, she persisted, at one point even electing a surgery so risky she was not expected to wake up. "If I hadn't taken the risk, I wouldn't be here today," she said in 2006. Her grit gave her a full decade more than anyone expected; she died just before this article went to press, in 2009.

Most people don't have the financial resources to seek such customized or experimental options, but even patients dependent on treatment approvals by an insurance company can choose the most aggressive courses that might confer even a slight survival edge. That explains why so many women with stage-one breast cancer opt for removal of both breasts instead of the watch-and-wait approach. It also explains why ovarian cancer patients subject themselves to multiple rounds of chemotherapy, often rejecting studies contending the treatment will fail.

"Even if it is a long shot, someone is going to fall at the end of the bell curve," notes Groopman.

Soldiering On

Research shows that, even while dealing with the disease, large numbers of cancer patients deploy their tenacity in other realms of life, as well. Take Elizabeth Cowie, 44, a career sergeant in the Army who was headed to Iraq with her troops. There was only one problem: Months before deployment, in a routine Army physical, Cowie was diagnosed with early-stage breast cancer. Instead of going home to attend to treatment, Cowie poured her energy into finding a way to get to Iraq along with the soldiers she'd trained. She forsook the more extreme course of mastectomy for circumscribed lumpectomy, dramatically shortening surgical recovery, and decided against weeks of radiation therapy in favor of a new technique she learned of, called Mammasite, which delivers radiation directly to the tumor over the course of days. She underwent the procedures quietly, without telling the soldiers reporting to her until she was declared cancer-free, and went on with her deployment, gritting her teeth only when her vest chafed the still-healing surgical wound. Cowie endured the heat of Iraq while still recovering, all the while watching over and counseling the soldiers she'd become so close to.

"There were days I was so sore and the heat was so oppressive and it was so exhausting," Cowie recalls. "But I had a commitment to the people I was with. The soldiers counted on me being there. Just knowing that made me stronger, and I couldn't let them down. I put one foot in front of the other; that is how I saw my mission through."

Cowie's can-do attitude is a trait common among the new survivors. According to University of Utah psychologist Lisa Aspinwall, a sense of purpose and positivity is adaptive in cancer's midst. In reviewing the literature on survivorship, Aspinwall found that 30 to 90 percent of patients reported benefits, from increased optimism to better relationships, *after* diagnosis was made. At first it seemed counterintuitive. But the positive, active mind-set "is likely to help patients manage what they need to do next," she explains. "Those in treatment must make dozens of decisions. To hold things together, you need to pay attention to options. Just think about it—negative emotions orient us to threats, but they also narrow our attention. That's not the best state for navigating a complex and changing situation, just what cancer is."

Post-Traumatic Growth

The benefits seen during the trauma, however, may pale against those reaped later, after survivors have had the chance to reflect. "It's hard to grow much when you are in the middle of a war," says psychologist Lad Wenzel of the University of California at Irvine, who works with women surviving gynecologic cancer at least five years. "Instead, strength and meaning unfold for survivors as they retell their stories, again and again."

There is nothing mystical about the power of hope. Hopeful patients managed their own illness instead of letting outsiders do it. They often chose the most aggressive treatments.

University of Connecticut psychologist Keith Bellizzi says the life event is so intense that some people use it to reconstruct their lives; they don't return to the same level of functioning but to a greater level. "Post-traumatic growth is above and beyond resilience," he says. "Life after cancer means finding a new normal, but for many the new normal is better than the old normal."

Bellizzi, 39, speaks from direct experience. He was a well-paid marketing professional when, at age 25, he was diagnosed with stage-three testicular cancer so advanced it had spread to his lymph nodes and lungs. A few months later, a CAT scan revealed a golf-ball-size mass in his kidney. Almost as upsetting as the cancer was the news that he might never have biological children of his own. "It was an opportunity to reflect on my life and face my mortality," says Bellizzi.

Following several surgeries, including removal of a kidney, along with aggressive chemotherapy, he made a vow: "If I survived, I would dedicate my life to the fight against cancer." Bellizzi kept his vow. He quit his lucrative job and went back to school, earning masters degrees in public health and in psychology and a PhD in human development and family studies. In 2005, he was one of 24 cyclists chosen to ride with Lance Armstrong on the Bristol-Myers Squibb Tour of Hope to heighten awareness of cancer research. He also has three daughters—and is a leading researcher in the field of post-traumatic growth.

Bellizzi's sense of purpose is just one type of growth that survivors report. Julia Rowland, head of the Office of Cancer Survivorship at the National Cancer Institute, points to enhanced and altered relationships. "You learn who's going to be there for you and who is not—you learn who your friends are," she says. Some friends, upset by the prospect of loss, may detach temporarily or even permanently. As some friendships fade, others may be forged, especially within the community of survivors. "You also learn to empathize," says Rowland, explaining how survivors acquire new depths of feeling.

Pleasures become more meaningful, too. As a team at the University of Pennsylvania found, those suffering chronic illness end up more immersed in art, music, and books. "Appreciation is often enhanced," points out Bellizzi. Many survivors literally stop to smell the roses even if they didn't before.

Not everyone diagnosed with cancer finds a new sense of purpose. "Some people have a glimpse of the possibilities but do not change. Cancer is just wasted on them."

The sense of self is often enhanced too. "Some survivors discover an inner strength they didn't realize they had," says Bellizzi. "A situation that might have seemed daunting before cancer may, after cancer, seem like something easily handled."

In one important study, Bellizzi looked at generativity—concerns, often arising at midlife, about the legacy one is likely to leave behind. Generativity can be expressed in many ways—making the planet a better place, giving children the love they need, being creative in work or intimate with family and friends. Midlifers surveying the past may vow to do more with the time they have left. But no matter an individual's age, Bellizzi found, cancer was a catalyst for generativity.

While cancer generally sparked more generativity in women than in men, all the survivors Bellizzi studied were more likely than those without cancer to forge a new life path reflecting their core values. Those reporting the most altered perspective "expressed an increased awareness of the fragility of life and the value of loved ones," he reports. "They also said they had learned not to worry about little annoyances." A patient with colorectal cancer said her disease had convinced her to put an end to meaningless pursuits; she resigned from her management position and spent time with her friends.

A Spiritual Dimension

Cancer can also promote a sense of inner meaning and add a spiritual dimension to life. Lisa Benaron, an internist and pediatrician from Chico, California, learned she had cancer in the midst of other traumas. Her sister-in-law, a dear friend, had just died of breast cancer. And her marriage was falling apart. Six months after her sister-in-law died, Benaron, too, was diagnosed with breast cancer. Although in stage one, her cancer was a particularly aggressive kind; further, she had the gene that signals ongoing risk.

Energized by her situation, Benaron focused on researching the best treatment options and chose the most aggressive course, to gain a few points of survival advantage. The chemo was debilitating, but she still recalls fondly the days after those sessions. They were, she insists, "great times. I didn't usually get enough time off to garden, or do yoga." She did then.

She made an effort to pursue the things she loved: kayaking, walks in nature, spending time with her daughter, Molly, then 7. "I took Molly to the Galapagos Islands on Easter break in 2004," Benaron recalls. "You could sit on the beach and the seals and iguanas would be right there within arms reach. Having cancer made me aware of how fortunate I was and how much beauty was in the world."

Her own journey wasn't complete, though, until a friend she met in the local cancer community, Theresa Marcis, sought her help to travel to Abadiania, Brazil, to see a healer named John of God. "When she was first diagnosed, Theresa had a large mass and stage-three cancer; the prognosis wasn't good," says Benaron. "But she was full of hope. She wrote the word HEAL in big burgundy letters on her kitchen walls."

Under ordinary circumstances, the logical, driven doctor would have had little in common with the free-spirited Marcis, a college English teacher. But under the influence of cancer, they became a team. Benaron helped Marcis navigate the mainstream medical minefield, and Marcis exposed Benaron to acupuncture, sound therapy, and other alternative techniques. "They were enjoyable and peaceful," Benaron recalls.

In 2008, doctors found that Marcis's cancer had spread to every bone in her body. Instead of conceding defeat, she journeyed with a colleague to Brazil to see John of God. Though her condition later worsened, she spoke of going back. When she was too sick to travel, Benaron went in her stead, "to give Theresa peace."

Still very much the logical physician, Benaron doesn't believe that John's interventions can cure. But she loved taking the trip as proxy for her gentle friend, who died hoping that John's powers would stretch from central Brazil to her home in California. "I came to realize through her that every person has their own path through life; she tapped into every good feeling within herself and threw herself into being spiritual. It helped me to see the importance of love and openness to others," Benaron says.

The California physician remembers meditating in Abadiania with a huge thunderstorm whipping up around her. "It was this gorgeous experience," she reports. "But I realized I didn't have to go across the world or down a dirt road to find it. You can be in the moment wherever you are."

Tyranny vs. Transformation

The idea that cancer can be uplifting or transformative has become controversial in the cancer community itself. Posttraumatic growth, while common, does not define all survivors. Young people, whose disease may be more challenging, often grow more emotionally from the experience than older people. "It's very disruptive to have cancer while raising your family and climbing in your career," explains Bellizzi, "and it's the intensity of the experience and the realization that life is finite that forges change."

Not everyone diagnosed with cancer transcends the past, finds a new sense of purpose, or becomes more spiritual. And in the midst of a deadly disease, the pressure to remake oneself can feel harsh. "It's wrong to pressure people to be optimistic or change their lives," says Utah's Lisa Aspinwall.

"Some will not be able to take advantage of having had cancer," says Breitbart of Memorial Sloan-Kettering. "Some people with poor prognoses just want to hasten death. Some have a glimpse of the possibilities but do not change. Cancer is just wasted on some people."

Still, cancer patients have undeniably entered a new era in which long lives are very much a reality, and they are changed by having looked death in the eye and beaten it back. The experience has made them stronger and forced them to reevaluate the very foundations of their lives. "The bottom line for me is I finally realized that I want to turn the negative experiences of having cancer into a positive," says Jasan Zimmerman, "and the more I do, the more I want to do. I don't want to miss out on anything."

Critical Thinking

1. Paraphrase the following: "Suffering is necessary to make us grow."
2. Label some of the qualities "discovered" by people with cancer.
3. Relate how a battle with death can transform a person.

Create Central

www.mhhe.com/createcentral

Internet References

Connect with Spiritual Side on Cancer Journey
www.mayoclinic.org/health/cancer-and-spirituality/MY02026

The Power of Hope: Reading between the (Head) Lines
www.psychologytoday.com/blog/reading-between-the-headlines/201307/the-power-hope

The Transformative Effects of Illness
www.ncbi.nlm.nih.gov/pubmed/9362651

Pamela Weintraub is a writer in New York.

Article

Prepared by: Claire N. Rubman, *Suffolk County Community College*

How to Fix the Obesity Crisis

Although science has revealed a lot about metabolic processes that influence our weight, the key to success may lie elsewhere.

DAVID H. FREEDMAN

Learning Outcomes

After reading this article, you will be able to:

- Generate a plan to deal with the behavioral issues of obesity.
- Explain why mass-market programs tend to fall short when it comes to maintaining weight loss.

Obesity is a national health crisis—that much we know. If current trends continue, it will soon surpass smoking in the U.S. as the biggest single factor in early death, reduced quality of life and added health care costs. A third of adults in the U.S. are obese, according to the Centers for Disease Control and Prevention, and another third are overweight, with Americans getting fatter every year. Obesity is responsible for more than 160,000 "excess" deaths a year, according to a study in the *Journal of the American Medical Association*. The average obese person costs society more than $7,000 a year in lost productivity and added medical treatment, say researchers at George Washington University. Lifetime added medical costs alone for a person 70 pounds or more overweight amount to as much as $30,000, depending on race and gender.

All this lends urgency to the question: Why are extra pounds so difficult to shed and keep off? It doesn't seem as though it should be so hard. The basic formula for weight loss is simple and widely known: consume fewer calories than you expend. And yet if it really were easy, obesity would not be the nation's number-one lifestyle-related health concern. For a species that evolved to consume energy-dense foods in an environment where famine was a constant threat, losing weight and staying trimmer in a modern world of plenty fueled by marketing messages and cheap empty calories is, in fact, terrifically difficult. Almost everybody who tries to diet seems to fail in the long run—a review in 2007 by the American Psychological Association of 31 diet studies found that as many as two thirds of dieters end up two years later weighing more than they did before their diet.

Science has trained its big guns on the problem. The National Institutes of Health has been spending nearly $800 million a year on studies to understand the metabolic, genetic and neurological foundations of obesity. In its proposed plan for obesity research funding in 2011, the NIH lists promising research avenues in this order: animal models highlighting protein functions in specific tissues; complex signaling pathways in the brain and between the brain and other organs; identification of obesity-related gene variants; and epigenetic mechanisms regulating metabolism.

This research has provided important insights into the ways proteins interact in our body to extract and distribute energy from food and produce and store fat; how our brains tell us we are hungry; why some of us seem to have been born more likely to be obese than others; and whether exposure to certain foods and toxic substances might modify and mitigate some of these factors. The work has also given pharmaceutical companies numerous potential targets for drug development. What the research has not done, unfortunately, is make a dent in solving the national epidemic.

Maybe someday biology will provide us with a pill that readjusts our metabolism so we burn more calories or resets our built-in cravings so we prefer broccoli to burgers. But until then, the best approach may simply be to build on reliable behavioral-psychology methods developed over 50 years and proved to work in hundreds of studies. These tried-and-true techniques, which are being refined with new research that should make them more effective with a wider range of individuals, are gaining new attention. As the NIH puts it in its proposed strategic plan for obesity research: "Research findings are yielding new and important insights about social and behavioral factors that influence diet, physical activity, and sedentary behavior."

How We Got Here

The desperation of the obese and overweight is reflected in the steady stream of advice pouring daily from sources as disparate as peer-reviewed scientific journals, best-selling books, newspapers and blogs. Our appetite for any diet twist or gimmick that will take the pounds off quickly and for good seems to be as insatiable as our appetite for the rich food that puts the pounds on. We, the public, love to believe in neat fixes, and the media oblige by playing up new scientific findings in headline after headline as if they are solutions.

It doesn't help that the scientific findings on which these headlines are based sometimes appear to conflict. For example, a study in September's *American Journal of Clinical Nutrition* found a link between increased dairy intake and weight loss, although a meta-analysis in the May 2008 *Nutrition Reviews* discovered no such link. A paper in the *Journal of Occupational and Environmental Medicine* in January 2010 postulated a connection between job stress and obesity, but in October a report in the journal *Obesity* concluded there was no such correlation. Part of the problem, too, is that obesity researchers are in some ways akin to the metaphorical blind men groping at different parts of the elephant, their individual study findings addressing only narrow pieces of a complex puzzle.

When the research is taken together, it is clear that the obesity fix cannot be boiled down to eating this or that food type or to taking any other simple action. Many factors contribute to the problem. It is partly environment—the eating habits of your friends, what food is most available in your home and your local stores, how much opportunity you have to move around at work. It is partly biology—there are genetic predispositions for storing fat, for having higher satiety thresholds, even for having more sensitive taste buds. It is partly economics—junk food has become much cheaper than fresh produce. And it is marketing, too—food companies have become masterful at playing on human social nature and our evolutionary "programming" to steer us toward unhealthy but profitable fare. That is why the narrow "eat this" kinds of solutions, like all simple solutions, fail.

When we go on diets and exercise regimens, we rely on willpower to overcome all these pushes to overeat relative to our activity level. And we count on the reward of getting trimmer and fitter to keep us on the wagon. It *is* rewarding to lose the weight, of course. Unfortunately, time works against us. As the weight comes off, we get hungrier and develop stronger cravings and become more annoyed by the exercise. Meanwhile the weight loss inevitably slows as our metabolism tries to compensate for this deprivation by becoming more parsimonious with calories. Thus, the punishment for sticking to our regimen becomes increasingly severe and constant, and the expected reward recedes into the future. "That gap between the reinforcement of eating and the reinforcement of maybe losing weight months later is a huge challenge," says Sung-Woo Kahng, a neurobehaviorist who studies obesity at the Johns Hopkins University School of Medicine and the Kennedy Krieger Institute.

We would be more likely to stick with the regimen if it remained less punishing and more reliably rewarding. Is there a way to make that happen?

From Biology to Brain

The most successful way to date to lose at least modest amounts of weight and keep it off with diet and exercise employs programs that focus on changing behavior. The behavioral approach, tested over decades, involves making many small, sustainable adjustments in eating and exercise habits that are prompted and encouraged by the people and the rest of the environment around us.

The research in support of behavioral weight-loss approaches extends back more than half a century to Harvard University psychologist B. F. Skinner's development of the science of behavioral analysis. The field is founded on the notion that scientists cannot really know what is going on inside a person's brain—after all, even functional MRIs, the state of the art for peering into the mind, are crude, highly interpretable proxies for cognition and emotion that reduce the detailed firing of billions of neurons in complex circuits to a few blobs of color. But researchers can objectively and reproducibly observe and measure physical behavior and the immediate environment in which the behavior occurs, allowing them to identify links between environment and behavior. That typically includes trying to spot events or situations that may be prompting or triggering certain behaviors and noting what may be rewarding and thus reinforcing of some behaviors or punishing and thus inhibiting of others.

The effectiveness of behavioral interventions has been extensively documented for a wide variety of disorders and problem behaviors. A 2009 meta-analysis in the *Journal of Clinical Child & Adolescent Psychology* concluded that "early intensive behavioral intervention should be an intervention of choice for children with autism." A systematic review sponsored by the U.S. Preventive Services Task Force found that even brief behavioral counseling interventions reduced the number of drinks taken by problem drinkers by 13 to 34

Advances in the Lab

The Biology of Obesity

The National Institutes of Health has spent nearly $800 million a year on studies to understand the neurological, metabolic and genetic foundations of obesity. In the process, scientists have uncovered complex biochemical pathways and feedback loops that connect the brain and digestive system; a new appreciation for the regulatory functions of fat tissues; subtle hereditary changes that make some groups more prone to obesity than others; and the strong possibility that exposure to certain foods and toxic substances might modify and mitigate some of these factors. Given that it will likely take decades to understand the various causes of obesity, more surprises are no doubt in store.

Brain: Scientists have long known that the hypothalamus and brain stem help to regulate feelings of hunger and fullness. Over the past several years researchers have found that the pleasure-reward centers of the limbic system and the evaluating functions of the prefrontal cortex are also heavily involved. Indeed, chronic overeating bears biochemical similarities to drug addiction.

Metabolism: The ability to burn and store energy varies greatly from cell to cell. In 2009 three studies in the *New England Journal of Medicine* demonstrated that at least some women and men continue to benefit well into adulthood from small stores of brown fat, which, unlike white fat, is associated with being lean. Brown fat helps to generate heat and is apparently more closely related to muscle than to white fat, whose primary purpose is to store excess energy.

Genes: Researchers have confirmed variations in 20-odd genes that predispose people to gaining weight easily. But further investigation shows that the effects are modest at best and cannot account for the current obesity epidemic. Genes may still play a role, however, through the environment's influence on which ones get turned on or off. So far most such genetic switches for obesity have been identified in mice, although a few likely human candidates are known.

percent for as long as four years. Review studies have found similar behavioral-intervention successes in challenges as diverse as reducing stuttering, increasing athletic performance and improving employee productivity.

To combat obesity, behavioral analysts examine related environmental influences: Which external factors prompt people to overeat or to eat junk food, and which tend to encourage healthful eating? In what situations are the behaviors and comments of others affecting unhealthful eating? What seems to effectively reward eating healthfully over the long term? What reinforces being active? Behavior-focused studies of obesity and diets as early as the 1960s recognized some basic conditions that seemed correlated with a greater chance of losing weight and keeping it off: rigorously measuring and recording calories, exercise and weight; making modest, gradual changes rather than severe ones; eating balanced diets that go easy on fats and sugar rather than dropping major food groups; setting clear, modest goals; focusing on lifelong habits rather than short-term diets; and especially attending groups where dieters could receive encouragement to stick with their efforts and praise for having done so.

If these strategies today sound like well-worn, commonsense advice, it is because they have been popularized for nearly half a century by Weight Watchers. Founded in 1963 to provide support groups for dieters, Weight Watchers added other approaches and advice in keeping with the findings of behavioral studies and used to bill itself as a "behavior-modification" program. "Whatever the details are of how you lose weight, the magic in the sauce is always going to be changing behavior," says nutrition researcher and Weight Watchers chief science officer Karen Miller-Kovach. "Doing that is a learnable skill."

Studies back the behavioral approach to weight loss. A 2003 review commissioned by the U.S. Department of Health and Human Services found that "counseling and behavioral interventions showed small to moderate degrees of weight loss sustained over at least one year"—a year being an eon in the world of weight loss. An analysis of eight popular weight-loss programs published in 2005 in the *Annals of Internal Medicine* found Weight Watchers (at that time in its pre-2010 points-overhaul incarnation) to be the only effective program, enabling a 3 percent maintained body-weight loss for the two years of the study. Meanwhile a 2005 *JAMA* study found that Weight Watchers, along with the Zone diet (which, like Weight Watchers, recommends a balanced diet of protein, carbohydrates and fat), achieved the highest percentage (65 percent) of one-year diet adherence of several popular diets, noting that "adherence level rather than diet type was the key determinant of clinical benefits." A 2010 study in the *Journal of Pediatrics* found that after one year children receiving behavioral therapy maintained a body mass index that was 1.9 to 3.3 lower than children who did not. (BMI is a numerical height-weight relation in which 18.5 is held to be borderline underweight and 25 borderline overweight.) The *Pediatrics* report noted that "more limited evidence suggests that these improvements can be maintained over the 12 months after the end of treatments." A 2010 study in *Obesity* found that continuing members of Take Off Pounds Sensibly (TOPS), a national, nonprofit behaviorally focused weight-loss organization, maintained a weight loss of 5 to 7 percent of their body weight for the three years of the investigation. The UK's Medical Research Council last year declared that its own long-term study had shown that programs based on behavioral principles are more likely to help people take and keep the weight off than other approaches. (The study was funded by Weight Watchers, but without its participation.)

Mass-market programs tend to fall short when it comes to enlisting a full range of behavioral techniques and customizing them to meet the varied needs of individuals.

But Weight Watchers and other mass-market programs tend to fall short when it comes to enlisting a full range of behavioral techniques and customizing them to meet the varied needs of individuals. They cannot routinely provide individual counseling, adapt their advice to specific challenges, assess environmental factors in a member's home, workplace or community, provide much outreach to members who do not come to meetings, or prevent their members from shooting for fast, dramatic, short-term weight loss or from restricting food groups. As a for-profit company, Weight Watchers sometimes even mildly panders to these self-defeating notions in its marketing. "Some people join us to drop 10 pounds for a high school reunion," says Weight Watchers's Miller-Kovach. "They achieve that goal, then stop coming."

To close that gap, a number of researchers have turned their attention in recent years to improving, expanding and tailoring behavioral techniques, with encouraging results. For example, Michael Cameron, head of the graduate behavioral analysis department at Simmons College and a faculty member at Harvard Medical School, is now focusing his research on behavioral weight-loss techniques. He is one year into a four-person study—behavioral analysts generally do very small group or even single-subject studies to more closely tailor the intervention and observe individual effects—in which the subjects meet together with him via online videoconferencing for reinforcement, weigh themselves on scales that transmit results via wireless networks, and have their diets optimized to both reduce caloric density and address individual food preferences. Favorite foods are used as a reward for exercise. So far the subjects have lost between 8 and 20 percent of their body weight.

Matt Normand, a behavioral analyst at the University of the Pacific, has focused on finding ways to more precisely track subjects' calorie intake and expenditure by, for example, collecting receipts for food purchases, providing food checklists to record what is eaten, and enlisting various types of pedometers and other devices for measuring physical activity. He then provides participants with daily detailed accounts of their calorie flow and in one published study showed three of four subjects reduced calorie intake to recommended levels. Richard Fleming, a researcher at the University of Massachusetts Medical School's Shriver Center, has in *Obesity* looked at ways to encourage parents to steer their children to healthier choices. He has found, among other techniques, that showing parents in person what appropriate serving sizes of foods look like on plates is helpful. Another successful Fleming trick: letting children pick out a small treat at a food store—as long as they walk there. "Kids can really respond to that reward for being active," he says.

Our environment is one in which ubiquitous, sophisticated marketing efforts prey on our need for sensory gratification as well as our vulnerability to misinformation.

Why are behavioral interventions effective? Laurette Dubé, a lifestyle psychology and marketing researcher at McGill University's Faculty of Management, notes that our environment is currently one in which ubiquitous, sophisticated marketing efforts prey on our need for sensory gratification as well as our vulnerability to misinformation. In addition, the poor eating and exercise habits we observe in our friends, family and colleagues encourage us to follow suit. In essence, behavioral interventions seek to reconfigure this environment into one in which our needs for information, gratification and social encouragement are tapped to pull us toward healthy food and exercise choices rather than away from them. "When we are getting the right messages in enough ways, we have a better chance of resisting the urge to eat more than we need," Dubé says.

Changing Policy

There is no one-size-fits-all solution, behavioral or otherwise, to the problem of obesity. But although behavioral interventions work best when they are customized to individuals, mass-market behavioral approaches such as Weight Watchers and TOPS are at least fairly effective. Why don't more people

What Works?

Four Steps to Losing Weight

Behavior-focused studies of obesity and diets have identified some basic conditions that seem correlated with a greater chance of losing weight and keeping it off: setting clear, modest goals and focusing on lifelong habits, among others. Most of these behavior changes fall into four main categories.

Initial Assessment

Research underscores the need to determine baseline measurements. How much does an individual weigh? What rituals and routines contribute to overeating (eating under stress) or underexercising (unrealistic expectations)? A physician, a nurse practitioner or a nutrition counselor can help with the assessment.

Behavior Shifts

Many people find it is easier to make small changes at first—such as taking the stairs instead of an elevator. Studies show that surveying the entire buffet before serving themselves will help people put less food on their plate.

Self-Monitoring

Recording body weight, counting the calories eaten and logging steps taken provide objective feedback on how well individuals are changing their habits. Behavior studies have found both low-tech paper logs and wireless monitoring systems to be of benefit.

Support Groups

Studies document the benefits of encouragement by others. Being part of a group—whether an exercise group, a formal support group or even a virtual group—lets participants share triumphs, bemoan setbacks and strategize solutions.

lose weight with them? The main reason is that people simply do not sign up for them, often because would-be weight losers are chasing fad diets or supplements or have read that obesity is locked into our genes. Weight Watchers, by far the most popular behavioral weight-loss program, counts only 600,000 meeting-attending members in its ranks in North America. That means that fewer than one out of 100 obese people in the U.S. and about one out of 200 overweight people are part of a formal behavioral-modification program.

Public policy may be changing, however. The U.S. Surgeon General's office and the CDC have both publicly lined up behind behavioral approaches as the main weapon in what is becoming a war on obesity. First Lady Michelle Obama's high-profile Let's Move campaign against childhood obesity consists almost entirely of behavioral weight-loss wisdom—that is, find ways to encourage children to eat less-calorie-dense foods, to become more active, and to enjoy doing it. The recent proposed ban of toys in Happy Meals in San Francisco suggests that more officials may be getting ready to pressure the food industry into easing up on contaminating the environment with what are essentially obesity-supportive marketing tactics. To make it easier and more tempting to buy healthier food in poorer, disproportionately overweight communities, the White House has proposed subsidizing the costs of fruits and vegetables. Approaching the problem from the other direction, New York City Mayor Michael Bloomberg is among those who have advocated modifying food-assistance programs to restrict the purchase of high-sugar beverages, and last year Washington, D.C., enacted a 6 percent tax on sugary drinks. New York City has also offered vouchers for buying produce at farmers' markets to low-income families and incentives to stores to offer healthier fare.

Some experts are trying to push the government to rewrite zoning and building codes to ensure that neighborhoods and buildings become friendlier to walkers, bikers and stair climbers. A 2009 study by researchers at Louisiana State University Medical School found that a mere 2.8 percent increase in a person's stair usage alone would keep off almost a pound a year. "The correlation between activity levels and healthy weight is one of the best-established ones in all of obesity research," says William M. Hartman, a psychologist and director of the behavioral program of the highly regarded Weight Management Program of the California Pacific Medical Center in San Francisco.

Increasing access to behavior therapy would help, too. Many overweight people might only need online behavioral monitoring, support and progress-sharing tools, which have proved moderately effective in studies. Others may need much more intensive, more personal interventions of the kind Cameron is developing. Given that obesity especially plagues the economically disadvantaged, fees for these programs may have to be heavily subsidized by the government and health care insurers. A weekly session with a behavioral therapist costing $50 would amount to $2,500 a year, or a bit more than a third of the $7,000 per year societal and medical costs of obesity—and the sessions might only be needed for a year or two to establish new, permanent eating and exercise habits, whereas the savings would continue on for a lifetime.

It is too soon to say whether the public will accept government efforts to push it toward healthier choices. In San Francisco, a community known to be especially friendly to public health initiatives, the plan to ban Happy Meals has provoked angry reactions, and Mayor Gavin Newsom vetoed it. Efforts by Let's Move to bring healthier food to school cafeterias have been intensely criticized by some as overly intrusive. Even if these efforts are eventually fully implemented nationwide, there is no way of being sure they will significantly reduce obesity. The current rate of obesity is far beyond any ever seen before on the planet, and thus a large-scale solution will necessarily be an experiment in mass behavior change. But the research suggests that such a grand experiment would be our best shot at fixing obesity and that there is reason to be hopeful it will succeed. Given that more and more scientists, public policy experts and government officials seem eager to get it off the ground, we may well have early findings within this decade.

More to Explore

About Behaviorism. B. F. Skinner. Vintage, 1974. A classic in behavior modification. You on a Diet: The Owner's Manual for Waist Management. Michael F. Roizen and Mehmet C. Oz. Free Press, 2006. Good layperson's guide to various aspects of weight management.

Determining the Effectiveness of Take Off Pounds Sensibly (TOPS), a Nationally Available Nonprofit Weight Loss Program. Nia S. Mitchell et al., in *Obesity*. Published online September 23, 2010. www.nature.com/oby/journal/vaop/ncurrent/full/oby2010202a.html.

The entry portal to the range of NIH research on obesity: obesityresearch.nih.gov.

Critical Thinking

1. What percentage of Americans are obese? What percentage are overweight? What percentage are normal weight or underweight?
2. What health risks are associated with obesity?
3. Which is a bigger reason for obesity: biology or lifestyle choices?
4. Why is behavior theory effective for many dieters?

Create Central

www.mhhe.com/createcentral

Internet References

Beyond the "i" in the Obesity Epidemic
www.mcgill.ca/desautels/channels/news/beyond-i-obesity

Boston Nutrition Obesity Research Center
http://bnorc.org

Determining the Effectiveness of Take Off Pounds Sensibly (TOPS)
www.nature.com/oby/journal/vaop/ncurrent/full/oby

Learn the Facts/Let's Move
www.letsmove.gov/learn-facts/epidemic-obesity

NIH Research on Obesity
www.obesityresearch.nih.gov

David H. Freedman has been covering science, business and technology for 30 years. His most recent book, *Wrong,* explores the forces that lead scientists and other top experts to mislead us.

Article

Prepared by: Claire N. Rubman, *Suffolk County Community College*

An Empty Nest Can Promote Freedom, Improved Relationships

A developing line of research suggests that many parents get a new lease on life when their children leave.

REBECCA A. CLAY

Learning Outcomes

After reading this article, you will be able to:

- Explain how the parent–child relationship can improve when a child leaves home.
- Detail the incorrect assumptions that students make about their parents as they become "empty nesters."

Every fall, psychologist Karen L. Fingerman, PhD, asks her students how they think their parents are coping with their newly emptied nests. And every year, students express surprise at what Fingerman's research has to say in response to that question.

"Students always think their parents are doing worse now that they're gone," says Fingerman, the Berner Hanley University Scholar and associate professor of child development and family studies at Purdue University. "Of course, you want to think that when you move out, your mom must be devastated, but that's not validated by the research."

Students aren't the only ones who believe in the so-called "empty-nest syndrome"—the depression, loss of purpose, and crisis of identity that parents, especially mothers, supposedly feel when their children leave home. Sociologists popularized the term in the 1970s, and the media have helped make its existence part of conventional wisdom. More recently, a number of psychologists have begun taking a more nuanced look at this transition—some of them because they themselves weren't experiencing the distress the popular literature says is typical when children leave home.

Now many of these researchers are busy debunking such myths as empty-nest depression and loss of purpose. While they acknowledge that parents do feel a sense of loss when their nests empty, they are also finding that this period can be one of increased satisfaction and improved relationships. And some findings even challenge the notion that an empty nest is hardest on women—if anything, this research suggests, it may be men who don't fare so well when children leave home.

Improved Relationships

A lot has changed since the idea of an empty-nest syndrome first surfaced. An unprecedented number of mothers now work outside the home, giving them a role beyond that of parent. And cheaper long-distance charges, e-mail, and lower airfares have made it easier to stay in touch once children leave home, some recent studies suggest.

"The empty-nest syndrome doesn't exist in the way it has been portrayed in the popular literature," says Fingerman, author of *Mothers and Their Adult Daughters: Mixed Emotions, Enduring Bonds* (Prometheus Books, 2002). "People do miss their children, but, based on what I've seen in my research, what happens is actually the opposite of the empty-nest syndrome."

According to Fingerman's research, most parents enjoy greater freedom, a reconnection with their spouses, and more time to pursue their own goals and interests once their children leave home. Parents in her studies report that seeing a child start down the path toward successful adulthood gives them a feeling of joy and pride. Most importantly, the parent/child relationship actually improves for many of them when children leave home.

In a study published in 2000 in the *Journals of Gerontology: Psychological Sciences and Social Sciences* (Vol. 55, No. 2), Fingerman interviewed women in their early 20s and their mothers, and women in their 40s and their mothers. The younger women and their mothers were "almost sappily positive" about their relationships, says Fingerman. Part of the reason for this upsurge may simply be the absence of the day-to-day stressors that come with living together and the contrast between children's often stormy adolescences and their emerging adulthoods.

"People may worry about losing their child when the child leaves home," says Fingerman. "In fact, they're not. They're going to have a more mature more emotionally meaningful and deeper relationship with them to look forward to."

Other psychologists' research reveals another unexpected benefit of the empty-nest period: a renewal of ties with other family members. "The research is very caught up in the parent/child relationship and the marital relationship, but there are a lot of other important relationships," says Victoria Bedford, PhD, an associate professor in the School for Psychological Sciences and the Center for Aging and Community at the University of Indianapolis. "This is not to say that the parent/child relationship and the marital relationship aren't important; they're just not the whole picture."

To fill that gap, Bedford studies the empty nest's impact on parents' relationships with their own siblings. In ongoing research on a group of 66 parents who were between the ages of 30 and 69 when Bedford started following them 16 years ago, first published in 1989 in the *International Journal of Aging and Human Development* (Vol. 28, No. 1), she has found that children leaving home allow parents to come together again with their siblings.

Fathers' Feelings

Helen M. DeVries, PhD, is one of the psychologists who started researching the empty nest when her own experience didn't conform to societal expectations.

"Everything said the empty nest is supposed to be this terrible loss and terrible transition for women," says DeVries, an associate professor of psychology at Wheaton College in Wheaton, IL. "I started wondering if I was just unusual and my friends were all unusual because we just weren't seeing our children leaving home as a terrible thing."

According to DeVries's research, it is actually men who are more likely to have a hard time when their children leave home.

In an as-yet-unpublished study of 147 mothers and 114 fathers with a child graduating from high school, DeVries found that mothers and fathers anticipate and experience their children's departures very differently. Although many of the women had been the traditional, stay-at-home mothers once thought to be most prone to the empty-nest syndrome, DeVries found that in reality they were looking forward to their children leaving home. They had started planning and preparing for the next stage, whether that meant going back to school, going to work or exploring new interests.

In contrast, the men in DeVries' sample didn't talk at all about preparing for the change, were less likely to view their children leaving home as a major transition and were less prepared for the emotional component of the transition. As a result, fathers were more likely to express regrets over lost opportunities to be involved in their children's lives before they left home.

Of course, says DeVries, all bets are off when the children fail to make a successful transition. One woman in her sample had a child who wasn't doing well; as a result, she felt reluctance about pursuing her own goals, guilt about her performance as a mother and a nagging sense of responsibility. Although DeVries is still codifying the qualitative data she has collected, she suspects that parents' ability to enjoy their empty nests is linked to children's successful negotiation of the transition.

The Refilled Nest

For some midlife parents, the empty nest isn't an issue simply because the nest hasn't really emptied. For instance, Linda L. Bips, EdD, an assistant professor of psychology and the former director of counseling at Muhlenberg College in Allentown, PA, has seen a huge increase in parental involvement in college students' lives.

"I went to college in the 1960s, when our parents just dropped us off, said goodbye and said they'd see us at Thanksgiving," says Bips, who recently self-published a book called *Parenting College Freshmen: Consulting for Adulthood,* available from her at LluBips@aol.com. "Parents are much more involved with their children now." At Muhlenberg, she reports, an ever-increasing number of parents are attending their children's plays and sporting events, becoming part of the parents' association and finding other ways to continue their involvement in their children's lives.

This involvement in children's lives doesn't end after graduation either. Empty nests are now refilling in record numbers as adult children return home after college or even after their first postcollege jobs. According to the 2000 census, almost four million young adults between 25 and 34 years old now live with their parents—possibly the result of a tough job market, delayed marriage, high housing costs and other factors. In any case, says Bips, "It's not an empty nest anymore."

Critical Thinking

1. Why do students incorrectly assume that their parents will not be able to cope with them leaving home?
2. What is the "empty nest syndrome"?

Create Central

www.mhhe.com/createcentral

Internet References

Empty Nest Syndrome

http://www.psychologytoday.com/conditions/empty-nest-syndrome

Six Steps to Getting Over an Empty Nest

http://www.today.com/id/5818627/ns/today-today_hidden/t/six-steps-getting-over-empty-nest/#.VDbY7xZNQVw

Rebecca A. Clay is a writer in Washington, DC.

Clay, Rebecca. "An Empty Nest Can Promote Freedom." *Monitor on Psychology* 34. 4 (April, 2003): 40–43.

Article Prepared by: Claire N. Rubman, *Suffolk County Community College*

Anxiety Nation

Why are so many of us so ill at ease?

SOPHIE MCBAIN

Learning Outcomes

After reading this article, you will be able to:

- Explain the term *pharmacological dissection.*
- Articulate the clinical definition of anxiety.
- Identify the World Health Organization's account of the country with the lowest reported level of anxiety.

For a condition that affects so many of us, there is very little agreement about what anxiety actually is. Is it a physiological condition, best treated with medication, or psychological—the product of repressed trauma, as a Freudian might suggest? Is it a cultural construct, a reaction to today's anomic society, or a more fundamental spiritual and philosophical reflection of what it means to be human? For most sufferers, the most pressing concern is whether drugs work, and if therapy is a good idea.

Our modern, medical definition of anxiety could be traced back to 1980 and the publication of the third edition of the *Diagnostic and Statistical Manual* (*DSM-III*), the doctor's and psychiatrist's bible for identifying mental illness. The authors of *DSM-III* suggested that, according to their new criteria, between 2 percent and 4 percent of the population would have an anxiety disorder. But three decades on, the *America's State of Mind Report* showed that one in every six people in the United States suffers from anxiety.

The most recent nationwide survey, which took place in 2007, found that three million people in the UK have an anxiety disorder. About 7 percent of UK adults are on antidepressants (often prescribed for anxiety, too) and one in seven will take benzodiazepines such as Xanax in any 1 year. Mental health charities warn that our anxiety levels are creeping even higher; they often blame our "switched-on" modern culture for this, or the financial crisis and the long recession that followed it.

And yet, it is difficult to quantify whether it is our feelings of anxiety that have changed, or whether it's just our perception of those feelings that is different: are we increasingly viewing ordinary human emotions as marks of mental illness? "In theory, it's possible that we've just watched too many Woody Allen films. That's a very difficult argument to definitively disprove," the clinical psychologist and author Oliver James told me.

If that seems like a slightly flippant way of framing the debate, that could be because James's books, including *The Selfish Capitalist and Britain on the Couch,* are premised on the idea that rates of depression and anxiety have reached record highs in the affluent consumer societies of the English-speaking world.

In January this year, Scott Stossel, who is the editor of the American magazine the *Atlantic,* published *My Age of Anxiety,* an account of his lifelong, debilitating battle with nerves. There has been a lot of interest in the book in both the United States and Europe. Stossel, who is 44, is a successful journalist and yet he is deeply insecure. He has been in therapy for three decades and has taken a cocktail of antidepressants, antipsychotic medications, and sedatives (not to mention more conventional cocktail ingredients such as gin, Scotch, and vodka) in an attempt to cope with any number of phobias, from the common (agoraphobia and fear of public speaking) to the more niche (turophobia: fear of cheese).

Stossel reveals in painful, intimate, and sometimes comical detail the humiliations of living with high anxious tension and very loose bowels. Despite the severity of his problems, he successfully concealed them from most of his friends and colleagues until the book was published. He told me when we spoke that in recent months co-workers have given him lots of hugs (which is sweet, but a little bit uncomfortable) and thousands of strangers have approached him because they so identify with the experiences he describes in the book.

"I was very nervous about coming out as anxious," Stossel says. "And now it's too late and I can't un-come out. It hasn't been a cure, but it has been something of a relief. I now feel there are practical things I can help with, like trying to reduce the stigma around anxiety."

He says we ought to view anxiety less as a "psychological problem" and more like a "medical condition, in the way gout or diabetes is. These are things that need to be managed and treated, and have an organic basis. It's not necessarily that you are weak, but that you have an illness."

Yet while we understand how our modern diet is making gout and diabetes more common, the causes of anxiety are more mysterious.

Anxiety has long been associated with depression, and often the two were subsumed under the notion of "melancholia": Robert Burton's great book *Anatomy of Melancholy* (1621) was as much about anxiety as sadness. But the *DSM-III* classified anxiety and depression as separate conditions: the former is related to feelings of worry, the latter to low mood, and loss of pleasure and interest. More often than not, however, the two occur together. The blurred lines between normality and illness, or depression and anxiety, make it very hard to grasp what it means to say that three million people in the UK suffer from anxiety.

If one in seven of us is taking pills to control or ward off anxiety, are we just medicalising an ordinary human emotion? Did the purveyors of the early antianxiety medicines such as Miltown—discovered in the 1940s, and the first in a line of blockbuster drugs including Prozac and Xanax—manage to create a new problem along with the solution they offered?

Stossel describes how in the 1950s a young psychiatrist called Donald Klein began randomly treating his patients with a new drug called imipramine. He noticed that patients on imipramine often remained very anxious but were less likely to suffer from acute paroxysms of anxiety. And so, having found a cure, he defined the problem—"panic attacks."

Until imipramine, panic attacks didn't "exist." This process of working backwards from new drugs to new illnesses is known as pharmacological dissection, and it is not uncommon. Yet even if modern drugs shaped our understanding of mental illness, that doesn't mean they made us sick.

As millions take pills, are we just medicalising an ordinary emotion?

Or maybe the UK's epidemic of anxiety isn't pathological at all but a product of historically unprecedented good health and affluence. Perhaps anxiety is a luxury that comes with wealth, freedom, and the privilege of having nothing fundamental to fear in our modern society.

This isn't an unpopular notion. A World Health Organization survey in 2002 found that, while 18.2 percent of Americans reported anxiety in any 1 year, south of the US border only 6.8 percent of Mexicans did. Of the 14 countries surveyed by WHO, Nigeria reported the lowest levels of anxiety, with only 3.3 percent of respondents experiencing anxiety in any year. Nigeria's per capita GDP is $2,690, about 6 percent that of the United States, and in 2010 84.5 percent of Nigerians were living on less than $2 a day, the international poverty line. Breaking out into a nervous sweat on the London Tube because you can't remember if you unplugged your hair straighteners is the kind of indulgence you can't afford if you're struggling to feed yourself, or so the argument goes.

However, it's not that simple. Again, it's very hard to tell whether feelings of anxiety vary internationally or if people label them differently. In countries with a large stigma against mental illness, people are less likely to report disorders, such as anxiety or depression. Yet the psychiatrist Vikram Patel, who recently featured on the BBC Radio 4 programme *The Life Scientific,* says his research in India and Zimbabwe has convinced him that rates of mental illness are the same all over the world.

The way we understand anxiety is cultural, says Beth Murphy, head of information at the mental health charity Mind. "If you're living on the breadline in a hand-to-mouth existence you might not recognise what you are feeling as anxiety, but it's quite probable that you're going to be pretty worried about where your next meal is coming from."

This raises another problem: if you are feeling anxious because it's very likely you could go hungry tomorrow, are you in any meaningful way unwell?

Just as sadness is natural but depression is an illness, most of the people I spoke to who suffered from anxiety instinctively drew a distinction between "good anxiety," the nervous adrenalin that helps you get stuff done and meet deadlines, and "bad anxiety," the destructive kind. Our common-sense interpretation of "bad anxiety" also suggests that the worries here should be disproportionate or irrational.

The *Diagnostic and Statistical Manual* used today identifies anxiety disorders according to how severe and persistent the feelings of worry are, and whether these feelings are accompanied by elements from a list of secondary symptoms, including sleep disturbance, muscle tension, poor concentration, and fatigue.

Although the anxiety should be "excessive" the focus is solely on the feelings, and not what caused them. This might go some way towards explaining the boom in prescriptions for mental illnesses; doctors sometimes prescribe antidepressants to someone who has suffered bereavement, something Oliver James described as "ludicrous." The counter-argument is: if a short course of drugs can make it easier to cope with the painful but completely healthy process of grieving, why not take them?

At its most extreme, anxiety is a debilitating, life-altering condition. I spoke to Jo, a volunteer at the charity Anxiety UK, and she told me that feelings of anxiety have "blighted" her life.

"It's stopped me from doing so many things that I would have liked to have been able to do and it's stopped me from living what I feel is a normal life, doing things like having relationships, perhaps getting married, having children, having a career. It's put paid to all that," she says bitterly.

Jo, who is in her fifties, has been overcome by anxiety since she was in her teens. She dropped out of school at 16, unable to cope with the pressure of exams, and when her anxiety peaks she is unable to work and is left isolated. Antianxiety drugs have helped ease the physical symptoms—such as headaches and irritable bowel syndrome—yet they've left her with "the same worries and fears."

What does anxiety feel like when it's at its worst? "It's an overwhelming feeling of being out of control, and overwhelmed by everything." Jo pauses, and then adds quietly, "It's not nice."

While researching this piece, I was struck by how many friends came forward with stories of anxiety-induced insomnia, phobias and stress, though mostly this didn't prevent them from working or socialising. I spent one strange dinner with a friend who is a lawyer. I noticed when we met that her hands were raw and bleeding slightly, and while we ate she repeatedly reached into her bag and disinfected them. Under stress from work, she had developed a huge fear of germs.

Another friend, a corporate lawyer, recently collapsed while out shopping after she suffered a panic attack. There's a recognisable stereotype of the neurotic, angst-filled high-flyer—and it has a historical precedent. In the 19th century, nervousness was seen as a mark of social standing, because only the new leisured classes could afford such sensibility. But how closely related are these manifestations of unease and anxiety to those feelings experienced by people who are incapacitated by their nerves or phobias?

The triggers for people's nervous complaints can be idiosyncratic. I chatted about this to Andy Burrows, a musician and the former drummer of the indie band Razorlight. He says he has never felt overly anxious about performing to huge crowds at Wembley or the O_2 Arena in London—a prospect that might make most people break into a sweat—but he has suffered from anxiety since his teens and is so freaked out by lifts and tunnels that he can recite from memory the average time that a London overground train spends underground. It takes 16 seconds to travel through the tunnel from Hampstead Heath to Finchley Road and Frognal Station "at regular speed," he says—and sometimes he just has to get off the train and walk between the two.

Of course, phobias can seem funny to an outsider. I can laugh with friends about the time I leapt up from my chair, tipped over my coffee and ran out of a café, because I suddenly couldn't cope with being in a confined space with a pigeon. And yet, for a brief few seconds, as someone with a fear of birds, I experienced a terror so profound that it overrode my usual instinct not to cause a scene.

In 2012, the National Health Service recorded 8,720 hospital admissions for acute anxiety. According to research for the Organisation for Economic Co-operation and Development, 40 percent of new claimants for disability benefits in the UK are suffering from mental illnesses, of which anxiety and depression are the most common. The effect of this is that Britain has a higher proportion of people claiming unemployment benefit for mental health conditions than any other developed nation. The estimated cost to the UK of mental illness is roughly 4.4 percent of GDP, through lost productivity and health-care costs.

What is going wrong? One problem is that we are not doing enough to support people with anxiety. The first port of call for most sufferers is their GP, and the response they get can vary. I know this because a few years ago, when I experienced a bereavement and a break-up in quick succession, I turned from a natural worrier into an unravelled bundle of nerves. I was unable to sleep, read, or concentrate.

Even sensitive GPs can be constrained in the solutions they can offer.

After a strange few months, spent mostly wandering aimlessly in London, as if somehow I might lose my panic down a backstreet, I burst into tears in front of my doctor. "Patient tearful but able to maintain eye contact," the GP typed on the large screen in front of us, leaving me feeling like some zoo exhibit. She advised me to book an appointment with someone who knew more about mental health.

In the end, I was lucky. The second doctor prescribed me a low dose of antidepressants (against his advice, I decided not to take these). Then, although the NHS waiting list for counselling was months long, my university counsellor could see me and within 2 months I felt almost normal again.

Even when they are very much aware of mental illness, GPs can often be constrained in the solutions they can offer. One in every 10 people in the UK has to wait more than a year for therapy and 54 percent have to wait for more than 3 months (people from black and ethnic-minority communities often wait the longest).

Anxiety is a broad, confusing label and is a condition with multiple causes. We are not the first generation to believe we live in an exceptionally anxious age, and yet in some ways, thanks to the development of drugs and talking therapies, anxiety is a peculiarly modern experience. Perhaps, at the very root of Britain's struggle with nerves—whether viewed in terms of its economic effects or from the perspective of plain, simple suffering, or whether one merely wonders why 3 million of us appear to be afflicted by a disorder we still can't quite define—is that we don't often talk about it.

In an odd way, it might be easier to admit in modern Britain that you're deeply sad than that you are anxious or scared. Collectively, we might be freaking out but most of us are suffering in silence.

Critical Thinking

1. Why do so many people suffer from anxiety in today's society?
2. How would our understanding of anxiety change if we viewed it as an illness instead of a psychological problem?

Create Central

www.mhhe.com/createcentral

Internet References

Anxiety Helpguide
http://www.helpguide.org/home-pages/anxiety.htm

Listening to Xanax
http://nymag.com/news/features/xanax-2012-3/

Medline Plus
http://www.nlm.nih.gov/medlineplus/anxiety.html

National Institute of Mental Health
http://www.nimh.nih.gov/health/publications/anxiety-disorders/index.shtml

Why Teenagers Act Crazy
http://www.nytimes.com/2014/06/29/opinion/sunday/why-teenagers-act-crazy.html?_r=0

SOPHIE MCBAIN is a staff writer for the New Statesman.

McBain, Sophie. "Anxiety Nation." *New Statesman* 143. 14 (April, 11, 2014): 24–27.

Article Prepared by: Claire N. Rubman, *Suffolk County Community College*

Bringing Life Into Focus

A generation of adults who came of age too early to be diagnosed with childhood ADHD is finding that later-in-life treatment can bring great rewards.

BRENDAN L. SMITH

Learning Outcomes

After reading this article, you will be able to:

- Articulate how ADHD negatively affects adults in their working lives.
- State a clinical definition of ADHD.
- Describe the abuse of ADHD medications by college students.

When he was attending law school at Wake Forest University in the 1980s, E. Clarke Dummit couldn't study in the library. It was just too quiet.

"I got in the habit of hanging out at a Krispy Kreme doughnut shop and drinking coffee while I studied my law books," he says. "I needed constant noise around me and a stimulant to focus."

Another decade would pass before Dummit saw a psychologist and was diagnosed with attention-deficit hyperactivity disorder. The diagnosis came as a revelation, and it helped him to fit together some of the jigsaw pieces of his life.

"It was fascinating. I've always had learning disabilities and had to work my way around them," says Dummit, now a 50-year-old criminal defense attorney with his own firm in Winston-Salem, NC. "I have focus when I really need to for a short period, but then my brain has to relax for a certain amount of time."

Dummit and other adults with ADHD also have to battle a stereotype that ADHD is a childhood mental disorder that doesn't affect adults. Most research on ADHD has focused on children, and the fourth edition of the *Diagnostic and Statistical Manual of Mental Disorders* (DSM-IV) lists symptoms for ADHD that apply mainly to children, such as losing toys or climbing on things. But a growing body of research is examining the effects of ADHD on adults and documenting that the disorder can have lifelong consequences.

ADHD can cause serious disruptions for adults in their careers, personal relationships, and higher education, says J. Russell Ramsay, PhD, an associate professor of psychology and co-director of the Adult ADHD Treatment and Research Program at the University of Pennsylvania School of Medicine. "Society in general values good self-regulation, being able to follow through on things, being reliable, completing tasks on deadline. These skills are important at school and work, and they are equated with good character," Ramsay says. "An individual going through life with ADHD often ends up saying, 'I must not be good enough. I must be lazy. I must be stupid.' These negative beliefs get reactivated and strengthened and may lead people to start giving up or limiting themselves."

Several studies have shown that more than half of children with ADHD will continue to have full symptoms as adults, while some level of impairment may affect up to 80 percent or 90 percent, says Ramsay, who has researched ADHD for more than a decade. "Many adults aren't growing out of ADHD. They're actually just growing out of the childhood definition of ADHD, such as running around and climbing on things," he says. "Adult ADHD research has been hampered because the current symptoms were designed for childhood and adolescence."

Diagnosing Adult ADHD

Many middle-aged and elderly adults grew up at a time when children with ADHD were just considered to be hyperactive or poor learners. ADHD first appeared in DSM-II in 1968, when it was called "hyperkinetic reaction of childhood (or adolescence)."

The symptoms included "overactivity, restlessness, distractibility, and short attention span, especially in young children."

When Dummit was growing up in the 1960s in Columbia, TN., he had trouble focusing in school so his parents took him to Nashville for an evaluation at the Peabody College of Education and Human Development, now part of Vanderbilt University. "No one diagnosed me with ADHD," Dummit says with a laugh. "They said my father was being overbearing and too demanding. My dad said, 'You're damn right,' and we marched out of there."

Today, in contrast, more than 5 million children have been diagnosed with ADHD in the United States, and the percentage of children who are diagnosed has increased each year over the past decade. But for Dummit's generation, who missed the chance to be diagnosed as children, psychologists, and psychiatrists must devise a way to identify ADHD in adults.

And even today, some people may not realize the extent of their ADHD symptoms until later in life. ADHD symptoms can sometimes be masked until adulthood because childhood often is structured by parents, school and other activities, says Stephen Faraone, PhD, a clinical psychologist and psychiatry professor at the State University of New York's Upstate Medical University.

"ADHD is a disorder characterized by the inability to regulate one's behavior, emotions and attention. As we get older, we have fewer people telling us what to do," Faraone says. "When we get to college or a job, we're expected to show up without having someone tell us what to do."

Paul Wender, MD, a pioneer in ADHD research, developed one of the first rating scales for measuring ADHD in adults—the Wender Utah Rating Scale—in the 1990s, when he was a psychiatry professor at the University of Utah School of Medicine. The questionnaire, published in the *American Journal of Psychiatry* in 1993, helped retrospectively diagnose adults with ADHD based on their childhood symptoms.

"The diagnosis of ADHD in adults has occurred more and more frequently in recent years, and it has improved dramatically over the past decade," says Wender, now a psychiatrist in private practice in Andover, Mass.

While the DSM-IV lists symptoms for ADHD that are mostly geared toward children, the upcoming fifth edition most likely will contain symptoms that apply more readily to adults, such as having racing thoughts instead of racing around the room. "Adults obviously aren't on top of their desks, but they are restless and unable to sit still," Wender says. Several other scales have been developed to help diagnose ADHD in adults since Wender's work. Faraone helped develop a self-reporting screening scale that was adopted by the World Health Organization. Published in *Psychological Medicine* in 2005, the 18-question survey translates childhood ADHD symptoms from the DSM-IV into adult situations.

In a nationwide telephone survey of 966 adults, published in the *Journal of Attention Disorders* in 2005, almost 3 percent of respondents reported they often had ADHD symptoms, while almost 16 percent reported occasional symptoms. The study by Faraone and Harvard Medical School researcher Joseph Biederman showed that individuals who reported ADHD symptoms were less likely to graduate from high school or college than those who reported no symptoms. Individuals who reported more severe ADHD symptoms were almost three times more likely to be unemployed than adults with no symptoms.

"In the workplace, we know from studies of work productivity and income that adults with ADHD are not likely to achieve as well as their peers," Faraone says. "The estimates range into billions of dollars each year in lost productivity related to adult ADHD."

"Playing Defense Every Day"

Drew Brody, a 39-year-old father with two young children in Santa Monica, CA., says he used to struggle through his daily routine because of ADHD. As a high-school tutor, he would lose track of time, miss deadlines and feel overwhelmed. "You're walking around with a fog around your brain. Just getting through normal daily behavior is hard, getting up, getting dressed, getting shaved, getting out the door on time," he says. "All of that stuff is 10 times harder than it should be."

Brody was diagnosed with ADHD about 7 years ago after his wife, a middle-school vice principal, suggested that he be evaluated. Brody began cognitive-behavioral therapy with a psychologist to identify coping mechanisms, such as time management skills, exercise, and a healthy diet. But his persistent symptoms interfered with the therapy. "After a year, I never really got my act together to do any of the improvements on a regular basis," he says.

Brody then was prescribed Concerta, the extended-release version of methylphenidate (Ritalin), and his life changed. He was able to start his own tutoring company, The Scholar Group, which now has 16 tutors who help students in more than 40 academic subjects and on standardized tests such as the SAT.

"It was a revelation," he says. "I don't think I would have created my business if I hadn't started taking Concerta on a daily basis. It's made a substantial change in my life. For bigger life decisions, I am able to think more clearly and work through the steps on how to get there."

His problems from ADHD haven't disappeared, but Brody says his symptoms are more manageable now than they were in the past. "Life with ADHD is like playing defense every day. Things happen to you and you have to address them," he says. "You're not proactively dealing with life. You're waiting to be late or to get in trouble because you can't get ahead."

Brody's experience is common for adults with ADHD who try cognitive-behavioral therapy without medication, says Ramsay, who wrote the 2010 book, *Nonmedication Treatments for Adult ADHD.* Therapy can be very helpful in teaching time management and organization skills, but ADHD symptoms can lead to late or missed appointments, failure to complete homework, and little progress on a treatment plan. Medication in conjunction with therapy can help bring ADHD symptoms under control through life coaching skills and counseling for underlying negative thoughts that can lead to procrastination and frustration, Ramsay says.

The public controversy about overmedication and overdiagnosis of ADHD is really a problem of misdiagnosis, which can result from quick visits to primary-care physicians, Ramsay says. "Some patients may get a diagnosis based on an all-too-brief evaluation and therefore may start treatment with a medication when maybe their symptoms are not a result of ADHD," he says. "Other people with ADHD may be misdiagnosed with some other mental disorder."

Stimulants on Campus

Several studies have shown that stimulants such as Ritalin or amphetamine salts (Adderall) are effective in treating ADHD in adults, but the drugs also can be abused, especially by college students who believe stimulants will boost their academic performance. In a survey of more than 1,800 students at the University of Kentucky, a third of the students reported they had illegally used ADHD stimulants, mainly by obtaining pills from fellow students with prescriptions. Most of the illegal users said the stimulants helped them stay up late and cram for exams, and they believed the drugs increased their reading comprehension, attention, and memory. The study was published in 2008 in the *Journal of American College Health.*

Every college in the United States faces problems with misuse of ADHD stimulants, but most students with ADHD are not faking their symptoms to get medication, says Lorraine Wolf, PhD, a neuropsychologist and director of the Office of Disability Services at Boston University. "Most students with ADHD are serious, hard-working young people who struggle in a college environment, but with accommodations and support they are very successful," says Wolf, an assistant psychiatry professor who researches adult ADHD.

Wolf's office offers time management skills for students with ADHD and provides academic accommodations, including extra time on tests and computer use during exams to help with spelling and grammar. Students must provide extensive documentation of severe ADHD symptoms before accommodations will be granted, Wolf says. "People who come to college with symptoms are pretty much going to have ADHD for the rest of their lives," Wolf says. "People become more refined in how they deal with it. They just get better at handling ADHD."

Almost 5 percent of teenagers in the United States were prescribed stimulants to treat ADHD in 2008, compared with just 2.3 percent in 1996, suggesting that many children aren't outgrowing their symptoms, according to a study by the National Institutes of Health and the Agency for Healthcare Research and Quality. The study was published online in September in the *American Journal of Psychiatry.*

Some college students who illegally use stimulants may have undiagnosed ADHD, according to a study of 184 college students in northern Virginia, published this year in the *Journal of Attention Disorders.* The study found that 71 percent of the respondents who misused stimulants also screened positive for ADHD symptoms. Students who illegally used stimulants were seven times more likely to have ADHD symptoms than those who didn't misuse the drugs.

Meanwhile, those symptoms aren't always entirely bad. ADHD can have some beneficial aspects, including the ability to multi-task, solve problems quickly and work with people, Wolf says.

Dummit, the criminal defense attorney in North Carolina, says he has embraced his ADHD and believes it helps him hyperfocus on detailed projects for short periods. He only takes a stimulant medication when he needs to concentrate for long stretches, such as during a trial. "I don't accept ADHD as an excuse for bad behavior, but I do try to talk openly about my strengths and weaknesses," he says.

Cognitive behavioral training resources for adult ADHD

- "Cognitive Behavioral Therapy for Adult ADHD" by J. Russell Ramsay, PhD, and Anthony Rostain, MD, MA (University of Pennsylvania Adult ADHD Treatment and Research Program).
- "Mastering Your Adult ADHD: Therapist Guide" by Steven A. Safren, PhD, et al. (Harvard Medical School/ Massachusetts General Hospital).
- "Cognitive-Behavioral Treatment of Adult ADHD: Targeting Executive Dysfunction," by Mary Solanto (Attention-Deficit/Hyperactivity Disorder Center at Mount Sinai School of Medicine).
- "Succeeding with Adult ADHD: Daily Strategies to Help You Achieve Your Goals and Manage Your Life" by Abigail Levrini, PhD, and Frances Prevatt, PhD,

APA LifeTools book for the general public (APA, 2012).
- "Nonmedication Treatments for Adult ADHD: Evaluating Impact on Daily Functioning and Well-Being" (J. Russell Ramsay, 2010).

Critical Thinking

1. Why is ADHD commonly thought of as a childhood disorder?
2. Do children with ADHD outgrow it or do they continue to deal with attentional deficits and other related issues in adulthood?
3. Can you develop ADHD in adulthood?

Create Central

www.mhhe.com/createcentral

Internet References

Adult ADHD

http://www.helpguide.org/articles/add-adhd/adult-adhd-attention-deficit-disorder.htm

Attention-Deficit Drugs Face New Campus Rules

http://www.nytimes.com/2013/05/01/us/colleges-tackle-illicit-use-of-adhd-pills.html?pagewanted=all

Diseases and Conditions Adult ADHD (Attention Deficit Hyperactivity Disorder)

http://www.mayoclinic.org/diseases-conditions/adult-adhd/basics/definition/con-20034552

The Selling of ADHD

http://www.nytimes.com/2013/12/15/health/the-selling-of-attention-deficit-disorder.html?pagewanted=all

Many Ivy League students don't view ADHD medication misuse as cheating

http://www.eurekalert.org/pub_releases/2014-05/aaop-mil042514.php#

Brendan L. Smith is a writer in Washington, DC.

Smith, Brendan L. "Bringing Life Into Focus." *Monitor on Psychology* 43. 3 (March, 2012): 62

Article

Prepared by: Claire N. Rubman, *Suffolk County Community College*

Brutal Truths about the Aging Brain

A graying world will have more of the experience that comes with age. It will also be slower, fuzzier, more forgetful, and just a bit hard of hearing.

ROBERT EPSTEIN

Learning Outcomes

After reading this article, you will be able to:

- Describe the four cognitive systems that tend to decline with age.
- Explain why it is easier for elders to remember things from their 20s than from a month ago.

As a graduate student at Harvard University, I worked with one of the most influential behavioral scientists of all time, B. F. Skinner. Beginning in the summer of 1977, we worked together nearly every day for more than four years, designing experiments and chatting about literature, philosophy, and the latest research. Although we were 50 years apart in age, we were also friends. We saw *Star Wars* together, had lunch frequently in Harvard Square, and swam in his backyard pool each summer. "Fred" (from Burrhus Frederic) Skinner was the happiest, most creative, most productive person I have ever known. He was also, needless to say, quite smart.

But the septuagenarian I knew was well past his intellectual peak. One day he gave me a set of tapes of a famous debate he had had with psychologist Carl Rogers in 1962. The Skinner on those tapes seemed sharper, faster, and even wittier than the man I knew. Was I imagining this?

Recently, Gina Kirkish, a student at the University of California, San Diego, and I analyzed tapes of three comparable samples of Skinner's speech: that 1962 debate, a 1977 debate, and a speech he gave from notes shortly before he died in 1990 at age 86. We found that the speech rate dropped significantly over time, from 148 words per minute in the first sample to 137 in the second to 106 in the third—an overall decrease of more than 28 percent.

Skinner's memory and analytical skills were also declining during the years when I knew him. Sometimes he had no recollection of a conversation we had had only days before. When I tried to talk with him about technical papers he had published early in his career, he often didn't seem to understand what he had written. And he had no patience for anything mathematical, even his own equations. On the other hand, Skinner was still much smarter than most of the people I knew my own age. When you fall from a high enough cliff, you remain far above ground for a very long time.

The sad truth is that even normal aging has a devastating effect on our ability to learn and remember, on the speed with which we process information, and on our ability to reason. Recent studies suggest that the total loss in brain volume due to atrophy—a wasting away of tissue caused by cell degeneration—between our teen years and old age is 15 percent or more, which means that by the time we're in our seventies, our brains have shrunk to the size they were when we were between 2 and 3 years old. Unfortunately, most of the loss is in gray matter, the critically important part of the brain composed of neurons, the cells that transmit the signals that keep us breathing and thinking.

Contrary to what scientists long believed, only about 10 percent of our neurons die during adulthood. The real loss is in the network of connections—the "dendritic trees" that allow a single neuron to be connected to a thousand others. Over the years, 25 percent or more of this network disappears. According to William Jagust, a neuroscientist at the University of California, Berkeley, adults are also losing dopamine, a critical neurotransmitter (the type of chemical involved in transmitting signals between neurons), at the rate of 5 to 8 percent per decade. "By age 80," Jagust says, "you've lost 40 percent or so of dopamine function. When you think about it, it's remarkable that old people can do so well."

Shrinkage, dopamine depletion, and lost dendritic connections are not the only problems facing the aging brain. Myelin, a substance that insulates neurons, deteriorates, and the number of nerve fibers that carry messages throughout the central nervous system also decreases. Chemical problems—such as an increase in calcium conductance, which might impair neuronal communication—also become more common in older brains, as do problems with gene expression and protein production.

With the global population of people over 80 expected to more than quadruple to nearly 400 million by 2050, the aging brain will become an increasingly big headache for humankind. Here are four cognitive systems that tend to decline as we age. Get used to these changes. You'll be seeing a lot more of them in the future.

1. Senses

Our ability to learn and remember is limited by the accuracy of our senses, our points of contact with the world. But vision, hearing, touch, smell, and taste are not just detection systems. The sense organs also comprise a primitive kind of memory, a temporary storage system or "buffer" for the brain. Much of the input to our sense organs reverberates in receptors, and that reverberation allows even weak stimuli—for example, images flashed so quickly that we have no conscious awareness of them—to impact decisions we make later on. Without the buffering ability of our sense organs, a great deal of information about the world would be lost to us. Unfortunately, as we age, our sensory systems deteriorate, and at the extreme, we become completely insensitive to a wide range of input. For example, high-pitched tones that we can detect at a mere 30 decibels when we are young have to be boosted to an earsplitting 90 decibels for the elderly to hear. (Physics buffs: That's about a million times the energy intensity.) And pupil size decreases as we age, so when it is dim, the elderly person's eyes pick up about a third as much light as people in their prime. Because the deterioration of sense organs limits our access to critical information—speech, text, music, street signs—thinking itself is impaired.

And loss of information is just part of the problem. Research by psychologist Monica Fabiani and her colleagues at the University of Illinois at Urbana-Champaign suggests that in older people the main problem might not be that the sense organ is rejecting input but rather that the brain itself is having trouble filtering out irrelevant information. In a recent study, Fabiani had people of various ages read a book while trying to ignore auditory tones piped through headphones. Overall, the older the individual, the more trouble he or she had ignoring the tones. "The background stimuli may flood your thinking with things that are irrelevant and that you cannot inhibit," Fabiani says. As a result, "you basically lose the capacity to perform tasks."

How Some Brains Stay Razor Sharp

Facing the specter of Alzheimer's disease, the most devastating and widespread manifestation of brain deterioration in old age, worried baby boomers have inspired whole catalogs of brain-fitness books and services. That's good news for publishers, vitamin companies, and computer game designers, but probably bad news for boomers themselves. Elizabeth Zelinski, a gerontologist at the University of Southern California, told me she was appalled at the explosion of miracle cures on the market, adding bluntly, "There's no evidence that anything works." (There is some evidence that some interventions work very narrowly or for short periods of time, but generally speaking, the new industry makes outrageous claims.) And don't hold your breath waiting for neuroscience to rescue you from your upcoming decline. When I asked neuroscientist Eric Kandel, a Nobel Prize winner in medicine, how long it will be before we achieve some reasonable understanding of how memory actually works, he replied, "a hundred years."

On the bright side, some people appear to overcome the ravages of a rotting brain by recruiting new brain systems or structures to take over functions of old ones. Neuropsychologist Yaakov Stern of the Columbia University College of Physicians and Surgeons points out that upwards of 25 percent of people who function perfectly normally while alive have brains that show serious signs of Alzheimer's in autopsy. People with more education have lower rates of dementia, suggesting that brains that get more of a workout create reserves that kick in when frontline systems start to fail.

Kandel, now 82, appears to be one of those rare souls who has somehow managed to keep Father Time at bay. He remains active in research at Columbia University, and his extraordinary productivity and creativity are exemplified by his weighty 2012 book, *The Age of Insight: The Quest to Understand the Unconscious in Art, Mind, and Brain from Vienna 1900 to the Present.* Kandel's daughter, attorney Minouche Kandel, speculates that her father's clarity and energy result from an almost fanatical regimen of healthy food—mainly fish—and regular exercise. "He's lived this healthy lifestyle for as long as I can remember," she says, "and he was doing it long before it was popular."

Through some combination of luck, good genes, and a healthy lifestyle, it is possible, it seems, for a fortunate few to stay razor sharp well into old age.

R. E.

2. Memory

Most people think of human memory as a single system. But because different kinds of information are retained differently, experts speculate that distinct types of memory systems exist in the brain. Some information stays with us for only a short time—generally no more than a few seconds unless we do something with it. For example, if somebody tells you a phone number and you do not immediately repeat it, it will very likely disappear, never to return. Research suggests the existence of a short-term memory system, consisting in turn of two subsystems: immediate memory (the temporary storage system that holds on to information we don't process in some way) and working memory (a system that allows us to retain information as long as we keep using it).

As we age, our ability to process new information in working memory is severely compromised. In a typical test procedure for evaluating working memory, cognitive aging researcher Timothy Salthouse of the University of Virginia asked people to perform arithmetic computations while also trying to remember the last digit in each problem. People in their twenties were typically able to solve four or five of these problems in a row and still recall the final digits without error. With each decade, performance deteriorated; people in their seventies could typically solve no more than two such problems in a row and still get the final digits right.

One of the simplest ways to assess memory is to read test subjects a list of words and ask them, after a short time has passed, to repeat as many as they can. In a 1990 study, Hasker Davis and his colleagues at the University of Colorado found that people in their twenties could typically recall 90 percent of a list of 15 words after a short delay. With each additional decade of age, the percentage of words recalled decreased. People in their eighties could recall only about half the words.

3. Knowledge

Some information in our short-term memory system is consolidated into a long-term storage system, where it remains available to retrieve for months or years. If a memory of anything from a good meal to a coworker's name persists for 5 years, there is a good chance it will persist for another 40. But as we age, the degradation of sensory and working memory systems makes it increasingly difficult for us to transfer information into long-term storage. That's why, if you are over 50, you are more likely to remember the lyrics to a Beatles song than to any song you have heard in the past 20 years. To put this another way, our ability to learn new things is extraordinary when we are young and peaks in our teens. We can learn after that, but it becomes increasingly difficult. In an early study by psychologist Jeanne Gilbert, English speakers of different ages were asked to learn Turkish vocabulary words. People in their sixties learned 60 percent fewer words than young adults in their twenties who spent equal time and effort on the task.

One of the most frustrating experiences we have as we age is accessing a particular word from long-term memory—the so-called "word-finding" or "tip-of-the-tongue" problem. Deborah Burke, a psychology professor at Pomona College who has studied this phenomenon for more than 20 years, explains that old people suffer from a disconnect between the meaning of a word—which presumably tells you that it is the correct word to say right now—and the sound of that word. It is, she says, "the most irritating and disturbing cognitive problem" reported by older adults. We do not know what causes the disconnect.

4. Intelligence

We also get dumber as we age. IQ remains fairly stable, but that is because it is a relative measure—a quotient (the Q) that shows where we stand relative to people our own age. The problem is that raw scores on intelligence tests actually peak in our teens, remain high for a few years, and then decline throughout life; IQ remains fairly stable only because people decline at roughly the same rate. And yes, even geniuses decline. I recently asked Nobel Laureate James Watson, 84, when he reached his intellectual peak, and he replied, "Twenty, maybe 21—certainly before we found the DNA structure." That seminal work had been done when he was 25.

Intelligence, like memory, is divided into types that decline somewhat differently. Factual information is the basis of what is called crystallized intelligence, and much of the crystallized knowledge we acquire stays fairly strong at least into our sixties. However, fluid intelligence—our ability to reason—declines dramatically in most people, in large part because we get *slow.* Generally speaking, on tasks involving reasoning, what a 20-year-old can do in about half a second takes a healthy 80-year-old more than two seconds—if, that is, he or she can do it at all. As Douglas Powell of the Harvard Medical School puts it in his recent book, *The Aging Intellect,* "No other single mental ability declines as rapidly during the adult years as processing speed."

Neuroscientists tackle the decline in reasoning and working memory under an umbrella concept called executive function. Somewhere in the brain there seems to be a coach: a system or structure that schedules and prioritizes, garnering resources, redirecting attention, or switching tasks as needed. Adam Gazzaley, a neurology professor at the University of California, San Francisco, has conducted research documenting how that coaching ability declines as we age. For example, older people are bad at multitasking, Gazzaley says, because they have trouble redirecting attention back to a task after it has been interrupted. On average, people in their seventies generally require twice as much time to do two things at once as do young adults, and they also make more errors on the tasks. That inability to focus takes its toll. "I would not be capable of doing groundbreaking work today," renowned physicist Freeman Dyson, 88, told me recently. When he was young, Dyson said, he could focus on a single problem nonstop for a week. "Today," he said, "I'm limited to two hours a day of serious work—which wouldn't be enough."

The deterioration of these four systems appears to be an inevitable part of normal, healthy aging, although the rate of decline varies among individuals. When you add disease to the picture, things truly look bleak. Half of Americans over 85 are suffering from Alzheimer's disease, which eventually robs people of their memories, identities, and the ability to function even minimally. Alzheimer's becomes increasingly common with age—so common that neurologist Gary Small of UCLA suggests that if we all lived to 110, we all would have it. These are the brutal truths we must face as we and our loved ones age.

Critical Thinking

1. What two processes are involved in the decline of the accuracy of the senses with age?
2. Why is crystallized intelligence much stronger than fluid intelligence in elders?

Create Central

www.mhhe.com/createcentral

Internet References

Changes in Cognitive Functioning in Human Aging
www.ncbi.nlm.nih.gov/books/NBK3885

Lifestyle Factors Affecting Late Adulthood
www.school-for-champions.com/health/lifestyle_elderly.htm

The Long Beach Longitudinal Study: USC Davis
http://gero.usc.edu/lbls/publications.shtml

What Happens to the Aging Brain?
www.psychologytoday.com/blog/memory-medic/201211

Article

Prepared by: Claire N. Rubman, *Suffolk County Community College*

Age-Proof Your Brain

10 Easy Ways to Stay Sharp Forever

BETH HOWARD

Learning Outcomes

After reading this article, you will be able to:

- Tell an elder how to delay memory loss and/or dementia.
- Predict which chronic health impairments lead to an early dementia and explain why.

Alzheimer's isn't inevitable. Many experts now believe you can prevent or at least delay dementia—even if you have a genetic predisposition. Reducing Alzheimer's risk factors like obesity, diabetes, smoking and low physical activity by just 25 percent could prevent up to half a million cases of the disease in the United States, according to a recent analysis from the University of California in San Francisco.

"The goal is to stave it off long enough so that you can live life without ever suffering from symptoms," says Gary Small, M.D., director of the UCLA Longevity Center and coauthor of *The Alzheimer's Prevention Program: Keep Your Brain Healthy for the Resf of Your Life.* Read on for new ways to boost your brain.

Get Moving

"If you do only one thing to keep your brain young, exercise," says Art Kramer, professor of psychology and neuroscience at the University of Illinois. Higher exercise levels can reduce dementia risk by 30 to 40 percent compared with low activity levels, and physically active people tend to maintain better cognition and memory than inactive people. "They also have substantially lower rates of different forms of dementia, including Alzheimer's disease," Kramer says.

Working out helps your hippocampus, the region of the brain involved in memory formation. As you age, your hippocampus shrinks, leading to memory loss. Exercise can reverse this process, research suggests. Physical activity can also trigger the growth of new nerve cells and promote nerve growth.

How you work up a sweat is up to you, but most experts recommend 150 minutes a week of moderate activity. Even a little bit can help: "In our research as little as 15 minutes of regular exercise three times per week helped maintain the brain," says Eric B. Larson, M.D., executive director of Group Health Research Institute in Seattle.

Pump Some Iron

Older women who participated in a yearlong weight-training program at the University of British Columbia at Vancouver did 13 percent better on tests of cognitive function than a group of women who did balance and toning exercises. "Resistance training may increase the levels of growth factors in the brain such as IGF1, which nourish and protect nerve cells," says Teresa Liu-Ambrose, head of the university's Aging, Mobility, and Cognitive Neuroscience Laboratory.

Seek Out New Skills

Learning spurs the growth of new brain cells. "When you challenge the brain, you increase the number of brain cells and the number of connections between those cells," says Keith L. Black, M.D., chair of neurosurgery at Cedars-Sinai Medical Center in Los Angeles. "But it's not enough to do the things you routinely do—like the daily crossword. You have to learn new things, like sudoku or a new form of bridge."

UCLA researchers using MRI scans found that middle-aged and older adults with little Internet experience could trigger brain centers that control decision-making and complex reasoning after a week of surfing the net. "Engaging the mind can help older brains maintain healthy functioning," says Cynthia R. Green, Ph.D., author of *30 Days to Total Brain Health.*

Say "Omm"

Chronic stress floods your brain with cortisol, which leads to impaired memory. To better understand if easing tension changes your brain, Harvard researchers studied men and women trained in a technique called mindfulness-based stress reduction (MBSR). This form of meditation—which involves focusing one's attention on sensations, feelings and state of mind—has been shown to reduce harmful stress hormones. After eight weeks, researchers took MRI scans of participants' brains that showed the density of gray matter in the hippocampus increased significantly in the MBSR group, compared with a control group.

Eat Like a Greek

A heart-friendly Mediterranean diet—fish, vegetables, fruit, nuts and beans—reduced Alzheimer's risk by 34 to 48 percent in studies conducted by Columbia University.

"We know that omega-3 fatty acids in fish are very important for maintaining heart health," says Keith Black of Cedars-Sinai. "We suspect these fats may be equally important for maintaining a healthy brain." Data from several large studies suggest that older people who eat the most fruits and vegetables, especially the leafy-green variety, may experience a slower rate of cognitive decline and a lower risk for dementia than meat lovers.

And it may not matter if you get your produce from a bottle instead of a bin. A study from Vanderbilt University found that people who downed three or more servings of fruit or vegetable juice a week had a 76 percent lower risk for developing Alzheimer's disease than those who drank less than a serving weekly.

Spice It Up

Your brain enjoys spices as much as your taste buds do. Herbs and spices such as black pepper, cinnamon, oregano, basil, parsley, ginger and vanilla are high in antioxidants, which may help build brainpower. Scientists are particularly intrigued by curcumin, the active ingredient in turmeric, common in Indian curries. "Indians have lower incidence of Alzheimer's, and one theory is it's the curcumin," says Black. "It bonds to amyloid plaques that accumulate in the brains of people with the disease." Animal research shows curcumin reduces amyloid plaques and lowers inflammation levels. A study in humans also found those who ate curried foods frequently had higher scores on standard cognition tests.

Find Your Purpose

Discovering your mission in life can help you stay sharp, according to a Rush University Medical Center study of more than 950 older adults. Participants who approached life with clear intentions and goals at the start of the study were less likely to develop Alzheimer's disease over the following seven years, researchers found.

Get a (Social) Life

Who needs friends? You do! Having multiple social networks helps lower dementia risk, a 15-year study of older people from Sweden's Karolinska Institute shows. A rich social life may protect against dementia by providing emotional and mental stimulation, says Laura Fratiglioni, M.D., director of the institute's Aging Research Center. Other studies yield similar conclusions: Subjects in a University of Michigan study did better on tests of short-term memory after just 10 minutes of conversation with another person.

Reduce Your Risks

Chronic health conditions like diabetes, obesity and hypertension are often associated with dementia. Diabetes, for example, roughly doubles the risk for Alzheimer's and other forms of dementia. Controlling these risk factors can slow the tide.

"We've estimated that in people with mild cognitive impairment—an intermediate state between normal cognitive aging and dementia—good control of diabetes can delay the onset of dementia by several years," says Fratiglioni. That means following doctor's orders regarding diet and exercise and taking prescribed medications on schedule.

Check Vitamin Deficiencies

Older adults don't always get all the nutrients they need from foods, because of declines in digestive acids or because their medications interfere with absorption. That vitamin deficit—particularly vitamin B_{12}—can also affect brain vitality, research from Rush University Medical Center shows. Older adults at risk of vitamin B_{12} deficiencies had smaller brains and scored lowest on tests measuring thinking, reasoning and memory, researchers found.

Critical Thinking

1. Name three categories of foods that are heart friendly.
2. Identify five herbs or spices that are antioxidants.
3. Why are friends important to brain health?
4. Which exercise stimulates brain circuits more: a daily crossword puzzle or learning something new?

Create Central

www.mhhe.com/createcentral

Internet References

Aging in Different Ways
www.brainfacts.org/across-the-lifespan/agingarticles/2012

Alzheimer's Disease Research Center
http://alzheimer.wustl.edu

AARP
www.aarp.org

Stockholm Gerontology Research Center
www.aldrecentrum.se/Havudmeny/English

Vitamin B12 Deficiency in the Elderly
www.ncbi.nlm.nih.gov/pubmed/10448529

Beth Howard last wrote for *AARP The Magazine* about medical breakthroughs, in the September/October 2011 issue.

Article

Prepared by: Claire N. Rubman, *Suffolk County Community College*

The Old World

Populations everywhere are getting older faster. This leads to more globalization—and more globalization means even older countries.

TED C. FISHMAN

Learning Outcomes

After reading this article, you will be able to:

- Explain how the economic climate is pitting young against old.
- Evaluate the evidence that more globalization leads to more older countries.

You may know that the world's population is aging—that the number of older people is expanding faster than the number of young—but you probably don't realize how fast this is happening. Right now, the world is evenly divided between those under 28 and those over 28. By midcentury, the median age will have risen to 40. Demographers also use another measure, in addition to median age, to determine whether populations are aging: "elder share." If the share, or proportion, of people over 60 (or sometimes 65) is growing, the population is aging. By that yardstick too, the world is quickly becoming older. Pick any age cohort above the median age of 28 and you'll find its share of the global population rising faster than that of any segment below the median. By 2018, 65-year-olds, for example, will outnumber those under 5—a historic first. In 2050, developed countries are on track to have half as many people under 15 as they do over 60. In short, the age mix of the world is turning upside down and at unprecedented rates.

This means profound change in nearly every important relationship we have—as family members, neighbors, citizens of nations and the world. Aging populations also alter how business is done everywhere. The globalization of the economy is accelerating because the world is rapidly aging, and at the same time the pace of global aging is quickened by the speed and scope of globalization. These intertwined dynamics also bear on the international competition for wealth and power. The high costs of keeping our aging population healthy and out of poverty has caused the United States and other rich democracies to lose their economic and political footing. Countries on the rise amass wealth and geopolitical clout by refusing to bear those costs. Older countries lose work to younger countries.

To see this process at work, look at China. In its march to prosperity, the country has encouraged hundreds of millions of its young people to move into cities. Chinese metropolises—some, like Beijing, ancient but newly sprawling, others, like Shenzen, built from scratch—are where the factories are. Foxconn Technology Group, for example, the giant electronics manufacturer that builds components for Dell, Hewlett-Packard and Apple in gigantic plants in Shenzen and elsewhere in urban China, will soon employ enough people to fill 60 percent of the jobs in Manhattan. Foxconn has close to 920,000 workers, nearly all of whom are under 25; in August, the company announced plans to add 400,000 more workers in the next year. But China's is a kind of Dorian Gray economy, its young and footloose global identity hiding a grayer reality. By and large, older workers have been excluded from its remade, globalized economy. They are left behind in their rural villages, or they are pushed from their urban homes into the ghettos of dour apartment blocks on the urban edge to make room for the new apartments and offices occupied by younger urbanites and the companies eager to hire them. Discrimination—"age apartheid" might be a better term—is one way to describe what's going on here: no country sorts its population more ruthlessly by age.

The problem for China is that it is rapidly approaching the point after which it will no longer be the relatively young country we see today. In 2015, China's working population below the age of 65 will begin to shrink. Meanwhile, the number of people over 65 will be rising to 300 million by 2050, a threefold increase. Richard Jackson, the director of the Global Aging Initiative at the Center for Strategic and International Studies, notes that China will be older than the United States within a generation, making it the first big national population to age before it joins the ranks of developed countries. One of China's biggest fears, expressed repeatedly in public pronouncements, is that it will grow old before it grows rich.

To avoid this fate, China is doing all it can to lure the world's production and capital while its work force is young. In large part, it does this by denying meaningful pensions and health care to its people today. Not only do the vast majority of elderly Chinese have little more than their meager savings, but today's workers have pensions so measly as to be irrelevant. To keep the cost of manufacturing in China low for the rest of the world, the young Chinese work force is, for now, rarely provided more than token pensions, health care or disability insurance. In aging, developed countries, older workers with long tenure are usually at their peak in terms of pay and the cost of their benefits. Here in the United States, for example, health care costs for workers who are between 50 and 65 are, on average, almost two times what they are for their peers in their 30s and 40s. When the median age of workers climbs in the United States, so does the cost of insurance their employers must buy for them. China's leadership clearly believes its young workers would lose their allure if the future costs of old age were added to their costs today. When state-owned companies trimmed their ranks of tens of millions of workers following the country's transition to a market economy, older workers—many only in middle age—were often let go with small pensions and replaced by younger workers. So what China offers now is workers with short tenure and negligible benefits (as well as something of a free social safety net in the form of all the relatively young, physically fit grandparents who move in with their children to care for their grandchildren).

Companies that move production to China or buy goods from Chinese suppliers gain the leverage they need to rewrite the terms of employment with their older workers at home or the ability to push those workers off the payrolls altogether. In a 2006 analysis of how aging work forces influence global flows of capital, the economists Ronald Davies and Robert R. Reed noted that because "older" economies have smaller work forces and higher wages, they push investment to younger economies, which offer higher rates of return. And high costs in older economies reach beyond wages—into taxes, which are used to pay for age-related public spending like social security. China's youthful labor force thus helps the country maintain its low-cost economic ecosystem and attract foreign investment that seeks the higher returns a "younger" economy offers, whether or not any particular pot of foreign money goes to employ young people.

China is not the only country in which a young labor force attracts global businesses and investors. Much of the developing world, particularly in Asia and Latin America, operates the same way. An outspoken champion of outsourcing, Nandan Nilekani, a former head of Infosys, the Indian technology giant, is well known for promoting India as a place to corral young workers in an otherwise aging world. Call it "global age-arbitrage."

The other part of the feedback loop, the role globalization plays in speeding up how fast a country ages, is tied to the two big reasons that populations grow older. First and most obviously, more and more individuals are living longer than ever before. Average life expectancy is increasing nearly everywhere. Longer life is itself a kind of byproduct of globalization, the result of the worldwide exchange of public-health technology, medical breakthroughs and, perhaps the most life-giving development of all, the spread of literacy. Every person who can read has access to the world of health information, including Internet sites and government pamphlets on diseases. Countries educate their people in order to make it possible for them to enter the mainstream of global commerce and that extends their life spans—making the countries older.

Above all, however, for communities or countries to age, people must have far fewer children. Today, almost no place in the developed world has a total fertility rate of 2.1 children, the replacement rate needed to keep a population from declining. The population of nearly every developed country is expected to shrink before midcentury. When emerging nations gear up for the global economy, they tend to take two steps that encourage smaller families: they extend educational and employment opportunities to young women, and they urbanize. Urban women postpone having children until they are prepared for and established in their jobs. Rearing children in the city is also more expensive. Cities serve the global economy, and the global economy drives people to cities. (According to the U.N. Population Fund, about half the world's population was urban in 2007, but by 2030 nearly 80 percent of it will live in the cities of the developing world.) The world gets older.

Such urbanization and globalization can take hold with remarkable swiftness. Japan was one of the youngest countries in the world until around 1950, and now its population is arguably the world's oldest. (Its median age will exceed 56 by midcentury, up from 43 today.) The median age in Western Europe today is just over 40; it will rise to near 50 by 2050. Population aging did not always happen so quickly. France was the first country in the world to see its share of 65-year-olds double, from 7 percent to 14 percent; this took about 115 years, starting in 1865. But China will experience the same doubling in 25 years.

One exception is the United States. The country is subject to the same two big trends—longer lives, smaller families—that are aging much of the world's populations, but we are not growing old as fast as countries in East Asia and Western Europe. Our median age will climb only 3 years, to 40, by 2050, a rate slowed by the arrival of young immigrants, including millions from Latin America.

Of course, immigration for one country means emigration from another—and an older population left behind. Spain, which rivals Japan as the world's oldest country, was for much of the 20th century one of the youngest nations in the West. Before 2000, it had virtually no foreign-born residents. Today, nearly 12 percent of Spain's population is foreign born. Among the arrivals are hundreds of thousands of Ecuadoreans (many of them female caregivers for elderly Spanish) whose absence at home increases the median age of Ecuador's population. More than one in 10 Ecuadoreans has left in search of work, and the loss of so many of the country's youngest and most enterprising workers means Ecuador has little chance of developing. Recently, its president initiated the Welcome Home Program to lure emigrants back with tax breaks and money to start businesses.

How do globalization and an aging population affect the American workplace? According to the Economic Policy Institute, 2.3 million American jobs were lost to China alone between 2001 and 2007. Susan Houseman, an economist at the Upjohn Institute for Employment Research in Kalamazoo, Mich., notes that older employees in manufacturing jobs who are low-skilled have been among the most vulnerable workers of all. And when older workers lose their jobs, they search longer for new ones than people do in other age groups. They find it hard to remake themselves with new skills and grow less employable over time and more desperate to accept low pay. This, along with the prospect of additional outsourcing abroad, drives down the earnings of those older workers who manage to stay employed. Looking at data ending in 2002, a team of researchers including economists from the World Bank and the National Bureau of Economic Research found that older workers suffered greater income losses because of foreign outsourcing than women and union workers.

Keep in mind that these results predate the recent recession and the even more difficult times that have resulted for older workers. The ranks of the unemployed who are 55 and older grew 331 percent over the decade that ended last December. U.S. unemployment levels for workers over 50 are now at their all-time highs, nearly double what they were three years ago. AARP's Public Policy Institute reports that from December 2007 to February 2010 the number of workers 55 and older who gave up looking for work rose more than fivefold, to 287,000 from 53,000. Far more people have retired early than anyone predicted. In 2009, there were 465,000 more applications for Social Security and disability benefits than there were the year before, as employers made it clear to older workers that they were not wanted. This increase was nearly 50 percent greater than what the Social Security Administration expected.

One conundrum for aging societies is how to keep older people employed at a time when economic conditions favor the young, whether nearby or far away. The workplace left to itself comes up with some solutions, but they require older workers to accept more "flexible" conditions, which often means joining the so-called contingent work force of part-timers, self-employed contract workers and temps hired through agencies. According to the AARP Public Policy Institute, 21 percent of workers over 65 are part time, compared with 16 percent for the overall work force. Self-employment is also climbing among older workers, and Americans over 50 are the most active group of entrepreneurs, often out of necessity. This partly explains an apparent contradiction: at the same time that unemployment among older workers is at a peak, the percentage of older people with jobs is also near a high, because more people must work to make ends meet.

In the United States, the transformation of older workers into a giant contingent work force is just getting started. This year, as baby boomers begin to hit 65, the "elder share" of the U.S. population begins a sharp climb. From 2010 to 2030, the number of Americans between 25 and 64 will climb by 16 million, but two-thirds of the increase will consist of people 55 and 64. Countries that are older than the U.S., that are further along in reshaping their workplaces, give a glimpse of the future. In Japan, retirees from the biggest companies are well provided for, but for many of the rest—workers at smaller companies, the self-employed—the fear of outliving their money is real. One in five elderly Japanese lives in poverty. So the Japanese stay on the job when they can. Since 2006, the number of Japanese still working after the customary retirement age of 60 has risen by more than 11 million. Most are officially retired but are back at their companies, under contract. They typically earn about half their former wages.

Will the world ever grow young again? Perhaps, but not anytime soon. Today, many of the places that are growing old the fastest are in the developing world, largely because that's where urbanization is most rapid. It is hard to conjure a situation in which people move back to the countryside and again have larger families. Instead, if past is prelude, today's young countries like China will be the countries that in the not-distant future go shopping for younger workers in younger places. Those places will be transformed by satisfying an older China's needs, and the cycle will repeat itself: when the world finds its next young place, that country may well age even more quickly than the formerly young countries that preceded it.

The rough adjustments that global aging imposes on populations can sound bleak. Nonetheless, the challenges do not trump what we gain by living longer. Remember, too, that smaller families enable parents to make greater investments in themselves and the children they do have. Still, as the world gets older, we need to anticipate how this extraordinary change might undermine our communities, weaken nations and push able older people to the side. There are also sobering geopolitical consequences to consider. It now looks as if global power rests on how willing a country is to neglect its older citizens. Faults in the welfare states of the West are highlighted by the world debt crisis. Fiscal woes driven by age-related expenses plague every level of government in the United States. Europeans take to the streets, strike and close down governments struggling to cover unsupportable pensions. The most advanced countries owe trillions in age-related public expenses. The most straightforward solutions, like higher payroll taxes to pay for benefits, raise the cost of doing business and chase off investors and producers to lower-cost economies. Mark Haas of Duquesne University has argued that aging forces all high-income democracies into triage mode. They can pay for income support and services for their elderly and drastically reduce financing for schools, defense, infrastructure and everything else, or they can decide older people will have to make do with far less.

China has gained new financial clout in relation to advanced industrial nations because it has grown rich enough as the youthful factory of the world to act as the developed countries' banker. Yet the Chinese government says the country is still too poor to put a more comprehensive social safety net in place. Perhaps, but it is the financial sacrifices of its people that give China the means to lend trillions of dollars to the United States and other industrialized nations. That's a bargain China may be happy to accept, but it, too, is caught in the irreversible dynamic of aging, and its demographic denouement is coming. By then, the United States will be older than it is now, but younger than most of the rest of the developed world, younger than much of the developing world and far younger than China. If we understand how aging populations and economic forces interact, perhaps we can make the most of our age and our youth.

Critical Thinking

1. Describe reasons why the United States' jobs are outsourced to China and India.
2. Predict what will happen to services for elders if more tax dollars are spent on crumbling infrastructure and schools.
3. Recognize the economic effects of increased longevity.

Create Central

www.mhhe.com/createcentral

Internet References

AARP Public Policy Institute
www.aarp.org/research/ppi

Aging and Globalization
http://sincronia.cucsh.udg.mx/powellfal/2011b.htm

Aging, Globalization, and Inequality: Book Introduction
http://baywood.com/books/previewbook.asp?id=AGA

Globalisation and Support in Old Age/London: LSE Research
http://eprints.lse.ac.uk/archive/00001032

Ted C. Fishman is the author of *Shock of Gray: The Aging of the World's Population and How It Pits Young Against Old, Child Against Parent, Worker Against Boss, Company Against Rival and Nation Against Nation,* from which this article is adapted.

Article

Prepared by: Claire N. Rubman, *Suffolk County Community College*

The Real Social Network

It's not only a neighborhood—it's a *village*. And it might just give you a chance to stay in your own home.

MARTHA THOMAS

Learning Outcomes

After reading this article, you will be able to:

- Distinguish between life in one's own neighborhood when old or moving to a retirement community.
- Describe the "village movement" among American elders.

On a bitterly cold morning a few years ago, Eleanor McQueen awoke to what sounded like artillery fire: the ice-covered branches of trees cracking in the wind. A winter storm had knocked out the power in the rural New Hampshire home that Eleanor shared with her husband, Jim. "No heat, no water. Nada," Eleanor recalls.

The outage lasted for nine days; the couple, both 82 at the time, weathered the ordeal in isolation with the help of a camp stove. Their three grown kids were spread out in three different states, and the McQueens weren't very close to their immediate neighbors. "We needed someone to see if we were dead or alive," Eleanor says.

But the McQueens were alone, and it scared them. Maybe, they admitted, it was time to think about leaving their home of 40 years.

Luckily, last year the McQueens found a way to stay. They joined Monadnock at Home, a membership organization for older residents of several small towns near Mount Monadnock, New Hampshire. The group is part of the so-called village movement, which links neighbors together to help one another remain in the homes they love as they grow older.

The concept began in Boston's Beacon Hill neighborhood in 2001, when a group of residents founded a nonprofit called Beacon Hill Village to ease access to the services that often force older Americans to give up their homes and move to a retirement community. More than 56 villages now exist in the United States, with another 120 or so in development, according to the Village to Village (VtV) Network, a group launched in 2010 that provides assistance to new villages and tracks their growth nationwide.

It works like this: Members pay an annual fee (the average is about $600) in return for services such as transportation, yard work, and bookkeeping. The village itself usually has only one or two paid employees, and most do not provide services directly. Instead, the village serves as a liaison—some even use the word concierge. The help comes from other able-bodied village members, younger neighbors, or youth groups doing community service. Villages also provide lists of approved home-maintenance contractors, many of whom offer discounts to members. By relying on this mix of paid and volunteer help, members hope to cobble together a menu of assistance similar to what they would receive at a retirement community, but without uprooting their household.

The earliest villages, like Beacon Hill, were founded in relatively affluent urban areas, though new villages are now sprouting in suburbs and smaller rural communities, and organizers are adapting Beacon Hill's model to fit economically and ethnically diverse communities. Each is united by a common goal: a determination to age in place. A recent AARP survey found 86 percent of respondents 45 and older plan to stay in their current residence as long as possible. "And as people get older, that percentage increases," says Elinor Ginzler, AARP expert on livable communities.

In its own quiet way, the village movement represents a radical rejection of the postwar American ideal of aging, in which retirees discard homes and careers for lives of leisure amid people their own age. That's the life Eleanor and Jim McQueen turned their backs on when they joined Monadnock at Home.

"To dump 40 years of building a home to move into a condominium doesn't appeal to me at all," Jim says. "The idea of Monadnock at Home is, I won't have to."

You could call it the lightbulb moment—literally: A bulb burns out in that hard-to-reach spot at the top of the stairs, and that's when you realize you're dependent on others for the simplest of household chores. "It's horrible," says Candace Baldwin, codirector of the VtV Network. "I've heard so many stories from people who say they can't get on a ladder and change a lightbulb, so they have to move to a nursing home. A lightbulb can be a disaster."

Especially when the homeowner won't ask for help. Joining a village can ease the resistance, says Christabel Cheung, director of the San Francisco Village. Many members are drawn by the opportunity to give aid as well as receive it. "A lot of people initially get involved because they're active and want to do something," she says. "Then they feel better about asking for help when they need it."

Last winter Blanche and Rudy Hirsch needed that help. The couple, 80 and 82, live in a three-story brick town house in Washington, D.C.; they pay $800 per year in dues to Capitol Hill Village (CHV). During the blizzard-filled February of 2010, Rudy was in the hospital for hip surgery and Blanche stayed with nearby friends as the snow piled up. On the day Rudy came home, Blanche recalls, the driver warned that if their walkways weren't clear "he'd turn around and go back to the hospital." She called CHV executive director Gail Kohn, who summoned the village's volunteer snow brigade. A pair of young architects who lived nearby were quickly dispatched with shovels.

The Hirsches have discussed moving; they've postponed the decision by installing lifts so Rudy can get up and down the stairs. Remembering her visits to a family member who lived in a retirement home, Blanche shudders: "Everyone was so old. It's depressing."

Avoiding "old-age ghettos," says Kohn, is a major draw for villagers. She touts the intergenerational quality of Capitol Hill, full of "people in their 20s and people in their 80s," and CHV organizes a handful of events geared toward people of different ages. One program brings high school freshmen and village members together in the neighborhood's public library, where the kids offer informal computer tutoring to the older folks.

Such social-network building is a natural outgrowth of village life. Indeed, Beacon Hill Village was founded on the idea of forging stronger bonds among members. "There was a program committee in existence before the village even opened its doors," says Stephen Roop, president of the Beacon Hill Village board. "Most of my friends on Beacon Hill I know through the village."

One fall evening in Chicago, Lincoln Park Village members gathered at a neighborhood church for a potluck supper. A group of about 80—village members and college students who volunteer as community service—nibbled sushi and sipped Malbec wine as they chatted with Robert Falls, artistic director of Chicago's Goodman Theatre.

What a Village Takes

Want to organize a village of your own? The Village to Village (VtV) Network offers information on helping villages get started. Membership benefits include tools and resources developed by other villages, a peer-to-peer mentoring program, and monthly webinars and discussion forums. Call 617-299-9638 or e-mail via the VtV website (vtvnetwork.org) for more info.

- To find out if a village exists in your region, the VtV website has a searchable online map of all U.S. villages now open or in development.
- The creators of Boston's Beacon Hill Village have written a book on starting a village: *The Village Concept: A Founders' Manual* is a how-to guide that provides tips on fundraising, marketing, and organizational strategies.
- Existing resources can make your neighborhood more "villagelike," says Candace Baldwin, codirector of the VtV Network. The best place to start is your local agency on aging. The U.S. Department of Health and Human Services offers a searchable index of these services (800-677-1116; www.eldercare.gov). —*M.T.*

Lincoln Park Village's executive director, Dianne Campbell, 61, doesn't have a background in social work or gerontology; her experience is in fundraising for charter schools and museums, and she lives in Lincoln Park. To village member Warner Saunders, 76, that's a big plus. "She doesn't see us as elderly clients who need her help," says Saunders, a longtime news anchor for Chicago's NBC affiliate, WMAQ-TV. "I see Dianne as a friend. If she were a social worker, and I viewed my relationship with her as that of a patient, I would probably resent that."

For Saunders, Lincoln Park Village makes his quality of life a lot better. He recently had knee and hip surgeries, and his family—he lives with his wife and sister-in-law—relies on the village for transportation and help in finding contractors. "I'd call the village the best bargain in town," he says.

Others, however, might balk at annual dues that can approach $1,000 for services that might not be needed yet. To expand membership, many villages offer discounts for low-income households.

At 93, Elvina Moen is Lincoln Park Village's oldest, as well as its first "member-plus," or subsidized, resident. She lives in a one-room apartment in an 11-story Chicago Housing Authority building within Lincoln Park. The handful of member-plus residents pay annual dues of $100 and in return receive $200 in credit each year for discounted services from the village's list of vetted providers. Since joining, Moen has enlisted the village to help paint her apartment and install ceiling fans.

But beyond home improvements, Moen doesn't ask a lot from the village yet—she's already created her own village, of a sort. When she cracked her pelvis three years ago, members of her church brought her meals until she got back on her feet; she pays a neighbor to help clean her apartment. Her community-aided self-reliance proves that intergenerational ties and strong social networks help everyone, not just the privileged, age with dignity.

Social scientists call this social capital, and many argue that we don't have enough of it. What the village movement offers is a new way to engineer an old-fashioned kind of connection. "As recently as 100 years ago most everyone lived in a village setting," says Jay Walljasper, author of *All That We Share: A Field Guide to the Commons,* a book about how cooperative movements foster a more livable society. "If you take a few steps back and ask what a village is, you'll realize it's a place where you have face-to-face encounters." He compares the village movement to the local-food movement, which also started with affluent urbanites. Think of a village as a kind of "artisanal retirement," a modern reinterpretation of an older, more enlightened way of life. And just as there's nothing quite like homegrown tomatoes, "there's no replacement for the direct connection with people who live near you," Walljasper says.

Strong, intergenerational communities—just like healthy meals—are good for everyone.

Bernice Hutchinson is director of Dupont Circle Village in Washington, D.C., which serves a diverse neighborhood. Many members are well-off; some are getting by on Medicaid. "But at the end of the day," says Hutchinson, "what everyone wants is connectedness."

Connectedness alone, of course, can't ensure healthy aging. What happens next—when villagers' needs grow beyond help with grocery shopping or the name of a reliable plumber?

To meet the growing health demands of members, villages boast a range of wellness services, and many have affiliations with health care institutions. Capitol Hill Village, for example, has a partnership with Washington Hospital Center's Medical House Call Program, which provides at-home primary care visits for elderly patients.

A new village—Pennsylvania's Crozer-Keystone Village—flips the grassroots Beacon Hill model: It's the first village to originate in a health care institution. Barbara Alexis Looby, who oversees the village, works for Keystone, which has five hospitals in the southeastern part of the state. A monthly fee gives members access to a "village navigator," who schedules medical appointments and day-to-day logistics like errands. Members also get discounts on Keystone's health services. Because the village and the hospital system are aligned, says Looby, "the boundaries are flexible. You care for people when they come to the hospital, and you are in a position to coordinate their care when they leave." Keystone hopes this integration will lead to fewer ER visits and hospital readmissions.

How long can a village keep you safe at home? It depends. But Candace Baldwin, of VtV, says that the trust factor between members and the village can help family members and caregivers make choices and find services.

Michal Brown lives about 30 miles outside Chicago, where her 89-year-old mother, Mary Haughey, has lived in a Lincoln Park apartment for more than 20 years. She worries about her mom, who has symptoms of dementia. Brown saw a flyer about Lincoln Park Village in a pharmacy and immediately signed her mother up. Through the village, Brown enrolled her mom in tai chi classes and asked a village member to accompany her as a buddy.

Just before Christmas, Haughey became dizzy at her tai chi class. With her buddy's help, she made it to the hospital, where doctors discovered a blood clot in her lung. Without the village, Brown is convinced, her mother might not have survived.

Through the village, Brown has also learned about counseling services at a local hospital to help plan her mother's next steps. "We can add services bit by bit, whether it's medication management or home health care. The village knows how to get those services."

Nobody knows what Mary Haughey's future holds, but the village has given her options. And it has given her daughter hope that she can delay moving her mother to a nursing home. For now, it helps knowing that her mother is safe, and still in her own apartment, in her own neighborhood.

Critical Thinking

1. Name several ways in which the village movement connects younger and older adults.
2. What is "social capital" and why is it advantageous to elders?
3. Which is more expensive: moving to a retirement community or paying an annual fee for elder services while staying in your current residence?

Create Central

www.mhhe.com/createcentral

Internet References

Beacon Hill Village: Home
www.beaconhillvillage.org

Liveable Communities: AARP Public Policy Institute
www.aarp.org/research/ppi/liv-com

U.S. Department of Health and Human Services
www.eldercare.gov

Village to Village Network
www.vtvnetwork.org

Martha Thomas is a Baltimore-based freelance writer.

Article

Prepared by: Claire N. Rubman, *Suffolk County Community College*

Elder Abuse Identification: A Public Health Issue

HELEN SORENSON

Learning Outcomes

After reading this article, you will be able to:

- Identify six ways in which elders can be abused.
- Describe some of the warning signs of elder abuse.

Elder abuse wears many hats. As defined by the World Health Organization, elder abuse is a single or repeated act or lack of appropriate action occurring within any relationship where there is an expectation of trust that causes harm or distress to an older person.[1] It can be manifested as physical, mental, financial, emotional, sexual, or verbal abuse. Abuse can also be in the form of passive or active neglect. Elder abuse is not confined to any country, any culture, or any age group (young-old to old-old). However, the very old seem to be most vulnerable. Determining the extent of elder abuse in any specific population is difficult, as much of it is unreported. There is a stigma associated with being abused that affects both the victim and the perpetrator, especially when it occurs within the family. Fear, loyalty, and/or shame may prevent the abused from taking any action to stop it. Suffering in silence for some seems to be a badge of honor. For those brave enough to report the abuse, it may not be considered a legitimate complaint coming from someone who has been diagnosed with delirium or dementia or from someone who is judged to "just be senile."

In all likelihood, respiratory therapists unknowingly care for patients who are or who have been abused. Unless questioned, the victim will usually not share information about the mistreatment. Brief encounters may not elicit information. Established relationships can develop between therapists/patients in smaller community hospitals, in home care, or in rehabilitation settings. These may be instances in which abusive situations can be addressed and stopped. Awareness of the possibility is the key.

Scenario

Doris and Frank live in a small house in the rural Midwest. Doris is 72, Frank is 84, and both are retired. Two years ago their daughter, who lives nearby, decided that Mom didn't really need all the "stuff" she had collected over the years. When Doris and Frank were away, she disposed of many items. After repeatedly asking her not to do this to no avail, they changed the locks on the house. Not deterred by this action, the daughter broke the window, got inside the house, and threatened to "burn the house down" if they ever locked her out again. When they disagreed, she struck Frank.

Will they report this? No, because she is their daughter, and it wouldn't be right. Are her actions justified? Is she legitimately concerned about their safety, or is this elder abuse? This is a difficult situation. Elderly individuals can be institutionalized (for their safety) after reporting abuse. Since most older adults prefer to remain in their homes, they do not report abuse. Another option is to take out a restraining order against their child, which may also have adverse consequences. What is needed is counseling for both the victims and the offender, which is a complex process and involves the local Department of Social Services. There are no easy answers.

Incidence of Abuse

Elder abuse is a public health issue that affects a significant percentage of the population and in the future is likely to get worse. A systematic review of studies by Cooper et al measuring the prevalence of elder abuse or neglect was published in 2008.[2] This summary of the best evidence determined the following: 25% of dependent older adults reported significant levels of psychological abuse, and 1% reported physical abuse. Twenty percent of the older adults who presented to the emergency department were experiencing neglect, and the incidence of financial abuse has been estimated to be about 6%–18%.[2] Another prevalence survey published in 2010 included data from 5,777 (60.2% female) respondents.[3] Abuse during a one-year period was as follows: 4.6% emotional abuse, 1.6% physical abuse, 0.6% sexual abuse, 5.1% potential neglect, and 5.2% financial abuse. Overall, 10% of those interviewed reported abuse of some kind. Factoring in demographic information, women and frail elders were more likely to experience verbal abuse. African-Americans were more likely to experience financial abuse, and Latinos were less likely than respondents from any other ethnic group to report any form of abuse. Overall, low social support increased the risk for suffering any form of mistreatment, and relatively little of this abuse was reported to the authorities.[3]

Understanding that abuse and mistreatment of older adults happens is the easy part of the dilemma. Determining the form of abuse, who is at risk, who is doing the abusing, and how it can be stopped is more difficult. The National Center on Elder Abuse (NCEA), in conjunction with the Administration on Aging, has provided a list of warning signs (see Table 1).[4] While one sign does not necessarily indicate abuse, it may raise a red flag that other signs may be present but not yet assessed. There may be many other logical reasons for the presence of the warning signs, but awareness of potential abuse is key to prevention.

Identification of Abuse

Warning signs of abuse may not be readily apparent to the RT providing routine therapy on a newly admitted patient. Respiratory therapists who work in intensive care may be more likely to notice bruises and burns, but their focus is generally on ventilation and respiration. RTs who work in home care or rehabilitation may be the most likely to pick up on the fact that "something is just not quite right" with their elderly patient. If during the course of a visit or an examination, any of the warning signs of abuse are noticed, it is time to ask questions. Any licensed health care provider is qualified to ask questions. Respiratory therapists routinely ask about shortness of breath, quality of sleep, and frequency of cough. If bruises are noted, asking "has someone hurt you" or "did someone do this to you" are not unusual questions.

To increase the odds of getting an honest response, it may be necessary to interview the older adult without others present. If family members or caregivers seem reluctant to leave you alone with the individual in question, this may also be a potential "red flag." If the patient seems afraid to answer two simple questions or seems elusive with a response, contact your hospital social worker or case worker for a follow-up. Respiratory therapy education does not always cover assessing for abuse; but despite lack of training, awareness is vital. Educators could add a unit on elder abuse to a disease management course or give reading assignments to students to increase their awareness of the problem. Classroom discussions can and often do result in attitudinal changes not measurable by examinations.

Questions for the RT to Ask

Questions that may elicit a response to warning signs or bruises include:[5]

? *Has someone hurt you?*
? *Did someone do this to you?*
? *Has anyone ever touched you without your consent?*
? *Does anyone yell at you or threaten you?*
? *Who cares for you at home?*
? *Are you afraid of your caregiver?*
? *Do you feel safe where you live?*
? *Who manages your finances?*
? *What happens when you and your caregiver disagree?*

Table 1 Warnings of Potential Elder Abuse

Warning Signs	Potential Causes
Bruises, pressure marks, broken bones, abrasions and burns	Physical abuse, neglect, or mistreatment
Unexplained withdrawal from normal activities, new onset of depression, change in alertness	Emotional abuse
Bruises around breasts, genitalia	Sexual abuse
Sudden change in financial status	Financial exploitation
Bed sores, unattended medical needs, poor hygiene, unusual weight loss	Neglect
Controlling spouses/caregivers, threats, belittling comments	Verbal/Emotional abuse
Frequent arguments between caregiver/older adult, tense relationships	Emotional abuse

Source: National Center on Elder Abuse, U.S. Administration on Aging, www.ncea.aoa.gov

Keep in mind that skin tears and bruises in older adults are not always the result of abuse, but assuming that they are "just signs of old age" may be doing a disservice to the patient.

Elder Abuse Screening Instruments

In an effort to facilitate early identification of elder abuse, a number of screening instruments have been created to help nurses detect mistreatment.[6–9] One of the more current instruments, the Geriatric Mistreatment Scale, is available in both Spanish and English versions and screens for five different types of elder mistreatment.[9] While useful, it is also important to realize that even when assessed, many older adults will not report and will not admit that they are the victims of abuse. Another screening instrument published by the American Medical Association and available at www.centeronelderabuse.org/docs/AMA_Screening_Questions.pdf suggests questions that physicians should incorporate into their daily practice. While presenting all aspects of elder abuse is beyond the scope of this article, a chapter authored by Tom Miller in "Elder Abuse: A Public Health Perspective" contains a very useful algorithm for elder abuse intervention designed for health professionals.[10] Unfortunately, sometimes it is the caregiver who is abusive.

Abuse at the Hands of Caregivers

In response to an increased awareness of elder abuse, in 1987 the Omnibus Budget Reconciliation Act (OBRA) enacted major reforms that ultimately led to improved training of caregivers working with elderly clients.[11] Additional initiatives across the country have attempted to address the problem in a variety of ways. An earlier publication estimated that at least 4% of elderly people are maltreated by their caregivers.[12] Reasons cited have been stress, dependency of the caregiver on the abused older adult for finances and living arrangements, and social isolation.[13] Marshall et al have offered that caregiver stress, rather than malicious intent, is often the cause of abuse.[14] Considering that neglect is also considered a form of abuse, how many patients develop bedsores for lack of being turned or have their call-lights ignored because they are "needy patients who whine a lot"?

Recognizing and Reporting Abuse

Health care professionals need to be able to recognize the "at-risk" factors for elder mistreatment. It is imperative to abide by all reporting laws and equally important is to maintain a therapeutic relationship with the potential victim. Communication and trust issues can make a big difference in the cooperation and willingness of older adults to share incidences of abuse. Legislatures in all 50 states have passed some form of elder abuse prevention laws. In March of 2011 Congress passed a comprehensive federal elder abuse prevention law.[15] Help for our older adults is out there; but first, abuse must be recognized. While not a comfortable situation to address, there are ways to let authorities know of a potential problem without violating the Health Insurance Portability and Accountability Act (HIPAA) rules and regulations. Anyone can report a case of elder abuse in good faith. The Elder Abuse and Neglect Act provides that people—who in good faith report suspected abuse or cooperate with an investigation—are immune from criminal or civil liability or professional disciplinary action. It further provides that the identity of the reporter shall not be disclosed except with the written permission of the reporter or by order of a court. Anonymous reports are accepted. While not easy to do, these actions may be as important as starting an IV, delivering a medication, or viewing an x-ray to get at the root of what is causing the older adult to suffer.

The following are resources that one can refer to for help if abuse is suspected or confirmed:

- Eldercare Locator: (800) 677-1116. Monday–Friday, 9 A.M. to 8 P.M. EST. Trained operators will refer you to a local agency that will help.
- The National Domestic Violence Hotline: (800) 799-SAFE (800-799-7233).
- National Committee for the Prevention of Elder Abuse: www.preventelderabuse.org.
- National Center on Elder Abuse/Administration on Aging: www.ncea.aoa.gov.
- Center of Excellence on Elder Abuse & Neglect: www.centeronelderabuse.org.

References

1. McAlpine CH. Elder abuse and neglect. Age Ageing 2008; 37(2):132–133.
2. Cooper C, Selwood A, Livingston G. The prevalence of elder abuse and neglect: a systematic review. Age Ageing 2008; 37(2):151–160.
3. Acierno R, Hernandez MA, Amstadter AB, et al. Prevalence and correlates of emotional, physical, sexual, and financial abuse and potential neglect in the United States: the National Elder Mistreatment Study. Am J Public Health 2010; 100(2):292–297.
4. National Center on Elder Abuse (NCEA), Administration on Aging website. www.ncea.aoa.gov.
5. Gray-Vickrey P. Combating elder abuse. Nursing 2004; 34(10): 47–51.
6. Yaffe MJ, Wolfson C, Lithwick M, Weiss D. Development and validation of a tool to improve physician identification of elder abuse: the Elder Abuse Suspicion Index (EASI). J Elder Abuse Negl 2008; 20(3):276–300.

7. Neale AV, Hwalek M, Scott R, Stahl C. Validation of the Hwalek-Sengstock elder abuse screening test. J Appl Gerontol 1991; 10(4):406–418.
8. Schofield MJ, Mishra GD. Validity of self-report screening scale for elder abuse: Women's Health Australia Study. Gerontologist 2003; 43(1):110–120.
9. Giraldo-Rodriguez L, Rosas-Carrasco O. Development and psychometric properties of the Geriatric Mistreatment Scale. Geriatr Gerontol Int 2012; June 14 [Epub ahead of print].
10. Summers RW, Hoffman AM, editors. Elder abuse: a public health perspective. Washington DC: American Public Health Association; 2006.
11. Hawes C, Mor V, Phillips CD, et al. The OBRA-87 nursing home regulations and implementation of the Resident Assessment Instrument: effects on process quality. J Am Geriatr Soc 1997; 45(8):977–985.
12. Pillemer K, Finkelhor D. The prevalence of elder abuse: a random sample survey. Gerontologist 1988; 28(1):51–57.
13. Penhale B. Responding and intervening in elder abuse and neglect. Ageing Int 2010; 35:235–252.
14. Marshall CE, Benton D, Brazier JM. Elder abuse. Using clinical tools to identify clues of mistreatment. Geriatrics 2000; 55(2):45–53.
15. The Elder Justice Coalition EJA Update, May 20, 2012. Available at: www.elderjusticecoalition.com *Accessed Sept. 11, 2012.*

Critical Thinking

1. How can a health-care worker maintain a therapeutic relationship with an elder who is being abused but does not want the abuse reported?
2. Why are people who report elder abuse immune from criminal or civil liability, even if they have betrayed their elder person's confidentiality and trust?
3. Under what conditions would you report suspected elder abuse?

Create Central

www.mhhe.com/createcentral

Internet References

Center of Excellence on Elder Abuse and Neglect
www.centeronelderabuse.org

Eldercare Locator
www.eldercare.gov

Eldercare Locator Resource Center
www.n4a.org/programs/eldercare-locator

National Center on Elder Abuse/Administration on Aging
www.ncea.aoa.gov

National Committee for the Prevention of Elder Abuse
www.preventelderabuse.org

Helen Sorenson, MA, RRT, FAARC, is adjunct faculty and an associate professor (retired) with the department of respiratory care at the University of Texas Health Science Center at San Antonio, TX.